in the
mouth in
here he
School of

rate in
llowship
and Economic
Research, and then, after three years as Land Research Officer in Western Nigeria, he founded the Sociology Department of the University of Ibadan, and became Senior Lecturer in Sociology there. He joined the University of Birmingham in 1964, becoming in 1966 Reader in West African Sociology.

Dr Lloyd has visited the U.S.A. on many occasions, and has lectured at several American universities. He is a member of anthropological, sociological and African Studies associations in both Great Britain and the U.S.A. His publications include *Yoruba Land Law* (1962), *The New Elites of Tropical Africa* (1966), *Classes, Crises and Coups* (1971) and *Power and Independence* (1974). In addition he has contributed to *Peoples of Africa* (1965), ed. J. L. Gibbs, *Political Parties and National Integration* (1965), ed. J. S. Coleman and C. G. Rosberg, and *Social Change: the Colonial Situation*, ed. I. Wallerstein (1966). He is co-editor of *The City of Ibadan* (1967). Peter Lloyd is married, and his wife, Barbara, lectures in Social Psychology at the University of Sussex.

P. C. LLOYD

Africa in Social Change

Penguin Books

Penguin Books Ltd, Harmondsworth, Middlesex, England
Penguin Books Inc., 7110 Ambassador Road, Baltimore, Maryland 21207, U.S.A.
Penguin Books Australia Ltd, Ringwood, Victoria, Australia
Penguin Books Canada Ltd, 41 Steelcase Road West, Markham, Ontario, Canada
Penguin Books (N.Z.) Ltd. 182–190 Wairau Road, Auckland 10, New Zealand

First published 1967
Reprinted with revisions 1969
Reprinted 1971
Reprinted with revisions 1972
Reprinted 1975

Made and printed in Great Britain by
Cox & Wyman Ltd, London, Reading and Fakenham
Set in Monotype Plantin

Contents

Maps of West Africa

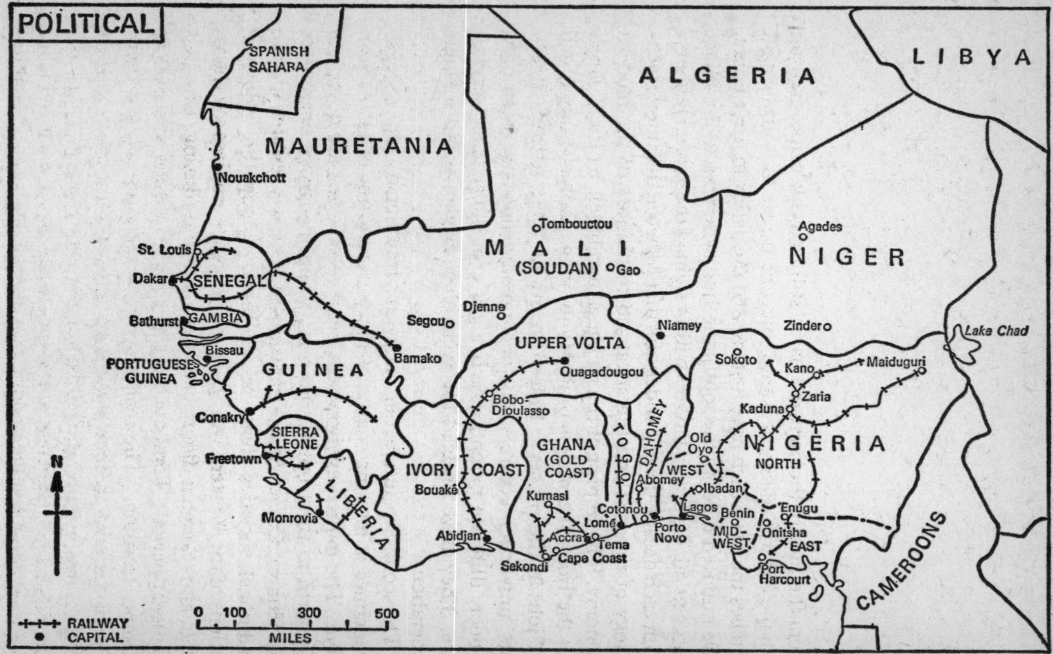
POLITICAL
SPANISH SAHARA
ALGERIA
LIBYA
MAURETANIA
Nouakchott
St. Louis
Dakar
SENEGAL
GAMBIA
Bathurst
Bissau
PORTUGUESE GUINEA
GUINEA
Conakry
SIERRA LEONE
Freetown
LIBERIA
Monrovia
Bamako
Segou
Djenne
Tombouctou
MALI (SOUDAN)
Gao
UPPER VOLTA
Ouagadougou
Bobo-Dioulasso
IVORY COAST
Bouaké
Abidjan
Sekondi
GHANA (GOLD COAST)
Kumasi
Accra
Cape Coast
Tema
TOGO
Lomé
DAHOMEY
Cotonou
Abomey
Porto Novo
Niamey
NIGER
Agades
Zinder
Lake Chad
Sokoto
Kano
Maiduguri
Zaria
Kaduna
NIGERIA
NORTH
WEST
Old Oyo
Ibadan
Lagos
Benin
MID-WEST
Enugu
Onitsha
EAST
Port Harcourt
CAMEROONS
N
RAILWAY
CAPITAL
0 100 300 500
MILES

Introduction

From the Sahara the nomad Tuareg still leads his camel caravan into the old walled city of Kano; today he passes the Airport and watches the jets which have just crossed the desert in three hours. Five hundred miles to the south, the Ijoh fisherman in the Niger delta sets out his prawn baskets within sight of the new oil refinery. With each decade the gap widens further between the simple technology of the past and the advanced techniques of the modern economy. The impact of the jet age is barely felt by the Tuareg. But the Ijoh fisherman is probably praying that his children will get jobs in the refinery. Indeed, many of West Africa's scientists, university lecturers, doctors and surgeons have been born to poor, illiterate parents practising a near-subsistence agriculture. They have bridged the technological gap in but a single generation.

The complex interaction between traditional and modern economies is but one source of the variety in the West African scene. The natural environment ranges from the bare deserts in the north to the tropical rain forests and mangrove swamps of the Guinea Coast. And a far greater diversity existed in the traditional societies than can be found among the industrial nations of the Western world. The vast savana empires of Ghana, Mali and Songhai flourished and withered during Europe's medieval period; Tombouctou was then renowned as a seat of Islamic learning. The contemporary emirates of Northern Nigeria parallel in their scale and in the complexity of their political organization the feudal kingdoms of Europe. Yet on the fringes of their domains are to be found societies in which a small group of hamlets constitutes the largest unit of political organization. Whilst the rulers of the savana kingdoms have embraced Islam, at least nominally, for hundreds of years, men of other societies have continued to worship ancestors and deities correlated with natural phenomena.

The colonial period, too, has produced its own diversities. Britain, France and Portugal each introduced to her colonial territories her own language, and legal and educational systems. Nigerians and Ghanaians can easily converse together, but communications with citizens of their neighbouring French-speaking states is difficult. German influence can still be seen in the former German colony of Togoland – a territory later divided in mandate between Britain and France; the British portion has since been incorporated into Ghana, while the French constitutes the present independent state of Togo. West Africa presents a kaleidoscopic pattern of images.

West Africa shares much with the rest of the continent: yet it has certain distinguishing features which justify our treatment of it as a unique area. Europeans have been visiting its shores for nearly five hundred years, bringing not only trade, but, in the latter centuries, education. Coastal towns, which can boast of a few families with several generations of education, have produced a succession of 'Westernized' elites, each with its peculiar characteristics. Although the colonial policies of British and French governments have differed in so many respects, they have been alike in freely allowing in the West African territories the indigenous development of export crops and in restricting or discouraging the permanent settlement of a European population (a feature for which the climate and the mosquito can equally claim credit). None of the West African states is thus a plural society in the manner of Kenya, Zambia or Rhodesia. The proportion of the population in wage-earning employment is much lower than in these latter countries. And so, while in such other African states most African workers have been drawn into relatively complex industrial economies, in the West African states there has been a greater development within the indigenous economies. The main concern of this book is thus with the adaptation of traditional West African society to modern conditions – traditional here denoting the far from static pattern of institutions deriving from the pre-colonial period and still remarkably persistent.

In recent years an increasing spate of books and articles has chronicled and analysed the rapidly changing political systems of the West African states as they pass from colonial status to independence. Many writers have been concerned with the 'prospects for democracy'; others, with the creation of stable governments which can direct economic growth. The economists studying the problems of the 'underdeveloped' countries turn increasingly to the sociologists in their search for the vital factors which intensify or inhibit 'the rate of take-off into sustained growth'. Both political scientist and economist seek to understand the impact of the processes of modernization upon the traditional societies. New social groups, and especially Westernized elites, are being created. What is the relationship between these various new groups on the one hand, and between them and their traditional societies on the other? How far are the patterns of Western industrial society, and in particular the stratification of society into social classes, being reproduced in West Africa? More and more the sociologist is being asked to define the preconditions for political revolution, for rapid economic advance, and the like. The answers are well-nigh impossible to give in the present state of our understanding of society. An examination of these themes is, however, the basis of this book. And in particular our attention will be focused on the development and character of the new elites, for it is upon these groups that the future of West Africa will largely depend.

Much of the literature which describes the rise of industrial society has in effect restricted itself to Western Europe and Japan, where capitalism has developed from an essentially feudal society, and dominant themes have been the rise of the bourgeoisie and the importance of the Protestant ethic. Traditional West African societies are for the most part, however, not feudal but tribal; nor does it seem likely that the small, private entrepreneur will play such an important role in the economic development of the West African states. The transition from tribal society to modern state-directed economies raises a new set of problems not covered by the classical studies. Continually we find apparent paradoxes. Modernization often seems to result in an intensification of tribal relationships rather than in their decay; or, it seems to be the society with the less highly developed social and political structure which accepts change more readily. Many of these paradoxes are, however, resolved when one studies individual societies in detail. And so one is caught between the need for detailed studies of small areas or individual problems, and the urge to generalize.

It is difficult to generalize about West Africa. The diversities of environment, in traditional society and in colonial heritage, have already been cited. Today West Africa embraces fourteen independent states and one remaining colony – Portuguese Guinea. Furthermore, national statistics, such as *per capita* income and the proportion of children in school, are apt to be misleading. Thus Ghana usually figures among the wealthiest territories, with the most impressive development of social services, while Nigeria ranks much lower, around the West African average. Yet conditions in Accra are little different from those in Lagos; the Ashanti cocoa-producing areas resemble those of Western Nigeria. Both Ghana and Nigeria have their areas of extreme agricultural poverty. Generalizations which embrace all the societies within any single state are not likely to be very meaningful.

Given these extreme diversities we must therefore eschew the encylopedic approach, the attempt to describe situations and institutions in each state and region. We must concentrate instead on the processes of social change. In abstracting, from the diverse and complex patterns of West African society, the principal variables, we may construct theoretical models which are illustrative of the contemporary changes. It is with such models that we might, subject to the availability of relevant data, make our predictions of political revolution, of economic advance or stagnation.

In selecting material, due coverage should be given to all parts of West Africa. But what is fair coverage? To give equal weight to each of the fifteen territories is to ignore the fact that Nigeria's population of fifty-six million far exceeds that of the remaining fourteen states combined; the ten million inhabitants of Western Nigeria (and the slightly greater number of Yoruba people) outnumber the combined populations of any two of the French-speaking states; the Kano emirate population alone outnumbers that of half the independent states together. Furthermore, the issues discussed in the following chapters have been studied far more extensively by British and American scholars than by the French; and the former have inevitably concentrated upon the English-speaking territories. For some states – Mauretania, Mali, Upper Volta, Niger and Portuguese Guinea – we have but the scantiest information on modern society. For slightly different reasons Guinea remains little known to Western scholars.

One amplifies the often sparse literature with one's personal experiences and impressions; it is here that bias is likely to be most pronounced. My own impressions are drawn from fifteen years' residence, research and teaching in Western Nigeria, supplemented by several visits to the other Regions of Nigeria and to Ghana, and much briefer visits to the French-speaking states. If, in the following pages, the English-speaking territories are more frequently mentioned in the illustrative material, and if references to Nigeria appear to exceed those to other territories, it is for the reasons cited. The tentative nature of so many of our assertions and the lack of data to substantiate them should serve to indicate the need for far more research into contemporary West African society.

Preface to the 1972 edition

The first revisions to the text were made in the 1969 edition when a few alterations were made and some recently published works were added to the bibliography; a few additional paragraphs in Chapter 13 reported events in Nigeria and Sierra Leone. In this edition, too, a few further textual alterations have been made and a brief additional bibliography added. Rather than embark upon a more extensive up-dating of the text – after a passage of but six years – I have added a Postscript outlining some of the themes which seem likely to dominate the 1970s.

Brighton, Sussex P. C. Lloyd

Part I
The Heritage of the Past

1 Traditional society

The map of West Africa shows an area bounded by the Atlantic Ocean to the west and south, and by wide arid wastes of the Sahara to the north. Eastwards, beyond the mountains of the Cameroons stretch the savanas of some of Africa's least-known regions – the territories of the northern Congo, of Chad and the Darfur province of the Republic of the Sudan. All but three of the West African states border the ocean, and they have coastal capitals – some of them sited on rocky peninsulas or lagoon islands, reminding us that they were once outposts of European influence. From each capital the railway lines run inland, but almost never to join those of neighbouring territories. Roads deteriorate or peter out as they near international frontiers. West African states today appear individually orientated to the Western world. But this is a phenomenon of recent centuries. It was across the savanas from the region of the upper Nile that the Negro first moved to West Africa; along this route probably came conquering groups, perhaps associated with Nubian kingdoms, who brought sacred kingship; by a similar route, too, possibly, came the Asiatic food plants now cultivated in West Africa – the banana and certain species of yam and cocoyam. It was probably the trade in gold from the mines of southern Ghana to the Mediterranean that stimulated the development of the empire of Ghana, and of its successors in the region of the upper Niger – Mali and Songhai. Today these northward and westward links of the West African peoples are being revived as Muslim political leaders look towards their co-religionists, and as possibilities of mineral wealth in the Sahara suggest the practicability of trans-desert highways.

The population of West Africa today numbers nearly one hundred million people. The recent population census of Ghana

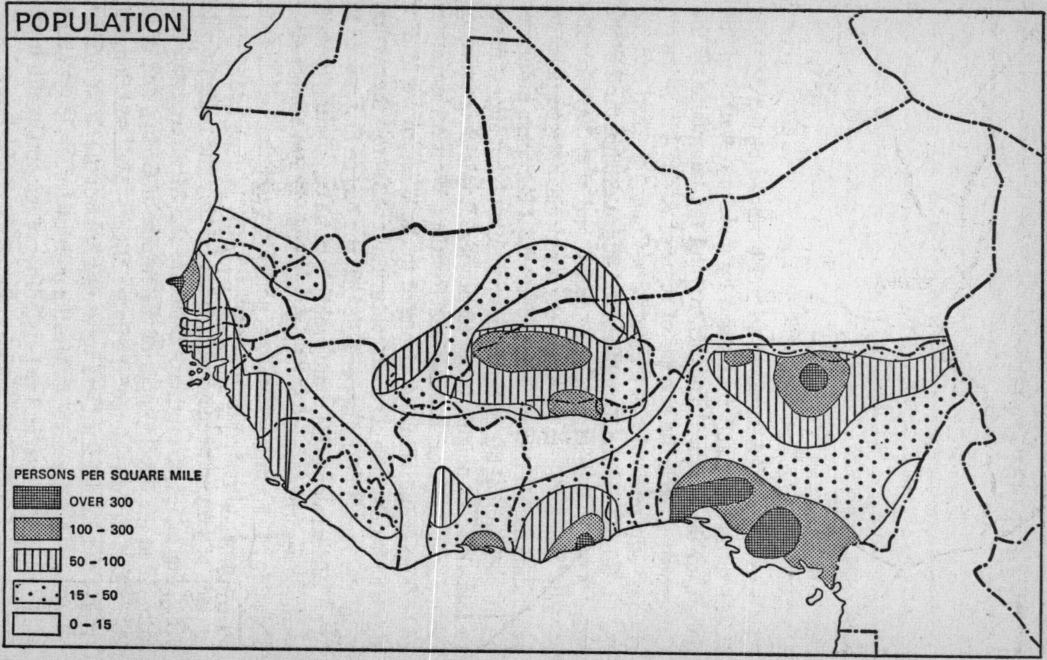
POPULATION
PERSONS PER SQUARE MILE
OVER 300
100 – 300
50 – 100
15 – 50
0 – 15

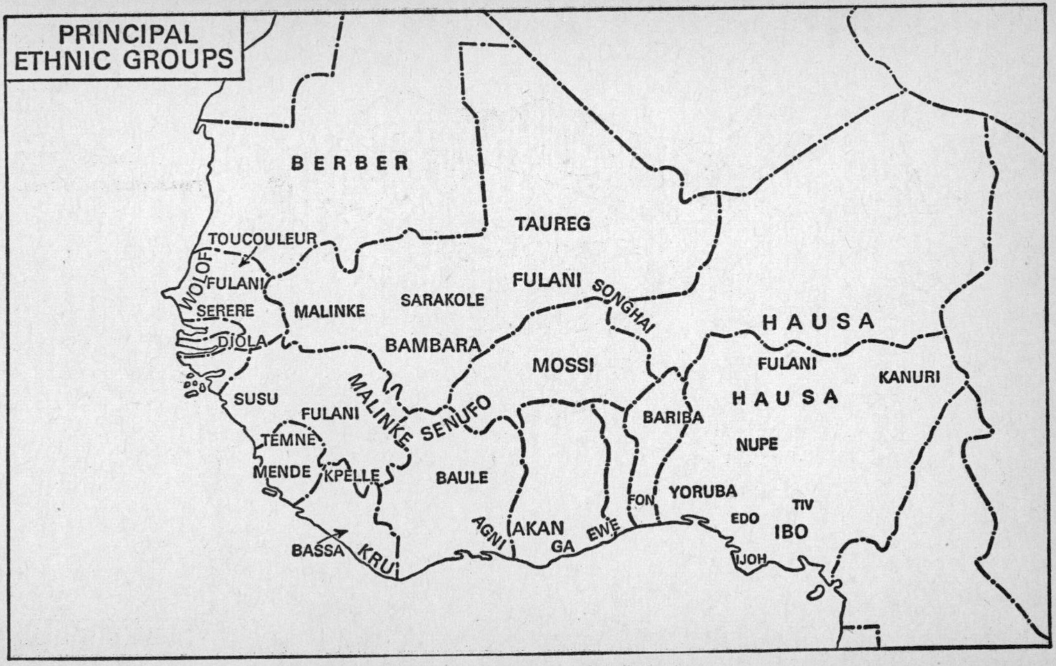
PRINCIPAL
ETHNIC GROUPS
BERBER
TAUREG
TOUCOULEUR
WOLOF
FULANI
SERERE
DIOLA
MALINKE
SARAKOLE
FULANI
SONGHAI
BAMBARA
MOSSI
HAUSA
FULANI
KANURI
HAUSA
SUSU
FULANI
MALINKE
SENUFO
TEMNE
MENDE
KPELLE
BAULE
BARIBA
NUPE
FON
YORUBA
TIV
EDO
IBO
IJOH
BASSA
KRU
AGNI
AKAN
GA
EWE

(1960) was detailed and of a high degree of accuracy. Nigeria's recent census (1963) gave the state a population of fifty-six million, an increase of twenty-three million over the previous count in 1951–2. Such an increase may certainly be attributed in part to better methods of enumeration and to rapid natural increase; but allegations are widespread that the Regions and Districts inflated their populations in order to claim a larger representation in the various legislatures. Dominant was the fear of the Northern Region that it would lose its majority in the Federal Legislature if the southern Regions together exceeded it in population. Lack of reliable census data is a serious inhibiting factor in the economic planning so ardently advocated by political leaders.

The demographic map shows three areas with marked concentrations of population: the Hausa-Fulani emirates, the Yoruba kingdoms, and Ibo country, all now within Nigeria. These three areas are so unlike each other that it is difficult to correlate population density directly with historical or ecological factors. The Ibo live within the rain forest in an area of poor sedimentary soils; but over much of the area the forest has been completely destroyed, replaced by a continuous belt of wild oil palms – the 'palm bush'. In some parts over a thousand people today live and farm within a single square mile. The compounds, consisting of a series of linked rectangular houses, are often dispersed through the bush so that it is only the open market place which indicates the functional centre of each little community.

In complete contrast are the capitals of the Hausa-Fulani emirates – Kano, Zaria, Sokoto and Katsina, for instance. Walled settlements, with populations today numbering several tens of thousands, they are administrative and commercial centres for large rural areas; in many respects they resemble the towns of medieval Europe. Many of their architectural styles are those found throughout the Sudan to the Arab shores of the Mediterranean. And their present high density of population is probably due to the political stability of the kingdoms in past centuries and their capture of population from neighbouring areas lacking centralized government; in some emirates at the turn of the present century half the population is believed to have been of slave status.

Very different again are the Yoruba towns. In the central part of Yoruba country, over sixty per cent of the population now lives in towns of more than twenty thousand inhabitants. Yet these walled and congested settlements are scarcely urban – three-quarters of their adult men are farmers commuting between their town compound and the hamlet at their farms perhaps five miles away. The high density of population within the forest areas is partly explained by the massive southward migration of Yoruba in the early decades of the nineteenth century after the collapse of the Oyo empire, wrecked by civil strife and Fulani attacks.

Throughout the remainder of West Africa the population is relatively sparse; twenty-five persons to the square mile is the approximate mean. Greater concentrations are seen in some stable kingdoms – those of the Mossi, for example, in Upper Volta – and along the banks of the Niger in the savana areas. In general, the more southerly forest areas, with their higher rainfall and shorter dry season, are better able to support dense settlement. Crops can be interplanted on the farm, and two harvests of maize each year are possible, thus increasing the return per unit of land and labour. But many of these areas have been colonized only in recent centuries. The Atlantic slave trade, which shipped six million Negroes to the New World in the last half of the eighteenth century alone, is often held responsible for West Africa's small population. But a high proportion of these slaves seem to have come from those very areas which are today most densely peopled – the 'Slave Coast', now comprising the southern portions of Ghana, Togo, Dahomey and Nigeria.

Most West Africans were in the past – as they are today – agriculturalists. The small surplus produced by the farmers sustained, among some peoples, a body of specialist craftsmen and of political and ritual office-holders. In other ethnic groups crafts were carried out by men who were principally farmers; the village priest worked his land as did any other man. Until the European advent the wheel was unknown in West Africa, and animals were used for transport but not to draw ploughs or to provide non-human power. The farmer worked with the simplest of tools – the short-handled hoe, the axe and cutlass. Systems of bush fallow rotation were usually followed: land cultivated for two or more years with a succession of crops, then left to revert to bush, the farmer moving to a neighbouring plot; the trees and bushes drew soil nutrients from the subsoil into their branches and leaves, and when these were lopped prior to re-cultivation, fertility was restored in the surface levels of the soils. Human or animal manures were not used, save in some savana areas where a symbiotic relationship existed – and still exists – between the nomad Fulani and the settled agriculturalists. The Fulani graze their cattle in the dry season on the stubble fields close to the village.

A wide variety of crops is now known to the West African farmer. There are a few peoples, mostly on the Jos plateau of Northern Nigeria and the adjacent Cameroons mountains, who still plant only an inferior small grain, *digitaria*. But most of the savana peoples have long depended on varieties of millet or guinea corn – crops which were perhaps originally cultivated in southern Ethiopia. The origin of rice cultivation in the Mande areas of the upper Niger remains a mystery. The only major food crop which appears to be indigenous to the forest areas is the yam – the white and guinea varieties. But to these have been added those from Asia already cited, together with the introductions from the Americas – cassava and maize. Of some introduced crops, only a few varieties are known to the West African farmer; but of those developed locally, a wide range of varieties is known – the Yoruba farmer today recognizes over thirty different types of yam. With such knowledge, farming becomes a complex task, as the various crops are fitted into a rotational system, and account is taken of local climatic and soil conditions.

Craft industries were more highly developed in West Africa than in other parts of the continent, though here too the technology remained simple. On the eve of the colonial era almost all peoples used iron tools, while basket making and pottery were universal. Cotton was widely grown in the savana and the forest margins, to be woven on both horizontal and vertical looms, and tailors made the cloth into gowns, often of complex design – such as the Hausa *riga* or the Yoruba *agbada* and *sokoto*. The royal courts gave employment to men producing regalia, luxury articles of clothing, and ritual objects for shrines. Throughout the forest zone a high artistic level was achieved in wood working, especially in the making of masks used in religious ceremonies. The brass heads of Ife in south-western Nigeria, of Benin and of other centres in the lower Niger valley, the earliest examples of which date probably from the fourteenth century, are now famous throughout the Western world.

The degree of specialization in agriculture and crafts led to a development of markets in West Africa on a far greater scale than elsewhere on the continent. Even in areas where most farmers were producing food primarily for their own domestic consumption, a considerable level of exchange existed. The established kingdoms provided security along the caravan routes; and although among the more backward peoples trade was conducted by barter, elsewhere local currencies existed, such as the cowry shell used by the Yoruba and neighbouring peoples. These currencies had most of the attributes of money as defined by economists. The degree of trading, particularly in the coastal areas, was increased with the exchange of slaves and later of palm oil for European imported goods. Indeed, commercial ability is still highly valued among some ethnic groups. The Hausa men today travel widely throughout the savana region and to the coasts of Nigeria and Ghana, while Yoruba men and women are today active in the markets of Abidjan, Bobo-Dioulasso, Ouagadougou and throughout Ghana.

The visitor to West Africa who travels inland from the coast is impressed by the slow change from forest to savana; within each ecological zone, the local scenic differences seem imperceptible. As he passes through a succession of equally small village settlements, the local differences in architectural style largely escape him. Yet the cultural differences among the peoples of West Africa are of considerable magnitude.[15]*

Almost all West Africans are negroid, with those of the savana tending to be darker skinned and taller than those of the coast. On the desert margins are the nomads of Berber stock. The Fulani seem to derive from a mixing of Berber and Negro peoples in the area of the Senegal river; they are notably lighter skinned and have aquiline features. In recent centuries the cattle-keeping

---

* Number references are to works listed under Further Reading.

Fulani have migrated through the savana to Northern Nigeria and the Cameroons mountains, where substantial concentrations today exist. The more negroid Toucouleur, also a product of this mixing of populations, have remained sedentary cultivators in Senegal. Whilst the Fulani have provided ruling aristocracies in many savana kingdoms, the Toucouleur today provide unskilled labour in urban Dakar; the contrast between two physically related peoples could scarcely be greater.

Many cultural traits are found widely diffused through West Africa, such as those associated with sacred kingship, while recurrent themes exist in myths of origin. It is certain that considerable movement of people has gone on in past centuries within the savana zone and from the savana into the forest. The sharp cultural discontinuities which exist, however, are most graphically illustrated by the distribution of linguistic groups. Most peoples south of the river Niger speak a 'Western Sudanic' language; Hausa belongs to the Chad-Hamitic group of the Hamito-Semitic languages, and the Songhai language, spoken in the Gao area of the Niger, remains unclassified. The Western Sudanic languages fall into several groups: Kwa, spoken in the forest areas from Nigeria to Liberia; Gur, spoken in Upper Volta and the northern parts of Ghana and the Ivory Coast; and Mende, the language of the western states, including much of Mali, Guinea, Sierra Leone, and most of Senegal. Bantu languages, also allied to the Western Sudanic group, are spoken in the eastern areas of Nigeria; it is from the areas near Lake Chad or the northern Cameroons that Bantu speech is thought to have diffused throughout East, Central and Southern Africa. This distribution reflects, in the eastern parts of West Africa, the boundary between savana and forest; and in the western parts, the penetration of Mande traders and ruling groups from their original homeland in the area between the Senegal river and the Futa Jallon plateau.

This simple division into linguistic groups obscures the considerable differences that exist, however, among the languages of neighbouring ethnic groups. Thus Yoruba differs from Edo, Nupe or Fon (all languages of the Kwa group and all neighbours of the Yoruba) by as much as English differs from Russian. And such contrasts, which can be pointed to throughout West Africa, strongly suggest the long existence of distinct cultural groups. Linguistic differences are paralleled by distinct patterns in food and habits of dress, in a multitude of cultural values, all of which tend to inhibit communication between peoples. Hausa is today spoken as a first language by twenty million people, while others speak it as a second language. The mutually intelligible dialects of both Yoruba and Ibo are each spoken by ten million. Yet on the Jos plateau over a hundred separate languages are said to exist, some of them spoken by members of but a few neighbouring villages.

Cultural differences between neighbouring peoples are further reflected in the myths of origin, by which many of them claim descent from single particular ancestors. Thus the one million Tiv of the Benue valley believe themselves to be descended, over fifteen or so traced generations, from a man named Tiv, who founded the human race. The Yoruba describe themselves as the descendants of Oduduwa, the first man, whom the supreme god let down from heaven on a chain to create the earth – though only crowned rulers are expected to be able to trace distinct descent. The term 'tribe', still so widely used, should perhaps be restricted to people both tracing such common descent and socially organized on bases of descent and age. But many ethnic groups do not conform to these criteria. One may reasonably describe the Ibo as tribally organized; collectively they recognize no common ancestor, and each small village group has its own origin myths, but they do nonetheless recognize cultural similarities which distinguish them from neighbouring peoples. Ibo consciousness of unity is perhaps largely a twentieth-century phenomenon, deriving from the much greater contact that the Ibo now have with neighbouring peoples. Hausa, however, is a linguistic term, properly applied to all Hausa speakers, nearly all of whom are citizens of one of the emirates, and most of whom are Muslim. Within some fairly large cultural areas, such as that of the Gur-speakers in north-central Ghana, the people are still not able to perceive the unity of the whole group, so local are their own horizons; they distinguish between themselves ('us') and neighbours ('them'), though neighbours who may be 'them' in one context become members of 'us' in others.

Our present knowledge of West African history is largely confined to the chronicles of the larger kingdoms. A few of these have had their own records, written in Arabic; several have been visited by literate travellers who recorded particular events. Their own legends incorporate lists of kings, with the major achievements of each. In contrast, the history of the 'stateless' peoples is contained in genealogies, which often place the mythical founding of the group only three or four generations above living elders; between the origin-period and the events of the most recent decades is oblivion. We still know almost nothing of earliest human society in West Africa; even the archaeological record is, at present, sparse.

Ancient Ghana, ruled by a Negro king with an impressive court, reached the height of its power in the tenth century A.D., when it controlled a large part of the present states of Senegal and Mali from its capital at Kumbi Saleh, north of Bamako. Then, in the mid-eleventh century, the empire was overthrown by the Almoravids, a puritanical sect of Muslim Tuareg. In the area of Lake Chad, the empire of Kanem flourished between the tenth and fifteenth centuries, with its rulers embracing Islam in the eleventh century. Ghana was succeeded by Mali, ruled by Mande rulers who later embraced Islam; and as this empire in its turn fell, Songhai rose to power.

These empires provided the internal security to facilitate trade; each lay to the east of its predecessor, perhaps reflecting the changing axis of commerce. As their rulers sent relatives to administer the provincial territories, members of these families, many of which still enjoy high prestige, became scattered throughout the savana. Although Islam became the court religion in these empires, it did not necessarily reach the masses; as the empires fell and village communities reasserted their autonomy, traditional religious practices were maintained. The Bambara of modern Mali have still not embraced Islam to any great extent.

Whilst the great empires rose and fell, lesser kingdoms displayed greater continuity. The Mossi kingdoms have been ruled by a single dynasty since the thirteenth century. The Hausa kingdoms are of similar antiquity; though, unlike the Mossi, their rulers embraced Islam. In the late eighteenth and nineteenth centuries the western savana areas were again organized into large empires by Al Haj Omar and Samory, though in neither case does a deep impact seem to have been made on village life. In the east, however, the fanatical Muslim Fulani overthrew the Hausa kingdoms in a *jihad* or holy war, on the pretext that their rulers and people were extremely lax in their Muslim faith. Much of the indigenous structure of these kingdoms was, however, retained, with the Fulani constituting a new ruling aristocracy from whom the highest political office-holders were chosen.

Centralized government developed late among the forest peoples. Migrants from the savana introduced sacred kingship probably a millennium ago. But the consolidation of petty chiefdoms into powerful kingdoms seems to derive principally from the European contact with the coast, with the development of new trade routes and the introduction of firearms. The powerful Yoruba kingdom of Oyo thus developed across the route from the lower Niger to the coast, albeit with the assistance of the horse, obtained from the north, rather than of guns. Brass plaques made in Benin in the sixteenth century testify to the importance of Portuguese weapons in the expansion of this kingdom.

Whilst the peoples of the savana have almost all, at one time or another, formed part of wide-flung empires, for most of them the opportunities to participate in government have been slight. They have continued to live in their village communities ignorant of the life in the capital. In the forest kingdoms, so much smaller in extent, political offices in the capital have been open to a much larger proportion of the people. The political elite have not been an alien ruling group. Then, within the forest zone are many peoples who have never known centralized government, whose largest political units are village groups with councils of elders. Such are almost all the peoples east of the Niger, the Ewe of Togo and Ghana, and most of the peoples of the southern Ivory Coast, Liberia and Sierra Leone.

Descent groups

We have stressed the distinctiveness of cultural groups, implying stable residential patterns; we have seen that, even within the greatest empires, village communities have continued with but little change in their social and political organization. It is perhaps for these reasons that groups defined in terms of descent remain the basis of the social organization of so many West African peoples.[30, 31]

Descent groups, variously termed lineages, clans or families, are the antithesis of the nuclear family upon which industrial society is so often based; they stress group loyalty rather than individual independence. As an individual moves from the rural area to work in the town, new loyalties compete with those to his descent group; yet in his absence from home he loses none of the rights conferred on him by his descent, and his membership of the group constitutes substantial economic and emotional security in situations of rapid change.

A descent group is a body of persons who trace descent, in male or female or both lines, from a named ancestor. New members are added by birth, while the dead are believed to retain their interests in and influence over the group from the other world, so that the group exists in perpetuity. Membership is described in terms of descent, but this may be fictive; adoptions and later absorptions into the genealogies are usually possible. Genealogies themselves are often foreshortened to three or four generations above living elders; their purpose is not to provide past history but to act as a charter for social behaviour among living members of the group. Far more important than the line of descent, usually used by ethnographers in classifying such groups, is the degree of corporateness that exists within the group.

In most descent groups the male members (if descent is traced in the male line) are co-resident, and so the territorial community coincides, in part, with the social unit. A few examples will illustrate this. A typical central Ibo village group, today comprising some twenty thousand persons, is said to have been founded by a man and a woman, now deified and perhaps associated with a local stream or some similar physical feature. They are believed to have had nine sons, who respectively founded the nine villages comprising the group. Each of these men had sons who respectively founded the quarters of the villages, and their sons in turn founded the individual compounds where their grandsons (as located in the genealogies) are now the living elders. The entire Tiv people, as stated above, trace descent from a single ancestor, located fifteen or more generations ago. The genealogical descent lines bifurcate in each generation; the members of each segment, at whatever level, occupy a territorially homogeneous area of land. The northern Yoruba trace descent in the male line; the Akan of Ghana, in the female line: the towns of each, however, are similarly structured. The town comprises a number of descent groups, the founder of each of which immigrated to the town at some time in the distant past. From the first migrant to the area, the 'founder of the town', are usually descended the members of the royal descent group, from which the king is selected. And in each case, the members of the descent group live together in a quarter of the town. The traditional Yoruba compound, which may house over a thousand persons, consists of a series of adjoined rectangular structures, each with rooms for its inhabitants leading off a verandah enclosing an open courtyard.

Co-residence itself indicates the corporate nature of the descent group. But the group may hold not only the land on which it lives but also that which it farms. Rights, often amounting to ownership, are vested in the group; the individual member participates in the meetings at which the management and allocation of the land is discussed, and has the right to the undisturbed use of the land allocated to him. He may claim as much land as he and his dependants can cultivate; but if he or his descendants fail to make use of the land, it will be allocated to others. Land is thus continually being redistributed within the group.

The descent group is usually exogamous – a man must choose his wife from a group other than his own (or perhaps other than those of his grandparents). The suitability of the proposed match is discussed by members of both groups, and the bridewealth paid by the man to his bride's family may be widely distributed among the members of her descent group. A creditor who finds difficulty in retrieving a debt may distrain upon the property of any member of the debtor's descent group. In those societies where the authority of political office-holders, if any, is weak, homicide is settled by the group of the murdered killing any member of the murderer's descent group – though the latter group may evade this retaliation by the transfer payment to the deprived group of a person, or of goods to enable the deprived group to gain a wife for one of its members and so eventually restore its numbers. In these, and other ways, the descent group corporately holds jural rights over its individual members.

In societies structured like this, a man's interests – his rights to land and to liberties of various types – may be represented through his descent group. The town or village council may be composed of representatives of the constituent descent groups – perhaps men judged to be the most senior by some process of ranking or elected by each group from among its members.

The cohesion of the descent group, established through its corporate rights over individual members, rights to land and political office, is often reinforced by its possession of deities peculiar to it and related in some way – perhaps as ancestors – to its origins. Furthermore, a medley of traits – appellations, facial marks, food taboos – may serve to distinguish the members of different descent groups in the community.

One must emphasize again that in not all societies does descent form the principal basis of association, and there are wide variations in the degree to which the groups are corporate bodies. One prevalent form of grouping which cuts across descent is that based upon age. Public tasks such as manual work in clearing paths or military service must be allocated on the basis of age, and many societies have systems of age grading, though no West African society compares in this with the Masai and other Nilo-Hamitic peoples of East Africa. Again, age sets – groups of men of like age (a three-year interval being common) – not only form the basis of age grades but also represent the collective interests of the young men in their disputes with their elders. A young man who feels that the elder members of his own descent group are working against him, bewitching him perhaps, may appeal to members of his age set for support.

Communities in which descent groups form the basis of social organization are thus composed of a number of identical groups of similar size, membership, age structure, occupations; and groups may be added to, or subtracted from, the community without markedly affecting the remainder. Such societies are said to have mechanical solidarity, on the analogy of the worm which can lose segments and still survive. Industrial societies are, in contrast, based upon organic solidarity; as with a living body, if any single part is removed, the whole will cease to function. Societies with mechanical solidarity have certain characteristics which determine some of the basic values held by their members – values which may persist when the members move to the modern town, however inappropriate these may be to the new situation.

Each corporate descent group in a community is competing with its rivals for the scarce resources of the community – wives, land, political power; for, as we have seen, the interests of the individual are expressed through the group. Loyalty to, and identification with, the group is dominant; the conflict with rival groups serves to reinforce the internal cohesion of each. Nevertheless tensions within the group still occur, for instance between half-brothers competing for the favour of their father. Such tensions, which might otherwise destroy the cohesion of the group, may in some societies be resolved by witchcraft or rather by accusation of witchcraft. Death or sickness is believed to have been caused by powers of evil immanent in near relatives, and perhaps used unconsciously by them. Divination may locate the source of the evil; and counter-magic or threats of violence may be used to combat it.

A further feature of such societies (as also of many small communities not primarily organized on the basis of descent groups) is the interdependence and multiplicity of roles. Any two men may be closely related to one another by ties of kinship, economically as trader and customer, politically as chief and follower, and so on. It is difficult for a man to alter the nature of any one of these relationships without affecting the others; and so the pattern of social relationships becomes somewhat static. (Conversely, changes in social relationships are more easily effected in modern society, where such a multiplicity of roles involving two particular individuals is less likely to occur.)

A final point concerns the status of the wife in societies organized on the basis of descent groups. One still hears the African wife described as a slave; the bridewealth paid for her represents a purchase price, while her overt subordination to her husband and other members of his descent group is most marked. But such a comparison quite misrepresents her status. By her marriage she does not gain full membership of her husband's descent group; her prestige among members of that group depends largely on the number of children that she bears. On the death of her husband, his rights in her perhaps pass to a junior brother; she inherits nothing from him, though she will be maintained by her sons in her old age. But the wife usually retains her membership of her own descent group, and its members will support her in her disputes with her husband. Since the woman is thus not alienated from her group, divorce may be easy. And it is further facilitated when the husband and wife do not form an occupational unit. Both the Ibo husband and wife farm, while certain other tasks are allocated on the basis of sex; and so divorce is less frequent than among the Yoruba, where the women never farm but engage in crafts or trade, having their own separate cash incomes, which are beyond the control of their husbands and which they may use to maintain themselves and their small children. Where the wife is not regarded as a member of her husband's descent group, and where divorce is frequent, the status of the husband in the community is not shared by his wives. Thus the prestige of the chief is not shared by his wives. Nor, conversely, does the wealth of a woman trader reflect prestige upon her husband. This is the opposite of the relationship in the modern nuclear family, where the social ranking of husband, wife and children is identical.

We have stressed the existence of descent groups in the social organization of West African peoples because such groups are important in societies of many different types. A distinction is often made between the 'stateless' or acephalous societies – societies lacking centralized government – and states or kingdoms; in the former, descent groups are often the dominant form of association, and order in the society is maintained largely through the balance existing between the groups within each community. Yet descent groups may form the basis of organization in the village communities of the centralized states as well, and even within the ruling classes of some such states.

Where order is maintained through the balanced opposition

between descent groups, the political units are certain to be small in scale. In fact, where most relationships are expressed in terms of kinship, it is often difficult to define the political unit. One may distinguish three levels: the smallest unit, within which disputes are settled by arbitration; a second or higher level, at which they are settled by controlled methods of warfare, like the feud; and the third level, at which unrestrained fighting may take place. Thus, between the numerous hierarchically arranged segments which compose the Tiv society, there are no recognized boundaries which may be held to divide the people into discrete political units. Relationships between Tiv are defined solely in terms of genealogical distance: against those more closely related, one fights with sticks and stones; against the distantly related, with bow and arrow, intending to kill rather than wound. In other societies the easily recognized ethnic units may not be political units. In the Ibo village group already referred to, disputes and such political matters relating to the public affairs of the community are almost invariably settled within the village; a group council, with representatives from each village, rarely meets. Village group cohesion is maintained instead through participation in the rituals concerned with the common founding ancestors and in the big market.

How can order be maintained when there are no persons holding any type of institutionalized authority, or when those in authority have little power by which to ensure obedience to their decisions? Of the Tiv it is said that there is no office of authority above the head of the individual compound – a group of a dozen huts with a population of fifteen or twenty adults and representing (in its male members) the smallest segment of Tiv society. When a dispute breaks out between two men – over rivalry for a woman, trespass on farm land, theft of a goat – each will call to his assistance the men of his own segment. Thus, if the disputants belong respectively to groups A and B, all the members of A will confront,

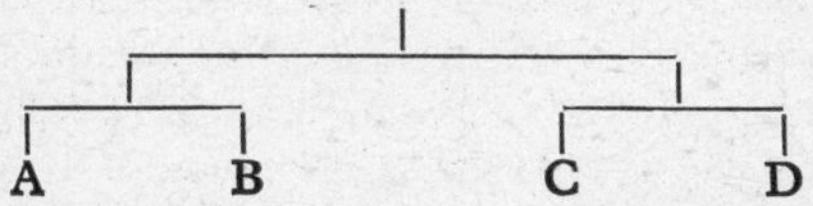

at the adjudication, the members of B; if the disputants, however, come from groups A and D, then the members of A and B will combine to face those of C and D. Ultimately a settlement is reached because the two segments are of roughly equivalent size, and neither can, in practice, coerce the other. This equivalence is maintained through a continual readjustment of the patterned genealogies and by the insistence on compensation for wrongs suffered. The values of the society strongly urge a peaceful settlement between closely related groups; the alternative would be anarchy. In achieving the settlement, however, a major role is played by 'men of influence', who lead the arguments of each faction. These are men skilled in the knowledge of customary law and history, men expert in manipulating rituals. Their power is thought to derive from possessing attributes of witchcraft, but their power can only increase by draining that of their near agnatic kin. The Tiv are a highly egalitarian people, and the *mbatsav* who builds up his power at the expense of others in the society is to be feared and resented. One is pleased to have his support in one's own disputes, but he may well side with one's opponent on another occasion.[17]

In other societies the role of referee between the competing descent groups is held not by elders who are members of the group but by men who, through their position in society, are seen as outside the conflict. Such are, in many societies, the priests of the major local cults. Again, these men have no physical power by which to ensure obedience; but as an ultimate sanction they may effectively excommunicate those who reject arbitration of disputes, by denying them the right to participate in the rituals. Alternatively the curse of the priest, so much more potent than that of other men, may be used to bring the recalcitrants to conformity.

A balance between opposed segments may be seen in other contexts. In some central Ibo villages, the constituent quarter and compounds combine into two equal groups. When the market area and the paths leading to it are to be cleared, each half vies with the other to finish first its share of the task, and the winners then enjoy themselves abusing the lazy losers. Market women are loath to tell tales against members of their own half who cut prices, but have no such compunction in disclosing the malpractices of members of the other half.[22]

One begins to recognize a distinctly political institution in the village council – comprising the oldest age set in the community, or sometimes representatives from each of the constituent descent groups. Often the oldest man, or the head of the descent group held to be *primus inter pares*, is described as the village chief. But such a council may have little power to enforce its orders. An aggrieved man may call upon it to meet and hear his case; it will summon the alleged wrongdoer and, if finding him guilty, may order restitution or compensation to the plaintiff and perhaps a fine of food and drink to be consumed by the elders. But if the guilty person refuses to accept this judgement, the village council can at worst expel him from the community, permitting the young men physically to drive him from its territory or, in extreme cases, kill him. Many of the slaves shipped across the Atlantic were men who had been taken captive in local wars; but many too, from the acephalous societies, were men who had been driven from their own communities, thus losing all protection from their kin and becoming slaves wherever they ultimately settled.

Social order may be maintained through the balanced opposition of descent groups only so long as the segments remain of equivalent size. When some groups gain in power at the expense of others – through control of land or of titled offices, for instance – and when this imbalance cannot be corrected through genealogical adjustment (as when the descent groups are of such diverse origins and attributes that the transfer of people from one to another becomes impossible), then a higher degree of authority is needed. This is provided, over large areas of West Africa, by the so-called 'secret society', or by sacred kingship.

Religious cults, the elaborate rituals of which may be known only to members, are common throughout West Africa. In some, such as the *Poro* of the Mande peoples or the *Ogboni* of the Yoruba, the cult elders perform important political functions. Membership of the cult may be open to all adult men, and most will join its lowest ranks; then, through the payment of fees, the giving of feasts and the performance of rites, some will rise through a series of ranks to the most senior offices. It may not be known, outside the membership of the association, which men these are. They do not represent their descent groups, though individual groups are not permitted to monopolize the leading positions. And these senior officials, sitting in council, may in extreme circumstances condemn a man to death, and themselves execute him at their meeting place, secure in the knowledge that the secrecy which surrounds their act and the supernatural sanctions which maintain the secrecy will suffice to prevent retaliation by the members of the condemned man's descent group. With loyalty to the cult transcending that to the descent group, a man may even order the death of his own brother.

Kingdoms

Ethnographers have tended to stress the common traits associated with sacred kingship throughout Africa: the identification of the health of the ruler with the fertility of the crops and of women; the installation ceremonies which symbolize re-birth; the taboo on seeing the king eat; and many others. Social anthropologists have described the interrelationship of political, religious, and social institutions; colonial administrators have seen in the African kingdoms a similarity with those of feudal Europe – overlooking the more apt comparison with the earlier Saxon kingdoms; and historians have postulated a 'Sudanic civilization' with a 'considerable fund of common political ideas'.

In the West African kingdoms, the king is advised by a council of chiefs, the individual members of which act not only in a political capacity but also as administrators, collecting from the mass of the people through lesser officials the annual tribute, and retaining a share of it as their own remuneration. Specialization of duties among the chiefs is not highly developed. The relationship between the king and his chiefs is, however, far from uniform, and distinct types of political structure may be recognized.[32] These differences are important to an understanding of the manner in which the colonial administrators were able to use traditional institutions in local government – and hence the degree to which these institutions have persisted to the present day.

It has been argued that political systems with a range of

specialized offices may be more easily adapted to modern bureaucratic systems; again, peoples who have been accustomed to selecting their representatives to a governing council will not find elections by ballot with universal suffrage alien to their values, though they may seek a stronger control over their elected parliamentary representatives than is usual in Western societies. Furthermore, the traditional political system helps to determine the stratification in society and the related current attitudes towards social mobility and achievement – attitudes which, in a modernizing context, importantly affect the rate of development.

In one type of kingdom, exemplified by those of the northern Yoruba and the Akan peoples, the town comprises numerous descent groups of heterogeneous origin. Each descent group elects from among its own members a titled chief, with a seat on the governing council, and the decisions reached by the chiefs are then communicated to the king, who announces them as his own. Indeed, it is the chiefs themselves who select the king from among the eligible candidates in the royal lineage. The king is seen as an arbitrator in the conflicts of interest between the various descent groups; without him the groups would never reach agreement, and the members of the community would disperse in anarchy. Educated Yoruba today term their rulers 'constitutional monarchs', to stress the fact that the king may not act except on the advice of the chiefs.

Yet the sacred aura of kingship, the wealth which could be accumulated within the palace (for all of it passed to the succeeding ruler, none to the closer relatives of the deceased king), and the opportunities enjoyed by the king to manipulate the disputes between chiefs, all combined historically to place considerable power in the hands of the reigning king. King and chiefs thus vied for power. Since the king had no direct control over the army and no substantial personal bodyguard of palace slaves, he was in a weak position to coerce the chiefs, who in the last resort could depose him, often by asking him to commit suicide. Attempts by a ruler to exceed the powers thought proper by his chiefs thus usually resulted in the re-establishment of the *status quo ante*. Extraordinary factors, however, such as great success in warfare (with a consequent increase in his wealth and in the numbers of his slaves), development of trade, or the introduction of new weapons, might provide the king with new opportunities for power, resulting perhaps in his ability to appoint chiefs responsible to himself alone and hence his escape from dependence on those elected by the descent groups.

Some such process probably accounts for the development of a second type of kingdom, exemplified by the pre-colonial states of Benin and Dahomey. Here all titled offices are filled by the king, who acts with the advice of his chiefs but not necessarily with their unanimous consent. The titles may be ranked in a series of grades, the membership of which decreases in number towards the top; and promotion in titled office depends less on the support of one's kin than on one's favour with those ranked above one and ultimately with the king. The chiefs are thus not primarily the representatives of their descent groups. In fact, the individual may be represented through a variety of associations – his descent group, age group, village, or title association. The most senior commoner chief is often regarded as leader of the opposition to the king and to the royal power, though remaining the king's principal adviser. On each specific issue the factions mobilize behind the two leaders. But the diffuse representation of interests and the rivalry among chiefs for promotion enable the king to retain considerable power as he manipulates the various groups. All the same, despite the apparent despotism of the ruler, advancement to high political office remains a possibility for any freeborn man in the kingdom.

A third type of kingdom is created by conquest. In the Hausa-Fulani emirates of northern Nigeria, the nomadic Fulani seized power from the erstwhile Hausa rulers by a *jihad* in the early years of the nineteenth century. The initial conquerors portrayed themselves as holy men, anxious only to restore the Muslim faith. Their sons, however, installed themselves as secular rulers and began transferring to their own kin the existing titled offices as well as creating new offices for them. Today the throne is shared by a number of descent groups or ruling houses, among which there exists considerable rivalry; for unlike the situation in the two types of kingdom outlined above, where the close kin of the king are denied political authority, among the Fulani the emir bestows upon his most favoured kin and followers the highest political offices, giving them not only power but also great wealth. Hausa commoners have no direct representation on the governing councils, though they may exert some influence in supporting rival Fulani claimants for office. The Fulani themselves stress Islam as a qualification for political office, and their domination is expressly identified with Islam. The Hausa acceptance of an inferior status is, however, facilitated by the high degree of inter-marriage between Fulani and Hausa, by the opportunities for acquiring wealth through trade open to the Hausa (and shunned by the Fulani), and by the recruitment to specified 'slave' offices from the lowest ranks of Hausa society. Ultimately, of course, the preservation of Fulani rule and the acceptance of the associated ideologies have rested upon Fulani powers of physical coercion.[24, 26]

In certain types of kingdom the descent group ceases to be a strongly corporate association and may even cease to be recognized as a social unit. A number of factors may operate singly or together. The descent group may cease to hold land as a result of substantial movement within the kingdom and the dispersion of group members. It may cease to hold a chieftaincy title, because such offices are allocated on other bases (as in kingdoms of the second type described above). Lastly, the cohesion of the descent group is weakened when an individual turns not to his co-members for support but to a person, perhaps unrelated to him, who is in a strategic position of influence. Thus in Benin a man seeks the patronage of those already influential at court to facilitate his own advancement. In a very different context the Hausa commoner, in difficulty with Fulani rulers over his tax assessment or some litigation, turns to a patron from among the ruling group, offering his allegiance and services in return for protection.

Stratification and achievement

These brief sketches of the traditional social and political organization of West African peoples have demonstrated some major differences among them. In some societies, and in particular those whose social organization is based upon descent groups, positions of political power or (as among the Tiv) influence are open to all members of the society; in others (the Hausa-Fulani emirates, for example) opportunities to attain high office are unequal, with members of a ruling class obviously preferred. Similarly, opportunities for amassing riches are more widely shared among African peoples than is sometimes recognized. One is still told that in the 'traditional' societies of the world, ascribed status is dominant – a man cannot escape the status into which he was born; conversely, that in modern industrial society achieved status is characteristic – a man's position in life is what he makes it. Both these statements are over-generalized. The image of 'traditional' society as an inert mass of men lacking initiative seems scarcely appropriate in West Africa today, where one may reasonably regard a major task of the politicians as assuaging the ambitious (and often unrealistic) expectations of their people for rapid economic advance. In many traditional societies there is considerable scope for competition and for rapid movement from humble to high ranking status; the values associated with such a situation are probably an important determinant in the rate of economic advance which is possible at the present time.

Few West African societies are, however, completely egalitarian. In the pre-colonial era domestic slavery was practised in most of them, and slaves were generally ineligible for political and ritual office, though in some centralized states the slaves of kings and chiefs were granted titles and might wield considerable power. Slavery is now abolished, but the stigma of the status still attaches to those of slave descent.

Many of the savana societies, such as the Wolof of Senegal, are described as having castes, though the term does not bear its Indian connotations. The descent groups of the freeborn were traditionally ranked, from the royal lineages at the top, through noble lineages related to the royal and the mass of the peasant descent groups, to the groups of craftsmen and professionals – the smiths, leatherworkers and praise singers – at the bottom.

Status based upon descent is rigidly ascribed. One cannot change ones' membership of a descent group – though, in systems of unilineal descent, adoption into one's mother's group is sometimes possible, and in those of cognatic descent the individual can choose to which of the many groups of which he is by definition a member he shall give his prime allegiance. Many of the traditional African crafts and professions are hereditary; where the market for their product is large enough, one may find all the members of the descent group practising a single occupation, like drumming, weaving, or blacksmithing. The economic affairs of the craft are managed within the descent group organization. Age, too, is an ascribed status; no man can become an elder before his time.

The descent group itself is, however, usually an egalitarian association. Within the particular group, all members are of equal jural and social status; none is, by virtue of birth, more privileged than others. In some societies this equality of status is stressed to a considerable degree. Thus, among the Yoruba, the chieftaincy title of the group is often held in rotation among the two to six segments which comprise the group, and a chief may not be succeeded directly by his own son. Every member of the descent group, therefore, may feel that, at some time during his own adult life, his own segment will be required to fill the titled office, and that he himself may be a candidate. Again, systems of inheritance by primogeniture are less common than those by which all children receive equal shares of the property of their deceased father – or, perhaps more commonly still, by which the property is divided into as many shares as there are wives with children, so that the children of one mother constitute a unit. It should be recalled here that land is not usually passed by inheritance in this way, unless it is in extremely short supply. A man gains, as a member of the descent group by birth, a right to as much land as he needs; he will perhaps tend to cultivate where his father did, but he may always ask for more land, and conversely land which he does not use will revert to the group for reallocation.

Within this egalitarian framework great differences of wealth and political power are possible, and the gap between the incomes of rich and poor may be as great as that now current in industrial societies. Wealth derives largely from farming and trading; craftsmen are poorly remunerated for their work even when artistically skilled. The wealth of the farmer derives in the main initially from his own hard work, together with some skill in assessing the potentiality of local soils and climate; later, it may result from the possession of a large cadre of sons (or, in the past, of domestic slaves). Of the vast quantity of food produced, much is needed to feed the producers themselves; but among some Ibo peoples, for instance, a man who achieves a very large barn of yams will throw a huge party, and earn a title which confers on him considerable prestige, if not political authority. Wealth from trading demands rather more astuteness in the manipulation of market conditions, but its rewards, in many societies, are correspondingly higher than those to be gained from farming.

In caste-like societies, such as those of the Hausa-Fulani emirates, the wealthy commoner cannot aspire to political office; for him wealth is an alternative to political power. The chiefs are wealthy too, of course; but their income comes from the tribute levied by them, and from farms attached to their position – in short, directly from their political office. In other types of society, wealth from farming and trade is frequently a prerequisite for political office. A candidate's wealth connotes a certain acumen, and he wins support by his generosity to his electorate. As a chief he is expected to be generous to all; kingship and chieftaincy serve to redistribute wealth between rich and poor, serving as an elementary agency of social security. As a chief, a man can devote less time to his farms, and almost none to his trade, and his income from these sources tends to be replaced by the tribute and gifts derived from his political office.

Most West African peoples probably believe still in some degree of predestination. As the soul of the newly born leaves the world beyond, the gate-keeper, on behalf of the supreme deity, gives it its 'fate' for this world. But within limits this fate can be improved or spoilt by the actions of the individual. Thus a father will train his sons to conform to the norms of the society (though he will believe, too, that only in having numerous sons will the chances be increased of his producing one able to achieve a high ranking status). To attain elective political office a man needs to be held in high regard by those of his descent group, to be a man who conforms to the norms of his society; he is not the deviant member of the group. Similarly, the trader works usually within his own society, and his business success depends heavily upon his popularity with his customers – his kinsmen and neighbours. The routes to the achievement of wealth or political office are limited. Where chieftaincy titles are held within individual descent groups, a man may aspire only to the title of his own group; he is ineligible for other titles. With other types of title association, slightly more choice is available as the individual moves upwards through the ranks. Competition for achieved status may thus be restricted to small groups of men, but within these it may be very intense.

Tension between individuals related so closely is difficult to manage, and witchcraft accusations are one method of coping with the situation. The man who fails to achieve his aspirations attributes his lack of success to the hostility, overt or covert, of his near kin. (Though not all peoples would go so far as the Tiv in believing that all success is achieved at the expense of other people.) This attitude is displayed today when young men who do not pass examinations ascribe their failure to the plots of jealous relatives rather than to their own lack of ability.*

The successful West African tends to symbolize his achievement by conspicuous leisure. The wealthy farmer sits in his compound, directing activities at his farm but mainly occupying himself with involvement in the public affairs of his community. Younger or less affluent men consider it an honour to carry the loads of one whose eminence has brought so much prestige to the whole of his descent group.

Few such achievements can be passed (as ascribed status) to one's children. The wealthy farmer acquires a large number of wives – one of the principal forms of conspicuous consumption possible in technologically simple societies – and his wealth is dissipated at his death in division among his many children. The wealth of the trader is similarly dispersed; his own business acumen may not be repeated in his children; his eldest sons may reach the age when they can work with him only when he is leaving trade for political spheres of activity. Chieftaincy offices cannot, in many societies, be transmitted directly to sons, though a son who has worked closely with his father may be a likely candidate for office at some later date. Capital accumulation is prevented by the inheritance patterns of polygynous and egalitarian

* See chapter 10.

societies; most men who achieve success do so by their own efforts and not through the wealth or office of their fathers. Correlated with this is the fact that achieved status remains, during his lifetime, personal to its holder; it is not shared by his wives or children, and does not determine their own relationships with members of their community.

It can be presumed that in every society some men are more ambitious than others, and hence more likely to achieve high ranking status than their fellows. It seems probable, furthermore, that in some societies the degree to which men desire achieved status will be greater than in others. The proclaimed values of societies indicate such differences: some stress the immutability of the ranking system of society and the virtues of obedience to authority; others stress the rewards of competitive effort. Psychological tests of West African peoples have not yet shown conclusively such differences, though popular stereotypes support one's assumptions. Among the Yoruba, the Ijebu are regarded as keen businessmen – an image similar to that held of the Jews in Western societies. Most Nigerians regard the Ibo as noisy and aggressive. How are such distinctions derived? Some would see their origin in social structure, with the achievement values transmitted through child rearing processes. Others attribute the differences to material conditions; both the Ijebu and Ibo (the latter especially so) live in densely settled and not very fertile areas; a man needs initiative and the willingness to emigrate for higher rewards if he is to live beyond a poverty level. It is perhaps indicative of different attitudes toward achievement that the 'typical' Ibo politician is a doctor or lawyer – having gained this status through hard academic work; the Yoruba politician takes a chieftaincy title to validate his claims to authority – though he, too, is usually well educated; the Hausa or Fulani political leader makes the pilgrimage to Mecca.[35a]

Whatever origins the differences in attitude towards achieved status may have, their importance is apparent as soon as urban conditions bring together men of diverse ethnic origins who must compete with one another for the new positions available in modern societies.

As scholars turn from examining African societies as examples of simply-organized peoples to assessing their potentialities for social and economic development, the concept of achievement motivation assumes a more vital role. The literature on the sociology of economic development in Western society has been dominated by the thesis that Protestantism and capitalism are closely correlated. Max Weber's Protestant man – ascetic, believing in his individual responsibility to God, seeing in hard work the route to salvation – provided the rational economic approach demanded of early capitalist enterprises. This thesis has been elaborated by the American psychologist, David McClelland, who defines the achievement motive as a need 'to compete with an internalized standard of excellence'.[35] McClelland holds that heightened achievement motivation within the members of a society is correlated with periods of rapid economic advance, both in pre-capitalist and modern societies. Hagen has incorporated this psychological theory into his theory of economic change. But the wealthy West African trader or chief shares few of the characteristics of the Protestant capitalist. Should ambition be equated with the inner-directed drive of the entrepreneur ? It may well be argued that Weber's thesis is not relevant to modern Africa, for economic advance is not here likely to be achieved through the small private businessman but by large state- or foreign-controlled enterprises.

Part 2
The Impact of the West

2 Trade and colonization

Early contacts

In 1434 Portuguese ships passed Cape Bojador in Mauretania; by 1475 Fernando Po had been reached, and in 1483 Portuguese sailors visited the capital of Benin, probably the most highly organized coastal kingdom at this period. The Portuguese were impressed by it and established a trading port at Ughoton (Gwatto) in 1486, but their main attention was directed to the 'Gold Coast' with its more valuable exports; the castle of Sao Jorge da Mina was erected at Elmina in 1482. Gold apart, the West African coast offered little to attract European trade until the discovery of the Americas provided a demand for slaves. A virtual Portuguese monopoly of trade in the fifteenth century was soon challenged by other European nations anxious to participate in this triangular pattern of Atlantic commerce. In the second half of the sixteenth century about 13,000 slaves were being shipped annually – a figure which grew to 27,000 in the seventeenth century, and to some 70,000 in the eighteenth.

The European traders built heavily armed forts on coastal promontories from which to conduct their business, and much of the international competition for trade was expressed in the capture, recapture and exchange of these bastions. Beneath the walls of the fort were clustered the huts and later the more imposing dwellings of the African traders and their families. In the Niger delta, however, the traders lived on hulks, anchored near the centres of established communities under the surveillance of the local rulers.The supply of slaves, and the subsequent distribution of the imported European trade goods, was almost entirely in the hands of the African. In some of the larger states, such as Benin and Dahomey, the trade was controlled directly by the king, and his income from custom levies and profits constituted a major factor in determining his relationship with his chiefs and people. The increasing importance of trade routes from the coast to the interior savana stimulated the development of larger kingdoms. Oyo undoubtedly gained its supremacy over neighbouring Yoruba kingdoms through its control of the trade route from the middle Niger to Badagri and Ouidah; its frequent wars with neighbouring Dahomey were perhaps an expression of rivalry for coastal control. Not all the slaves, however, reached the coast by these major routes, to be held until sale in the traders' forts or barracoons; in the Niger delta ships would wait for three months to assemble a cargo of some four hundred slaves, individually sold as their local owners felt the need for cash or imported goods. Samuel Crowther, later to become the first Christian bishop in Nigeria, changed hands in domestic slavery on four occasions between his capture in a local war in Oyo and his eventual transportation from Lagos.

The European traders did not usually go far inland from their coastal forts and hulks; the African traders were anxious to retain their monopolistic role as middlemen. Portuguese embassies penetrated to Mali and perhaps reached Tombouctou in the mid-sixteenth century, but did not establish active trading. This contrasts markedly with their penetration of Central Africa from their coastal bases at Luanda and Lourenço Marques. From their headquarters at St Louis, established in 1659, and Gorée, captured in 1677, the French at the end of the seventeenth century began to penetrate the hinterland of the Senegal river; but the profits from the small trade in gum, wax, ivory and slaves, did not warrant the expenses of control over such a large region. The small population of the savana, together with the hostility of those controlling the trans-Saharan trade, contributed to the failure of European efforts in this area. European traders visited the capitals of coastal kingdoms like Abomey and Benin but did not travel farther into the forest belt.

Confined to their small forts and hulks, the Europeans had only a small direct impact on the social and political structure of neighbouring peoples. In just one case did a large settlement develop – that of St Louis which at the end of the eighteenth century had a population of seven thousand including six hundred Europeans and a substantial mulatto community. The French settlers of this period were usually prepared to educate their offspring by their mistresses, though as the nineteenth century progressed, liaisons with local women became less permanent, and fathers were less inclined to accept responsibility for their children. A few Africans were sent to England for training; from Cape Coast, Philip Quacoe was trained for the priesthood at Oxford in the 1760s; he established a small school on his return, and from 1765 to 1816 was chaplain (for the Society for the Propagation of the Gospel) at Cape Coast Castle.

Many African traders learned at least a smattering of English or French; Antera Duke of Calabar kept a diary in pidgin English which was preserved in Scottish mission archives and has recently been published. And these traders often obtained posts as clerks or interpreters for their junior relatives, several of whom were subsequently given magisterial posts in their communities. These men were, in some sense of the term, a local elite. But their adoption of certain articles of European dress and their literacy notwithstanding, they remained members of their descent groups and retained their relationships with their kin in their own societies. Their status was not always, or even often, assumed by their own children. Instead, entire communities profited from their position as middlemen between the Europeans and the interior peoples.

Proselytizing was a major aim of the early Portuguese travellers; for them, the conversion of slaves served to justify the trade. But their religious efforts were largely unsuccessful. Attempts to establish mission stations in the Senegal area failed. After showing a preliminary interest in the new faith, the kings of Benin lost interest, and Portuguese contact with their kingdom was confined to trading. A more spectacular success was achieved in Warri, the kingdom of the Itsekiri people living just south of Benin, which had once been dependent on Benin but which probably used its relationship with the Portuguese to establish its independence. From the sixteenth to the eighteenth century a succession of priests lived in the capital – usually for short periods, as death quickly claimed them. A prince of the early seventeenth century spent ten years in Portugal, to return with a white wife of noble birth, and their son later became king. But the practice of Christianity seems to have been confined to the court. By the mid-nineteenth century there remained in Warri only a few customs derived from Christian rituals, Portuguese words for imported goods assimilated into the local tongue, some of the more indestructible heirlooms of important families, and a consciousness among the Itsekiri of a special relationship with the European and of a superiority to neighbouring peoples. Contact with the European was purposively used by the indigenous African rulers to buttress their position against their own people, or neighbouring ethnic groups. Assimilation of Western ideas and values was minimal.

The effect of the industrial revolution in Western Europe on the pattern of trade, and the upsurge of missionary activity in the nineteenth century, changed the earlier pattern of relationship between European and African.

The anti-slavery movement so prominent in England towards the end of the eighteenth century ultimately achieved not only the banning of the slave trade but also the settlement of colonies for freed slaves. In 1792, a party of nearly twelve hundred sailed from Nova Scotia for Sierra Leone; they had been slaves in the American colonies, freed by British troops in the War of Independence, and taken northward with unfulfilled promises of land to farm. The American Colonization Society sent over sixteen hundred freed slaves to Monrovia and other points along the Liberian coast between 1822 and 1892. These and like settlements within this area suffered many vicissitudes, but ultimately survived. Their people were mostly illiterate, and few had any skills; all had lost contact with the ethnic groups of their origin, and had participated, if only to a slight degree, in Western life. To the Freetown groups of settlers were added a far greater number of men and women who were landed there from slavers captured at sea by British warships. Some seventy thousand in number, compared with three thousand from the Americas, they were settled in village communities around Freetown. (In the Liberian settlements, on the other hand, those freed from the slave ships comprised only a third of the number of the American settlers.)

In 1799, Wilberforce and his friends founded the Church Missionary Society, and Sierra Leone became the first field for its endeavours. Governor MacCarthy envisaged the missionaries as acting as government agents in the villages of the freed slaves, and the Africans themselves, lacking a common language or culture, feeling no bonds with the indigenous people and envying the greater prosperity of the ex-American settlers in Freetown, rapidly embraced the mission teaching. In this manner was created the creole population of Freetown – a group which not only monopolized the trade and high ranking offices in Sierra Leone well into the twentieth century, but also largely provided the early Westernized elite in Nigeria.

To the coastal towns of Nigeria and Dahomey during the nineteenth century, and in particular to Lagos and Porto Novo, came other freed slaves from Brazil. Many of these were trained craftsmen and were responsible for introducing the 'Brazilian' styles of architecture seen in Bahia; but some of the earliest arrivals made their contribution only as slave traders. Whatever their occupations their role in introducing Western values to Africa was less marked than that of the creoles of Sierra Leone.

In the first half of the nineteenth century French Catholic missionaries gained a shaky foothold in the Ivory Coast and Dahomey; in Dahomey they could claim a mere five thousand converts by the end of the century and had twenty-two priests working in the country. In 1845, the Fathers of the Holy Spirit established a mission on the Island of Gorée but made little headway in a predominantly Muslim region. Even today, with nearly three hundred priests (almost half of them Africans), only five per cent of Senegal's total population is Christian.

In the British spheres of influence, predominantly Protestant missions achieved a much greater measure of success. Methodist missionaries landed at Badagri in 1840, and evangelists from this and other mission societies soon moved to interior Yoruba towns such as Abeokuta, Ibadan, and Ogbomosho. Here they were usually tolerated except for brief periods of persecution, their early congregations consisting largely of the men and women who had, at this period, returned to their homelands from Sierra Leone. Far-sighted chiefs and wealthy men often sent sons to the new schools, to learn the techniques of reading and writing so obviously important in dealing with Europeans. Other converts tended to come from the lower ranking members of the society. For at no point did the rulers and chiefs embrace Christianity as the official faith of their kingdoms.

The policy of the C.M.S., enunciated by its Secretary, Henry Venn, was to build up a church staffed by African priests. Almost all of those ordained in the early decades were, in fact, from Sierra Leone. In 1860, Samuel Crowther was ordained Bishop, and much of his life, both before and after consecration, lay in extending the work of the Church to the lower Niger valley. But this policy of Africanization was to be suddenly reversed at the end of the century. An evangelical revival in Britain provided an increased number of candidates for the mission fields, and the conquest of malaria made the employment of Europeans the practical proposition which it certainly had not been earlier in the century. The missionaries themselves, by emphasizing the more primitive and sordid aspects of African life in their letters and reports home, had done much to effect the changed image of the Negro from that of the 'noble savage' prevalent during the early years of the century to that of the sin-ridden creature subsequently common. The later missionaries were intolerant, too, of the compromises effected by the indigenous clergy between their acquired faith and traditional values; and they were reluctant to assume offices inferior to African priests.[86] A similar change occurred in the sphere of government. Africans had risen to high positions in the coastal towns during the nineteenth and early twentieth centuries. In the Gold Coast, H. Vroom had acted as Secretary for Native Affairs; J. A. M'Carthy, a Sierra Leonean, was Solicitor-General in the 1890s and acted on occasion as Attorney-General. In Lagos, Sir Henry Carr was appointed Deputy-Director of Education in 1907. But with the advance of colonial rule, the more senior posts became closed to Africans, and the numbers holding such offices markedly declined.

Education, fostered by the missions, developed rapidly. As early as 1814, a school to train teachers and missionaries had been founded in Sierra Leone; this was re-established at Fourah Bay in 1827, and later became West Africa's first university. In 1845 the C.M.S. opened a grammar school in Freetown, to provide academic instruction and not merely religious teaching, and other mission societies soon founded their own schools. Furthermore, many of the European missionaries worked to establish local crafts and industries and to improve farming. Just as it was the respectable middle classes in Britain who were the backbone of the Christian congregations, so it was surmised by evangelical Protestants that an African bourgeoisie could best regenerate the continent. The C.M.S. Yoruba mission established the Lagos Grammar School in 1859 not so much from a belief in the value of secondary education as to provide a job for the ambitious Sierra Leonean, the Rev. T. B. Macaulay (whose son, Herbert, was later to found one of the first nationalist movements in Nigeria). This and other secondary schools were immediately popular among the African populations, who saw in an academic education the surest path to new offices and to wealth; the industrial training centres, in contrast, enjoyed a marked lack of support, and most of them vanished.

For almost four centuries Western Europe's knowledge of West Africa was virtually limited to the coastline and a few of the most southerly kingdoms. Not until 1795 did Mungo Park travel inland from Bathurst to Segou on the river Niger; ten years later, following the river downstream, he died near Bussa. Indeed, the Niger was still popularly thought to flow eastwards into Lake Chad. Clapperton and Richard Lander were probably the first Europeans to traverse Yoruba country when they followed the trade route from Badagri to Old Oyo in 1825, subsequently crossing the Niger at Bussa. Five years later the Lander brothers retraced this route, but sailed down the Niger to discover its mouth in the well-frequented delta. In the early 1850s Heinrich Barth travelled extensively between Bornu and Tombouctou. These journeys fired the imagination of many Europeans who saw, in the towns of the savana, rich prospects of trade and evangelism.

Government policy was opposed to any costly extension of imperial power, but the momentum of events took command. British and French consular officials made treaties with coastal peoples in attempts to monopolize trade and influence among them. The European trading community and the missionaries resented official interference, but demanded greater protection from their governments. Then, in their attempts to end the slave trade and keep open the routes of legitimate commerce, the consular officials became more and more deeply involved in the local politics of the coastal peoples; support given in war became a recognition of protectorate status. Lagos was annexed in 1861, and Britain's power over the Fanti states increased as she sought to protect them from Ashanti attacks.

Various expeditions by mercantile interests were made up the river Niger, culminating in the granting of a charter to the Royal Niger Company in 1886 to trade and to administer the areas controlled. Such penetration, however, was opposed by both the European merchants on the coast and those African coastal middlemen whose monopolies were threatened.

It was the French who first made a systematic attempt to penetrate the interior. From 1854 to 1865 General Louis Faideherbe was Governor of Senegal. He not only established French rule as far up the Senegal river as Kayes, but laid the foundation of administrative and educational systems, and pioneered the development of groundnuts as an export crop. Only after the 'partition of Africa' in the 1885 Treaty of Berlin, however, did the colonial powers begin to occupy the vast areas assigned to them. Conakry was occupied by the French in 1887. Five years earlier the French had re-established their protectorate over Porto Novo, but their advance into the interior was resisted by the kings of Dahomey; Abomey was captured in 1893, and its ruler deposed. In the savana the French were opposed by Samory and Rabeh, each of which African leaders claimed (though barely administered) vast territories. In the Yoruba kingdoms, British consular officials and local clergy had negotiated a peace between the warring factions and had made treaties with them to ensure peace, freedom of trade, abolition of human sacrifice, and the like. Such treaties were repeated in 1893 and were signed after full discussion with the various rulers and their chiefs. The Order-in-Council of 1901 establishing a protectorate over the area was not so discussed. When Sir Frederick Lugard became Governor of Northern Nigeria in 1901, succeeding to the administration of the Royal

Niger Company, he quickly sought to establish British rule beyond the banks of the Niger and Benue rivers. With an incredibly small force of three hundred men, he marched on the capitals of the emirates; the Fulani fled and, massing at Sokoto, fought and lost the single short but decisive battle.

Thus by conquest and by treaties the West African states, as we know them today, became colonial territories. Boundaries were fixed which often followed local divisions yet cut across major ethnic groupings. In each territory a centralized form of government was established, its form deriving from the metropolitan country, and the expatriate members of the new administration controlling a wide variety of services. The colonial governor was responsible only to the parliament in the metropolitan capital; he was advised primarily by his senior civil servants, and to some extent in the British territories by a Legislative Council composed at first mainly of British traders, later of nominated and finally of elected African members. Over the colonial territories, the new administrators sought to ensure law and order, while promoting a minimum of development; and how far these aims were fulfilled was determined largely by the small number of personnel available. Thus, after his conquest of Northern Nigeria, Lugard had only nine political officers to control a population of some twenty million people.

Colonial rule

The British and French colonial governments pursued contrasting policies, which have been succinctly distinguished as Association and Assimilation (in French usage); Paternalism and Identity (in British usage); or, when translated into methods of native administration, as Indirect and Direct Rule. But these three pairs are not exact parallels, and the actual policies did not always conform to the stated principles. French policy stemmed largely from the Revolution, when edicts abolishing slavery had declared that 'all men, without distinction of colour, domiciled in French colonies, are French citizens and enjoy all the rights assured by the Constitution'. British policy rested more on empirical foundations, though it found ultimate expression in

Lugard's *Dual Mandate*, published in 1920 after his retirement from the colonial service and virtually the only textbook of administrative policy used by British officials.[40, 41, 42, 43]

The French proclaimed that Africans could assimilate French culture and that those who did so would be accepted on terms of full social equality by all Frenchmen. The stereotype of the British attitude towards Africans was that they could never become Black Englishmen; that their attempts to imitate British behaviour led to ridicule; and that they should develop their own culture. The contrast in these two policies was, however, much modified by administrative practices.

The residents of the coastal settlements in Senegal for long enjoyed substantial political rights. In 1848, some 12,000 Africans of St Louis and Gorée became French citizens, even though most were illiterate and non-Christian. They were even entitled to send a representative to the French Assembly in Paris, and though this right was withdrawn in 1854, others enjoyed by citizens – to be judged in all penal cases according to French law to be immune from the *indigénat* and compulsory labour, to be represented in French parliamentary bodies – continued until Independence. (Under the *indigénat* the freedom of colonial subjects to express opinions and to form associations was restricted; administrative officers could summarily punish many offences.) But the number of Africans who gained this status remained small. In 1936 there were only 78,000 such citizens in Senegal and only 2,400 in the remaining French West African territories. The rejection of assimilationist policies of citizenship began in the mid-nineteenth century, with the establishment of the more authoritarian Second Empire of Louis Napoleon; and whilst Faideherbe pursued assimilationist policies in social services for the residents of St Louis and Goree, the administrative system which he established in the conquered territories was harsh on the 'subjects'. Had the French granted citizenship to all their colonial populations, the African representation in Paris would have outnumbered the French – a situation which had never been envisaged.

French educational policy lay in the establishment of schools with similar curricula to those of the metropolitan country. Indeed, local languages were not taught in primary schools. The financial provisions for education were so small however that only the training of a very small African elite could be achieved. In contrast, a policy of Indirect Rule was applied by the British in Northern Nigeria; Christian missions were forbidden to operate within the towns of the Muslim emirates, and education stressed Islam and local crafts. Elsewhere, however, the government and mission secondary schools (with the Government Katsina College for teacher training, from which so many Northern Nigerian politicians graduated) tended to be run on English public school lines. Local history and geography tended to be ignored, not so much from principle as because no expatriate teachers knew any. The Christian missions themselves saw their schools as instruments of evangelization, and were largely responsible for the dissemination of new values among their pupils.

The African educated in the French territories did, in fact, embrace French culture, and his loyalty to it far exceeded any parallel felt by his counterpart in British territories; thus Blaise Diagne of Senegal could proclaim 'we French natives wish to remain French, since France has given us every liberty.' In Dakar and Paris such men moved freely in European company. But, the absence of any legal colour bar was countered in Africa itself by the resistance of the *petits blancs*, the small-scale businessmen and artisans of little skill, who formed the backbone of the resident French communities.

In contrast with the highly uniform and centralized system of local administration adopted by the French, British colonial administrative policy remained empirical. Considerable initiative remained with the District Officers in the field, and conscious attempts were made to use indigenous political institutions as instruments of colonial rule. It was argued that, in situations of social change, the slow adaptation of traditional structures would cause far less disturbance and tension than the introduction of new ones. And in the 1930s, this view tended to find support from the writings of social anthropologists, who stressed the functional importance of all traditional institutions. It was not always appreciated that whilst offices might be maintained, the roles which their incumbents were expected to play might be considerably altered, producing tense periods of role conflict. Prior to 1939, it was widely held that the parliament of a self-governing Nigeria might be based not upon the existing Legislative Council (where the Westernized elite of Lagos was extending its power) but upon a federation of Native Authorities. A correlated view was that Africans should not enter the colonial administrative service, since this was but a superstructure which would be withdrawn as obsolete upon eventual independence. This general policy was, however, applied in markedly different forms, as adaptations to local situations were effected.

British administrative policy has been termed Indirect Rule – but there seems to be little agreement on the essential components of this concept. Paramountcy of African interests is generally understood as basic, but this has little to do with any specific type of administrative system. Indirect Rule implies, too, the participation of Africans in the administrative machine; but this may be as bureaucrats in an essentially alien structure or as traditional office-holders in the indigenous one. Even the indigenous political structures may be utilized in a variety of ways. At one extreme, the traditional councils may be allowed to function as in the pre-colonial era, with responsibility for local matters; the colonial administration then exists by the side of the traditional system, responsible for tax collecting and the provision of modern services. At the other extreme, the colonial administration attempts to work through the traditional political structure so that, ideally, there is only one system of local administration. Indirect Rule is perhaps most properly used of such a system; but the term has not always been so precisely applied.

The various uses to which the colonial powers put the traditional political systems found in their territories are important to examine. They had a distinct effect upon the maintenance of such systems, upon the prevalent values relating to power and authority, upon the roles of chiefs in modern society.

Throughout most of the nineteenth century the relationship between the British government and the rulers of West African kingdoms was determined through treaties made and enforced by the consular officials. The problems of administering large indigenous populations arose first in the southern Gold Coast. Legislation in 1874 and 1883, which remained in force until 1927, gave recognition to local rulers, allowing them to make by-laws and to exercise limited civil and criminal jurisdiction in local courts. The rulers collected no tax for the colonial government, whose revenues came largely from customs and excise duties. The provision of local services was in the hands of the District Officers, and the colonial government could not make grants-in-aid to bodies such as the traditional councils of chiefs over whose treasuries they had no supervision. These councils often had large incomes, however – from rents for land leased to immigrant cocoa farmers, and from timber and mining fees and royalties paid by expatriate companies. The alleged mismanagement of these monies led to frequent destoolment of the traditional rulers and to a consequent decline in the prestige of the office. Only in 1939 did legislation provide for local treasuries subject to control by the colonial administration. But this reform had barely taken effect when the structure of native administration was replaced by local government in the late 1940s.

Parallel with this *laissez-faire* attitude towards the political role of traditional rulers in their home areas was the attempt to draw them into the government of the colony. Councils of chiefs were set up which discussed government policies, though merely in an advisory capacity, and some chiefs gained seats in the Legislative and Executive Councils – gratefully, since such offices tended to protect their holders against popular attempts at deposition. Predictably, the Westernized elite saw the traditional rulers as rivals for power and, on occasion, blocked moves which would enhance their local authority, while their close association with the colonial government tended to brand the traditional rulers as 'stooges' in the eyes of the mass of the people. This declining status of the traditional rulers and chiefs among the Akan peoples in Ghana forms an interesting contrast with that of the Yoruba chiefs in south-western Nigeria. The traditional political structure of the two peoples is very similar; and both areas are wealthy cocoa producers. The major difference lies in the roles accorded to the traditional rulers in the colonial administrative system.[45, 46]

A very different solution to the problems of administration was instituted by Lugard in Northern Nigeria. The suggested restoration of the Hausa dynasties, usurped by the Fulani *jihad* a century earlier, was seen as too great an ethnographic problem for the minute political staff. Instead, Fulani from rival ruling houses replaced those deposed by the British conquest. Lugard's administration was meagrely financed by the British government, but a ready source of money lay close at hand in the traditional taxation system of the emirates, and this was accordingly used. But with the success of the system came the issue of remunerating the emirs. Were they to be paid salaries, and should their treasuries be subject to administrative control? Lugard himself wished to exercise a close control over the native authority treasuries and retain whatever surplus they had for colonial funds; but he was opposed in this by his subordinates, who argued successfully for far greater financial independence. Later, as the emirates received government grants, they maintained their own public services – water works, hospitals, schools.

The traditional role of emir was an autocratic one; he consulted his chiefs and advisers but was not responsible to them. And such a role, of course, could easily accommodate British over-rule; only minor adjustments were necessitated in the relationship between emir and his chiefs. Being so dependent upon the emir and his subordinates, the colonial administrative officer was obliged to protect the emir's traditional role; emirs were shown considerable respect (and Lugard devised a complicated set of rules defining the degrees of respect to be accorded chiefs of different rank). With the traditional dominance of the emirs reinforced by the tenets of Islam, the safeguarding of the faith from Christian competition was an essential facet of British policy. Later commentators argued that the native authority system, as practised in the Northern Nigerian emirates, tended to ossify a feudal system rather than promote development along indigenous lines. Perhaps. And, with but a few modifications, the system continues today.[26]

The administration of the emirates became a colonial showpiece for its efficiency and cheapness. District Officers from other areas in Nigeria and beyond were sent out to 'find the chief' on whom could be devolved the powers of a gazetted Native Authority. The problem looked easy in the Yoruba kingdoms, and a native authority system was accordingly instituted in 1917. But in the new system, the Yoruba *oba* was no longer dependent upon his council of chiefs – in most kingdoms, men elected by the members of their descent groups; he leaned for advice on the British administrative officer. It was the latter, and not the chiefs, who now held the right to depose the *oba*. Whilst colonial policy did not counter local interests and aspirations – as was the case most of the time – the *oba* could satisfy the role expectations of both the administrative officer and his council of chiefs. But as educated *oba* exploited their status to become benevolent autocrats in their towns, they aroused the opposition of their chiefs, and though many suffered short periods of exile, their eventual victories led to a severe reduction in the prestige of the chiefs among their own people. Reforms of the 1930s which led to the recognition of *oba* and chiefs in council as the native authority (rather than the *oba* alone) and which encouraged colonial officials to see the status of the *oba* safeguarded for decades to come, did not alter the basic contradiction in the system. (Whilst the chiefs lost their battles against the autocratic *oba*, the young literates later elected to local government councils, and backed by nationalist political parties, soon succeeded in reducing the *oba*'s powers.) This contradiction was, of course, inherent in the native authority system. If a chain of authority was to run from the Governor through his subordinates in the administrative service and hence through the office-holders in a traditional political structure, the office-holders in the traditional structure had to be responsible to those above them. But their traditional roles were often ones of dependence upon those below them – kings upon chiefs, and chiefs upon the people who elected them.[46]

These issues were repeated in the administration of acephalous societies with an added dimension. In attempts to 'find a chief', men were often selected whose traditional roles had little to do with political authority. They were ritual experts or merely presided over councils of elders with equal status. Indeed, the introduction of Indirect Rule on the Northern Nigerian pattern to the Ibo peoples and their similarly organized neighbours of Eastern Nigeria proved impossible. From the beginning of the century, administrative officers had created 'warrant chiefs' – men who often had no traditional authority but who seemed powerful enough to act as British agents in recruiting labour. Then, when direct taxation was introduced in 1927, widespread rioting, led by Ibo women, disclosed the extent of hostility to these warrant chiefs. In the 1930s, therefore, councils were instituted which were based upon traditional political units and their representation. These, however, tended to be much too small to function efficiently as local government units.

In both traditional states and stateless societies, under systems of both direct and indirect rule, the village head usually continued to be selected in the customary manner, and he was the bottom link in the chain of colonial authority, responsible for maintaining order, collecting taxes, and recruiting labour for public works. The incompatibility between the demands of the administrative officers and the expectations of his people made the position of this village head an invidious one. A tactful man might succeed in appearing a satisfactory office-holder to both parties; a more ambitious one might exploit the situation to his own advantage. In the early years of colonial administration the peoples of many villages, in both British and French colonies, tried to safeguard their traditional head by putting forward to the administrative officers a younger man – a 'straw chief'.

The institution of Direct Rule in the French colonial territories stemmed in part from the policies of assimilation, in part from historical factors. The conquered savana empires of Samory, Rabeh and Al Haj Omar did not provide an administrative framework such as Lugard found in Northern Nigeria. Where, as in the Mossi territories of Upper Volta and the Fulani emirates of the northern Cameroons, local rulers still effectively controlled their kingdoms, these men were drawn into the French system as *chefs supérieurs*. The greater part of the French colonial territory was, however, divided into *cercles* and *cantons*, units which frequently, and sometimes deliberately, cut across ethnic and traditional political boundaries. The key personnel were the two thousand canton chiefs – each in charge of an administrative unit averaging 8,000 people – and these were selected by the colonial administration. Men from families traditionally holding ruling office were preferred, but the prime qualification seemed to be ability and loyalty to France, as demonstrated by literacy, and by service in government offices, in the army or police. The canton chiefs controlled an average of twenty-four village chiefs; but they were themselves subordinate to the French *commandant du cercle* and could be punished by him through dismissal, reduction of salary, or reprimand. The difference in the relationship between French commandant and his canton chiefs on the one hand, and the British District Officer and traditional ruler on the other, was most marked: the British official spent much of his time touring, visiting the chiefs in their own compounds, and according them overt respect; the canton chiefs were expected to report regularly to their headquarters for instructions, and might wait for hours outside their commandant's office.

French rule fell more harshly than did British on most of the colonial people. More judicial cases were settled by French officials than in British territories with their complex system of customary courts; yet the French official usually knew little of customary law. Under the *indigénat* the French administrative officer could punish without trial. Compulsory labour for public works was less cleverly disguised.

In the 1920s reports were widespread of corruption and maladministration by the canton chiefs – as might reasonably have been expected of men who were in no way responsible to those over whom they held authority; and laxity of control over them during the depression of the 1930s and the Second World War, when there was a shortage of administrative officers, permitted abuses to continue. The chiefs turned increasingly to the colonial administration for protection. In 1947 those in Guinea sought a bill of rights to define their status; and in 1953 chiefs throughout the colonial territories were granted civil service terms of appointment and dismissal. Indeed, in the years immediately following the Second World War, these chiefs formed an elite group with substantial vested interests, and as Independence loomed closer, the French administration sought at first to transfer power to them rather than to the more highly educated and politically conscious leaders.[41, 43] Yet when, as in Guinea in 1957, their abolition was mooted, there was little said in their favour, even by French administrative officers.

The colonial economy

In each of the West African territories a colonial economy was developed; even Liberia, despite its political independence, was no exception. The modern sector was organized around the production of a few raw materials, employing very few skilled persons and, in many cases, large amounts of migrant labour. Manufacture of consumer goods or even the processing of raw materials was virtually absent. Private capital came entirely from abroad, and its profits were remitted there, while public capital was used to develop the non-productive infrastructure needed by the expatriate commercial interests. The majority of the white collar jobs existed in the civil service. Societies were thus created with a small literate elite, with few artisans but with a mass of unskilled labourers, who spent part of their life in urban areas and most of it in their villages. Some farmers increased their income by raising exportable cash crops while continuing to grow foodstuffs in the traditional manner, but many more remained largely untouched by the economic changes in their country.

After the flurry of activity in the late nineteenth century, when the European powers apportioned Africa among themselves and sought to establish some form of domination over the land allocated to them, West Africa lapsed into comparative stagnation. Its exports were not in great demand in Europe; nor did its subsistence agriculturalists provide a market for Europe's manufactures. The British and French governments (and the German until 1914) ran their colonies on shoe-string budgets. The British, indeed, insisted from the beginning that each territory should be self-supporting. Southern Nigeria thus relied initially on its income from customs and excise; and since Northern Nigeria shared little of this revenue, Lugard was obliged to develop for his own needs the Fulani system of direct taxation. The French colonies, on the other hand, were integrated with their metropolitan country to a high degree. French officials were frequently paid from Paris; France paid higher prices than those ruling on the world market for many exports from her empire; and budget deficits in the colonies were erased with grants from the metropolitan treasury. This integration does not seem to have resulted in any greater development of the French territories; but it did make it far more difficult for them to assert their political independence from France.

The economy developed only slowly, with the period of colonial rule marked by two world wars and a general economic depression during much of the interval, so that grants and staffing were for many years drastically cut. In the early 1920s the colonial governments expressly acknowledged their obligations not only to govern but to develop their territories economically and politically. At the same time, however, they asserted that – or behaved as though – what was best for the metropolitan powers was also best for the colonies, so providing ample occasion for generations of African nationalists to complain that their economies were being developed merely to serve European material interests. It was at this period that the development of education and social services was stressed – to produce a peasantry prosperous enough to provide a market for manufactured goods. But with the depression of the 1930s and the Second World War, rather little had been achieved by 1945; and it was in the near- and post-independence periods that the greatest economic advance was achieved, both in mere scale and in the degree to which each state endeavoured to develop an integrated economy of its own.

Agriculture. Agricultural products provided nearly two-thirds of West Africa's exports in 1961, with almost all these crops grown by African peasant producers.[49]

Total exports from West Africa (in £ Million)		*Main Exporters (in £ Million)*
Cocoa	120	Ghana 70, Nigeria 34, Ivory Coast 14
Groundnuts	85	Nigeria 39, Senegal 37
Palm products	41	Nigeria 33
Coffee	34	Ivory Coast 29
Cotton	14	Nigeria 13

The trade in palm oil, and slightly later in palm kernels, replaced the slave trade in the early and middle years of the nineteenth century. The oil palm grows wild in southern Nigeria on land cleared of forest for farming; it has just to be protected by the farmers as they fire the bush prior to each new cultivation cycle.

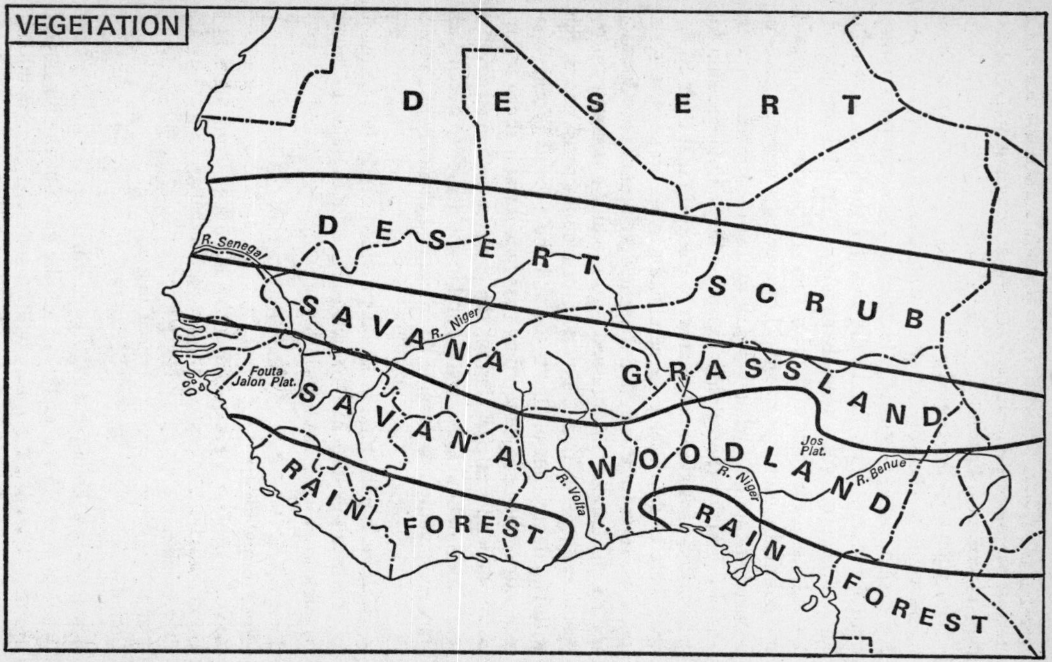
VEGETATION
DESERT
DESERT SCRUB
SAVANA
GRASSLAND
SAVANA
WOODLAND
RAIN FOREST
RAIN FOREST
R. Senegal
R. Niger
Fouta Jalon Plat.
R. Volta
R. Niger
Jos Plat.
R. Benue

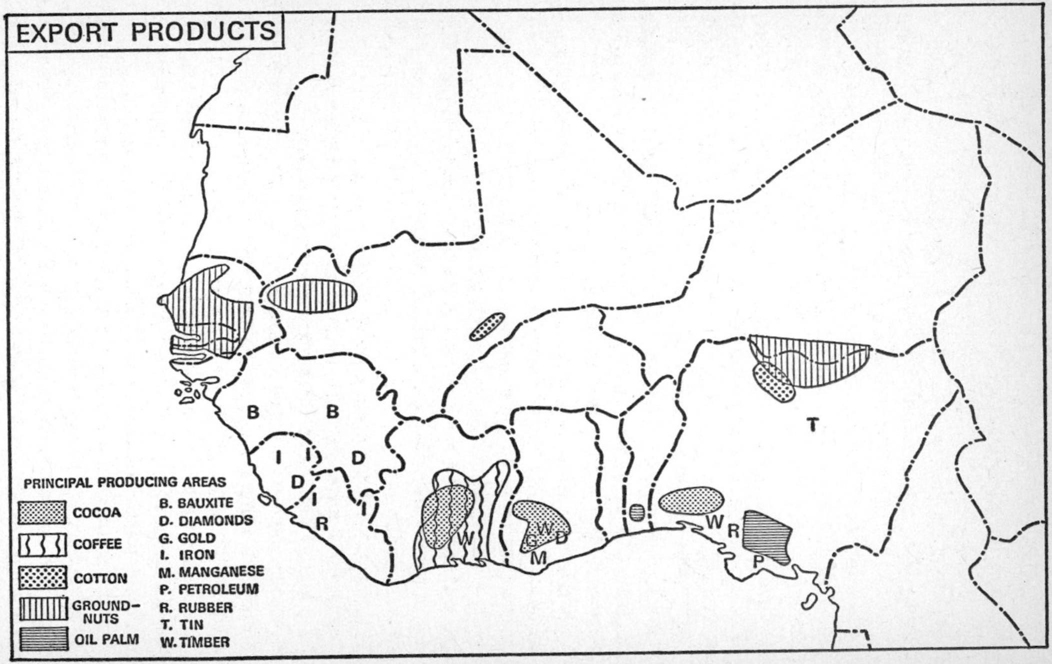
EXPORT PRODUCTS
PRINCIPAL PRODUCING AREAS
COCOA
COFFEE
COTTON
GROUND-NUTS
OIL PALM
B. BAUXITE
D. DIAMONDS
G. GOLD
I. IRON
M. MANGANESE
P. PETROLEUM
R. RUBBER
T. TIN
W. TIMBER

The farmer collects the fruit and, with the aid of his womenfolk, prepares the red oil from the fibres and extracts the kernel from its nut. Much of the oil is sometimes used locally as an essential ingredient of soup – thus Western Nigeria has exported palm kernels but very little oil while the East exported both oil and kernels. Output of this crop has risen only slowly; Nigeria's export of palm products did no more than double between 1910 and 1950. It remains a small-scale activity, and plantations produce only 7 per cent of the present West African total.

Groundnut cultivation began in Senegal in the mid-nineteenth century, and in the early years of this century production there amounted to 125,000 tons; output rose to 500,000 tons before 1939, then fell dramatically, and rose to a new peak of 900,000 tons in recent years. Nigerian production, from the Northern Region, and especially from the area between Kano, Zaria and Sokoto, began soon after 1910 and rose rapidly in the 1930s and 1950s. Individual holdings are small in both Senegal and Nigeria, and yields are low; the average cultivator gets but a small income. In the Casamence area of Senegal the government has established 15-acre plots, mechanically cultivated, on which groundnuts are planted in rotation with cereals and a green manure crop: elsewhere groundnuts are planted as a sole crop in successive years, reducing soil fertility.

Cocoa was introduced into Ghana in 1879, and the first exports from there were in 1896. The country's production rose to 310,000 tons in 1936, and then fell back until the early 1960s, when the average annual production reached 420,000 tons, rising to nearly 600,000 tons in 1964–5. Nigeria's rate of production has followed a similar pattern.

The extension of cocoa growing has been due almost solely to the initiative of the Akan and Yoruba farmers. Holdings are generally small; in Nigeria, half of them are of less than half an acre in extent, giving the farmer an approximate gross return of £50 per acre with the producer's price at £100 a ton. Cocoa should be planted in newly cleared forest (hence its greater extent in Ghana, where the density of population is lower), and food crops may be interplanted with the growing cocoa, so reducing the costs of establishing the farm. In fact, so little labour is needed on a cocoa farm, save for harvesting, that it yields an attractive return to the grower. Nevertheless, there are few farmers for whom cocoa is the sole crop; most grow enough food for their own families. Indeed, it is probable that cocoa farming has not seriously reduced the quantity of food grown; it has been instead an additional source of income. Disease has threatened the crop. In the 1950s, the cutting out of old trees suffering from swollen shoot was the only remedy for the virus disease, though one opposed by the farmers, who saw no reason for cutting down trees still bearing; much of the success of the programme in Ghana was due to the popularity of Nkrumah's Convention People's Party among the farmers. Spraying the trees with insecticide to eradicate the capsid bug, quite an elaborate technique for West African farmers, has been quickly taken up by the cocoa growers. The spraying, together with the intensified planting of trees in the early 1950s when cocoa prices were very high, has led to the increasing size of the crop in the present decade.

This increased production has been a mixed blessing, however, to the governments of Ghana and of Western Nigeria, much of whose revenue has come from export duties on cocoa. In the late 1930s Marketing Boards were established, ostensibly to stabilize the income of farmers by fixing in advance a price for the season. In the early 1950s, when the world price rose to £500 a ton, the Western Nigerian farmer was receiving only £120; the balance, less the costs of handling and shipping the cocoa, was retained by the local Board and used in subsequent years to finance much of the development of the Region. But rising production resulted in lower world prices, and governments were then loath to incur unpopularity by reducing the farmers' price. The Marketing Board's surplus vanished, whilst the total receipts of the farmers in fact increased – in Ghana during recent years from £35 million in 1959–60 to an average of £42 million in 1961–3 and £58 million in the bumper crop year of 1964. With import and export duties rather than direct taxes having provided the revenue for colonial governments, one of the most difficult tasks faced by the leaders of the newly independent states is to retrieve from the masses the wealth produced by the increased production of the 1960s.

Coffee, the main export of the Ivory Coast, accounting for a half of her total exports, was introduced there in the late nineteenth century, but was widely grown only from the 1920s. In general, the colonial governments prohibited or discouraged the immigration of European settler farmers to West Africa; but in the 1930s a few came to the Ivory Coast to grow coffee and cocoa. They never numbered more than 250 there, but by 1942 accounted for over half the coffee produced. Africans were quick to follow their example, though with small, low-yielding plots; and their enthusiasm led to a five-fold increase in the output between the late 1930s and the late 1950s.[49, 131]

This brief survey of export crops has focused on the wealthier states. But the poor ones are no less dependent upon one or two products. Palm products account for half of Dahomey's total exports; groundnuts, for almost all those of Gambia, and over half those of Mali. Live cattle exports account for two-thirds of Upper Volta's visible exports, while migrant labour is probably her main source of income.

These crops, grown by peasant farmers, on a small scale and with traditional tools, have not led to any marked changes in indigenous methods of agriculture. The wealthiest cocoa farmer still grows his food crops in the manner of his forefathers. The Agricultural Departments in the colonial governments each had their stations directing research towards the improvement of local farming methods. But their success was limited – due to the shortage of extension officers and the apparent impracticability of many proposed reforms. Few attempts seem to have been made to take the African farmer and his techniques as the starting point for change; rather were the experiments of the research stations offered to the African. Thus attempts to introduce continuous cultivation of land through the use of green manures and the complete renewal of the bush struck the farmer as requiring much more labour for only slightly greater yields. Of far greater value has been the development of disease-resistant strains, of maize for instance, or higher-yielding varieties; these have been quickly adopted by the farmers. Much of the current research is devoted to assessing the effect of inorganic fertilizer on raising crop yields and profitability – for most fertilizer must be imported at substantial cost. Mixed farming schemes are also being explored, but these too must be investigated over many years before it can be confidently asserted that soil fertility may be maintained by methods other than the bush fallow.

Both the British and French governments embarked on schemes of large scale mechanized agriculture without success. A groundnut farm established at Mokwa in the Niger valley near to Jebba was abandoned after a few years; at one period the cost of destroying (for a single season) the pyramidal termite mounds was equivalent to the final selling price of the crop! Mechanical cultivation led, too, to erosion of the soil by wind. The Office du Niger, established in 1932 to develop irrigated farming in the middle Niger at Segou, had by 1959 cost over £30 million, yet only 13,000 acres have so far been cultivated out of an originally projected total of 2,500,000. Poor soils, cotton parasites and weaver birds together resulted in low but costly yields. The Sokoto rice scheme, in the Sokoto valley, has been rather more successful. But, in general, these schemes have used vast sums of capital to produce little more food and employ few people.

The migration of men and women to the towns inevitably leads to a demand for greater food production from the farmers. But how much has so far been achieved is difficult to measure. To some extent the need has been met by the expansion of cassava growing. Introduced to the coast by the Portuguese, cassava never became popular, largely because of the difficulties involved in its preparation to remove toxic substances. During the present century, however, its production has rapidly expanded in certain areas, notably southern Nigeria. It is a high yielding crop, tolerant of poor soils (including those exhausted by other crops); many varieties may be left in the ground until required for up to four years – thus obviating problems of storage and consequent loss; it is propagated by a length of its stem, not pieces of edible tuber as in the case of yam. Indeed, cassava flour has become the staple diet of urban workers, in place of the more nutritious and more expensive pounded yam. But much of the deficit in food is met by imports – of wheat flour for bread, milk, and other items of elite diets. One-tenth of the imports of tropical African countries tends to be of foodstuffs, drinks and tobacco – a proportion which rose to a fifth in the more affluent Ghana of the mid-1950s.

Industry. The remaining third of West Africa's exports are of plantation products, timber, and minerals.[49]

Total exports from West Africa (in £ Million)		*Main exporters (in £ Million)*
Timber	35	Ghana 15, Ivory Coast 12, Nigeria 8
Diamonds	28	Sierra Leone 16, Ghana 7, Guinea 3
Rubber	20·5	Nigeria 11, Liberia 9·5
Iron ore	17	Liberia 12, Sierra Leone 5
Petroleum	12	Nigeria 12
Bauxite and alumina	12	Guinea 12
Gold	10	Ghana 10
Manganese	7	Ghana 6
Tin	6·5	Nigeria 6·5

Rubber was Liberia's principal export and provided 39 per cent of government revenues before the development of her iron ore reserves. The Firestone Plantation Company, a subsidiary of the well-known American company, secured in 1926 a concession of one million acres, of which over 70,000 had been planted by 1940. These form the most modern rubber plantation in the world and include a latex-processing plant and a small workshop for rubber sandals and other items. Since 1945 Firestone has encouraged the production of rubber by peasant farmers, providing them with seedlings and, until 1962, buying the entire crop. But low yields and small farms are again the rule; though independent farmers now produce 15 per cent of the country's total, four-fifths of the farmers account for only a tenth of this. The Nigerian rubber boom, dating from the late 1940s, was the work of peasant farmers in the Benin and Warri areas.

The extraction of West Africa's mineral wealth is almost exclusively in the hands of expatriate companies, with the notable exception of 'illegal' diamond mining in Sierra Leone. Furthermore, a few companies dominate the field in each case. Liberia's rich iron ore is exploited by four companies, two of which are closely allied. Most of Nigeria's present production of oil is commanded by a Shell–B.P. subsidiary – a company which began exploration in 1937 and was rewarded with success only in 1957. In some cases small companies may operate profitably – for instance, in the open-cast mining of alluvial tin on the Jos plateau of Nigeria, already linked by rail to both Lagos and Port Harcourt. But the Shell–B.P. subsidiary had invested nearly £70 million by 1962 in exploring and developing oil production under the most difficult conditions – sinking shafts 10,000 feet deep into the mangrove swamps of the Niger delta. The development of the Nimba mountains iron ore in Liberia has necessitated a similar capital expenditure; this new area lies 165 miles from the sea through thick forests, and a new port and railway line had to be built to serve it.

Liberia's iron ore industry dates only from the 1950s; and most of the ore is concentrated near the mines before export. Similarly Shell–B.P. is building an oil refinery near Port Harcourt. But such local processing was not common in earlier decades. Although tin has been mined for export at Jos for fifty years, the first local smelter was opened only in 1961. The local processing of cocoa and groundnuts have similarly been extended in recent years.

West Africa was almost completely lacking in manufacturing industries before 1945. The textile mill established at Bouake in the Ivory Coast in the 1920s, and the shoe factory at Rufisque in 1940, were among the isolated exceptions. Thus few industrial skills were imparted to Africans, save through the public services – the workshops of Public Works Departments, the railways and the electricity corporations.

This brief description of West Africa's principal exports vividly contrasts the wealthier and poorer countries. Thus the combined exports of Ghana and the Ivory Coast are twenty times those of Mali, Upper Volta and Niger combined – three states with a slightly larger total population than that of the former two. If agricultural products and manufactures for local consumption are considered, the disparity becomes smaller, but not appreciably so. The gross national product *per capita* in Ghana and the Ivory Coast is approximately £70, while that of Dahomey, Upper Volta and Niger – the poorest states – is only £14.

Commerce. It is not difficult to see why so much of West Africa's mineral wealth should be developed by international concerns;

the investment in the Nimba iron ore mine is equivalent to one-sixth the value of all West Africa's exports in 1961. It is not so easy to understand how commerce, too, came to be dominated by a few large expatriate companies. At the turn of the century Lagos, for instance, had a number of fairly prosperous business-men. But these were not able to compete effectively with the expatriate merchants, since they lacked credit with foreign suppliers and were unwilling to combine among themselves. The British merchants in competing with one another did combine. One such amalgamation, the United Africa Company, had with its subsidiaries an annual turnover in the early 1950s of between £200 million and £300 million. It was, on its own, responsible for a third of Nigeria's imports and over two-fifths of the non-mineral exports. Its activities stretched to industrial enterprises, shipping lines and timber concessions. A whole chain of African middlemen extended from the expatriate firm to the ultimate consumer or producer, breaking down the imported goods into small quantities, and bulking the crops of peasant farmers. Indirectly, indeed, such firms have provided much of the credit available to the African, by making cash advances to traders and farmers for the cocoa crop or supplying goods to be paid for in a month's time. Many a man has started as an agent for the U.A.C. or similar firm, and accumulated enough capital to trade independently. Yet a number of factors, including the lack of credit, seem to inhibit the growth of these entrepreneurs into major importers; their lack of skill and knowledge of business organization prevents their entry into minor industrial fields.

The operations of the expatriate companies, together with systems of protective tariff, ensured that the trade of the West African colonies should remain largely with their metropolitan countries. Thus France in the mid-1930s took over three-quarters of her colonies' exports, while Britain's share of the exports from her territories ranged between nearly two-thirds for Sierra Leone and a little over one-third for Ghana.[55]

Education. The missionaries set up primary schools in the nineteenth century to promote evangelization and provide teachers so that this process might be continuous. Then, towards the end of the century, their schools were subsidized from colonial government funds, and the governments themselves entered the educational field.[87] The official aim, of course, was purely secular – to produce an executive class to staff the growing bureaucracies and provide a cultural bridge between the expatriates and the African masses. Indeed, the rift between Church and State in France led to the discontinuance of government subsidies to mission schools in the French colonies in 1903, and though many of these schools continued to operate, especially in the coastal areas, the majority of schools in the French territories were soon government run. This permitted, perhaps, a greater degree of coordination between educational expansion programmes and estimated manpower needs than obtained in the British territories. Here the competition among mission societies together with the expressed desires by the educated Africans for more advanced education led to the establishment of far more secondary schools than existed in the French colonies.

Nevertheless, government expenditure everywhere remained low, amounting in the mid-1930s to only 4 per cent of total revenue in Nigeria and the French territories, and 7 per cent in Ghana. Thus in Ghana in the mid-1920s there were only 236 primary schools, with a total enrolment of 35,000 pupils. And such gross totals often obscure the low number of pupils who complete their primary education – for in this early period many children attended only the first few years of school. In Ghana, in 1911, a total enrolment of 19,000 included nearly 11,000 in the infant classes, only 2,000 in Standard 1, and fewer than 400 in Standard 7. Secondary education, indeed, came later to Ghana than to Nigeria. The first schools were Adisadel, founded in 1910 by the Anglican missions, and Mfantispim, founded in 1913 by the Methodists, both at Cape Coast. Then, in 1924, Achimota College was opened in Accra by the colonial government, and by 1938 it was running classes from kindergarten to university level. This school illustrated the tendency for the colonial governments to maintain a single institution as a showpiece, bestowing great prestige on those who passed through it; in 1938, government expenditure on Achimota was one-quarter of that spent on all other education in the colony.

Mission competition did not extend to the Muslim emirates of Northern Nigeria, and educational expansion there was very slow. It is perhaps significant that Katsina College, where so many of the Northern Nigerian political leaders were educated, is a teacher training college and not a secondary school, a feature it shares with the William Ponty School at Dakar, *alma mater* of the French-speaking leaders. Attendance at Koranic school replaced, for the Muslims, the perfunctory two or three years at a Christian mission school in the coastal areas.

Whatever the educational aims of the colonial governments, progress was tardy. In the savana areas of the French colonies, the proportion of children attending school in the 1930s was approximately 2 per cent. Not until 1929 did Ghana's secondary schools produce their first Cambridge School Certificate holders; and only 82 passed this examination in 1938.

Curricula were closely tied to those of the metropolitan country – even when it was recognized that education was designed to fit an African into his own society. Expatriate teachers knew nothing of African history or geography to teach their students. And so in the 1950s one could meet a youth with a good pass in School Certificate geography, able to describe the difference between crystalline and sedimentary rocks, but unaware that his own village lay across the boundary of the two!

When the post-war universities were opened in Accra and Ibadan, their teaching staff and African supporters alike envisaged their structure along Oxbridge lines. Fifteen years later the University of Ibadan was still debating the place of the classics in its curriculum; the most effective argument for its retention appeared to be that it was still taught in so many secondary schools and these schools needed teachers.

A colonial assessment. It is easy to cavil today at the slow rate of economic development during the half-century of colonial rule. So much more might perhaps have been done had the development of backward territories been seen by the industrial nations as a first priority. Nevertheless, the difference between the condition of African society at the end of the nineteenth century and at the end of the Second World War is staggering. The colonial powers provided the infrastructure on which progress in the 'independence' period has depended: a fairly efficient administrative machine, reaching down to villages in the most remote areas; a network of roads and railways; and basic services in health and education. West African exports of primary products brought considerable wealth to the people. Attention is usually focused on the minerals, showing that only a small proportion of their value has reached the African in wages or royalties; but two-thirds of West Africa's exports are of crops produced by peasant farmers who receive a substantial proportion of their overseas selling price.

The policies of French and British governments alike contained contradictions. The French sought to assimilate the African to their own culture, but were willing to meet only a minute part of the cost of such a programme; they trained an African elite which later reacted strongly against the assimilation process, emphasizing instead its own *négritude*. The British sought to develop indigenous African institutions, the logical result of which would have been to devolve power upon a legislature of traditional rulers; yet they trained an executive class to work within Western-style bureaucracies, so encouraging these men to aspire to higher offices than the colonial government was prepared to grant. The subsequent frustration gave birth to the nationalist movements.

Towards independence

The turning point in the colonial experience came at the end of the Second World War. A more liberal attitude towards the backward parts of the world pervaded Europe, and self-government for African peoples was envisaged, even if at a distance of decades rather than years. West Africans fought in the Middle East and Burma with Allied armies, but were disillusioned when they could find insufficient jobs in the modern sector on their return. Yet the speed of political and social advance – almost all the French and British colonies had attained independence by 1960 – would, in the late 1940s, have surprised African and European alike.

In 1946 elections were held in France and her colonies, now

termed the 'French Union', for a constituent assembly to draw up the constitution for the Fourth Republic. The West African territories were allotted ten seats – five for French (white) citizens and Africans of the same status, and five for the erstwhile 'subjects'. Among those elected were Léopold Sédhar Senghor and Félix Houphouet-Boigny, later to become Presidents of Senegal and the Ivory Coast respectively. And in the ensuing decade African leaders increasingly participated in the political life of the French capital. 1946 saw other reforms, too: the right of association – to form political parties or trade unions – was granted to Africans; forced labour and the *indigénat* were abolished; the native courts no longer had jurisdiction in penal cases, which henceforth had to be tried under French law; and citizenship was granted to all inhabitants of the colonies whilst allowing them to retain their personal status under customary law (so permitting, for instance, polygyny, which would be illegal to anyone subject to French law). These radical reforms were, however, followed by a quiescent ten years, during which new political groups and parties developed in the colonies and competed for mass support.

In 1956, the *loi-cadre* was passed by the French Parliament, creating in each territory a separate but not yet fully independent assembly, elected by universal adult suffrage. Executive councils were to become embryo cabinets in a ministerial system, and local government reforms made possible the substitution of elected councils for administration through the chiefs. Then, in 1958, all the territories of French West Africa except for Guinea, which demanded independence, voted in a referendum to remain in a French Community, with greater autonomy than hitherto. By 1960 all had gained full political independence, though their economic ties with France continued to be very strong.[54, 131]

British policy seems to have been more consistent than that of the French governments, which first tended towards assimilation in the French Union and later, after the experiences in Indo-China and North Africa, sought to cast off those political relationships which might prove embarrassing, whilst retaining close economic links. Following perhaps the precedent of India, it envisaged a cautious but planned approach to self-government. In 1947 the Labour government urged the establishment of local government councils in the colonies; for not only were the Native Authorities too small in scale and wealth, and with too few literate members, to be able to carry out schemes for improved social services, but local government councils were seen as training grounds for political leadership – as they had been for many Labour Members of Parliament. The first elected legislative assemblies were set up too soon afterwards, however, to permit recruitment from local government councils, and the first parliamentarians were lawyers and school teachers, often without previous political experience. New constitutions followed each other with great speed, as the politicians exploited the flaws in each to gain greater autonomy. Thus Ghana gained full independence in 1957, and declared herself a Republic in 1960. Nigeria was a little slower, having first to produce a satisfactory Federal constitution; she gained internal self-government for her constituent Regions in 1957, and full independence in 1960. Throughout West Africa, the gains made by one state were quickly claimed by others; and later states in the race for independence had a much shorter and smoother passage through the bargaining process with the metropolitan power.

Paralleling the grant of political rights to the colonial territories was the rapid expansion of economic aid. The British Colonial Development and Welfare Fund, and the French F.I.D.E.S. (Investment Fund for Economic and Social Development), provided investment capital to the West African territories at a far greater rate than hitherto. Thus, for the single decade 1946–56, French investments were double those of the previous four decades. Furthermore, most of these investments were in the form of outright grants rather than loans, while in the early 1950s France continued to pay for over a third of the civil and military expenses of her West African territories. The annual post-war expenditure of British C.D. and W. funds was twelve times that of the equivalent pre-war scheme. Then, as the West African states approached independence, they were able to negotiate with international financial organizations like the World Bank and the International Monetary Fund.

Higher prices for some export crops – especially for cocoa in the early 1950s – brought a flush of money to the peasants. Yet, in general, the terms of trade have been such that the real income of West African farmers and workers has not risen greatly during the past two decades; the improvements in their lives have been the better communications, the hospitals, and the new schools which enable a greater proportion to enter the modern sector of the economy and enjoy the benefits associated with it.

Political development. The Western-educated elite bargained with the colonial governments for the transfer of power, and their claims were enhanced by some popular demonstrations from urban workers and exservicemen. But the masses remained largely apathetic, partly out of ignorance, partly because colonial rule brought few recognizable hardships which could be set against the perceptible benefits. The metropolitan powers introduced to their colonies parliamentary forms of government, modelled mainly on their own institutions, and based on universal adult suffrage (though in Northern Nigeria only adult males were enfranchised). Thus, while the new politicians collectively sought to achieve their aims for the development of their country, individually each was responsible in most cases to a rural electorate, not unsuspicious of the new elite and demanding tangible rewards.

The African politicians acceded to a system autocratic in character, geared to a limited rate of expansion, and far more totalitarian than the government of the metropolitan country in its control over the social and public services and the pricing and marketing of exports. The transition to a ministerial system, where the senior civil servants advised rather than directed, produced tensions as men learned new roles (ministers, too, had to learn to treat their advisers with respect). The departure of expatriate civil servants and the rapid expansion of the civil service to meet the expansion of social services, led to a rapid Africanization of senior posts. Government expenditure rose fourfold in Ghana between the mid-1950s and mid-1960s, and by 1960 Ghanaians outnumbered expatriates by five to one in the senior ranks of the civil service. Even in the relatively backward Northern Region of Nigeria, indigenous officials in 1959 held a quarter of the administrative posts.

Local government councils established during the past two decades have been unable in most cases to perform the tasks expected of them. Many have continued to be too small to manage social services on the scale required, while councillors and their staff have often been unsure of their roles. Allegations of self-seeking and corruption have been rife. Men elected to win new services for their respective wards have lacked authority to enforce higher local taxes. The political parties, anxious to gain local popular support, have tended to use local government councils to this end; ministers have favoured councils of their own political persuasion, and the elected councillors have become the nucleus of the local party branch. This process has been formalized in Guinea, where the ruling party, the Parti Démocratique de Guinée, is responsible for policy making, and its village councils are local sounding-boards and administrative bodies, responsible to a minister of local government for the collection of tax and maintenance of order. The weakness of local bodies together with the general shortage of trained administrators lead to an increasing centralization of government services.

With local government councils frequently reflecting traditional political units in their two or more levels of organization, with large parliaments in each of the former French territories and in each of Nigeria's Regions, West Africa is said to have a greater ratio of legislators to population than any other part of the world. Whilst this produces a relatively large political elite, it results equally in political units which are not economically viable. The common services and organs which united the French territories in Dakar, and on a smaller scale those of the British territories, have quickly disappeared. Some would hold that France encouraged the 'balkanization' of her West African empire, hoping thereby to retain the allegiance of each small weak state, and Britain is similarly accused of having nourished Nigeria's regionalization. On the other hand, the more prosperous African states have been notably reluctant to belong to any form of federation wherein their own wealth might be used to finance the development of poorer areas. Political power once gained is not easily surrendered to supra-national bodies. Attempts at close union – as between Senegal and Mali, or

Ghana, Guinea and Mali – have either broken down or else never developed beyond formal statements of intent by the political leaders.

Social services. 'Freedom For All, Life More Abundant' – the Nigerian Action Group's slogan could well have been adopted by the politicians of any state. Unable to reward their electorate with a radical redistribution of wealth, by cancelling the obligations of an indebted peasantry, or granting ownership rights to tenant farmers, the politicians have promised improved social services and more jobs. Furthermore, it has been persuasively argued that a population sound in health and basically literate is an essential prerequisite of economic development (though illiterate cocoa farmers manage well enough to spray their crops, quickly learning the techniques from others when they themselves cannot read the instructions on the tin).

Such policies produce their dilemmas. Village dispensaries and maternity centres, however rudimentary, have led to a reduction in infant mortality rates, high though these continue to be; in many rural areas one-half of the children born do not survive their fifth birthday. A population increase of 2 per cent a year tends to keep the *per capita* income low and even, in some territories, reduces it, despite a national increase in wealth. It results in a population with a very high proportion of young people, a significant feature when so much government expenditure is for education and child welfare. Thus, as the diagram opposite illustrates, nearly half of Ghana's present population is below the age of 15, compared with less than a quarter of that of England and Wales. (The latter have, however, a larger and still increasing proportion of aged dependants over 65 – 10 per cent against 3 per cent in Ghana.)

Educational expansion has been most rapid in the coastal areas, where there already existed a well-laid foundation and a population avid for achievement. Thus Ghana and the southern Regions of Nigeria instituted universal primary education in the mid-1950s. But expansion of teacher training programmes had to proceed simultaneously, so that, for a few years, the primary schools were staffed with untrained teachers, reducing the quality

Age distribution: Ghana 1960 and England and Wales 1951

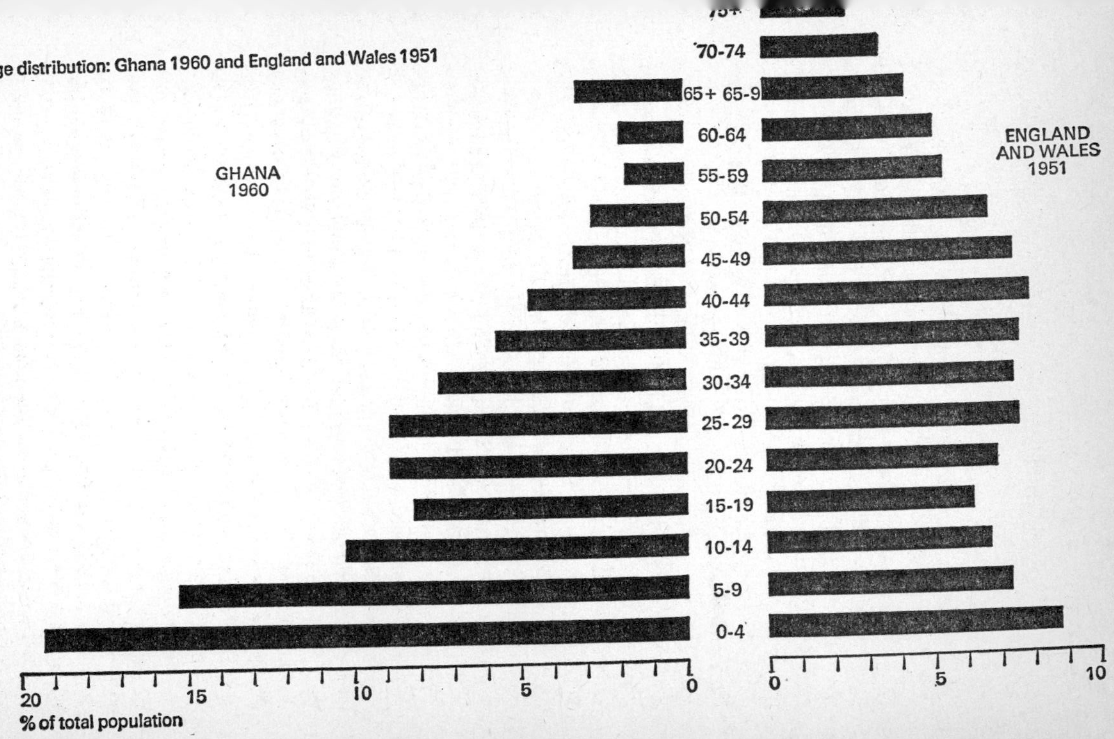

of the education provided and leading to a popular belief that the new school leaving certificates were much inferior to those of an earlier period. Expansion in particular areas has often magnified differences within states. Thus, in Northern Nigeria, 11 per cent of children attended primary school in the early 1960s; but whilst the figure for the Kabba-Yoruba is 83 per cent, that for most of the Muslim emirates remains below 5 per cent – in Sokoto it is only 3 per cent. One possible outcome of such a situation is that, whilst political power resides basically in the hands of the Fulani aristocracy, the majority of civil servants come from the non-Muslim areas outside the emirates.

A similar expansion has occurred in secondary education. Thus in Western Nigeria the number of schools trebled in less than a decade, from 59 in 1954 to 177 in 1961, as each small town strove to enhance its status with a school of its own. At the same time, the structure of the education system and the curricula of the schools have remained little changed. Academic subjects continue to be stressed, though the content of the teaching in history and geography now has a greater African bias. Technical schools are advocated – but few are established, largely because of the difficulty of recruiting staff and assembling the necessary equipment. Thus, while manpower commissions stress the need for technicians, the schools continue to produce administrators. To the towns of Ghana and southern Nigeria young men stream to seek, on the basis of their school certificates, clerical jobs which do not exist. Political leaders recognize that in the immediate future well over half the youth of their countries must find employment in agriculture; yet they are loath to recommend a division of primary education into agricultural and academic, so determining from the earliest age which children shall gain entry to the modern sector and ultimately to the privileged elite. The poorer countries may evade this issue for several years by braking their expansion of primary education.

Economic dilemmas. Experts rarely agree on the best measures to be taken by the developing countries of the world to ensure a steady growth towards prosperity and towards living standards more comparable with those of the industrial nations. Their conflicting advice poses serious dilemmas for the West African politician.

What proportion of a government's revenues should be spent on social services? In the budgets of the government of Western Nigeria, forty per cent of the recurrent expenditure has been allocated to education alone, and a similar burden in Eastern Nigeria obliged the reimposition of school fees in the higher classes of the primary schools. In Ghana's first two Five Year Plans, non-productive expenditure comprised more than four-fifths of the total, though a recurrent theme was the need to switch to investments directly productive of revenue. A familiar trend is for the planned increase in administrative posts to be exceeded, and for investment in industry to fall short. The building of schools and dispensaries comes naturally to the civil servant; the setting up of factories demands new techniques and skills. Many worthwhile projects fail to win the support of international loan agencies because West African governments lack the men able to prepare adequate plans and budgets. Politicians attempt to stem the drift to the towns; but how profitable is the extension of rural water and electricity supplies if industry persists in locating itself at the major ports?

Economic development on the scale necessary – whether of agriculture or industry – demands massive inputs of foreign capital. Yet this appears to increase the dependence of the West African states upon the industrial nations. The possibilities of increasing the indigenous contribution seem slight. Can the popularity of the government withstand a much heavier taxing of the peasantry? Improved banking and saving facilities have little impact when the farmer spends his savings on education and a large house.

On what productive development should money be spent? The drift of the school leavers to the towns necessitates an increased production of food by those remaining in the rural areas. And allied to this is the desire to make farming more attractive for literates; parents are unlikely otherwise to urge their children to farm in the same manner as themselves after they have made sacrifices to give them six or more years of schooling. Schemes of improved farming can, however, be costly. The Western Region of Nigeria planned settlements of twenty-acre farms, largely planted with export cash crops; the cost of establishing each settler amounted to over £3,000, to be repaid, all being well, within twenty years. But such schemes seem unlikely to increase the production of indigenous foodstuffs. Nor do mechanized schemes seem any more promising. The state farms of Ghana have proved conspicuously unprofitable. Investment in increased agricultural extension services presupposes that one knows how the peasant farmer can increase his output, but this is in fact far from certain.

Much of the recent investment in industry has been in the extraction of newly discovered raw materials – the oil of Nigeria, the iron ore of Liberia, Sierra Leone and Mauretania. The pattern of the colonial period seems to be perpetuated, even though local refineries are now being built. The West African states themselves seek manufacturing industries, especially of consumer goods which may replace imported manufactures and so reduce the drain on foreign exchange. For many countries a brewery has been the first major plant, and those which soon follow include textile, tobacco, flour, cement, and footwear industries. Many firms now assemble their products at the West African ports rather than in the country of manufacture. But almost all the states provide too small a market for production on a sufficiently profitable scale; Nigeria is the conspicuous exception. With political uncertainties, too, West Africa is not a promising field for the foreign investor. He may be attracted if the local government provides a large share of the capital and promises tariff protection or tax concessions. But this locks up government funds for long periods. Whatever the provisions in their economic plans, governments are generally able to establish only those industries which foreign companies are prepared to sponsor. Their desire to locate them in rural areas so as to stop the urban drift is thwarted by the industrialists themselves, who seek the services and skills in the already established centres and accordingly turn these into still larger islands of development. Most industries are highly capital-intensive: a textile mill may employ one person for every £1,000 invested; an oil refinery, one for every £10,000. An investment of £1,000,000 will thus provide employment for a thousand or fewer persons;

but Western Nigeria alone produces over 100,000 primary school-leavers a year.

Much expenditure is on prestigious schemes with small direct economic reward but of unknown social benefit. Presidents Tubman and Houphouet-Boigny and former President Nkrumah each had a palace built costing over £5 million. Yet initially these are often seen by the masses as symbols of nationhood; in them their leaders can entertain without shame the rulers of the most powerful states. Ghana's Volta project becomes a focus of national effort. Nigeria, as the largest West African state, feels that she ought to have an iron and steel industry – even though her raw materials are of low quality; the industry's chance of viability was then even further weakened in the compromise whereby the plant was divided between the Northern and Eastern Regions, because their political parties controlled the Federal government.

Industrial development along these lines does little to increase intra-Africa trade, an objective of Pan-Africanists, who see it as a means both to provide more diversified economies overall and to strengthen the cause of African unity. At present Nigeria's trade with other African countries amounts to only one per cent of her total; that of Ghana and Sierra Leone, to 4 per cent and 2 per cent respectively. In an effort to maximize its own manufacturing capacity, each state sets up similar industries. Road and rail links between states have not been improved. For every frontier which has been opened for a freer passage of people and goods, another has been closed. Only recently has the teaching of French begun in the schools of the ex-British colonies, and few French-speaking Africans are fluent in English. Inter-territorial communication, of all types, remains difficult.

3 The changing rural scene

Two-thirds of West Africa's exports are the products of her peasant farmers. But only a minority of the population participates in the affluence they create. The wealthy areas are islands of prosperity. The cocoa- and coffee-producing regions of south-western Nigeria, Ghana and the Ivory Coast are the richest, for these crops command high prices relative to the labour expended. Here the traditionally-styled compounds are fast disappearing, replaced by modern bungalows with corrugated iron roofs and the occasional two-storey building. As new houses face the roads, the boundaries between the compounds of the descent groups become difficult to trace. A bustling market place with its lorries, and the shops lining the main thoroughfares give an impression of both great economic activity and the rapid disintegration of traditional social structures.

Perhaps a sixth of West Africa's farmers live in such areas. One-quarter farm in the less affluent areas, where groundnuts, cotton and the oil palm yield cash incomes less substantial than those gained by the individual cocoa or coffee farmer. And more than half the farmers grow no crops for export. It is difficult to estimate what proportion of them are selling surplus food crops to neighbouring towns or to the export-crop areas. There are many areas, remote from the main trunk roads and centres of population, where the economic activity of the village has changed little during the colonial period; there areas tend to export their labour. In some areas, opportunities seem to have been ignored. Within sight of the residential quarters of Jos, a flourishing mining centre, the indigenous people live in their cactus-ringed compounds, growing food only for themselves; it is immigrant Hausa who produce the vegetables for the expatriate and elite population. Ibo living east of Enugu are prepared to lease land for rice growing to immigrants from the densely settled Ibo areas to the south-west; they will not grow it themselves.

The ease and speed with which people accept a new crop or a new method of farming depend on a variety of factors. There are the *technological*: do the changes involve new tools? do the new labour requirements fit into the existing agricultural calendar, so that the major effort does not fall within the already busy planting or harvesting season? (As some mechanized schemes have shown, it is useless to plough twenty acres with a tractor for a farmer who can only weed four acres with his hoe.) There are the *institutional*: are the patterns of land holding, on which the social structure is largely founded, altered by the changes? There are the *ideological*: what incentives exist in the society to achieve wealth?

One frequently reads of the need to stimulate a demand for imported goods so that a need for cash is felt. But in many traditional societies wealth is sought as a mark of prestige and as a means of attaining political office; export crops here provide new opportunities for achieving traditional goals. One is often apt to view the impact of a Western economy as disruptive of traditional social structure; yet it is possible for a substantial degree of economic development to take place within the indigenous institutional framework. In fact, traditional structures may be strengthened; thus, whilst new associations and the development of social strata weaken the inclusive cohesion of the descent group, shortage of land may reinforce the hold of the group over its individual members.

Looking at the African rural areas, one may choose to stress either the forces of change or the persistence of traditional institutions. The observer whose framework of analysis is a rather static image of traditional society will point to the 'cracks' in the structure effected by mission education, colonial government, or greater affluence. His comments seem more predictive of disintegration than of the development of new structures. If, on the other hand, one sees the traditional institutions in terms of conflict and competition between individuals and groups, one is more likely to stress the persistence of these groups as changing conditions are exploited to achieve the goals of the indigenous society.

I prefer the latter approach on theoretical grounds. It also seems particularly appropriate in examining West Africa, where, despite the accession to relative wealth, the institutions of the indigenous societies seem to have been maintained to a greater degree than in the other parts of the continent. This is an important factor in discussing the political development of the new West African states and particularly in describing the relationship between the Western-educated elite and the masses.

Labour migration

For the areas where the farmers grow neither surplus food crops nor an export crop, the main source of cash incomes is wage labour. But because these areas are economically so backward, local employment is scarce, except perhaps where the government decides to construct a major highway. To find work, men travel seasonally, or for periods of two or three years, to the richer regions. From Sokoto they go to the Jos tin mines, the Zamfara valley groundnut-producing areas, and to Ibadan, Lagos and Accra.[79] Mossi men from the Upper Volta travel south to work on the cocoa and coffee farms and in the towns of Ghana and the Ivory Coast. On their return what impact do these men make on their home rural areas?

Their journeys have broadened their horizons; they become aware of the affluence of neighbouring regions and the comparative poverty of their own. But the man who enjoys the former is more likely to stay in these regions than try to exploit opportunities at home, while it is the less ambitious who are content to save what they can and return to become absorbed in the traditional way of life. The average Mossi migrant in Ghana, working on the cocoa farms, hopes to save about £2 10s. a month, or at the most £10 for his season's work. This small sum is spent on buying luxuries for friends and relatives at home – cloth, trinkets, or perhaps a bicycle. Most are quickly disbursed and confer little lasting prestige on the giver, while the bicycle may soon be sold to purchase seed for a new crop. Migration does not create a wealthier category of men in the village.[10, 69]

The West African seasonal migrant learns little from his

sojourn abroad. In Ghana, the migrant Mossi lives under the surveillance of a local Mossi chief, establishing few relationships, except in the impersonal commercial sphere, with the non-Mossi. He is unlikely to embrace Christianity or Islam, save perhaps in the most perfunctory manner (though not all immigrants are from areas unconverted to a world religion). Agricultural techniques learned, for instance, on Ghanaian farms, or on the Niger Irrigation Project in Mali where many Mossi work, are not appropriate to the climate or soils of his homeland. Some men who have been away for a considerable period, however, reject farming on their return, preferring to be traders or craftsmen and thus bringing a greater specialization of tasks to their communities.

The most marked effect of migration on the still largely subsistence farming communities lies not in any radical change of the social structure but in a slow loosening of social controls. Mossi marriages, for instance, are still largely arranged by parents. But when an individual finds his personal choice of a spouse thwarted by the elders, the young couple can abscond to Ghana, to return a few years later when the *fait accompli* will be accepted. Divorce is not approved, but a wife may move to her lover's house during her husband's absence. The sanctions which can be operated by a small tribally structured community cease to be fully effective when they may be evaded by temporary emigration.

Cash crops and new wealth

The introduction of a cultivated tree crop, the use of whose product is still scarcely understood by the farmer, may seem a revolutionary step in an economy where hitherto only annual food crops were grown. Cocoa growing has, however, spread with considerable speed and without any external pressure on the farmer; the visible rewards have provided a sufficient incentive.[57,58]

The technique of cocoa cultivation requires no tools that the farmer does not already possess. Methods of drying and fermenting the beans are simple, and little labour is expended on the crop save at harvest, when immigrants and local women are recruited to assist. Other methods, demanding greater skills and an increased output of labour, would certainly result in higher yields, but these, except for spraying the trees to control capsids, have not been adopted by the farmers.

Cocoa growing has, moreover, not led to any substantial change in the pattern of land tenure. The Akan or Yoruba farmer applies to the head of his descent group for forested land on which to grow the crop and he is granted the use of an area for as long as he requires it – a type of grant no different from that made for rotational cycles of annual crops. The trees and their crop belong to their planter and pass on his death to his heirs – his sons among the Yoruba, his nephews among the matrilineal Akan. This, too, introduces no new principles, however, for farming is not a collective activity among West Africans. The traditional pattern of land right usually gives the farmer no power to alienate the land on which his cocoa grows. Thus in most parts of Yoruba country the farmer may pawn his cocoa – allowing the creditor to reap the harvest until the debt is repaid – but not sell it to a buyer from another descent group. An unredeemed pawn may in fact be regarded as a sale – but the fiction is maintained of the continuing rights possessed by the descent group over its land.

The land of the Akan people is only half as densely populated as that of the Yoruba, and the increased amount of forest in the former areas has encouraged a substantial immigration of farmers from the grassland to the east and south-east. These immigrants, arriving in groups, have tended to reproduce the land holding patterns of their diverse home areas. As immigrants, they owe little allegiance to the traditional rulers of the area in which they have settled, though they contribute considerably by their land rents to the incomes of the rulers. And within their own communities, their social organization is still based upon their descent groups.[57]

The growing of export crops and, more especially, the recent rapid increase in population have in some areas increased the pressure on land to the point where there is barely enough for everybody. The usual initial reaction is to insist that a man farms 'where his father did', and requests for land from maternally related groups are received much less favourably than in the past. One is much more dependent upon one's own group, and can less afford to offend its elders. The enhanced cohesion that this produces in the descent group is paralleled in the case of urban land. Frequently this gains a high economic value and, among the Yoruba, for instance, is sold. The descent group thus becomes a land management agency, whose profits from transactions are shared among all members. Ultimately, land shortage results in increasing individualization of land holding; a father's farms are shared among his own sons, who are unlikely to be able to find additional land. Even smaller segments of the descent group acquire the right to alienate land by lease or sale. This process has probably gone furthest among the Ibo of south-eastern Nigeria, in whose central districts population densities of over one thousand per square mile are recorded.

Neither cultivation of export crops nor land shortage has produced a landless rural labour force. Most cocoa farmers rely on seasonal migrant labour or on local men who are themselves farmers but who need immediate cash. In one Yoruba town the biggest cocoa farmer during the early 1950s – his annual income from the crop amounted to about £4,000 – had ten permanent Igbirra labourers, immigrants from the savana area fifty miles north-east, who were settled on his land, growing their own food crops. But such cases are rare. Land shortage does not deprive a man of his legal rights to the land of his descent group – only of his practical chances of getting more than a minimal area. In such situations his neighbours are unlikely to be able to feed extra mouths, and his response will be to move to the towns to seek employment.

The continued holding of land by descent groups has inhibited the development of rural landlessness whilst permitting the cultivation of export crops. It may, however, be detrimental to future economic development. The descent group may, in attempting to allocate land equally to each segment, or to preserve sufficient land to grow foodstuffs for its members, impede the development of large areas by an individual member with capital. Such systems of land holding do not favour the introduction of enclosed, or even mixed, farms. On the other hand, when the government seeks to acquire land for public purposes, it can far more easily negotiate with the heads of a few descent groups than with the hundreds of individual members. The inability of the individual farmer to alienate his land preserves him from indebtedness to money lenders; but it also makes it difficult for him to raise credit on his valuable improvements to the land – a cocoa farm, store, or a substantial house.

In West Africa men have always been active farmers, and their cultivation of export crops has not greatly changed their relationships with their wives. Other changes have, however, affected the status of wives. The Ibo man, for instance, customarily cuts down the oil palm fruits, and his wife prepares the oil, to sell it on her husband's behalf; but she retains the kernels, and cracks and sells these for her own profit. The introduction of oil mills increases the quantity and quality of oil extracted and so raises general income levels; but the new mills also process the kernels, thus depriving the women of employment and income, and making them increasingly dependent on their husbands. They have, indeed, rebelled against the new mills. Elsewhere in Ibo country, the increased growing of cassava for the urban market has provided the women with new opportunities; the men thought it beneath their dignity to grow such a crop – yam growing is for men – and so the women cultivated it on their plots, to increase their personal incomes. Thus, whilst some changes enable the farming wives to gain greater economic independence from their husbands, others tend to render obsolete those occupations which have traditionally given the women their freedom.

Export crops can often be cultivated within indigenous systems of land tenure, causing in themselves no widespread population movements or breach in the traditional social structure. But these crops do bring considerable wealth directly to the rural areas, so that new categories of prosperous men are created, and new associations are formed. A stratification of society into classes may increasingly cut across the earlier descent group divisions.

Some of the most prosperous men are, naturally, farmers; but their numbers are few, for the export crops tend to be grown on small plots by a large number of men. The richest men are usually the traders – the produce buyers, the retailers of imported goods, and the lorry owners – with most of such men engaging in a number of different enterprises. And as the wealth circulates through the community, greater opportunities are provided for the specialist craftsmen – tailors, goldsmiths, carpenters, and builders – men who (save perhaps for the entrepreneurial builder) never become very rich but who achieve, by local standards, a relative prosperity.

The rich farmers are all natives of their community, and many are illiterate; decades earlier, such men would have been equally prosperous yam or guinea-corn farmers. Many of the traders and craftsmen, too, are natives of the towns and villages where they now operate. Few have received a full primary education. Most continue to live in the compounds of their own descent groups. And their wealth is spent on modern status symbols. The Yoruba man, for instance, uses his savings progressively to acquire a corrugated iron roof for his traditional house, a two-storey house, education for his children, a car, and a much more elaborate house. Inasmuch as these men are living and working among their own people, and as their prosperity depends largely on their personal popularity with their customers, they tend to be conservative, upholding the values of their society. Lavish generosity is expected – and usually yields its rewards; the man who saves to reinvest is likely to be branded as a miser. Although living styles may borrow much from the West, ultimate goals may still be expressed in traditional values. Wealth from trading is seen as a stepping stone to political office. The story is told of a Dahomeyan trader who seemed to exhibit all the entrepreneurial characteristics of the early capitalist; and then, suddenly, he sold all his business assets to acquire a ritual office, giving him (presumably in his own estimation) a much greater power over his community.

The wealthy men do become leaders, not only within their own descent groups but in the community at large. Men hesitate to take a dispute arising from a complex commercial transaction to elderly, illiterate lineage heads; instead, they ask a rich trader to arbitrate, giving him the traditional gifts for his services. The rich man thus builds up a following of men unrelated to him. In the rural area, or in the small provincial town, few associations exist to distinguish these men from the masses. Produce buyers and lorry owners may meet to fix uniform prices and rates; but the leisure time of these men is spent in their own compounds, with their kin, followers and customers, rather than in social pursuits with men of like affluence. Many of the new associations seem modern or non-African in structure. Thus the Yoruba craftsmen have formed associations which closely resemble the guilds of medieval Europe; but their monopolistic tendencies, the rules of etiquette at meetings, are all obviously drawn from the existing market women's organizations and from age group associations.

Much of the cash income of the rural area finances the new social services – the schools, dispensaries, and a variety of benefits provided by the local government. These employ literates, whom one might expect to be powerful agents of change in the communities where they work. Their education has alienated them from traditional society to a greater degree than that experienced by illiterate but wealthy traders. Yet most of them work in communities other than those into which they were born. As employees of a missionary body or of government, they have been subject to frequent transfers. They have little opportunity to develop permanent relationships with those among whom they work. They are regarded as strangers by the local people and seek companionship among men of similar education and status. Their impact, beyond the compass of their employment, tends to be small.

The literate living in his home town is not always in a better position to influence his community. His status is ambiguous. As a teacher or clerk, his loyalty to his employer is seen to conflict with that to his descent group or village. If he is a farmer, people ask why he has not made better use of his education; if a letter writer, a public scribe, he is seen as fomenting disputes, as profiting from litigation. Where literates are few in number, they are frequently afraid to press for changes, lest they be blamed for any untoward results. Whilst the illiterates may bc glad of his advice in setting up a new school, the literate man, usually quite young, lacks the authority to recommend the higher taxes needed to pay for it. One important result of the rapid increase in the scale of social services in rural areas during the past decade is the greater number of local men who staff them. When the Yoruba town seeks to establish its own secondary grammar school, it puts pressure on a locally-born university graduate to head it. Such men become drawn into local affairs far beyond their official spheres.

The greatest changes will, however, be effected only when primary school leavers stay at home to farm.[62]

New values

The Churches. The missionaries introduced to the rural areas of West Africa a faith with a new cosmology, in which ancestors and native deities had no place, and churches with a world-wide membership in contrast to the purely local nature of the indigenous cults.

Many of the early adult converts were 'outsiders' in their communities – men and women of low social rank or strangers. Respected men sent their sons to school, expecting them to learn the new techniques of reading and writing, and were horrified when the young people, probably at the instigation of a zealous priest or teacher, flagrantly violated local taboos and thus endangered the prosperity or fertility of the whole community. Their ostracism drove the converts into exclusive groups, practising their new faith with considerable fervour. Christians refused to take chieftaincy titles on the grounds that these involved rituals repugnant to them, and the existing chiefs refused, in turn, to modify the ceremonies. Yet conversion proceeded, for the schools were the main agents of proselytization; unbelievers were made to feel not only uncomfortable in school but also ineligible for post-primary education in missionary colleges.

In many areas, especially in southern Nigeria and Ghana, nominal Christians now constitute three-quarters of the population. The churches have become institutionalized. Yet many of the catechists and priests in the Protestant churches have received only a minimum of education – perhaps two years in a theological college after primary school for a catechist; four years, for a priest. These men are not, by contemporary standards, highly educated. Little or no study has been made of the doctrines actually preached from their village pulpits, and so they are likely to be much closer to local beliefs and values than to the official doctrines of the churches. Monogamy is expected of communicant members of the churches but not of the mass of the congregations. Church associations are often based upon locally recognized status divisions: the sexes may be separated at Sunday services, while the chiefs may sit in the front pews and be allowed to retain their headgear. Chiefs and Christians have agreed on modified rituals so as to enable the latter to achieve those political offices for which their other qualifications – age, wealth, and perhaps education – make them the most suitable candidates. Even the traditional ceremonies of installation for a Yoruba *oba* are today frequently followed by thanksgiving services in church and mosque.

Whilst membership of the churches has increased rapidly, their offices – church wardens and councillors – have tended to be restricted to communicant, monogamous, and, in practice, literate men. These offices are highly respected. The churches thus offer avenues whereby men who would, by their age or other criteria, be ineligible for traditional political offices, can achieve prestigious positions in their communities.

Islam too has been gaining converts in the coastal areas. Today there are as many Muslims as Christians among the Yoruba. Yet Islam is for these simply a personal faith; the Yoruba kingdoms have not become theocratic states like the emirates. Nor has Muslim law ousted Yoruba customary law in any sphere, least of all in marriage and land holding. Islam has always appeared more tolerant of indigenous social structure – though, at the present time, its adherents appear more strongly opposed to participation in traditional rituals or secret associations than do most Christians.

Politics and Authority. If land rights constitute one cornerstone in the structure of traditional society, the patterns of authority constitute another. To a considerable degree the general maintenance of indigenous institutions depends on the extent to which the boundaries between communities were respected by the colonial administration and to which the roles of traditional office holders were upheld. In the British territories, as we have seen, the application of Indirect Rule was directed towards maintaining these roles and boundaries. The French, on the other hand, either ignored the rulers of the larger political units or used them in a minor capacity; frequently the new administrative divisions cut across traditional ethnic units in a deliberate policy of destroying local loyalties. Yet the smallest units, the villages, remained intact; their chiefs, usually appointed according to customary law, were recognized as agents of French rule. It is probable that during the colonial period village meetings continued to be held in the traditional manner.

In examining the impact of the colonial period on the kingdoms of the British territories, least change seems to have occurred in the Hausa-Fulani emirates, where the new native authorities closely followed the traditional units. The autocracy of the emir was retained, and though his subordinate chiefs were made heads of administrative districts instead of holding dispersed fiefs, his control over them was little modified – even if, instead of being able to appoint and remove chiefs on grounds of political loyalty and expediency, he had to argue his case before the British officials in terms of administrative competence or negligence. The traditional conflicts between rival royal houses were merely continued through accusations of corruption, like the misappropriation of taxes.[26]

Similarly, in Yoruba country the traditional kingdoms were retained as units of native administration. But here the role of the *oba* was altered as he increasingly looked for guidance and depended for support not on his chiefs but on the District Officer. In exploiting this situation, and in a genuine attempt to introduce reforms in their communities, educated *oba* fell foul of their chiefs. The *oba*, however, was backed by the administrative officers and, in the long run, won; the chiefs became discredited in the eyes of their people. The literate *oba* created the image of an autocratic but benevolent ruler, who might be approached directly, and as such, many of them became highly popular in their kingdoms. They ceased to observe many of the traditional rituals associated with their offices – but then the people, too, had lost faith in these. The major annual ceremonies continued to be held, albeit in an air of carnival festivity. The modern *oba* performs new leadership roles in church or mosque. His substantial salary has enabled him to maintain an affluent style of life – with modern palace buildings and large car – that few of his subjects can match. (The salaries of his chiefs, however, are often lower than the income of an unskilled labourer; their poverty contributes to their loss of prestige.)

For a brief period, from the 1930s to the early 1950s, the literate *oba* was often the best-educated man in his town who was also a native of it; local literates were transferred elsewhere, and those working locally were strangers. This tended to enhance his prestige, and his authority among his subjects. Only recently has he been eclipsed by secondary school teachers or senior government clerks who have occupied new posts in their home areas.

The traditional role of the *ohene* in the Akan kingdoms of Ghana was very similar to that of the Yoruba *oba*. Yet a variety of circumstances has contributed to their relatively reduced prestige at the present time. British administration in the Gold Coast tended to parallel the traditional government rather than work through it in a native authority system. British officials were thus less interested in protecting local rulers from the assaults of their people, and destoolments were frequent. A common ground for complaint lay in the misuse of the substantial rents received from strangers growing cocoa and of royalties or fees from mining and timber concessionaires; incomes of this kind did not reach the Yoruba *oba*. The Akan kingdoms, moreover, contained a relatively high proportion of strangers. (The 1960 census reveals that in the present Ashanti Region, 49 per cent of the men were enumerated in the localities of their birth; 19 per cent came from other localities in the same Region; and 32 per cent came from other Regions or from abroad. Equivalent proportions for the much more backward Northern Region were 77 per cent, 14 per cent, and 9 per cent respectively.) These strangers, owing no loyalty to the local traditional rulers, were more likely to be attracted by nationalist political parties, and especially to the modernist Convention People's Party. The rulers themselves came increasingly under attack as they first participated in colonial administration through membership of the Legislative Assembly and later collaborated with the older Western-educated elite against the C.P.P. Yet in spite of their more uncertain status and future, the Akan traditional rulers still hold office, maintaining much of the dignity of their roles and symbolizing for many the institutions and values of the past.[46]

Independence has, in the modern state and in the new local government areas, created larger political units than those of traditional society. The rivalry between nationalist political parties has brought to the provincial town and village stark divisions which did not exist in the traditional system. Yet although the authority of the traditional rulers is being increasingly weakened, modern politics, in exploiting traditional conflicts, often tends to reinforce indigenous institutions.

The boundaries of the present constituencies and wards generally follow those of the colonial period and of traditional communities, so that local rivalries can now be fought out in terms of contemporary politics. Candidates in remote areas hold, not without reason, that their constituents do not understand the major issues of an election, and are principally concerned that their representative in the far-off capital should be one of their own group. Thus elections in the mid-1950s in the northern part of Ghana have been described in terms of competition between chiefdoms to get one of their own members into office, or of rivalry between two segments of a ruling group.[67, 68] Nor is the dominance of local issues to be found only in the most backward areas. The major factions in a prosperous Yoruba town may be those formed in a recent contest for the throne, each later becoming identified with a political party. The opposition between the capital of a kingdom and its subordinate towns may similarly be expressed in political terms. The rivalry between Ibadan and Ijebu which developed in the nineteenth century over the control of trade routes to the coast and was continued in the twentieth as Ijebu strangers in Ibadan seized the opportunities to lease land and build houses for letting to immigrants, was further perpetuated in political contests. The Ijebu have been identified with the Action Group, many of whose prominent leaders came from this area, while the Ibadan have supported first the rival National Council of Nigeria and the Cameroons (N.C.N.C.), subsequently renamed the National Convention of Nigerian Citizens and later the Nigerian National Democratic Party (N.N.D.P.).

The political divisions in Yoruba country, where loyalties have, throughout the past fifteen years, been divided between two political parties or alliances, form a stark contrast with the overwhelming support that the Ibo have given to the N.C.N.C. The reason lies partly in the nature of the segmentary Ibo society. Neighbouring villages oppose one another but unite against other village groups; these in turn unite against similar sized units; and at the highest level, the Ibo unite against other ethnic groups. In a sense, Yoruba society is similarly segmented – into opposed kingdoms, opposed metropolitan and subordinate towns; but the opposed units are here not equivalent, nor is the type of segmentation similar at each level.

Political divisions do, in fact, exist within Ibo communities. The almost unanimous support given to the N.C.N.C. on polling days masks the intense struggles that have taken place in the nomination process, as each of the three or so village groups composing a constituency seeks to ensure the official candidature of one of its own members. Such village groups often hope to surmount the distractions of rivalry by giving the nomination to each group in turn; but this plan is incompatible with the hopes of the existing legislators to remain in office and with the view of party headquarters that nomination should, in part, be a reward for loyal service at the capital. One major split in the N.C.N.C. during the 1950s followed ethnic lines, for the secessionist group was identified with the Aro – a people whose home town lay on the eastern extremes of Ibo country but who had gained considerable power in the pre-colonial period throughout the Ibo area as traders and as controllers of an important oracle.

Another rift in the N.C.N.C. occurred when the party headquarters imposed on a number of constituencies its own nominees as candidates, and many of these were defeated by local worthies who stood as 'Independent N.C.N.C.'. This incident reflects the dependence of the new nationalist parties on the local elites. With party organization at a minimum level and with the divorce of the Western-educated elite from their home areas, direct contact between politicians and mass electorate becomes slight. The support of local opinion leaders – the traditional chiefs and wealthy men – becomes vital to them. In overtly supporting one party, however, these men then place themselves in opposition to the adherents of another party – a role unknown to traditional rulers.

To the extent that they manipulate local conflicts and loyalties, which usually have little connexion with national issues, politicians at all levels – national, regional, and local – are contributing to the maintenance of those traditional institutions and values involved.

The persistence of descent groups. Export crops, world religions, colonial rule and modern nationhood have each, in varying degrees, drawn the societies of West Africa from their mutual isolation and self-sufficiency. Although two-thirds of those in the rural areas are still farmers, the modern economy has created more specialized tasks and offices. Men establish a wider range of relationships, forming new associations. Yet the communities which enter the modern world are not ones in which the traditional social structures are collapsing, the people avidly seeking new interests and values. They tend to be ones in which indigenous associations have maintained considerable cohesion. Unless this is understood, one cannot appreciate the attitudes of the Western-educated elite and its role in the political process.

Many traditional associations have, it is true, become obsolete. Age grades have been deprived of their functions as local wars are banned, and public work is carried out through local government departments. Indigenous religious cults have been slowly disappearing. But descent groups have remained the basis of social organization.

Most men continue to reside in their own compounds, albeit perhaps in individual houses of more modern construction. Land is still held corporately by the descent group, with its increasing shortage or high market value enhancing group cohesion. Modern political units perpetuate traditional conflicts and loyalties. A man still relies on his descent group for his social security. The primacy of descent group allegiance does, in fact, impede the development of other associations, the functions of which tend to be specifically limited.

Today the individual has greater responsibility. The law of modern states does not recognize the collective liability of the descent group, and group members have few jural rights over each other. In exploiting the opportunities provided by new types of occupation, the individual moves outside the sphere of his own descent group. But among the relationships which he may manipulate to achieve new goals are many traditional ones. Maternal kin and age-mates may prove allies. And the descent groups may modify their structure themselves to give opportunities for leadership to the educated or wealthy; the elders may play a more passive role in meetings, relying heavily on the advice of younger men.

Of the Ibo it has been written: 'paradoxically, of all Nigerian peoples [they] have probably changed the least while changing the most . . . many of the basic patterns of social behaviour . . . have survived and are part of the newly developing culture.'[61 p.142] The same might be said of many other wealthy coastal societies, where development has taken place within the indigenous structure. Finally, in examining the wealthier rural areas like this, one must not forget that there are many others, where economic change and mission proselytizing have been on a much smaller scale and where, in consequence, departures from the traditional way of life have been relatively slight.

4 Urban life

In few parts of the world can the contrasts between town and country be as marked as in West Africa. In states where the majority of people are farmers living in village settlements, the capitals have in many cases grown into cities with populations of a quarter of a million or more; urban areas of intermediate size are relatively few. While economic development has led to only limited change in the social structure of the villages, the new towns are peopled by recent migrants who are creating by their presence completely new patterns of relationship. Today village houses have been given corrugated iron roofs, and a few shops often overlook the traditional market. In the capital, architects, released from the need to match their buildings with the existing styles, have designed some of the most exotic of modern buildings. Governments, anxious to provide visible expressions of progress both for their own people and for visitors from abroad, have spent freely on public construction.

In these towns a completely new range of occupations is open to the African migrant from the rural areas. Women can no longer assist their husbands as they once did on the farm, but can earn separate incomes from trade or paid employment. Employment in office and industry creates bureaucratic patterns of relationship not found in traditional society. New associations develop to protect these new categories of workers. The cinema, the bars and night clubs provide entertainments unknown to the village. The extremes of affluence and poverty exist side by side in the town as new forms of social stratification develop. At the apex stand the expatriate community and the African elite, reference groups for the aspiring masses. Only in these towns is the educated and wealthy elite community of sufficient size for its members effectively to define new values and patterns of behaviour.

The modern towns are ethnically heterogeneous. And as men of different groups increasingly live side by side, one might expect them to develop greater tolerance of each other's customs, to develop a stronger sense of national allegiance. But they are also competing for employment. Differences in educational level or in achievement drive lead to the association of the meaner tasks with certain groups. Stereotypes of those from other ethnic groups take on more force as one enters into rivalry with them. Ethnic hostilities grow, and 'tribalism' becomes more pronounced.

The town is the focus of political life. It is here that the nationalist parties developed. Their leaders, in power today, are far more influenced by pressures from the urban elite or by strike threats from the workers than by rumblings of discontent in the villages. The congregation of the elite and of the workers in so few urban settlements clearly stimulates their organization into groups expressing their respective interests.

Lastly the town is the locus of most innovation. Here the individual may escape the restraints of his family and kin, of traditional elders and tribal values. How many men choose to do so is another matter; for, as we shall see later, the African townsman tends to remain in a very close relationship with his kin and community of origin.

The growth of towns

Towns have existed in West Africa for centuries. The capitals of the great empires of Ghana, Mali and Songhai were impressive centres; Tombouctou and Djenne still live on as faded relics of those distant ages. The capitals of the Hausa and Yoruba states in the past millennium sometimes had populations approaching 50,000. But these centres were scarcely urban. Although walled and densely settled the Yoruba centres were aggregates of the huge compounds of descent groups which constituted the town; their social organization was based upon criteria of descent and age. Four-fifths of the people in these towns were farmers; and the towns themselves were largely self-sufficient both in foodstuffs and in crafts. The Hausa towns functioned more in the manner of medieval European cities – as administrative and commercial capitals of a surrounding rural hinterland. But a large part of their population, too – perhaps a half or more – consisted of farmers. Residence in compounds by members of a single descent group was the usual pattern.

The new towns have grown rapidly. The oldest of them developed around the coastal forts of the European traders – as at Cape Coast or Gorée. Then, as trading expanded, the new settlements became established. Around the indigenous town of Lagos, with its own *oba* and chiefs, settled the returning captives from Sierra Leone and from Brazil, together with the European merchants. As traders moved up the river Niger, they developed a major market centre at Onitsha waterside – the nucleus of a new town whose modern suburbs have now encompassed the indigenous village of the Onitsha people. With the colonial era, these towns were sometimes selected as the headquarters of administration; in other cases, sites were chosen – as was Kaduna in Northern Nigeria – in open country. New settlements were created in the mining centres – Jos, for example – and ports were developed as the export trade increased.

The most phenomenal expansion in the size of these towns, however, has taken place since the Second World War and especially since Independence, which has led both to an extension and to a greater centralization of government activities. New industries have been established in the existing centres, to exploit the available supply of local skilled labour, of power and of transport facilities. The entreaties of the politicians, that industrialists should locate their factories in the rural hinterland and thus bring wealth and employment to these areas, have largely gone unheeded. The primary school leaver, reluctant to farm, thus still turns to the town in search of employment.

The population of Lagos was estimated to be approximately 75,000 at the outbreak of the First World War; by 1950 it had grown to 230,000, and by 1962 to 675,000. Abidjan was a late starter; it had only 10,000 people in 1931, but by 1960 this figure had increased eighteen-fold. Accra, too, had fewer than 20,000 people before 1914, but between 1948 and 1960 grew from a population of 135,000 to 325,000. Dakar doubled its population in the same period to nearly 400,000, and Bamako has almost quadrupled its size since 1945, to exceed 100,000 at present.

Some of these towns – Lagos, Abidjan, or Dakar, for example – are not only the seats of government, but also the major ports and industrial centres of their states. In other areas, a greater specialization of function among towns exists. Thus in Eastern Nigeria, Enugu is the regional capital and a centre of coal mining, but is of little importance as a trading centre; Port Harcourt is a major port and now the centre of the oil industry and smaller manufacturing enterprises; Aba, only twenty miles distant, has a beer and a soap factory, but is primarily a market town serving the southern and eastern parts of Ibo country, with half the adult men – as at Onitsha – being traders, mostly self-employed.

The capitals of the French-speaking states have had much larger European populations than their English-speaking counterparts. In the mid-1950s, Dakar Europeans numbered 30,000, at that time 13 per cent of the total population in the city. Conakry had almost as great a proportion of Europeans, while Abidjan's 9,000 formed 7 per cent of the city's population. In contrast, less than 2 per cent of the populations of Lagos and Accra were Europeans.

We should compare the sizes of these African capitals with the population of their territories. Abidjan has 5 per cent of the total population of the Ivory Coast; Dakar, developed as a capital for all French West Africa and as its major port, now contains one-tenth of Senegal's population; Accra's inhabitants represent 5 per cent of the population of Ghana.

With the rapid growth of the West African towns in recent decades, it is obvious that most of their present residents must have been born in the rural areas and have migrated to the town in search of work. Few censuses have proved sufficiently detailed material to illustrate this migration; but that of Lagos in 1950 has some interesting figures. Of the city's population of 230,000 at that date, 73 per cent were Yoruba and 12 per cent Ibo; 37 per cent had been born in Lagos (and this proportion must have included many small children of migrant parents), 39 per cent had been born in the Western Region, 11 per cent had been born in the East, and 8 per cent in the North. Within the Western

Region, the districts neighbouring Lagos – Abeokuta and Ijebu Provinces – provided not only more than half the migrants from the Region, but also a much greater number of migrants in proportion to their own populations. Ijebu in Lagos numbered 50 per 1,000 Ijebu in their home country, compared with 7 per 1,000 for Oyo and Ibadan Provinces. The rate of migration from the latter areas was almost the same as that from the heavily over-populated Owerri Province in Ibo country; the rate from other parts of the Eastern Region was substantially lower. These figures, and similar ones for the other territories, suggest that the city draws most heavily for its immigrants on the area of its immediate hinterland. As the Lagos census suggests most Ibo will, in fact, seek work in towns of the Eastern Region; and even here a predilection for the nearest town is apparent.

In examining the character of the West African town dweller, therefore, we must remember that he is an immigrant, and that we are dealing with a perhaps transitional period when these immigrants form a majority of residents. Their children, born and growing up in the town, and having little contact with the rural areas, will have very different attitudes towards town life. Again, a large proportion of the present immigrants to the towns have come relatively short distances. With modern roads and frequent bus and lorry services, they can, without much difficulty, travel home for annual holidays or even for week-ends. This situation contrasts markedly with that of many workers on the Zambian Copperbelt or in Johannesburg, who have travelled a thousand miles to find employment.

In the nineteenth century, the houses of the European traders and government officials in Lagos and Freetown were closely juxtaposed with those of the local community. Europeans, in fact, often lived in houses built by and rented from the local merchants. Then, with the advent of the colonial period, governments developed segregated areas for European populations – though British and French practices differed – to produce towns of contrasting character. The British developed residential areas well away from the existing centres of population – in Lagos, on Ikoyi island, for instance. Large houses were set in spacious grounds, and the secretariat area of government offices, with other non-residential buildings like the club and perhaps the nursing home, were adjacent. Where new towns were built, the European residential area and that of the African population met at a commercial centre, which contained the railway station, banks and post office, and the stores of the large trading companies. In Northern Nigeria the new residential areas were all developed outside the walls of the old cities and were, as in the case of Zaria and Kano, formed into separate settlements for stranger Northerners, for southern Nigerian immigrants, and for Europeans. At Ibadan, the largest pre-colonial African town, the new residential areas almost ring the old city. In contrast, the capitals of the French-speaking states, being of more recent development, have at their heart the French residential area, more densely settled than counterparts in British territories and with a greater provision of services – local shops, garages and cafés for the relatively larger community. Government offices and the large open market share this central area. But the residential areas for Africans are sited beyond its limits.

Governments and other employers of large expatriate staffs have invariably provided housing for their senior officials. As these posts pass to Africans, so do the houses attached to them, and in government residential areas, university campuses and the like, one now finds multi-racial communities. But, save in the mining areas or at industrial sites far from established towns, employers have not usually built housing for the junior African staff, and this has been provided instead by local African entrepreneurs. Men have invested their savings in houses which could be rented, often room by room, to immigrants, and so there has developed in the new towns a category of wealthy landlords. Civil servants, enjoying the luxury of government subsidized housing, build houses for rent to the expatriate staff of new or expanding commercial firms. For profits from landlordism tend to be high. Only recently have the more affluent among the migrants to the towns, envisaging permanent employment, begun to build their own houses or to buy, by way of mortgage, a house on an estate developed by a public corporation. But the masses have neither the inclination to buy property in the town, nor the necessary capital. West African governments have yet to develop large-scale and mechanized building techniques to provide cheap housing for artisans and clerks.

The private development of African housing areas has tended to reduce the segregation of immigrants by ethnic group or socio-economic category. Ibo migrants become tenants in the family houses of Yoruba who have lived in central Lagos since the mid-nineteenth century. In a large house let out as single rooms, one is unlikely to find all, or even most, of the rooms occupied by persons of a single ethnic group or locality.[76] Although members of one ethnic group may tend to settle in certain suburbs, they are not often exclusively restricted to these. Thus Toucouleur who comprise the largest immigrant group in Dakar (after the indigenous Lebou and Wolof) are to be found in appreciable numbers in most wards of the city.[80] When houses are built to individual order by local contractors, little uniformity in style characterizes the new suburbs. An educated man buys or leases a plot and erects an elegant house to be occupied by his family alone; on the neighbouring plot is built a house designed to accommodate forty families in single rooms, sharing cooking and toilet facilities. In Nigeria, the Western Region Housing Corporation has developed at Ibadan an estate in which the better houses, now costing about £4,000 each, line the main roads, while the smaller ones, costing £1,500 to £2,000 and falling within the means of the executive grades of the civil service, lie to their rear. Thus, only on the erstwhile expatriate residential areas do the African elite live exclusively with their own kind. Yet residential proximity does not necessarily imply friendly social interaction. Elite children may be forbidden to play with their poorer neighbours, and be taken instead in their parents' car to approved playmates.[97, 100]

The immigrants

In much of the literature on African urban life written in the past three decades, the terms 'urbanization' and 'detribalization' are freely used. In leaving his village society, the African becomes 'detribalized'; in learning the new norms and values of town life, he becomes 'urbanized'. But these concepts have tended to obscure the degree to which relationships in the town may still be patterned according to traditional norms. The migrant, taking employment as a labourer in a large company or government department, must learn the behaviour appropriate to bureaucratic structures. But on arriving in the town, he will most probably have lodged with distant relatives or other people from his home community, and his behaviour towards these will follow that of the village. With every new contact that he makes, the immigrant has the choice between patterns of behaviour from his village days and some new pattern.

Generalizations about life in urban society tend to stress the superficiality, anonymity and transience of personal relationships, contrasting these with the dense network of close personal relationships to be found in the small and self-sufficient village community. The former generalizations seem, in fact, to be most appropriate to middle class suburbs of Western industrial cities, and especially those of recent rapid growth; the slums of the old cities have quarters which are in social structure not unlike African villages. The West African towns cannot easily be divided into compact territorial sub-units, each encompassing persons in a restricted socio-economic status. Indeed, to the individual immigrant the city presents a wide range of opportunities. He can, as many of the illiterate and unskilled workers do, maintain social relationships, save for those of the workplace and market, only with members of his own ethnic group or home community. On the other hand, he may consciously exploit to the full the opportunities offered by town life, rejecting relationships with kin and past friends when these seem to be a handicap to further achievement. The residents of East London in South Africa have been described by Mayer as falling clearly into two groups – the 'Red' and the 'School' people; the former, though living in the town, reject town norms and maintain, as far as is possible, the values appropriate to village life, while the latter reject the village instead.[83] Nowhere in West Africa is such a distinction so clearly marked; for the literate town dweller, in almost all cases, maintains fairly close links with his village of origin. Neither town nor village rejects the life of the other. Instead, the residents of each continually adapt their behaviour to every new situation.

Attitudes towards town life are conditioned largely by the motives of the migrant in leaving his village and by the expected length of his stay in town. From the areas economically most backward, areas lacking cash crops, the men travel to earn the money for their taxes – taxes which the colonial government decreed should be paid in cash and not in kind. Young men go to earn enough to pay the bridewealth for their first wives, to acquire a bicycle or similar status symbol for themselves or luxuries with which to woo their brides. In a few rural areas the density of population is becoming so great that there is not sufficient land to provide an adequate living; it is from the rural parts of Ibo country that emigration is heaviest, and some villages report half their adult men absent at any one time. School leavers, unwilling to farm in the manner of their parents, go to the towns to seek wage employment. Personal factors often determine which men and women migrate most frequently or for the longest periods. Quarrels or accusations in the village encourage a man to leave; today he will probably go to the town, whereas in the past he would perhaps have taken up residence with his mother's kin. In those societies where divorce is comparatively rare and a stigma attaches to the divorced woman, impeding her remarriage, she will today go to the town to earn a living, perhaps by trade, perhaps by prostitution.

Traditions of emigration develop which perpetuate the established patterns. In many savana societies migration southward in each dry season replaces the raiding forays of the pre-colonial period; the young men are not considered adult until they have made the journey to Lagos or Accra once or twice. The migrants tell glowing stories of the luxuries and pleasures of the distant cities – in most of which they have been far too poor to participate. The northern towns of Yoruba country are far from poor, but lying beyond the forest belt they cannot grow cocoa. It is from these towns that many of the traders found in northern Nigeria and the neighbouring territories come. From Ogbomosho it is usual to travel to Jos; from Shaki, on the other hand, it has become customary to travel to the inland towns of French-speaking territories – to Parakou, Ouagadougou and Bobo-Dioulasso.

The migrants may be most conveniently classified into three

groups: the seasonal, the short-staying, and the long-staying. The seasonal migrants come predominantly from the savana, where the long dry season, during which little or no work is needed on the farms, permits the young men to travel vast distances to seek employment. Annually, a quarter of a million men from Sokoto Province and neighbouring territories travel southward. From the Upper Volta a third of a million men (nearly all seasonal migrants) work in the coffee and cocoa plantations of the Ivory Coast; moreover, 200,000 people from Upper Volta were enumerated in the latest Ghanaian census – one third of them women, who had probably come with their men to stay for a year or more.

On the tin-rich Jos plateau, the ore is still dug from some open cast mines by hundreds of men and women with shovels and head-pans; many workers come for only two or three weeks, and the supply of them, strangely, remains sufficient throughout the year. These seasonal migrants do not, of course, take their wives with them on their journeys; in the towns they tend to live several men to a room or even sleep on verandahs. They can be employed on only the most menial tasks, for they never learn any skills during their short periods of work. In Yoruba country, for instance, they do not usually work on the cocoa farms but are employed building houses – mud walled constructions being put up only during the dry season. Informal labour markets develop where the contractors may hire, early each morning, their requirements for that day.

Many of the short-stay migrants – men who remain in the town for a year or two before returning to the village, perhaps only for a similar period – are termed 'target workers'. They come to town to earn sufficient for a specific purpose, and when they have achieved their aim they return home. They tend to live poorly while in town, maximizing their savings, and they also usually learn no skills.

Save for the educated youths, there are perhaps few men who arrive in town with the intention of staying permanently. But those who make good, with success in trade or through the acquisition of a skill which guarantees permanent employment and a better wage, will tend to remain in the town. The possibilities of gaining a similar income in the village grow less, while their urban affluence, demonstrated by their beneficence on visits home, enhances their prestige in the village. Those, on the other hand, who fail to make good in the town are reluctant to return to their villages penniless; they are more likely to stay on, hoping for better luck, until their kinsmen lose patience with their indigence and forcibly repatriate them.

With the rapid growth of West African towns, it is difficult to assess the stability of their populations. Most men will have resided in them for a short period only, whatever their long-term intentions. Few surveys have been conducted to measure the stability of urban residence and the patterns of migration. It has been calculated, for instance, that of the Toucouleur in Dakar, fifty per cent are seasonal migrants and only fifteen per cent long-staying ones. It seems probable nonetheless that there is, in West Africa, a quite rapidly increasing tendency for men to stay longer in the towns, and to have their wives and children with them. This may partly be explained by the increasing shortage of land in the rural areas or by the increasing immigration to the town of literates. It is probably also due to an increasing proportion of semi-skilled and skilled work in urban employment. In Nigeria during the past decade, the number of employed persons has increased but slightly, relative to the visible expansion in government services, commerce and manufacturing; many of the activities which formerly absorbed large numbers of unskilled labourers – road building, for instance – are now mechanized.

Urban employment

Wage employment in West Africa is characterized by three marked features – the smaller number of persons involved in it; the dominance of employment in construction, transport and commerce at the expense of manufacturing; and the high proportion of employees in the public sector.

The recent Ghanaian census records two-thirds of the country's adult males as farmers. (In other states, this proportion is much higher.) And of the remainder, nearly half are self-employed or working for members of their own families. In all, less than 25 per cent of the adult men are in wage employment. In Senegal, dominated by Dakar, the proportion is almost as great, but in the other territories the figure falls to around 5 per cent. Nigeria has, for instance, but half a million wage employees in a population of over 50 million. Of the *self-employed* non-agricultural workers in Ghana, the greatest number (over 40 per cent of the total) are in 'manufacturing' – or craft industries; commerce and trading claim a quarter of them. Of the Ghanaian *wage earners* in non-agricultural employment, one-third are in service occupations – as clerks, teachers, nurses, policemen, etc. One-fifth are employed in construction industries, and an eighth each in mining, in commerce, and in transport. Only 7 per cent are employed in manufacturing industries. And these figures describe, it must be remembered, the pattern of employment in West Africa's wealthiest state.

Four-fifths of those working in Ghana in service occupations are employees of government or of public corporations; government and the private firms share almost equally the employees in construction and transport. Only in commerce and manufacturing is the private sector dominant. Thus, two-fifths of all Ghanaian wage earners work in the public sector; the government is their employer, and it is to the politicians that they must look to ameliorate their conditions of employment. In such a situation, too, the government's conditions of employment have a determinant effect on those in the private sector. In the economically least developed countries, the public sector's share of employees tends to equal that of the private sector.

These various types of employment are not evenly distributed among the ethnic groups of each state. Wage earning is more developed among those groups living nearest to the centres of employment and these same groups provide, too, a higher proportion of the skilled and semi-skilled workers, the longer-staying migrants. In some areas education, perhaps as a result of mission activity, took an early root, and these have tended to retain their advantage. Thus Dahomey provided many of the clerks in neighbouring French territories, since she produced more literates than she could employ herself. Southern Nigerians filled most of the posts demanding skill and literacy in Northern

Nigeria, even in the Native Authorities (of the Zaria Native Authority's employees in 1950, southerners comprised one-sixth). Recently, indeed, the indigenous peoples have come to resent the monopoly of so many prestigious offices by 'strangers' and have demanded their replacement by local men. Some ethnic groups seem to prefer certain types of work. Thus in Lagos in 1950 a similar proportion of Yoruba and Ibo in the city were clerks, but the proportion of Ibo policemen was over eight times as great as that of Yoruba, and most of those employed in domestic service were Ibo and Edo. Members of a particular single locality may corner certain specialized commercial activities: in Onitsha, market people from a single village group may hold a near monopoly in a particular commodity; in Dakar, the news-vendors come from a single Toucouleur locality.

Wage rates in West Africa are low. Whilst the salaries of expatriate staffs in government and commercial firms were related to those obtaining in the metropolitan countries – with added perquisites to compensate for the discomforts of tropical life and, perhaps, the necessity of maintaining two homes – the wages of African workers were related to the income of subsistence farmers, and to the belief that all workers were migrants who did not have to maintain their families in the town. Thus, in Lagos in 1964, an unskilled daily paid labourer would earn less than £100 a year in full employment (and the same work would earn him only £70 in Kano, or £45 in the rural areas of Northern Nigeria). Artisans in Lagos received £135 a year at the bottom of the scale, and £290 at the top. A primary school leaver employed as a messenger might earn £100 a year; a primary school teacher, with three years of a teacher training college after primary school, would commence at £120. A young man with full secondary education and with qualifications for entry to university could expect to earn, as a clerk in a government office or as a teacher, about £240. And, generally, these figures are reproduced in all West African states. The Liberian police constable earns £8 a month; the primary school teacher, £10; the teacher with a high school certificate and teacher training, £28 a month. Whilst 'colonial-type' salary scales operated it was extremely difficult for an African to rise from the ranks of the junior service posts into the salary grades appropriate to expatriates and university graduates. Today this is being changed in several states with the introduction of extended scales for higher executive posts.

The majority of the African wage earners fall into the lowest-paid categories. In Ghana in 1957, 14 per cent of those employed in the public and private sectors earned less than £75 a year, and a further 50 per cent earned between £75 and £120. Only 9 per cent earned more than £240 a year. And similar proportions would doubtless emerge for other states, were reliable data available.

Some indication of what these sums mean in terms of living standards are revealed by the report of a Nigerian commission of inquiry into wages held in 1964.[81] On the basis of estimates of minimum expenditure put forward by trade unions and of their own inquiries into dietary needs, the commissioners concluded that in Lagos a minimum wage of £16 a month (excluding savings) was necessary to maintain a young unskilled labourer with a wife and child at the level of the Poverty Datum Line – a line 'which allowed no margin for anything other than the essentials of existence'. A similar figure of £10 10s. a month was calculated as appropriate for the more remote rural areas of Nigeria. These figures were approximately double the existing wage scales; yet to raise wages to them would, the commissioners realized, disrupt the national economy. The report accordingly recommended much lower scales, and these were then further reduced by the Nigerian government. The conclusions from these various sets of figures seem to indicate that well over half, and perhaps three-quarters, of West Africa's urban workers are living in conditions of extreme poverty. Yet it is these men who have entered the modern economy and who, living in close proximity to the luxury and affluence manifest in city life, have the highest aspirations.

Translated into living standards, these low wages mean overcrowded housing and poor diets. In Lagos today the rent of a single room in a well-constructed house (with electricity and water laid on, and washing and cooking facilities communally provided) is £2 10s. a month. But many tenants pay less if they have lived in the same building for many years, and many tenants, too, find far inferior accommodation. Some of Dakar's outer suburbs consist of rows of round mud and thatch huts. Few married workers can afford more than a single room. Bachelors club together to pay the rent. In an Accra survey of the mid-1950s, two-thirds of the households occupied a single room; and of these households, one-half consisted of from three to six persons, one-sixth of more than seven. Urban diets tend to be poor, as the workers purchase only the basic starch foods, without the addition of fruits and vegetables that enrich the farmer's meals. Transport costs in the town are high; the residential areas of the expatriates and the African elite tend to be adjacent to their places of work, while those of the lowest-paid workers are farthest away. The Nigerian commissioners presumed that the Lagos worker would want to save ten shillings a month in addition to the £16 needed to meet his basic expenditure. In fact many hope to save much more than this, perhaps through savings clubs. But such savings can only be made at the expense of accommodation or food.

Migrancy and poverty both contribute to the high ratio of working men to women of equivalent age in the towns. In Accra and Sekondi-Takoradi, the number of women aged 25–44 is only two-thirds that of men. In Lagos in 1950 the ratio of adult men born in Western Nigeria to women was 2 to 1, and of Eastern Nigerian men to women 3 to 1. A factor here is age. Sixty per cent of the Ibo in Lagos were aged between 15 and 34 years, many of them obviously young men in search of the high bridewealth demanded in their home communities. Similarly, in Tema, 57 per cent of the population was aged between 15 and 44 years – the Ghanaian national mean for this category being 43 per cent. 'Target workers' in south-eastern Nigeria find it advantageous to leave their wives in the village when they travel to the town. With the help of their male relatives, the women can grow enough on their farms to maintain themselves and their children and even to send their husbands the occasional food parcel. The men live in shared rooms and maximize their savings to buy bicycles, sewing machines or similar capital goods. Western observers are often perturbed by this division of the family. But, as in many West African societies, the Ibo woman anyway practises a two-year sexual abstinence after the birth of a child; she is protected by her husband's parents and brothers; and the children of absent fathers do not lack adult male supervision in the traditional compounds. The large number of single men in the towns might suggest that drunkenness and prostitution create a serious social problem; but, in fact, the incidence of these seems remarkably low. Again poverty may be a causative factor, but the strong desire to save and the control exercised by ethnic associations themselves serve as powerful checks.

The migrant who settles in the town for a long period will usually try to have his wife with him; and unless she is literate, when she may work as a teacher or clerk, the wife will probably trade. In Accra nearly 90 per cent of the employed women were engaged in commerce, most of them either as petty traders or as makers of cooked food. Earnings were low; three-quarters of the established traders who bought on credit from the large importing firms had estimated profits of below £45 a year, while perhaps a half of all petty traders made less than £20 profit annually. Yet these sums, however small, are welcome additions to the household income, and in addition give to the wives a degree of economic independence from their husbands.[72]

Even though they have their wives living with them, many men are not fully reconciled to town life. They send their wives home at the time of childbirth; and their children home to the village school, believing that discipline there will be stronger and distracting influences weaker. Almost all men state that they wish to return to their home communities before their death so that they may be buried in their traditional compounds. But these are, of course, men who spent all their youth in the villages; their own children, born and reared in the town, will almost certainly think differently.

5 The Western-educated elite

The leaders of the pre-colonial African societies were their chiefs and priests, their influential men, their wealthy traders; and it was with such men – we may call them the traditional elite – that the early Europeans negotiated. Later in the colonial period these same men were often used in systems of native administration as instruments of colonial rule. In the Gold Coast and Nigeria, educated traditional rulers, sitting in councils of chiefs or on the governors' legislative councils, were apt to see themselves as heirs to British power. But in every West African territory power passed at Independence to a Western-educated elite, members of which had led the various nationalist movements. The official language of government business today is in each state (save Northern Nigeria, where Hausa is widely used) either English or French.

The members of the traditional elite were, of course, recognized as such only in their own kingdoms and communities. They did not gain general recognition throughout the newly created colonial territories. Western influences and colonial rule resulted in the establishment of schools which provided clerks for the civil services, catechists and teachers for the missions, and a few men who became independent professionals. Many of these, and especially the more highly educated among them, lived in the colonial capitals and through the nationalist movements sought to wrest power from the expatriate rulers. And in so doing they identified themselves more with the entire colonial territory than with their own ethnic groups or local communities.

It is with this relatively small Western-educated elite that the future of the West African states largely rests. For this elite now wields political power. It is the innovating group responsible for mediating between European and traditional African values. The rate of economic development will to a large extent depend on the ability of the new leaders to seize the opportunities open to them. It is thus important that we examine the character of this elite, its social structure and the possible effects of this upon its members, its attitudes both towards the Western world and towards traditional societies.

A difficulty arises in defining at all closely the membership of the Western-educated elite. We may base our classification upon levels of education and of wealth, but the size and quality of the educated population varies from one state to another: in one state the trained primary school teacher appears as relatively highly educated; in a neighbouring state the young university graduate receives less recognition. Again, such a classification does not guarantee that the categories so formed are social groups. The term elite cannot be used with precision. A decade and more ago the term 'middle class' was frequently used to designate the educated Africans. It was appropriate then inasmuch as these Africans did occupy an intermediate position between the European ruling group and the mass of the population, though the term class was hardly appropriate. The term 'elite', used so commonly today, is convenient because it suggests the superior status of its members; it connotes, too, positions of influence – which the educated African certainly holds in redefining traditional values. Furthermore, an elite is thought of as an open group, access to which is not restricted by birth or family antecedents – and the present West African elites have certainly recruited their members widely.

It is common to refer to the elite of each West African state in the singular form, as a single group. Yet in Western societies, one frequently lists a number of separate elites – the political, the business, the religious, the artistic – though several of these may be closely related to form an 'establishment'. In some respects there is much less differentiation within a West African elite; members live in a single small community in their country's capital, and most of them have had a common educational experience. Yet there are significant differences within West African elites. These differences have markedly affected the political history of their states and will almost certainly determine to a significant extent their political and economic future.

The early elites of the various colonial territories differ markedly. The creoles of Sierra Leone, the Americo-Liberians of Monrovia, and the Sierra Leone immigrants to Lagos stand in contrast with the Gold Coast elite which, though settled around the European forts, maintained close links with kinsmen in the coastal kingdoms. Those educated in the emirates of Northern Nigeria during the inter-war years retained a close association with the traditional rulers, in contrast with the similarly qualified teachers of the French colonial territories. Differences of this order have frequently influenced the relationships between nationalist leaders.

With the expansion of educational facilities and the intensification of nationalist struggle, a new generation of the elite arose. The younger and more highly educated men resented the dominance of those still ranked above them, and the younger nationalists accused their elders of too great an accommodation with European rule, of being 'Uncle Toms'.

A third generation of the elite has been produced in some states by a diversification of the means of attaining an elite status. No longer is education almost the sole qualification; members of the political party in power (men who often through misfortune or lack of ability received little education) may rise to positions of considerable political power through their demonstration of loyalty to the party leaders and their influence over the masses. Thus the highly educated civil servant is resentful when his advice and decisions are challenged by party officials.

Thus the rapidity of social change is producing in West Africa a succession of elites with different criteria of achievement and different sets of values. And among these groups there is rivalry to control the political system of the newly independent state.

The rise of the elite

One of the most clearly distinguished elites is the creole type of Sierra Leone, of Liberia, and of nineteenth- and early twentieth-century Lagos. The term creole is applied only in Sierra Leone, but the other elites mentioned have the same characteristics, deriving from their alien origin. Differences among the three groups result from the fact that the Americo-Liberians of Monrovia were, from the beginning, in political control of the country, while many of the Sierra Leone emigrants to Lagos recognized their Yoruba origins, maintained tenuous relationships with their supposed communities of origin, and felt a closer identification with traditional societies.

The creole elite developed around these settlements which ultimately became capitals of the modern colonies and states. On their arrival they were poor and little skilled, but they were able to seize the new opportunities for commerce and political office which developed during the nineteenth century. Christian missions provided not only the education through which many of these opportunities were realized but also the basis of a community life so necessary to this ethnically heterogeneous collection of freed slaves. Many of the creoles prospered in trade and became comparatively wealthy men, but their commercial status began to decline at the end of the nineteenth century. Increasing competition arose from the large expatriate trading companies and the Lebanese merchants, while the creole traders themselves tended to invest their savings in house property, the regular income from which was used to educate their descendants and thus enable them to hold professional offices, with a far greater economic security than that provided by commerce. This channelling of creole achievement into the independent professions was further encouraged when, with the imposition of colonial rule, prestigious positions in government and church became almost impossible to attain.[85]

In order to distinguish themselves from the indigenous peoples, the creoles tended to identify themselves closely with the European communities and their values. Their houses were styled after those of the white traders and missionaries or after those of their transatlantic experience. Furnishings, furthermore, closely followed European patterns, with upholstered settees and chandeliers in vogue. European dress was usual, with wing collars and crinolines the essential accompaniment of high status. Attempts to introduce African forms of dress to the creole groups were conspicuous failures. Eating habits, too, differed markedly from those of the indigenous peoples, with local foodstuffs prepared according to English or New World recipes. Exchanges of social visits and dinner invitations were common.

To a substantial extent the adoption of European styles of living was fostered by the Mission churches. For in the nineteenth century the distinctions between Christian principles and the values of the English Victorian middle class were not often clearly drawn, and the acceptance of one presaged acceptance of the other. Moreover, the churches continued to play a dominant role in the social life of these communities. In Lagos, for instance, high general prestige in the town was closely correlated with an active participation in church affairs. The distinctive patterns of creole social life were reinforced by the virtual endogamy of the group; and since creole numbers were so small, it is easy to see how in three or four generations a very close network of kinship bonds was created.

In the nineteenth century, identification with European style of living and values was relatively easy. In spite of a growing belief among Europeans in the African's innate inferiority, the white trading and consular communities lived, in Freetown and Lagos, among the creole elites. They attended the same churches, and since few men had their families with them, they tended to find their recreation in clubs freely attended by Africans. Visits to each others' homes by Europeans and Africans were more frequent than they were to become in the twentieth century.

Creole society was not completely closed, however. Indigenous youths would initially be employed as domestic servants and might on achieving better jobs be accepted as social equals in creole circles. Others, from interior ethnic groups, who settled in the capital as traders or clerks, might assiduously assimilate creole behaviour patterns to earn recognition by the elite. But in general the creole attitude towards the indigenous peoples was one of scorn and hostility. Creoles tended to adopt many European stereotypes of the 'depraved native' – such sentiment effectively impeding the adoption of the culture and values of the indigenes – and did little to advocate or advance education in the interior, for such could only result in an increasing threat to their monopoly of prestige status in the capital.

In economically backward Liberia, this creole group has maintained its dominant position, due no doubt to its control of the government since the foundation of the state. In Sierra Leone and Nigeria, however, the creole ascendancy has passed. The economic expansion in these countries has created far more opportunities for educated persons than the small monogamous creole families have been able to fill. And whereas the colonial governors were apt to select their African advisers from among residents of the capital, the modern parliaments distribute their seats throughout the country. Many Lagos politicians who had lived all their lives in the capital were obliged in the 1950s to seek adoption in the constituencies from which their forebears had once emigrated and of which they might thus claim to be native.

The early elite of the Gold Coast contrasts in many respects with the creole groups. In the settlements around the coastal forts, at Cape Coast or Elmina for instance, there developed families whose members tended to monopolize the local commercial and political offices during the nineteenth century. As with the creoles, these tended to bear English names – the Bannermans, Brews, Casely Heyfords, etc. – and to adopt to a substantial degree the Victorian style of life. But these men and women were not descended from alien slaves. Most were from local groups, though some families derived from the union of a European trader and a local woman in the late eighteenth or early nineteenth century. In such cases, the trader was often responsible for the education of his mulatto offspring, though the youth generally grew up with his maternal kin.

The foundations of these families often preceded the periods of strong mission activity, and the influence of Christianity over them was a relatively late phenomenon. Their male members tended to marry local women and thus established a wide network of kin relationships in the coastal Fanti kingdoms, relationships which were exploited to gain commercial advantage or political influence in these kingdoms. Instead of the opposition to indigenous society which marked creole attitudes, indeed, the early Gold Coast elite as a group mediated between the Europeans and the traditional societies. Nevertheless, as these families accepted Christianity at a faster rate than other peoples, and as, in the second half of the nineteenth century, their members tended to monopolize the most prestigious positions in local communities, intermarriage among them tended to increase. This educated elite began to develop a character distinct from that of the traditional elite of kings and chiefs, and whilst on some occasions they would jointly oppose the colonial government, on others the two groups would see themselves as rival heirs to power, and each would strenuously oppose any extension in the influence of the other.

Inasmuch as this elite had its roots not exclusively in a small area of the capital but throughout the coastal kingdoms, it has not been so markedly eclipsed as its creole counterparts. Yet in Ghana, too, the rapid expansion of the bureaucracies has meant that the older elite has been able to fill, from its own ranks, only a small proportion of the posts.

The development of an educated elite in the coastal areas was markedly different from the elite development in the emirates of Northern Nigeria. British rule did not extend over this area until after 1901, and in their desire to preserve the integrity of the indigenous political structure and the Islamic faith which upheld it, the colonial administrators prohibited the Christian missionary bodies from proselytizing. Educational expansion, largely the result elsewhere in Nigeria of mission attempts at conversion, was accordingly slow. The output of the schools, and especially of the teacher training colleges – the only form of post-primary education available to the Hausa youth for several decades – was more closely geared to the needs of government. Scholars tended to be drawn from the ruling Fulani families, or from other families, perhaps of slave origin, closely associated with the palaces. And they sought, and found, employment in the Native Authorities, for the size and wealth of these provided offices with salaries and power rarely matched in local government elsewhere in Nigeria. Furthermore, the educated Native Authority employee sought to use his opportunities as a civil servant to reach a traditional titled office. Within the past decade Northern Nigerians of ministerial rank in Regional and Federal legislatures have vacated these offices to assume important traditional posts in their own communities; the present Emir of Kano was, before his accession, Nigeria's ambassador to Senegal. Thus, a body of educated men was produced which did not feel alienated from traditional society and did not experience competition from Europeans for the high ranking offices.

In upholding Muslim culture, the British in Northern Nigeria prevented the creation of an educated elite taking Western styles of living as its reference point. The literate Hausa does not adopt Western dress; Hausa remains the official language of local government; traditional house styles are substantially maintained within the walled towns.

Historical and ethnic factors have produced as wide a variety in the character of the early elites in the French-speaking states as in their English-speaking neighbours. In general, however, the French-speaking elites are of much more recent formation; only in Senegal can there be found three generations of Western-educated men. By 1945, indeed, very few Africans from the French colonies had received an education abroad, and again most of these were from Senegal. Those who had attended secondary schools in West Africa had done so alongside the children of resident French families, and so, whilst the educational system was openly assimilationist, it produced at the same time in the African students a resentment that the contents of the courses contained little relevant to their own country. The existence in practice, too, though not in law, of a subtle colour barrier between Africans and Europeans further encouraged nationalist sentiments among the former. Only in Senegal, where most of those educated in the early years were citizens and jealous of the privileges accorded to them by the French administration and denied to the masses, was identification with the French substantially fostered.

In each of the French territories except Senegal, one of the political parties in the early post-1945 period was based on the appointed chiefs whom French administrators sought to raise to power in preference to the more radical elements. These chiefs were themselves rarely well-educated, but with the scarcity of others who had secondary or university education they did constitute an elite. In Guinea the opposition to the chiefs' party came from the trade union leaders led by Sékou Touré. Guinea had been among the economically more backward of the French West African territories before 1945, but subsequent development of iron and bauxite mining produced a large industrial labour force which could be organized with relative ease, and by the mid-1950s the territory possessed a greater number of trade unionists than did any other French-speaking one save Senegal. In both Guinea and Mali many of the members of the early elite, both chiefs and educated men, were from Fulani families. Their own culture tended to stress some of the puritanical elements in Islam, while Fulani history, especially the nineteenth-century empire-building of Samory and Al Haj Omar, with their resistance to the French, nourished nationalist pride. Puritan Islam and, in Guinea, the trade union origins of the present political leaders, have produced in Bamako and Conakry an elite far more spartan in its style of living than that of any neighbouring capital.

In the Ivory Coast, the French administration encouraged the planting of coffee by Europeans, while among the African planters were civil servants and chiefs. Discrimination during the inter-war years in favour of the Europeans formed a primary target of attack by the nationalist movement, which thus drew together the chiefs and the Western-educated Africans in a manner contrasting sharply with their rivalry in the other territories. The Ivory Coast chiefs, through their economic interests, were also more independent of the French administration than those of the remaining French territories. President Houphouet-Boigny himself was both a canton chief and a wealthy planter.

European Elites. For the whole colonial period, the term elite should most properly be applied to the European residents of the colonial territories. In their hands lay political and economic power. It was from them that the Western-educated African nationalist leaders sought to gain control of their countries. But the European population acted, too, as a reference group for the African elite, with its behaviour determining in part the African reaction to the impact of Westernization.

In the nineteenth century the European traders and government officials had tended to live in close proximity to the educated Africans. With the rapid increase in their numbers during the twentieth century, however, the Europeans segregated themselves in residential areas which the ordinary African citizen of the town would not be likely to visit unless on special business. The European way of life was a mystery, disclosed for the most part to Africans only through the reports of domestic servants. The residential areas had their own clubs, from which Africans were explicitly or effectively excluded. And as the proportion of European wives and children who resided with their husbands increased, the recreation of the men increasingly revolved around their families and family friends. The administrative officer in the lonely bush station became less inclined to play tennis with his senior clerks or discuss with them the history and culture of their ethnic groups.

Almost all Europeans employed in government service or the large commercial firms enjoyed a higher standard of living than they could have achieved in their metropolitan country. The status symbols of the European upper middle class – the large house, car, and ample leisure time – were deemed essential to efficient working in tropical countries. And these privileges gave a cohesive character to the expatriate group, however markedly its members might be bureaucratically ranked within it.

The European population of the colonial period was a transient one; all its members expected to retire to their home countries at a relatively early age. (Retirement in the British colonial service was permissible at 45 years of age, and obligatory at 55.) Yet many did expect to spend the greater part of their working lives in the colonies and felt that they had a mission to perform there. To the extent that they did not feel threatened by African competition for their jobs, they could – and often did – assume a benevolently paternal role towards the African. The administrative officer ruled his rural district like an eighteenth-century squire.

The African's image of the European was that which the latter chose to present on public occasions – the conscious public image of middle-class European society stressing reserve, propriety, probity and group cohesion. It was not apparent to the African who never left his country that these attributes were not typical of white society in general. In fact his illusion tended to be reinforced by his choice of fictional reading; Marie Corelli and Rider Haggard were the most popular authors among English-speaking Africans. For most Africans of this period the first close acquaintance with Europeans was with their working class landladies in Britain and France. On the one hand, this experience dispelled their stereotyped image of European behaviour; on the other, it often presented to them models of house furnishing and child rearing.

The past two decades have produced considerable change in the structure of the European population in the West African states. In all of them it has increased in size, often rapidly. The new arrivals tend to be associated more with industry and commerce than with government. They come to Africa for short contract periods and have less of a commitment to, or interest in, the country of their sojourn. An increasing number are performing tasks for which Africans ought to have appropriate qualifications; this seems especially so in French-speaking territories, where the lack of educational development has resulted in a marked shortage of Africans to fill necessary executive and minor technical posts. In the English-speaking territories the number of university graduates currently being produced suggests that almost all offices of an administrative nature could soon be Africanized. Thus, while the new European arrivals to West Africa are less imbued with the paternalist sentiments of their predecessors, they are increasingly threatened economically. For they and their families are still privileged, enjoying relatively high standards of living.

A recent survey in Dakar has shown that less than five per cent of the European population there have frequent contact with Africans beyond that occasioned by their duties. Those who do interact tend to be those whose social status and style of life in Africa differ little from what they would enjoy in their home country, those who are religiously or politically militant, and those who see their vocation in serving a developing country. To these broad categories may be added a small group of those who seem to have rejected their own cultures in favour of African alternatives; in patronizing African tribal arts, they have given a lead to many educated Africans whose approaches to their own heritage had hitherto been rather timid.[92]

Although those Europeans who interact frequently with Africans tend to be marginal to the European community as a whole, their behaviour does weaken the cohesiveness of the group. And this weakening of cohesiveness is furthered by the ethnic heterogeneity of the recent migrants. No longer do they come overwhelmingly from the former metropolitan country, but include the overtly egalitarian Americans and citizens of other developing countries. Many are employees of international organizations. The European community thus disintegrated into a large number of small groups based on ethnic origin, social class and other criteria. Whilst the African's contacts with these groups might be slightly more intense than in the colonial period, they provide him with not a single reference group but a variety of behavioural patterns with which he may identify or which he may reject.

Education and social mobility

The early West African elites, though defined as having received some Western education, varied widely both in levels of educational attainment and in occupation. With the growth of government and its services, and the consequent expansion of the elites, the importance for entry to the elite of educational qualification had increased. Today, there are relatively few posts for which specific levels of attainment – a primary school leaving certificate, the West African School Certificate, a university degree – are not required by employers. This situation is common to most industrial countries; but, unlike these, West Africa lacks extensive private industry and business where these criteria are less stressed. Entry to the elite and the subsequent character of this group are thus determined by the educational system.

The colonial powers bequeathed to the West African states educational systems which were more egalitarian in many respects than those of the metropolitan country. There were virtually no private schools in the colonial period; mission schools were at least supervised by government officers and, in recent years, subsidized from government revenues. It has been possible for a boy born to humble parents in a rural area to pass from his village school to secondary school and thence to university at very little cost to his parents or kin. Such examples, though rare in occurrence, have provided inspiration for thousands of youths.

Certainly the proportions of those who pass from primary to secondary schools, and from the latter to post-secondary institutions, have been relatively low. The numbers of children cited as attending primary schools often gave a false impression, for the bulk of them were often in the lowest classes, and relatively few ever reached the highest. In Guinea in 1957, where some 37,000 children attended primary school, those passing the first and second *baccalauréat* (roughly equivalent to the G.C.E. Ordinary and Advanced Levels respectively) totalled only fifteen in each examination. In the wealthier Ivory Coast there were fifteen times as many students in primary schools as in all kinds of post-primary institutions. In the Western Region of Nigeria, which has had probably the highest rate of secondary school attendance in West Africa, only six per cent of those who left primary school in 1960 were, at the beginning of 1961, in the lowest classes of the secondary grammar schools. For those who successfully complete their secondary education, admission to an institution of higher learning is perhaps slightly easier.

Entry to secondary schools, as to a local African university, is by competitive examination (in the latter case, often on the basis of marks obtained in School Certificate and G.C.E. examinations). It is difficult for the very dull son of wealthy or influential parents to survive long in such a system, although an element of nepotism and corruption is often present. Far greater, however, are the financial obstacles to the bright son of poor parents.

In some English-speaking states primary education is now free, or almost so. The southern Regions of Nigeria abolished primary school fees and provided schools for all children between 6 and 12 years of age (though attendance is not compulsory). The parents, however, still have to provide books, pen and ink, and school uniform, the costs of which may well deter them from keeping their son at school.

Secondary school education is heavily subsidized – but is still not cheap to the parent. Most schools were founded as boarding schools – for the obvious reason that their scholars were drawn from a very wide area. Even in 1961, of Western Nigeria's 177 secondary grammar schools, only 7 per cent were exclusively day ones, and only 43 per cent were prepared to accept any day scholars. An egalitarian tendency exists here; for it is argued that the day-boy would be unlikely to find at home an atmosphere conducive to study and that his performance in examinations would be poorer. With the children of both wealthy and humble families living under the same conditions in school, their chances of examination success are not disparate. (Missionary bodies, furthermore, hoped to have a greater influence in shaping the values and beliefs of their scholars in a boarding school.) But boarding sends up the cost. Tuition and boarding fees amount in Nigeria, for instance, to about £75 a year – a sum equal to the entire earnings of an unskilled worker. In Ghana the government has proposed to abolish tuition fees, but boarding fees (perhaps amounting to £40 a year) will remain. No figures exist for the number of children who achieve admission to secondary grammar schools but are unable, for financial reasons, to take up their places. Nor does one know how many bright children never trouble to sit a secondary school entrance examination, knowing that their parents could never afford to send them to the school. One does encounter frequently, however, the youth whose school fees for the first year or two were paid from accumulated savings, and who spends the rest of his school career in constant fear of dismissal for not paying his fees and in periodic absences from school while efforts are made to raise the money from distant kin and benefactors.

Similarly, the costs of a university education are heavily subsidized. Nigerian universities charge between £150 and £200 a year for tuition and boarding fees (representing about one-eighth of the total cost); those educated in English universities must spend double this amount. It is often proposed that all secondary and university education should be free. But this is usually countered with arguments that the rewards paid to the successful school leaver or graduate in a higher salary is so great that he or his family (whom he will eventually repay for their efforts on his behalf) should contribute at least part of the education costs.

Formal scholarships and the indulgence of school principals, who connive at the failure to pay fees by bright but indigent pupils, have enabled many a poor boy to get a good education. But these courses of aid do not increase as fast as the educational system expands. In a very few years during the 1950s the proportion of undergraduates at the University of Ibadan in receipt of scholarships fell from eighty per cent to forty per cent; or, in other words, over half the university places went, at the end of the decade, to those who could afford the fees.

The subsidizing of education thus does not enable boys from poor homes to receive higher education, whilst it relieves the wealthier parents of paying the full costs of such schooling. Furthermore, a greater part of the benefits received by these children as higher salaries is likely to be returned to their families, as payment for further members' school fees, than will be received by governments as tax to finance further education and scholarships.

No educational system is so egalitarian that it can overcome differences in home environment and afford equal opportunities to all social classes. It seems probable that the 1944 Education Act in Britain, which made secondary education free there, did not result in a significantly higher proportion of working class children attending grammar schools, though more may have succeeded in reaching universities. In West Africa the differences in the family environment of primary school children are vastly greater. In the secondary school entrance examination, all the advantages lie with the child from the elite home, who has grown up with parents literate in English, who has had books to read and toys to play with, and who has received, at some cost, extra school private tuition to cram him for the examination. The boy from the crowded compound without electric light, who spends his evenings doing domestic chores or playing, is seriously handicapped.

As the number of secondary schools increases, so do differences in quality appear. The reputations of the schools become ranked, both by the degree of success which their pupils show in examinations and in the prestige which the school can bestow on its pupils throughout their later life. Ghanaian scholars, in assessing the prestige of the secondary schools of their own country, produced a rank order which correlated to an uncannily high degree with examination success. The fees of the prestigious schools tend to be no higher than others (in fact, they may be lower), and so it is, in one respect, as easy for a poor as for a wealthy boy to enter them. But the competition to enter these schools is so great that odds are even more in favour of the children from elite homes. Thus, Ghana's two top schools have a higher intake of scholars from professional and well-educated families than do other schools, and a similar situation seems likely to obtain in other countries.

The considerations raised here may be illustrated by data from samples of secondary school pupils in Ghana and the Ivory Coast.[87, 88] By taking the proportions of fathers of secondary school boys in different educational and occupational categories, and then comparing these with the proportions of such men in the total population, a selectivity index may be calculated; this index illustrates the chance which sons of fathers in these categories have of attaining secondary education.*

Fathers' education	*Selectivity Index: Ghana*
None	0·4
Primary 1–6	1·5
Secondary 1–6	6·9
Teacher training college	10·4
University or equivalent	13·0

Fathers' occupations	*Selectivity Index: Ghana*	*Ivory Coast*
Professional, higher technical and administrative	4.9 (combined)	25·7
Clerical workers and teachers		5·9
Private traders and businessmen	2·9	2·1
Skilled workers and artisans	1·1	3·4
Semi-skilled and unskilled workers	0·1	0·2
Farmers	0·6	0·8

* The Selectivity Index = The percentage of students with fathers of a given characteristic / The percentage of all adult men with such a characteristic

Thus the son of a Ghanaian university graduate has over eight times as good a chance of entering secondary school as has the son of a man with primary education. Further figures for girls at secondary school show an even greater bias in favour of those with educated parents. And the figures for the Ivory Coast show a greater bias than in Ghana in favour of the professional groups.

An Ibadan sample indicated that it was extremely rare for a man to receive less education than his father. Thus, whilst there has been abundant mobility, over a generation, to occupations requiring better education and commanding higher salaries, there has been little movement in the reverse direction.[100]

The above figures stress the advantages which elite parents have in obtaining a good education for their children, but they tend to obscure the fact that a high proportion of present secondary school pupils and undergraduates still come from humble homes. So rapid has been the educational expansion that the early elites have been far from able to fill all the new places provided. Thus, in the sample of Ghanaian secondary school children cited above, over a third of the scholars had fathers who were farmers; a third had fathers of professional and similar occupations; and a fifth parents who were private traders or skilled workers. (Though, of course, nearly two-thirds of Ghana's adult men are farmers; 16 per cent traders or skilled workers; and only 7 per cent professionals.) The Ibadan sample revealed that of Yoruba with university degrees living in the city, a third had fathers without a full primary education, and only a third had fathers who had received some post-primary schooling. A Ghanaian survey of the early 1950s showed that 26 per cent of the undergraduates in the University College had fathers with little or no education, compared with 30 per cent who had fathers with secondary or higher education; again 26 per cent were children of farmers or fishermen, and 23 per cent were children of professional men.[89] Similarly, two-thirds of the sampled pupils in the Ivory Coast secondary schools had non-literate fathers.

Thus the members of the present elites in the West African states, together with those who will become members in the coming decade, are still drawn predominantly from humble homes. Although the early elites have been able to ensure comparable status for their own children, they have been outnumbered by the new entrants from the masses.

Just as education is not distributed equally among the children of the various socio-economic categories, so too certain ethnic groups have a disproportionate number of educated persons. Those groups living near the coast which accepted missionary teaching and schooling at an early period have tended to perpetuate their superiority in this respect. With their greater numbers of educated people, they appear to monopolize the most prestigious offices, at the expense of those ethnic groups among which education has been slow to develop. Such differences tend to exacerbate the rivalries among ethnic groups.

The elite today

Whilst one must stress the rapidly increasing size of the Western-educated elite and its recruitment from all sections of the population, the fact remains that its numbers are still very small. The West African states provide a variety of statistics, unfortunately not often comparable, illustrating the size and composition of the group.

The Ghanaian census of 1960 gives the total number of men and women employed in professional, technical and related occupations as 60,000 – of whom 27,000 are teachers and 5,000 are nurses and midwives. Not all of these 60,000 are Western-educated, however; for this category includes 5,000 native doctors (specialists in traditional African medicine) and 2,700 priests in traditional cults. Nor are all African; for included in these figures, as in those of the administrative, executive and managerial category, are the non-Africans (numbering in all in the two categories nearly 12,000 of whom perhaps 5,000 are occupied males). Only 13,000 persons are employed in administrative, executive and managerial posts, of whom 5,000 are administrators – a category which includes nearly 300 elected representatives, 800 chiefs, 900 government administrative officers, and 3,000 executive officers. These two categories – professional, etc. and administrative, etc. – account for only 4 per cent of the total male occupied population.

The same census also gives us the educational background of

the Ghanaian population: 280,000 men (from a population of 6,700,000) have completed middle school; 25,000, secondary (grammar) school; 16,500, courses in commercial, technical or teacher training; and 3,760 have university degrees.

Similar figures are not available for other states, but an impression of the size of the elite may be obtained from the output of the educational institutions. In the early 1920s Nigeria possessed only 30 university graduates – fifteen of them lawyers and twelve doctors, mostly drawn from the Lagos creole families. By the early 1950s there were 150 lawyers and 160 doctors; in the early 1960s, the number of lawyers was 2,000 or more. In 1945 there were under 190 Nigerian students studying in Britain, two-thirds of them in universities; in the early 1960s, this number had exceeded 5,000, with nearly, 1,000 in universities (and to this should be added the 5,000 students at universities in Nigeria and others in the United States of America). In 1933 only 19 Nigerian students passed the Senior Cambridge School Certificate; by the late 1950s the figure had exceeded 2,500, again with most of the successful candidates coming from the southern Regions. Relative to the size of their population, this rate of success was, for the southern Regions of Nigeria, twenty times as great as that of Guinea at the same period; but it was, too, twenty times smaller than that of England and Wales. In 1957, the Ivory Coast had approximately 500 students in France, and this number trebled by 1960. Its secondary school output, however, remained low; in 1957 only 63 students passed the first part of the *baccalauréat*, and 45 the second part – and many of these were resident Frenchmen. Almost all the successful Ivory Coastians went on to university. The simultaneous expansion of primary, secondary and university education in all states during the 1950s has for a short period resulted in a relatively high proportion of students passing from one level to the next; later, the competition to enter the universities will become stiffer again.

Statistics of taxable incomes are generally suspect in Africa; yet they do help to amplify data on occupation and education. In Western Nigeria in recent years only 0·5 per cent of adult men have earned more than £500 a year. Senegal, with a total population of three million, has only 50 indigenous civil servants earning about

£2,400, and a further 275 earning between £1,200 and £2,400 a year. 350 Senegalese in private employment have a mean income of £850 a year.

These statistics all point in one direction – the Western-educated elite is still extremely small (and this will be seen later to be a most important determinant of its social characteristics). The elite is also a youthful one. Again we must rely on Ghanaian census data, although the situation in other countries is probably very similar. Of the 60,000 professional and technical workers cited above, two-thirds are under the age of 34 years (the proportion of Western-educated is probably higher, since the native doctors and priests are among the elderly). Again, nearly half of the 13,000 administrators, etc., are under 35. In the more junior posts, 78 per cent of the 32,000 clerks are below the same age limit. Striking as these figures appear, they are somewhat modified by the fact that the whole population is weighted youthwards, as a result of the diminishing infant mortality rate in recent decades. Nevertheless, the elite is composed predominantly of young men, still early in their careers and hoping and planning for advancement.

We have already seen that half of the wage earners in West African states are employed in the public sectors, and the dominance of the public sector is even more marked in the employment of the elite. Of Ghana's 60,000 professionals, etc., only 10,500 are self-employed, and the latter figure includes the nearly 8,000 native doctors and traditional priests, leaving only 2,000 or more Western-educated persons in this category. 40,000 – two-thirds of this total – are employed in the public sector, and the remaining 8,000 in the private sector. Of the 13,000 administrators, etc., only 3,200 are self-employed, compared with 6,100 in the public and 3,700 in the private sector. In other words, the vast majority of the well-educated Ghanaians, whose opinions might be expected to have a powerful effect on government policy, are themselves employees of the government. When the modern West African state seems to be a rather fragile structure, it is these public servants who grow fearful for their government positions.

Of comparatively recent growth is the military elite – the officer corps of the growing armies. Both Nigeria and Ghana, for instance, had, in 1966, armies of 8,000 men, with approximately 300 officers. These national armies were developed from the locally based battalions of the Royal West African Frontier Force, and Africanization has been recent. The first Ghanaian was commissioned during the Second World War, and he later joined the Foreign Service; the present officers of the Ghanaian army were commissioned from 1950 onwards; and in 1961, British officers ceased to hold executive positions. In Nigeria under a third of the officers were indigenous at this date (and three-quarters of these were Ibo); but by 1966 the Nigerian army had been almost completely Africanized.

Large numbers of Africans from the French colonial territories served in units of the French Army – Guinea alone provided 22,000 in 1958 – and units of the French Army containing a high proportion of Europeans in the non-commissioned ranks were based in West Africa. National armies were developed after 1958, however, making little use of men demobilized from the French units. Guinea's army, developed within the Parti Démocratique de Guinée, grew to 4,800 by 1964. That of Senegal was smaller – only 2,500 – but 5,000 French troops were still based at Dakar in 1964 (a number which declined to 2,500 in 1965).

Of the self-employed elite, the lawyers often form the largest single category. A few architects, accountants and like professionals are self-employed, but even in these occupations the majority are probably employed by the large public corporations and private businesses. Nigeria's well-known novelists do not live by writing alone – most are highly placed civil servants. For the elites in the early decades of this century, medicine provided an occupation conferring great prestige and independence from the colonial government; but today most doctors work in government- or government-aided mission hospitals.

Few of those who leave the schools and universities become private businessmen. Most of them have received a strictly academic education and have very little technical knowledge or skill. They do not have capital of their own, and their families are loath to spend more on them when there are other children to train. The immediate rewards, too, of a salaried post are far more alluring than the slow growth of profits. Many educated Africans undoubtedly have native entrepreneurial skills, but the openings for them in trade, transport and the like, are those in which risks are greatest and competition most severe. Banks are loath to lend money for such enterprises, especially when the applicants have so little security. Family members, on the other hand, who do provide capital are apt to seek too great a share of the profits as dividends, allowing too little for reinvestment and so inhibiting the growth of the enterprise.

Many Africans are, however, entering the commerical world as employees of the large expatriate businesses. They may rise to become district managers of the wholesale out-stations; in the head office they are the personnel managers, information and publicity officers. Rarely do they occupy those positions responsible for the economic policies of the firm. In the new industries there tends to be strong competition for the technically competent men who can be sent to the overseas factories and be trained for supervisory posts.

A few of the Western-educated West Africans have taken posts not in the modern but in the traditional sector, notably in former British colonies where they fill traditional political offices. Nigeria and Ghana each has a lawyer among its *oba* and *ohene*, and many other traditional rulers were once clerks or teachers. Even Northern Nigerian emirs are becoming increasingly literate. It would be erroneous to imagine these traditional offices as being filled by elderly, illiterate men, impervious and perhaps hostile to Western ideas. The educated among them form a highly significant bridge between the indigenous societies and the modern state.

As has already been noted, dual salary scales operated in the once colonial territories – one scale designed for African employees and based on the incomes of farmers, the other for the expatriate official which paralleled salaries in the metropolitan country. Discrimination in reward, indeed, was one of the principal complaints of the emerging educated African elite, and it was inevitable that men who eventually attained 'senior service' posts should be eligible for the same salaries and privileges as expatriate staff enjoyed. Thus a Nigerian university graduate will commence with a salary over £700 and will, as a permanent secretary in a ministry, receive between £2,500 and £3,000. The Nigerian government has maintained an expatriation – later renamed inducement – allowance for expatriate staff, amounting to about one-third of the basic salary. The university colleges at Ibadan and Accra in an egalitarian move consolidated the basic salary and inducement allowance and paid expatriates and Africans alike (this move was justified in part by the fact that some of the first African staff at these colleges were from other colonies and were as much expatriate as their European colleagues). But recently the University of Ghana has reintroduced differential salary scales; and in Nigeria, for instance, where salary scales have fallen below those obtaining in Britain, the British government supplements the salaries of its own citizens.

Privileges accorded to expatriate officials have, in like manner, been inherited by their African successors in office. The more senior among them have moved to large houses in the government residential areas and pay a rent amounting in Nigeria to 8·5 per cent of their salaries. (Many such men have built private houses, with loans from government corporations, for which they charge commercial rents, several times as high.) The same conditions for leave tended to apply to Africans as to expatriates – in Nigeria, the rate of a week for each month's service still obtains – and for a period Nigerians were entitled to free passages to England for themselves and families each leave. Civil servants with salaries above £500 have, in the ex-British territories, continued to be eligible for an advance, at low interest rates, to buy a car, and for basic and mileage allowances to run it. In Nigeria the advances are now made, on hire purchase terms, by a private company; but 2·4 per cent of the Western Nigeria government's recurrent expenditure has gone on basic car allowances to its civil servants. Most Africans, not unnaturally, take advantage of this privilege, and possession of a car is apt to be the main criterion distinguishing the elite.

It is felt by the governments concerned and by citizens at large that these perquisites of public office (shared, too, by those in the private sector, for the companies are competing strongly with the government for skilled personnel) ought to be drastically reduced. And in the past decade there has certainly been some whittling away of them. But in the last resort those exercising the privileges are most loath to forgo them; the new entrants to the public services are unwilling to deny themselves the privileges held by their seniors.

In all the former colonies of West Africa, Africanization of the public service has, if with varying degrees of vigour, been pursued. Not only are Africans to replace expatriates in the existing offices, but the many newly created posts also are to go to local men and women. Yet only in Ghana and Nigeria have the educational institutions been able to meet the demand with any real measure of success. In Ghana only 14 per cent of the senior government posts were held by Africans in 1949; by 1954 the proportion had risen to 38 per cent. In Nigeria, progress came later, though no less rapidly. Not until 1954 was there any large intake of Nigerians into the Western Region's civil service. In 1961 almost all the posts of permanent secretary in that Region were filled by Nigerians (the one expatriate being a West Indian); by the end of 1963, 80 per cent of the posts in the senior administrative and technical grades were held by Nigerians, and most of the expatriates in this category were on contract. The expatriate colonial service officials quickly retired. Some were reluctant to work in an independent state, while more were anxious to take the generous compensation offered to them; with the top posts reserved in practice for Africans, prospects for promotion (and of eventually higher pensions) seemed slight. Nigeria (especially its southern Regions) and Ghana have been able to fill their teaching posts with Africans as well as staff the administrative services. Thus over one-third of the staff at the University of Ibadan are now Africans. In Western Nigeria recently only a third of the teachers in secondary grammar schools were university graduates; yet a majority of these, and most of the non-graduates, were Nigerians. In the French-speaking states the virtual drafting of educated men into the government offices has not only been insufficient to staff these adequately – very many senior posts are still held by Frenchmen – but has also depleted the schools of African teachers. In Mali in 1960, only one out of thirteen secondary school principals and only a third of the total teaching staff of these schools were Africans.

Africanization policies have resulted in rapid promotion for those who first gained a foothold on the ladder. The Western Nigerian permanent secretaries appointed in 1959 had had an average of ten years' service in the administrative grade. The first Nigerian professors at the University of Ibadan gained their chairs between five and ten years from the date of obtaining a doctorate or their first teaching post. Appointment to these high ranking posts seems to have been based largely on seniority. The education of these men had often been protracted unduly with their intermittent employment, so that they did not graduate from university until their late twenties; but they were still only in their late thirties or early forties on gaining these topmost posts, and they seem likely to occupy them for a decade or more to come. For the slightly later entrants to the public services, promotion has been much less rapid, and threatens to become very slow for present entrants, since the public services seem to have expanded to the financial limits of the governments. Thus, the suggestions made in Nigeria that the civil service compulsory retirement age should be raised from 55 years (the age applicable to expatriate colonial service officials) to 60 years are met by cries from the junior civil servants that their career prospects would be severely jeopardized. On the one hand, manpower experts claim that Nigeria is still very short of skilled personnel; on the other, graduates in the arts and social sciences are finding it increasingly difficult to find employment. Whereas the governments formerly found employment for almost every university graduate automatically, they now hold competitive examinations to select the favoured few.

Such a situation is not likely to occur in the French-speaking states for a few years at least; indeed, the poorer countries among them may never be able to afford an expansion of educational services on such a scale as to provide an apparent excess of educated men.

Prospects of rapid promotion and the increasing scarcity of posts combine to engender among the elite a high degree of competitiveness and insecurity. Those who have reached the top may feel inadequate in their posts and threatened by those ranked below them who are nevertheless far better qualified. The latter, in their turn, become disgruntled at the barring of their own promotion prospects by the 'time-servers', whose seniority rests upon a year or two in age or entry into the service. In states where the vast majority of the highly educated are in the monolithic public service, where universities are few, and where a small number of expatriate firms dominate the economy, the opportunities for the free flow of talent from one sphere, or one employer, to another become very limited.

Styles of living. The great differences in salary between the young university graduate earning £750 a year, the secondary school leaver with £250, and the unskilled labourer with only £75 a year, result in the very distinct style of living enjoyed by the elite. These styles are basically Western.

Many members of the elite have moved into official houses occupied by expatriate civil servants and originally designed for them. Some of the largest were built with only two bedrooms, in the expectation that the occupier might have his wife with him for only part of his tour, and his children never or rarely. Such houses are clearly inconvenient for Africans with several children; they certainly restrict their present occupants to nuclear family households. Many men are, in fact, only too pleased to use the house as an excuse to keep away the would-be parasitic near-relatives. These families tend, however, to employ a large number of servants, some of whom may be junior relatives receiving free board and, in return for domestic services, payment of their school fees. When the wife is working, a nursemaid is necessary for the children; when both spouses need the single car to carry them to work, a driver must be employed. A gardener is needed to maintain the spacious grounds of the house in neat order – for few Africans were taught in their youth to bother with growing flowers, and most continue to value the exemption from physical labour traditionally accorded to men of high status.

Among the houses of the elite there is a general uniformity of furnishing styles. Houses belonging to the government and public corporations are usually provided with basic furniture in a limited number of patterns, and the variety provided by the city shops is again small. In these circumstances, differences in style tend to reflect wealth rather than taste. The more affluent families will have a larger car, a bigger radiogram or television set. Such possessions make it easy for others to measure one's scale of income; though, in fact, one rarely needs to provide such consumption indicators, for the official staff lists give, for oneself and most of one's friends, exact age, rank and salary. Certainly there is detectable among the African elite a greater preoccupation with minor aspects of the salary scales and privileges than in societies where close friends and neighbours are not employees of the same organization, competing with each other for promotion.

Similarity of employment and a limited range in living styles both contribute to the cohesion of the elite. This cohesion is even further enhanced by the close network of friendship patterns that exist among members. Little study of social networks has, as yet, been conducted in West Africa; but a project of limited scope carried out at Ibadan in 1963 gives indications which are probably valid for other areas too.[100]

Members of the elite asked to name their ten best friends almost invariably chose persons of similar elite status and of the same sex, though not necessarily of the same occupation. Thus a single set of best friends included civil servants, private lawyers, and university lecturers. Nearly one-half of the friends came from the same ethnic group as the informant. One-half of the friends cited were, in addition, thought to be close friends of one another. Nearly two-thirds of the friendships seemed to have originated in school or college; this might perhaps be expected in a group of young people, but the proportion did not markedly fall among older informants. Perhaps the sudden transfer of young people from traditional homes to boarding-schools encourages deeper and more lasting bonds than would occur in day schools, where closer ties are maintained with siblings and with the friends of one's parents in the rural area. How far the close friends cited today were in fact the close friends of school days is difficult to judge. The number of secondary schools through which members of the present elite have passed tends to be very small. The graduate returning from abroad and given employment in Ibadan finds himself not in a community of strangers but among men from his home area and classmates from his old schools; relatively new close friendships may be projected backwards into the past.

A close-knit network of friendships is further fostered by the small size of the elite and the concentration of its members in the national or regional capitals. Even where they are not congregated in affluent suburbs, the possession of a car and its free use makes interaction among them easy. Formal entertaining through dinner parties or the paying of purely social calls seems less frequent than among the European residents; but very large parties to celebrate marriages or christenings are common and call for elaborate arrangements. Many of the marriages are, in fact, between persons from families with a number of educated members, and these new ties provide fresh relationships among the elite.

If one compares the living style of the West African elite with that of men similarly employed in an English or American city, the differences appear marked. The much-remarked-on anonymity of Western city life, especially for its professional middle classes, is conspicuously absent in Africa. A closer parallel would probably exist with the elite or upper class of Western societies – the families which are products of the most prestigious schools and universities, which have intermarried to an extensive degree and belong to the same few exclusive clubs.

The degree of cohesion in the African elites is sociologically significant for a number of reasons. It is the members of these groups who are creating new patterns of values for modernizing African societies. Within close-knit groups these new values will become generally accepted at a faster rate than in groups with a more open network of social relationships; the values will thus be identified with the entire elite by the mass of the population and form, for them, a new reference point for their own behaviour. On the other hand, the forces of social control are much stronger in close-knit groups. The member who deviates from the accepted behaviour patterns is both isolated and made to feel his isolation to a more marked degree. Innovation by existing members of the elite group may become more difficult; conformity may be strongly emphasized within the elite.

The sub-elite. In this chapter our attention has been directed at the wealthier and better educated members of the elite; in the previous chapter, it was directed primarily at the manual workers in the towns. In between these two categories are the clerks and the teachers in primary schools. Their salaries, falling within the £150–£500 a year range, are often closer to the incomes of the farmers and craftsmen than to those of the university-trained elite. Their attempts to Westernize their style of living are inhibited by their poverty. Yet their achievements in this sphere may well provide a more practical model for their less educated kin than do those of the elite, which may be admired but cannot be copied.

These clerks and teachers are furthermore still young men and women. The 1960 Ghanaian census revealed that nearly four-fifths of the country's clerical workers were under 35 years of age. Most of them do not see their present status as the ultimate point of their career. Whatever vocational training they may have received so far, they still hope by private study to gain the qualifications necessary to enter a university, or through good fortune to be selected for a course overseas which will give them a status similar to that of the graduate. Three years of education alone stand between their present jobs and the career prospects available to the elite. Many Africans at present at university have worked for as many as ten years since leaving school; their ultimate success stands as an example to their juniors that one should never give up hope.

The members of this sub-elite occupy an important position in those states with wealthy elites of relatively substantial size. Continually aspiring to enter the elite and to share in its affluence and privileges, they run a high risk of failure, and bitterness and disillusion seem likely to be their lot.

Part 3
Changing Institutions

6 Processes of change

The previous chapters have sketched, in broadest outline, the magnitude of the changes which have been taking place in West Africa during the present century. With the export of cash crops and industrial raw materials, and more recently, with the development of local manufacturing industries, African states have been drawn much farther into the world market economy. Modern towns have mushroomed within sight of traditional villages. The colonial territories created by the European powers have become independent states, with their national governments ruling areas far larger and more populous than any traditional political units since the medieval savana empires. Uniform systems of law overlie and to some extent replace the multitude of customary legal systems. Bureaucratic principles of organization prevail in the modern sector – in the civil service and in the larger commercial firms – in sharp contrast with the dominance of descent grouping in traditional societies. Small Western-educated elites now wield power; yet the members of these privileged groups have been drawn very largely from the humble homes of illiterate farmers.

To a substantial degree the West African states have been provided with the prerequisites of modern and industrial societies. But in each case the metropolitan power bestowed upon the colonies her own institutions. The early forms of central government, the educational and legal systems were all imposed upon traditional African societies – in no instance did they develop naturally out of them. What would have happened had the European nations maintained their trading relationships with the African peoples but not assumed government over them, is anybody's guess. Liberia, of course, has never been a colony, but it does not furnish us with an example of indigenous development, for its ruling groups have always been recruited from the alien Americo-Liberians. The colonial period thus created the political basis for the modern states and provided them with an infrastructure necessary for future economic and social development. The pace of subsequent development has grown increasingly rapid as these states have approached and then gained their independence. Their aspirations, reflected in their economic plans, can only be fulfilled with the continued import of capital and skills from abroad; yet it is accepted that the realization of these plans depends to an equal extent on the mobilization of resources within each country. Success here presupposes the adaptation of traditional society to meet modern needs. Thus our attention focuses not on the degree to which African states can borrow from the West, but on the speed and smoothness with which they can modify indigenous institutions. The emphasis on changes within these societies begins to overshadow that on changes effected from without.

Sociologists are, therefore, returning to evolutionary theories in their attempts to understand these processes of change. Such theories, widely accepted in the nineteenth century, became discredited when their proponents postulated a unilinear series of stages through which all societies passed (thus inferring that backward peoples had a long way to go before catching up with the Western industrial nations – if this, indeed, was ever possible); or seemed more interested in the origins of human institutions, basing their reconstructions of history on evidence of doubtful value. They neglected the diffusion of techniques and ideas; but, in so doing, they did properly stress the process of change within societies, even though their explanations of this process now seem naïve and unacceptable. Today, as the technological gap widens between the latest discoveries of the industrial peoples and the tools and methods of peasant farmers and craftsmen in the underdeveloped areas, it is nevertheless presumed that the poorer nations of the world can develop rapidly to approach the living standards of the industrial societies. Furthermore, the latter are acknowledging to an increasing degree that it is their responsibility to aid the former in their struggles against poverty, even though practice may lag far behind perception and precept. Yet development will not be attained merely by munificence, even supposing the munificence to be available; the richer must encourage the poorer nations to realize the potentiality of their own resources. Hence the scholars seek to discover the mechanisms by which rapid social changes can be effected, while men of affairs seek to direct their practical aid to those points where it will lead to further and continued economic growth.

The efforts of the scholars are directed along two major channels. The first approach attempts to establish the prerequisites of industrial society. From a comparison of the existing industrial and non-industrial societies of the world, one may abstract institutions prevalent in the former but not in the latter and deduce that these are accordingly essential to the maintenance of industrial society. Such institutions may be listed as including bureaucratic forms of organization, a developed system of social stratification, and a universal legal system. The development of any of these institutions is then held to promote progress towards a modernizing society. At one extreme, however, these prerequisites are formulated in terms too vague to permit of practical application. At the other, there stands the industrial evangelist who believes that the African should adopt the same forms of political, economic and social organization as predominate in his own country (just as the nineteenth-century missionary tended to see the acceptance of Christianity as inseparable from the adoption of Victorian family life and the development of entrepreneurial activity).

The second approach to the study of development lies in discovering the principal innovators in a society. Who are they? To what extent are they restrained or even totally inhibited by other members of their society? How, in practical terms, may one encourage them? In studies of the development of the already industrialized nations, attention has been focused upon the private entrepreneur and his qualities. Yet it is unlikely that such men will contribute greatly to the economic expansion of West Africa; the scale of industrial developments and the reliance upon foreign capital and skills place the initiative in the hands of indigenous civil servants and expatriate entrepreneurs (themselves more often managers of large corporations than small private businessmen). Theories in this field have stressed the importance of a class of entrepreneurs, the incipient bourgeoisie, who, denied access to political office and its privileges, find recompense in heightened commercial activity (unlike the wealthy trader of many traditional African societies, who virtually buys political office as a symbol of his success). Others have stressed the unequal distribution in different societies of 'achievement need' – the inner drive which impels men to attain or seek to attain a self-imposed standard of excellence. Such motives derive, according to some, from methods of child rearing, and it would seem to follow from this that a calculated attempt to instil achievement motivation into young children might pay substantial dividends later in economic development. Such theories are not yet sufficiently widely accepted, however, to justify attempts at changing family relationships. Nonetheless, the child rearing practices of elite parents do differ from those of their own forebears, and these will probably affect the children's personalities and the values dominant in future generations.

Throughout this book emphasis is placed on the changes occurring within West African society, on the adaptation of indigenous institutions. Sociologists have not always studied change in this manner, and although many of yesterday's theories are now outmoded, they are perpetuated in many popular attitudes current today. 'Culture' was taken as the frame of reference in the past, rather than 'society'; and 'culture' was defined as a set of traits, diverse and yet stable, which included both material objects and behavioural patterns. In the African context, the distinction between African and European cultures was most marked. Social change was interpreted as a process of acculturation in which persons of one culture – usually the African – borrowed items from the other whenever their own was unable to furnish an appropriate trait. And at the crudest level it was possible to count the number of borrowed traits as an index of acculturation. Such an approach is not accepted by sociologists today. Yet it is reflected in the surprise often shown by Europeans when they suddenly find an African acquaintance – well dressed, in Western clothes, speaking fluent English or French, and apparently completely Westernized – holding opinions about family relationships quite contrary to those of European society or participating in a traditional religious rite. Similar is the disquiet felt by Europeans on seeing the parliamentary form of government established in the new states working in a manner different from that of the former metropolitan country and from the intentions of the men who introduced it.

The sociologist is primarily interested not in unrelated items of behaviour, which may be termed the customs of people, nor in their material goods, which are only symbols. His interest lies in the relationships which exist among people and which determine their generalized patterns of behaviour. Social change is a change in these relationships – changes both in the form of relationship among people and in the number and type of relationships in which the individual participates. Thus in contemporary African society the relationship between father and son in urban areas or among the elite often differs markedly from that found in the traditional society; the urban dweller forms new relationships – with his employer, with trade unionists – which did not exist in Africa before the colonial era. These are the changes we are concerned with here.

Every individual member of society has certain basic interests or needs, both material and emotional. He must earn a living to support himself and his family; he seeks security – in both the economic and the psychological senses. To further these interests he sets himself certain goals which are broadly determined by the technology of the society, by the values held by its members, and by his own personality. But these goals can rarely be achieved in isolation, and he must combine and cooperate with others in various associations. The family, the descent group, and the age group are associations typical of traditional African societies; the craft guild, the trade union, and the political party are typical of modern societies. Sustained interaction among members of such associations is possible only when each behaves in a manner predictable by the others, and such behaviour is termed the norm, or the role of the person concerned.

The predictability of behaviour may depend variously on a

common set of values held by the members of the association and on the experience of past actions. Thus, one may believe that theft will be punished either because, in common with the members of the society, one believes it to be wrong, or because in one's own experience it is usually punished. If one's behaviour approximates to the standards expected, one is praised and rewarded; if one deviates from the expectations of one's fellow members, they will apply sanctions in an effort to ensure conformity. But members of an association are rarely equally powerful in their abilities to coerce their fellows; some are able to wield sanctions that ensure virtual compliance with their own expectations, while the weaker feel impelled to act not according to their own goals but to satisfy the expectations of others. The sociologist sees in the association not merely an assemblage of individuals, but the pattern of relationship among them, with each member performing a role appropriate to his status or position in the association. Such a pattern of relationships is usually termed the structure of the association. The term structure may imply a static pattern; it can perhaps best be described in static terms. Yet it is not necessarily unchanging.

A society is comprised of a number of associations, which together constitute its total structure. A man may perform a number of roles within a single association; in the family, he is both husband and father. But as a member of different associations he has a wide and varied range of roles. These roles should be mutually compatible; incompatibility leads to emotional strain as the individual seeks a means of satisfying the expectations of others, and to frustration as the others impose sanctions upon him for his failure to comply with their expectations. One is apt to see these roles presented as rather narrowly defined patterns of behaviour. But in all roles there is some degree of latitude open to the individual – often the gap between the highest expectations, expressed in terms of moral values, and a much lower level which one can be content with without fear of punishment by one's fellows. In situations of change, however, some roles may be very poorly defined. The elite father feels that he ought to be less authoritarian towards his children than his own father was to him. But how much less? His peers have no agreed standard. Some roles operate within specific contexts only; others are more diffuse. Thus one tends to expect certain standards of behaviour from a traditional chief in all his activities; in modern society, the clergyman can never escape his clerical status. But in general, diffuse roles are more common in traditional than in modern society. The flexibility in the definition of roles gives the individual freedom to manoeuvre in his attempts to achieve his own goals.

We may thus look at the structure of society from two viewpoints. On the one hand, we observe the relationships among members of given associations, the striving for compatibility in these relationships, and the adjustment in the relationships as individuals are obliged to alter their expectations of the roles of other members. On the other hand, we observe the individual, member of numerous associations and trying both to attain the goals he sets for himself and to satisfy the expectations appropriate to his various roles. A study of the manner in which an individual resolves the incompatibilities among his roles is perhaps the task of the psychologist; but inasmuch as many men are in the same predicament, and as their solutions to their problems result in a redefinition of one or more roles, the study is relevant to the sociologist.

Functional and conflict models

This bare outline of the concept of social structure has ignored the rivalry among various current theories on the nature of society. Here two contrasting viewpoints are provided by the 'functional' or 'integrational' schools and the 'conflict' school, with each presenting a model of society, valid in that it is logically consistent. The usefulness of each depends on the questions that one poses. If one asks 'what keeps this society going?', the functional model is apt to provide the answers. If one asks 'how do societies change?', the conflict model may be more appropriate. But the choice of models by a man analysing his own society, is likely to reflect his perception of his own position in society. Those men in privileged positions thus see their roles as functional within an integrated society; the underprivileged stress their conflict with the privileged. (This distinction is often most clearly shown in divergent views of class structure held by members of the different classes; the upper classes stress integration; the lower, conflict.) Much of modern conflict theory derives ultimately from Karl Marx. Functional theories have dominated Western sociology in recent decades, due variously to the reaction against the excesses of evolutionary and diffusionist theories, to the repugnance felt for Marxism, and to the stress placed by anthropologists on the functional integration of the small, simply-structured communities which they have studied.

The functional or integrational model of society emphasizes the consensus of values held by members of the society. The roles of the individual are formulated in accord with these values, and role expectations therefore tend to be complementary. The norms of the society are accepted and upheld by all its members. Through procedures of socialization, the young are taught these norms and values while new members of any association are indoctrinated. The man who behaves in a manner contrary to that expected of him is usually termed a deviant (rather than an innovator – the former term is pejorative), and the other members of society will attempt to coerce him by varied sanctions into maintaining the society's norms. The *status quo ante* is thus restored, and one speaks of the society as being in a state of equilibrium – meaning either that the pattern of relationships is static, unchanging, or that any change is followed by a return to the former position.

Such a model contains no provision for changes within the structure; but proponents of functional theory cannot deny the reality of change. It tends to be accounted for in three ways. First, the deviation of the individual may not be countered or contained by the sanctions of others; his innovations, if they amount to this, may be accepted and result in a restructuring of roles. Secondly, while the functional model may seem apt for single institutions or simply-structured small communities, the complexities of modern societies are such that it is most unlikely that the values and norms of each institution or group will be in accord. Hence, individuals will experience incompatible role expectations and in resolving these will alter their roles. But the main source of change lies outside the institution or society; and change is thus seen, thirdly, as the outcome of adapting relationships to meet external forces. Thus, in describing earlier the changing role of traditional rulers, we might have postulated perfect compatibility in the role expectations of the ruler, his chiefs, and his people. The administrative officer then enters the scene, demanding that the ruler takes his orders from him rather than from the chiefs (and threatening the deposition of a 'bad ruler'). The ruler becomes more of an autocrat, or he may try to appeal directly to his people for support, bypassing his chiefs. A new pattern of relationships is established, though the actors remain the same.

The basic premise of the conflict model is the incompatibility of individual interests, stemming from the unequal distribution of wealth, power or security in society. In striving for the common ends men may or may not agree over the means to be pursued. Rival candidates for a titled office will probably pursue their contest in an identical manner; but disgruntled workers may assert their claims through strike action, whereas the employer demands arbitration. In the conflict model, the stress is upon power – the ability of each party to realize its aim in the face of opposition from others. This element is largely absent from the functional model. In the conflict model, it is postulated that each party to a conflict will formulate its own system of values, appropriate to its interests, and that it will endeavour to win acceptance for these among the members of the opposing party. Thus, Fulani domination in the Hausa states of Northern Nigeria is not, as yet, resented by the commoners, for justification has been successfully incorporated into the Islamic faith. In the conflict model, society is seen in a state of perpetual bargaining, as each individual and group seeks to maximize success.

These two models, almost diametrically opposed in their premises, are, it must again be emphasized, means to the interpretation of society. The use of either tends to determine both the choice of data in describing society, and the type of social change which is discussed. Nor should the convergence of the two models be overlooked. The functional model can account for social change to a substantial degree. In the conflict model, it is not impossible that rival contestants may completely reconcile their interests. More probably, they may reach a point at which they feel that continued pursuit of their goals will not yield a greater success to themselves, and so terminate the contest, accepting as inevitable the inequalities between the parties; a latent source of conflict thus remains.

It may seem paradoxical to argue that conflict contributes to the cohesion of society, that it has its 'functional' aspects. But a contest between individuals may stress the underlying norms of a society; in competing for a chieftaincy title, the rivals assert their own qualifications for its agreed roles and so confirm these roles in the minds of the people. Again, a contest between two groups tends to reinforce the cohesion within each. Africa's present political leaders may strengthen the unity of their own people by exciting hostility to other nations, describing them as 'neo-colonialists'.

The functional model explains change as the result of forces external to the system; in the conflict model, change is inherent in the continual bargaining between those with incompatible interests and goals. So much of the change that we see taking place in West Africa today seems to result from the impact of the West on tribal societies, that we are apt to view it exclusively from the viewpoint of the functional model. But in so doing, we tend to ignore the conflicts which are inherent in traditional society and which are given new forms of expression in modern life.

Thus, on the one hand, we describe the new techniques introduced from the West which oblige men to create new relationships. Manufacturing industry cannot be carried on in communities organized on the basis of descent groups; towns imply the geographical mobility of people. New actors are introduced into traditional institutions – such as the colonial administrative officer into the government of a local community – necessitating the reformulation of relationships. On the other hand, we see that the new roles available, the new forms of wealth and power now existing in West Africa, may be manipulated by the African to achieve goals initially conceived in terms of traditional values. We are apt to view the introduction of every Western technique or moral value as creating change in the indigenous patterns of relationship; we must examine, too, the degree to which these Western imports can be assimilated into the indigenous social patterns without seriously affecting them. Thus, in the chapter on changes in the rural area we stressed the ability of a community to incorporate development into its structure rather than the disruptive consequences of the new techniques and institutions.

Incompatibilities

Both the conflict and the functional theories of society portray social change, the change in social relationships, as resulting from a resolution of incompatible roles or interests. Let us explore this process a little farther.

The individual may find himself in a situation where other persons make demands of him that are incompatible. The African civil servant is expected by his superiors to be completely impartial and impersonal in his dealings with the public, while his kin expect him to find jobs or perform favours for them; the values of bureaucracy are not compatible with those of the descent group. Again, the expectation of others may be incompatible with the individual's own goals; his aspirations to reach a high office in the modern sector clash with the desire of his kin that he should return to his village to assume a chieftaincy title for which his status in the community renders him the most suitable candidate. Such incompatibilities produce in the individual feelings of guilt and anxiety as he attempts to formulate his own course of action. This course will, ultimately, derive from his appreciation of his own goals and values, and of the sanctions with which others will attempt to determine his conduct. The outcome may be of three types.

First, the individual may succeed in establishing a role for himself which differs from that initially expected of him but which, as a result of bargaining or negotiation, is accepted by others. In other words, a new pattern of complementary relationships is established. Secondly, there are various methods of evading the problem of incompatibility. Roles may be compartmentalized; a man's behaviour among his elite colleagues may differ radically from that expected in his village; but inasmuch as his close kin do not observe him in the elite surroundings, nor his colleagues during his village visits, he may act in each situation in an expected manner without fear of sanctions save from his own conscience. Again, difficult roles may be delegated; a Christian chief may ask others to carry out the installation rituals repugnant to him, thus satisfying both the local Christian community and those non-Christians who feel that the due performance of the rituals directly affects, for instance, the prosperity of the community. Roles which seem too difficult may be eliminated, the relationships severed, perhaps with the justification that one is too busy to fulfil all one's expected commitments. Such action is considerably easier in a complex modern society, where roles tend to be highly specific, than in tribal society where they are multiple or diffuse – where the man with whom one has quarrelled may be, in his several roles, one's chief, the controller of the land on which one farms, and a close kinsman.

Finally when the individual cannot resolve these incompatible expectations or side-track them, his anxieties and frustrations tend to become aggravated and to manifest themselves in aberrant behaviour – in aggression or in fantasy.

Problems of role incompatibility are not peculiar to societies undergoing rapid change. The incidence of witchcraft beliefs in tribal societies indicates the degree of tension that may exist within the descent group. But the sudden introduction of new relationships does, surely, increase the possibilities of incompatibility, though tension may be reduced if the new roles are poorly defined. The creation of new goals may lead to an increase in frustration, when men do not fully understand the means of attaining them and set for themselves unrealistic aspirations. Whilst societies which have undergone little change over long periods usually develop means whereby these tensions are managed, so that they do not disrupt the society or incapacitate individual members, in situations of rapid change the traditional means may no longer be effective; explanations in terms of witchcraft or of tribal religious beliefs may no longer be acceptable. It usually takes time for new methods to become institutionalized.

A consideration of the bargaining processes between two individuals or groups who find their respective goals incompatible is at the present time often studied by sociologists within the framework of the theory of games – a set of statistical procedures developed from games of skill (bridge, for instance) by which the future moves of the players and the outcome of the game may be predicted. Most conflicts between individuals or groups would seem to fall within the category of 'non-zero-sum' games – that is, games in which the result is not a simple win or lose for the respective players, but one in which degrees of success or failure have infinite variety and do not necessarily balance each other out. Thus, each player is continually manoeuvring so that his chances of success are greatest, and the threat of loss occasioned by the other's moves least. Although the games theory provides a useful tool in understanding sociological situations of conflict, its ability to predict outcomes is vitiated by the complexity of these situations, by the number of independent variables involved.

The methods of resolving incompatible interests and goals may range from unrestricted fighting at one extreme to the most amicable discussion at the other, with the contestants sitting around a table and each anxious to understand the other's point of view. In most societies a number of processes, usually intermediate between these two extremes, are evolved. (Some sociologists would, in fact, see society as a 'system for managing tensions'.) These processes may determine the behaviour expected of rival individuals and, perhaps, the role of arbitrators. Many of these processes, appropriate to traditional African society, however, cannot function in modern and urban conditions. Thus, when husband and wife quarrelled in the village the near kin of each attempted to resolve the dispute by appealing to both parties to observe the local norms. In the cities today, the kin are too distant to perform these functions, and moreover the norms of marital relationships are less clearly defined in the new situations. One attempt to provide a new process may be seen in the use made by elite women of meetings of charitable organizations. An aggrieved wife will discuss her problems there with other wives, hoping that they will subsequently urge their husbands to put pressure on her own to meet her demands; the support of her descent group which she has lost is replaced by that of the club members.

In what manner may the resolution of incompatible interests produce changes in the social structure? The range of results in the 'non-zero-sum' game is infinite. In terms of sociological situations, a range lies between the outright rejection of the goals of the weaker contestant, in favour of those of the stronger, and the compromise between the two, resulting in a redefinition of the relationships between them. If we think in terms of groups rather than of individuals, other outcomes become apparent. The dominant group may accede to some of the claims of the weaker without altering its own composition. For instance, a council of elderly and traditionalist chiefs may accept the demands of the younger literates that a school be built in the village. Alternatively, the demands of the weaker group may be met by changing the composition of the dominant one; a few young literates are given seats on the village council so that, being party to its decisions, they can no longer overtly oppose them. Ultimately, the young men may feel that action taken through their descent group is ineffective, that they should form a new association devoted to the development of the village, and that the traditional council of chiefs should be replaced by a governing body better fitted to introduce improvements – a local government council, perhaps, on which their members are strongly represented. The outcome of any particular conflict of interests is determined by a number of factors and can be predicted only to the extent to which these are known and capable of valuation.

In the following chapters it is proposed to select a few spheres in which we may study the process of adapting traditional associations, their norms and values, and the establishment of new associations owing more, perhaps, than seems at first sight obvious, to the indigenous social structure of West Africa.

7 The family

Changes in family structure are closely correlated with the processes of modernization and industrialization. Sociologists, indeed, often argue that the nuclear family is a necessary concomitant of industrial society. Only when the nuclear family is isolated from the wide groupings of kin and descent, it is held, can there be the geographical mobility that is essential if men are to move from one job to another, seeking to use their talents to the utmost. Only in the nuclear family can a man pursue his occupational goals free from claims by his kin. The values which prevail in the nuclear family usually differ from those of the descent group. Instead of the hierarchical ranking of the latter and the correlation of authority with age, there exist in the nuclear family relationships which are more diffuse and affectionate; greater stress is usually placed on individual initiative and achievement than on the sense of affiliation and the importance of getting on well with one's fellows that infuses the descent group. Those who were born into traditional families but are now among the Western-educated elite may display these varied traits in their own personalities; more important, perhaps, is the impact which their new values and their present social status will have on the personality of their children. One correlates individualism and individual achievement with innovation and progress in rapidly changing societies. Yet bureaucracies are apt to stress affiliation as a necessary quality in their members; one is expected to work as a team. American sociologists (and the vast majority of the profession are from the U.S.A.) tend to see the middle class family of their own country as the indispensable element of industrial society. Yet the example of Japan shows that a country may become highly industrialized and yet retain strong extended family groupings. It is difficult to assess the type of family structure that West Africa *needs* at the present time.

Yet, even if we cannot always evaluate the effect of changes in family structure, we cannot ignore that they are taking place. As men and women move into the modern towns, their relationships with their descent groups are inevitably weakened to some degree – in what manner and to what degree, we shall discuss later in this chapter. An important factor in West Africa is that the migration to the towns has so far been on a relatively small scale; the majority of the people remain behind, in their traditional compounds, and the descent groups survive as viable units. Were they not such, they would lose, at an even faster rate, the allegiance of the absent members. The reality of the changing social structure is reflected in the persistent arguments – 'is the extended family a handicap to development?'

In the West African states the patterns of change in family structure must be extremely varied. Marked differences occur within the traditional patterns of relationships, and the effect for instance of migration to town will not be the same in each case. Thus the Ibo woman who has always worked with her husband on his farm, forming a joint economic enterprise, will experience a change when, in the town, she pursues an occupation separate from that of her husband; the Yoruba woman who has always worked independently of her husband will not find town life in this respect any different. Again, town life will affect, in markedly different ways, the family relationships of those with contrasting social status – the member of the elite, the junior clerk or artisan, the unskilled labourer.

Nevertheless, all who move into the modern sector of West African life must, in some degree, modify their family structure; and in this situation of change, tensions are inevitable. Many men and women are uncertain of the type of marital relationships they want; they find difficulty in adapting their traditional values to those which they have recently acquired, through their Western education, through the cinema and magazines, through their observation (and, frequently, misinterpretation) of patterns of behaviour in European homes. Once formulated, the expectations of the educated men and women differ from those of their parents.

Again, although husband and wife may have received an equal measure of Western education and broadly profess the same values, their expectation of their respective marriage roles may well differ, producing strains which can lead to divorce. Modern situations may exacerbate conflicts common in traditional society – such as the rivalry between half brothers, or the desire of the Yoruba wife to become economically more independent of her husband, which runs counter to his need for her services.

Marital roles

The individual selection of a spouse was certainly not absent in traditional societies, though most of the marriage procedures may have been conducted by the parents and brothers of the young couple, and betrothals in infancy were common within many ethnic groups. Today one often hears of the unskilled urban worker who, having saved enough to make a partial payment towards the bridewealth, sends home to his parents and asks them to find in the village a suitable wife whom he might marry on his return from the town. But most educated West African men met their wives at school and college – some of the women were, perhaps, sisters of their classmates – and their parents were asked to ratify their mutual choice.

In traditional societies stress was placed, in the choice of a wife, not only on the health and character of the woman but also on that of all the members of her descent group. The ties created by the marriage tended to bind descent groups which in other contexts rivalled each other within the small village community. In a somewhat similar manner today, marriage between individuals who both belong to families with a number of well-educated persons tends to reinforce the cohesion of the new elite. The young educated men now expect to court their wives and to develop, before marriage, strong emotional attachments. Many of their attitudes have here been influenced by the cinema and popular overseas magazines. They also expect their wives to be educated. To some degree the man seeks companionship from his wife when, in the urban situation, he is separated from most of his kin. In a more practical vein, he seeks a wife who will furnish a home and be able to entertain guests in a manner appropriate to his status.

One sometimes meets the man who married in his early twenties, when he was perhaps a primary school teacher, a girl with just a primary education. Later, by dint of study and hard work, he goes abroad to a university, leaving behind his wife and children. On his return, he becomes one of the elite – but his wife is still accustomed to cook on an open fire, speaks English haltingly, and is shy with the well-educated friends of her husband. He is torn between his loyalty to his wife and his embarrassment at her inability to cope with his new mode of life. Such men, together with politicans whose rise in status is often even more meteoric, may often send their wives to domestic science courses to complete their education.

Of a sample of Yoruba university graduates living in Ibadan, over two-thirds had wives with at least a complete secondary school education or its professional equivalent, while only one-tenth had wives with no more than a primary school education. The tendency is for men to choose a wife with a slightly lower qualification; only twenty per cent of the Yoruba graduates had wives of the same status.[116] This is largely inevitable, for in all the West African states the education of women has fallen far behind that of men. To some extent this lack of educated women has been rectified by the ease with which women can gain in nursing both professional training and the prestigious experience of study abroad. Whereas a parent can expect to spend £500 a year for three years to send a son to a British university, he has to find only the boat fare and an outfit allowance for his daughter – her hospital provides her with board, lodging and pocket money throughout her training. But in any event, most men prefer wives of slightly lesser education. In the modern sector of the economy, men and women can occupy similar posts, in teaching or administrative work, and the scarcity of educated women may result in a promotion rate more rapid than that of their husbands; this situation would be uncomfortable for men in most societies, but is certainly so in those where male dominance is still expected – at least by the men. One notices in the West African university – Ibadan is a typical example – that the women undergraduates are not often courted by the men students, but usually by much older civil servants and the like. The men undergraduates criticize the women for their airs and graces; a factor in this attitude may well be that the women tend to come from homes with at least a well-educated father and probably an educated mother too, whereas the majority of the men are from humble homes.

The degree to which traditional attitudes have been adopted, Western values assimilated, differs between the sexes, and the difference is probably developed early in school careers. A study in Ghana revealed that boys at secondary school, on being shown drawings of women in traditional and Western dress, tended to select the former as illustrating desirable wives; secondary school girls, however, identified their future selves as the women in Western dress. Furthermore, the education and professional training of the women result in their desire to pursue their careers throughout their marriage, a factor of considerable importance in understanding their marital relationships.[99]

When the number of well-educated women is small, the search for a suitable wife often results in a man selecting a woman from an ethnic group other than his own. This is apt to upset the parents, who would prefer the marriage to create a meaningful alliance with a neighbouring family. It tends, too, to deter the young couple from interacting so intensely with their respective kin and from participating in the affairs of their home community. However, as the number of educated women rises, so may one find an increasing tendency to select a wife from one's own locality. Thus, over one half of the sample of Yoruba graduates at Ibadan, cited above, had wives from their own ethnic sub-groups of the Yoruba (though not necessarily from their own town or village), and this proportion tended to be higher for the ethnic sub-groups in which the education of girls had been more widespread. The frequency with which the gay Don Juans eventually settled down with girls from their own home areas suggests either the continuance of marked ethnic divisions or strong parental pressures.

A survey of literate men in the Dahomeyean capital of Porto Novo showed that only one per cent had married without the explicit consent of the respective families, and three-quarters had made at least part payment towards the traditional bridewealth.[74, 98] Today the educated parents of an educated daughter are less apt to demand bridewealth; they expect, perhaps, a recompense of the sums they have spent on their daughter in financial assistance she in turn will give towards educating her junior relatives. Though the young couple may have little interest in traditional betrothal ceremonies – involving their parents and elderly relatives with themselves as rather minor participants – they usually acquiesce in them. Thus, whilst they prefer a church wedding with a formal reception to which they can invite their educated friends, they place no barrier to the giving by their families of the traditional feast in the compound. Most well-educated men and women marry not by customary law but under ordinances, enacted by the colonial governments and retained by the independent states, enjoining monogamy and perhaps intestate inheritance according to the law of the erstwhile metropolitan country; divorce is possible through High Court actions, but is a procedure far more costly and complex than that allowed by most customary laws.

Most educated women are today in employment outside their homes. For some, such as the Yoruba, this is a traditional pattern. In many of the early elite families, dominated by evangelical missionary values, however, the wife's place was seen to be in her home and in economic dependence upon her husband. Today the demand for improved social services is such that every woman feels that she should use her talents and training. Some skills are so rare, indeed, that one finds them practised where a Western observer would least expect them; the chief justice's wife makes wedding and birthday cakes for the elite, the minister's wife has a thriving dressmaking business with a similar clientele. Husbands are anxious that their wives should augment the household income, though where there is a tendency towards marital instability they may be jealous of the opportunities that their wives enjoy to meet other men; where shared interests are few, they suspect the competition of wealthier and more successful men. Women, like their menfolk, feel an obligation to repay the money spent on their own education by training younger relatives.

The disposal of the wife's income sometimes raises problems.

Men would often prefer that their wives hand over the whole of it to them, though they are happy then to let their spouses have some money with which to indulge safe fancies. Suspicious of the man's inclination towards polygyny and uncertain that upon his death she will be his foremost heir (unusual in customary law), the wife is unwilling to give all to the husband. A joint bank account is a novel idea, little accepted as yet – since it implies a check by the wife on her husband's private spending. In many families one finds an arrangement whereby the husband is responsible for items such as house rent, school fees, and food, while the wife is responsible for clothing herself and her children, and for house furnishings such as curtains. In the Porto Novo study cited, the wives in over a third of the elite families clothed themselves and their children – the same proportion as kept their earnings.

Within the home, the educated husbands maintain the traditional attitude of repulsion to manual work; but most of this is carried out not by their wives but by servants – essential when the wife is out at work all day, and easily afforded with the high salaries received by the educated and the relatively low wages of domestic servants (often lower than those of unskilled manual workers, but including free lodging and other perquisites). Educated men do, however, participate more actively in child-rearing, stressing perhaps the importance they attach to these aspects of parenthood. The traditional custom by which men and women eat separately gives way to family meals, though the employment of husband and wife, together with the children's schooling, may make it difficult to find times when all can eat together. In the more secular modern elite families, morning family prayers, often regarded as essential by their own literate parents, have tended to lapse.

Some traditional attitudes towards sex die hard. Although the educated person claims disbelief in such traditional superstitions as that intercourse spoils a mother's milk, and although the use of contraceptives is increasing, many still practise a two-year period of abstinence after the birth of a child. Many educated Yoruba men and women feel, too, that it is desirable (if not often possible) for husband and wife to have separate bedrooms.

Education is so often seen merely as a means to a career, that cultural interests, in which husband and wife might share, are often minimal; West African towns provide few opportunities for the lover of music or theatre. Men take their wives to the formal balls, but not to dances at the night-clubs. Thus, although the servants can take care of the children in the evenings, husband and wife go out together infrequently. The study of Ibadan elite showed that each spouse had a separate circle of friends, most of them gained through school or university, with few acquired through the spouse. At parties one tends to find the women sitting together at one end of the room, and the men gathered at the other, with the topics of conversation rarely interchangeable.

The general pattern that emerges – for the Yoruba elite, and probably that of other ethnic groups – is one in which domestic roles are segregated to a considerable degree; separate spheres of activity and responsibility are clearly defined for husband and wife respectively and there is little overlapping or sharing of roles. Such a pattern is not typical of middle class professional families in Western societies, families where the husband has a similar occupational status to that of the members of an African elite. The pattern has more in common with descriptions of working class family relationships of a few decades ago – with one important difference; the wife in Africa earns an income and is not completely dependent financially upon her husband. (Perhaps an even better parallel exists with Western upper class or aristocratic families, but these have not been studied by sociologists.)

The pattern of segregated roles derives in part from the traditional relationships in African societies, the values of which have not been modified by the contemporary occupational roles and the separate close-knit networks of friends that the elite spouses acquire. But its continued persistence is also due to the close ties which men retain with their own parents and near kin. Many educated husbands still say that their mothers are more important in their lives than their wives; one can always get another wife, never another mother. Men will first discuss matters such as building a new house or changing jobs with parents or brothers. Tension between the husband's mother and his wife, if the former lives with her son, seems to be even more acute in Africa than in the England of the music-hall jokes.

Two responses by the wives in such situations seem to occur frequently. One is to seek a more egalitarian form of marital relationship; the other, to claim rights of emancipation, with this last tending to emphasize segregation of roles rather than an egalitarian sharing of them. Educated Yoruba women, for instance, seem ignorant of the legal disabilities suffered by English women in the nineteenth and earlier centuries and against which they rebelled in the first decades of the twentieth century. The traditional rights of Yoruba women – to enter into contracts, and to easy divorce, for instance – exceed those granted in most Western societies until very recently. Their own rebellion is against the overt subservience demanded of women, a factor which in traditional society perhaps balanced their economic independence. But in demanding equality of rank with their husbands in the house, they do not necessarily seek a greater sharing of roles, a higher degree of mutual respect, or a greater element of romantic love – indeed, this last feature is often described as alien to African values and an undesirable import from Western societies.

Notwithstanding these claims, the African elite wife is, in general, placed in a position of demanding a more egalitarian marital relationship than her husband wishes to offer. Unlike most wives in traditional societies, she bears her husband's rather than her father's surname; she is Mrs X. In gatherings of women she is ranked more by her husband's status in society than by any status due to her own education or ability. And since the husband is usually better educated, his wife has been raised in status. Her husband is able to provide her with a better standard of living than she could gain for herself – and almost certainly better than her parents could offer her should she decide to leave her husband. Furthermore, her separation from her own kin tends to be greater than that experienced by her husband. Such factors lead women to claim the desirability of monogamous marriage far more often than do their menfolk; they seek a more equal division in inheritance, not a smaller share than is allocated to men.

The husbands on the other hand, maintain ties with their own kin which are frequently incompatible with loyalty to their wives.

They remain anxious to have male children, and these hopes are reinforced by their parents, who still value descent group continuity. When their wives produce daughters only, or are sterile, they tend to make 'outside marriages'. And these, of course, threaten the status of the wife, who sees her husband's income dissipated on other women, and on children not her own. In part, her desire to pursue her own career is an effort to insure against her husband's infidelity. But, at the same time, it may strain the marital relationship still further.

In emphasizing the tensions that may arise between husband and wife in situations of rapid social change, one suggests, perhaps, that a greater degree of marital unhappiness exists in modern Africa than elsewhere. There is, in fact, no evidence of such a gloomy situation. Divorce statistics are not available for a comparison of rates in the traditional societies with those among the educated town dwellers from these societies. In many cases, indeed, the latter rates may be lower, not only because the cost and complexity of divorce procedures are much greater in the High Courts than in the lower courts dealing with marriages under customary law, but because of the great stigma attached to divorce by missionary influence. Marital happiness derives from the compatibility of the expectations which both spouses hold of their own and each other's roles. There are many women less well educated than their husbands who gladly submit to his patriarchal authority; other spouses mutually enjoy a much more egalitarian relationship.

Whilst trying to present a generalized picture of marital relationships among the West African elite, we have seen, too, that a wide variety of patterns can and does exist. It is tempting to see all these along a continuum from most traditional to most egalitarian, and to postulate that the position on the scale of any couple would be determined by their degree of education, itself perhaps denoting a degree of acceptance of Western values. However, evidence does not support such a hypothesis; the education of the parents of each spouse seems to be an important variable. Should one then divide one's subjects into the first and the second generations of educated people? But this ignores the differences which occur over the decades in the character of the first generation elite. Those of thirty years ago – the parents of today's second-generation educated men and women – tended to be a small minority group of Christian converts, hostile to traditional values and highly receptive to mission teaching. Those who are today the first educated persons in their families are the product of a more secular education, and are more receptive to nationalist ideologies with their stress on the values of traditional society. Thus, not only are there differences between the values held by these two sets of educated people, but one would expect in consequence that their child rearing practices would vary accordingly.

The elite of today contains a substantial proportion of members who were born to illiterate parents; many who were born to educated parents – the national or local Western-educated elite of a generation ago; and a few from families with a longer experience of education. A study of educated Yoruba in Ibadan suggests that a more egalitarian marital relationship exists among children of educated parents. These have tended to intermarry among themselves, suggesting not only that their parents favoured such alliances but that the young people themselves recognized a similarity of interests. Such couples tend also to have smaller discrepancies in their respective levels of education and ages. Neither age alone nor the exact standard of education reached by the elite couple seem to be important factors; a strongly traditional marital relationship may well exist between persons each of whom has a doctorate degree and a considerable period of residence in England, whilst some egalitarian couples are without university or overseas experience. The egalitarian relationship itself tends to be manifest in a greater degree of joint financial control over the household budget, in a larger number of shared friendships, and in a home furnished more in accordance with contemporary design – prints of Van Gogh replacing the portrait of the husband in academic robes.

Parents and children

Few contrasts could be greater than that between childhood in a traditional West African compound and in an elite home. In the latter, the child is reared within the nuclear family and with the aid of a few domestic servants; in the former, the child is surrounded both by a number of adult relatives, most of whom take a hand in disciplining him, and by scores of children as playmates. The elite family, however, is not always a very small group. In Ibadan most educated Yoruba women seem to have five or six children in a completed family. Their training has often postponed their marriage until their mid-twenties, but children arrive at fairly regular two- or three-year intervals thereafter. Economic factors are not a strong deterrent to a large family. In the tropics, the cost of clothing is low and education is heavily subsidized by the state. Although many elite women feel that four children are sufficient, the desire of their husbands for more sons leads to additional births. Elite fathers have, by the standards of their traditional polygynous societies, relatively few children; elite mothers, on the other hand, tend to have more children (or, to be precise, more surviving children) than do the women of traditional societies.[97]

Educated fathers seem anxious to reverse the authoritarian role so common not only in traditional societies but also in many early elite families with their Victorian moral codes. They realize that their children's future depends not on 'fate' or the 'will of God' but on the encouragement that they are given to develop their initiative, to express their own interests and personalities. Thus mothers actively train their children to walk and talk, instead of waiting for the child to develop such techniques in his own time. The father helps in looking after his children when he does no other form of domestic work. Although the educated father spends the whole working day in his office, he probably spends at least as much time with his children as does the traditional father. Sometimes the highly permissive attitudes of the father are not balanced by a more authoritarian role performed by the mother; she continues to 'spoil' her own children in the traditional manner. In most elite homes, indeed, less stress is placed on the obedience of children; they are not expected to drop everything at the call of their parents, and are required to do few domestic tasks (these often being done by servants). Solitary amusement is approved, whereas in many traditional societies the boy who sits alone, not playing with his mates, is apt to be accused of communing with the spirits.

The hopes which elite parents have for their children's success are often no higher than those of traditional parents. Differences arise in the manner by which the respective parents pursue their aims. Traditional parents are apt to cite specific occupations – especially those like medicine or law which carry much prestige among the masses. They have, on the other hand, little accurate understanding of how these occupations may be attained; they pray to God for their son's success, and thank God when he passes his examinations. The educated parent not only realizes the determining effect of educational qualifications, but knows how to manipulate the educational system. A tutor is hired to cram his children, so that they may gain entrance to the better secondary school; and influence with their headmasters (perhaps former classmates) enables a poor performance in an entrance examination to be overlooked. The home environment of the elite child, with educated parents, with books and toys, gives him a marked advantage over the child from a humble home. (Though, with both parents at work, the elite child, while very young, spends much of the day in the care of ill-educated nurse girls.) Elite parents are more likely to praise or reward their children's success as an encouragement to further effort. The elite child is spurred on to realize his own potential ability; the child of the traditional home strives to fulfil the expectations of his parents – though this element is not absent in elite families where children are expected to attain at least the same status as their parents.

Elite children can scarcely fail to notice their privileged position in society. Though they may attend primary schools where the majority of pupils are from humble homes, they arrive in their fathers' cars, while others trek for two or three miles. Often their parents were themselves born in humble homes and deny 'class' differences in their society; yet they tend to be highly selective in choosing playmates for their children, often rejecting those from poorer homes as being rude or dirty. Elite parents tend to be more tolerant of aggressive behaviour in their children's play; in the traditional compound, fighting between children can lead to quarrels between co-wives, adding to their existing jealousy and perhaps raising heightened fears of witchcraft, so that cooperation between children is more highly stressed.

Kin and community

The well-educated men and women of the elite, the skilled and unskilled factory workers, the clerks and teachers usually live in the modern town, far from the compounds of their parents and brothers. Only in a few instances – Ibadan or Porto Novo, for example – has a traditional settlement become an administrative or commercial centre, with the result that some of its sons can work in the modern sector of the economy and still continue to live in the compounds of their birth. The occupational roles of the modern sector are usually quite unlike those of the traditional economy. Yet in spite of the differences in roles and the distances separating kinsmen, the urban-dwelling West African seems to maintain a very close relationship with the remaining members of his extended family in the rural area.

Many members of the elite, and in fact a majority of the urban adults, are relatively young. Their parents are frequently still alive. Strong emotional ties continue to bind parents and children, and men and women visit their homes as often as they can. The affluent, with their own cars, may make the journey several times a year; the unskilled labourer, perhaps once in two years. The short distance of urban migration is an important factor here; distances between town and rural home are measured in tens and hundreds of miles, but not in thousands.

In spite of the emotional ties, one would expect the great differences in style of life and in values between the urban elite and their often illiterate parents, still practising a near-subsistence agriculture, to make communication between them very difficult. For as we have already seen, it is not unusual for the brilliant young hospital surgeon or university lecturer to come from a humble home. Parents and children seem to belong to different worlds. That such difficulties appear to be largely obviated is due to the recognition of these differences by those involved. Humble parents have no ambition to abandon the traditional way of life to which they are accustomed. Yet they may realize that the future of their country lies in its modern sector, and that the most high ranking status will be in the new bureaucracies, in political office, and in the factories, not in the spheres of local trade and chieftaincy. Inasmuch as they hope for their children's success – and this would seem to be the case among most of the tribally organized West African peoples – they see this success as lying in the modern sector, to be achieved largely through education. This is clear in the degree to which the farming communities have saved and often pooled resources to pay for the secondary or university education of some of their members. The folk at home are often unable to appreciate the abilities necessary for academic success or the nature of the occupations which are its rewards. But they have learned to recognize the symbols of such success – the large car as a sign of wealth, the neat suit and tie apparently signalling acceptance into the world of the European. Many young men who return from abroad with a university degree would prefer to relax at home in traditional dress or at least in a casual shirt and slacks; their parents demand that they appear before the village in their English winter clothing. The prestige of the parents in their little community depends upon the recognized success of their children. In the traditional genealogies, the names of many ancestors of no great personal ability have been retained for future memory because they were fathers of important men. Thus, in areas where university degrees are still rare, the returning graduate receives a processional welcome, followed perhaps by a church service of thanksgiving for his success and safety.

In their turn, the young educated men and women are sometimes intolerant and impatient of traditional ways and values. A few are ashamed of them. It is among these that one finds the rare case of the man who returns from overseas with a complete Western outfit for his mother, so that she may be a 'civilized' woman and not an embarrassment to him. But such rejection of indigenous society, more common in earlier decades, has usually been succeeded by a repudiation of assimilationist tendencies. The African seeks the roots of his own culture; he endeavours to preserve in it the elements which seem distinctly African. His parents in many cases represent this traditional culture, and he thus respects their way of life. Indeed, many seek from their own elder kin a fuller appreciation of their heritage, the learning of which was denied to them at school and by their long absence from home.

Between the generations there may thus exist a mutual respect. The difficulties which arise tend to be in the practical sphere. The mother is frightened by her daughter-in-law's electric cooker – and is perhaps a little caustic when it seems unable to produce soup as tasty as she cooked on the open fire. For the elite family, a visit home is often quite an expedition as they pack their beds, tinned foods, boiled water and other accustomed comforts not available in the village. Children maintain their aged parents in the style of life to which the latter are accustomed; they do not try to convert them. They will, however, pay for the best medical attention they can afford when the old people fall sick. The main direction of financial assistance is towards the younger members of the family.

The first-generation members of the Western-educated elite have, among their brothers and sisters, men and women following a very wide range of occupations. Usually one son alone has been to secondary school or university; the financial resources of his parents, and perhaps of his entire community, may have been invested in him as he won admission to successive educational establishments. Thus a senior civil servant working in a West African capital may number among his brothers a primary school teacher, a carpenter and a farmer working on his father's land. Here, too, the emotional ties among the siblings remain strong even though they may see relatively little of each other.

Whether or not his family financed his own schooling, therefore, the educated West African almost invariably feels a strong obligation to raise the status of other members of his family, primarily by helping them to gain an education and secondarily by assisting them subsequently to find the best jobs appropriate to their qualifications. This feeling of obligation reciprocates the expectation of the family that their one successful member will bring not only prestige but material rewards to the whole group.

The first charge on a man's beneficence is the education of his own junior brothers and sisters. In societies where women bear issue throughout their reproductive period, the eldest and youngest children may be twenty years apart in age. Thus, when an elder son graduates from university and begins to earn a substantial income, some of his younger brothers are just beginning to attend secondary school; the elder brother can then pay their fees. The unlucky brothers are those so close in age to the educated one that their chances of schooling are lost before he can assist them. When it is the youngest son who alone is educated, his responsibilities are first towards the children of his elder brothers (some of whom may be nearly his age). Women, too, are expected to repay their own families for the education they received, though their assistance is more often limited to their own siblings, nieces and nephews, and does not extend to those more distant kin whom a man might feel obliged to support. This expectation reinforces their desire to earn an income separate from that of the husband, for he cannot be asked to assist members of another descent group.

Many southern Nigerians earning £2,000 a year are spending as much as a quarter of this sum on the education of their kin; junior clerks may spend a higher proportion. Undergraduates have been known to use their own scholarships to pay their brothers' secondary school fees before their own bills, thus risking (but usually evading) expulsion from their university. An Ibo doctor trained in Dublin apparently failed to support his kin on his return, so his family sued him in the High Court for the repayment of the 'loan'; the result of the case depended on the technicalities of legal language, but its significance lies in the general support which the aggrieved family felt it should receive. Once again it should be noted that investment in education brings not only prestige to the family but also considerable financial reward. The secondary school leaver will earn from £250 to perhaps £750 a year during his working life, with his average annual income some £500. The university graduate rises, by increments, from £750 a year to over £2,000, with his average perhaps £1,500 a year – or £1,000 a year more than the income of the secondary school leavers. Thus, in crude terms, an investment of £500 in an education (heavily subsidized by the government) at a West African university will yield a gross annual return averaging over 200 per cent during the three following decades. The popularity of education is hardly surprising.

Young Africans frequently assert that the advantage of living far from the family compound lies in freedom from the persistent and less reasonable demands of their kin. They do not claim that their general responsibility can be evaded. Distance enables them to plan their expenditure on their families, directing their resources to the most worthy causes. Were they at home, every case of hardship would have to be assisted, or the risk run of causing serious offence. The unskilled urban worker carefully spaces his visits home, for on each of them he is likely to spend between a quarter and a half of a year's income in gifts and charity.

The young secondary school leaver or university graduate, in receiving as a result of his education a much higher income, has no lack of goods on which to spend his money. But his own children will be small and attending free or relatively cheap primary schools for several years. It is in this period, therefore, that he may best be able to assist his kinsmen. Schemes of investment – in life or educational assurance policies, for instance – are not yet popular, probably because savings are so often directed to the family. The corollary is, of course, that a man relies in turn on his family should he be unable, through loss of job, sickness or early death, to complete the education of his own children.

As the members of the elite aspire to give university education to all or most of their children; as they send them to expensive fee-paying schools to ensure that they pass the relevant entrance examinations; as the expansion of higher education results in an ever decreasing proportion of scholarship places; so the expenditure of these men and women on their own children increases. It may become increasingly difficult both to educate one's own children to the desired level and to fulfil the expectations of one's family. Family elders may argue that one ought not to give all one's own children a university education when one's nephews are unable through poverty to take up the secondary school places offered to them. Yet one's wife will press hard for the education of her own children, her husband's nephews being of little matter to her. Inevitably the wealthier men will tend to put the interests of their own nuclear families before those of their more distant kin, and to this extent the cohesion of the traditional descent groups will be severely weakened. However, in the transitional period of the present, this conflict is only slowly becoming apparent. One of its possible symptoms is the emphasis with which some young West Africans assert that responsibility and loyalty towards one's kin is an ineradicable feature of African culture, and contrast this adversely with the individualism of the Western middle class family.

We have stressed the continuing strength of the relationships between the townsmen and their kin in the rural area. But how far do these ties affect the entire home community? In describing the financial assistance rendered to the family, it is clearly the closer kin who are most benefited. A man cannot educate all the youths of his own descent group. In helping his closer kin, therefore, the gap between this segment of the group and others is widened. In the past, too, a wealthy or politically powerful man would probably have benefited most those closely related to him; but his wealth would have been expressed in more than one wife and hence in numerous children, so that his segment of the descent group would ultimately dominate others in size as well as in affluence. The descendants of the modern elite member of the group will remain few in number.

Yet while the bonds created by his financial assistance tie a man only to his closer kinsmen, other factors draw him into the life of the community. The parents of the successful man will, to maintain their own prestige, attempt to draw their son into the affairs of the community, urging that his advice be sought or that his influence in the capital be exploited. Nor will the community be slow in seeking such support. In their effort to attract social services to their own villages (usually at the expense of their neighbours), they are likely to rely heavily on their best-educated members, whether at home or abroad. Again, the expectations of the community are usually matched by an acceptance of responsibility by the elite.

In an old-established town like Lagos, descendants of the mid-nineteenth century immigrants describe themselves today as Lagosians, adding only if pressed their Egba or Ijebu origins. It seems likely that the more modern towns will eventually develop their own 'native' populations, too. But most of their present residents who have come from the rural areas assert a desire to return to their homes on retirement. As an investment, and as a pledge of their good faith, they build a house at home during their working years. Thus among these peoples, such as the Ibo, for whom the pull of the home area is strong, one might abuse an affluent man for not building at home and for apparently denying his origins.

For the poorer urban worker, his village community provides the only source of security for retirement and old age. As a member of his descent group, he may assert his rights to farm as soon as he returns home, and he will take the place on the councils of his descent group and village ascribed to his age. The wealthier man may look to his home community for political office, in the traditional hierarchy, in local government, or as a representative in the national assembly.

Within the modern town the ties with the home area are maintained through the ethnic associations (examined in the next chapter). And at the meetings of these associations, those who have not visited their homes for several months are provided with all the latest gossip by those who have most recently returned. Each traveller also, of course, reports to his village on the doings of its members in the town, of the generosity of some members and the lack of interest shown by others in the problems of their countrymen. The migrant returns to his rural home not only feeling that he has never lost emotional contact with it, but also possessing a complex record of service to his community.

Individualism and the modern family

In this discussion of changing family relationships in West Africa, achievement has been stressed in two senses. First, the relationships between husband and wife and between parents and children in the educated home may promote in the personality of the children a much stronger drive to individual achievement – a desire to attain an internalized standard of excellence, irrespective perhaps of the opinions of others. We have also seen the pressure which the traditional family, among many West African peoples, exerts on its individual members to attain positions of wealth and prestige. In a society not undergoing rapid change, one would expect the values expressed by the family to accord approximately with the processes of child socialization. In changing societies, however, it is possible that elders may interpret the traditional values of achievement in a contemporary context, expecting success in modern occupations, whilst patterns of child rearing do not equip the young for the tasks involved.[97]

The continuance of strong ties with the extended family is frequently described as an impediment to the modernizing process and to economic development. In the West African context this assertion needs considerable qualification. The extended family, it is claimed, leads to a dispersal of savings which might otherwise be productively employed. Needless gifts are made to relatives. The unemployed live parasitically upon their wealthier kin; they scorn jobs which seem below their status. This is a valid criticism. But much of the assistance given by the affluent is to the genuinely poor and needy, for whom the state provides no support; indeed, the governments of West Africa could not possibly afford elaborate social security services. And, as we have seen, family savings are often aggregated and invested in education, thus benefiting the whole society. It is argued, furthermore, that the drain on his income disinclines the prosperous man to seek wealth (just as in industrial societies high rates of tax are said to deter men from effort and initiative). Yet the West African does not see the issue in this light. The expectations of his family can be a spur to further effort; the respect and allegiance of those supported provide rewards in themselves for the many who maintain such traditional values. Obligations to employ in a business the members of one's own family may impair its economic efficiency – but very few modern West African enterprises are organized on this scale. The clerk may seek an opening for his brother in the office; but the appointment, confirmation, and promotion of the brother depend on his ability.

The extended family is sometimes seen as enforcing conformity upon its members, as discouraging change. This is perhaps most marked in peasant societies, where sons follow the occupations of their fathers, and the stratification of society is seen as immutable. But we have already seen that in many West African tribal societies, men born to humble farmers could become wealthy and powerful men as traders or chiefs; their own children, moreover, could not inherit such status, but had to make their own way in life. Modern society has merely provided new roles in which the traditional striving for wealth and power may be expressed. The young educated West Africans, in pursuing their goals, may behave in such a manner as would, in the rural area, earn the censure of the elders; but living in the towns, they may escape much criticism, being judged at home by their success rather than by their means of attaining it.

8 Urban associations

When men and women leave the rural areas and emigrate to the modern towns they lose, to some extent, the benefits of their membership in the traditional association – the descent and age groups. In their absence, they do not forfeit their rights in these associations, for these may be resumed immediately on their return; but whilst they live in the town the rural associations cannot afford them the social security or the recreation enjoyed by those locally resident. Yet the townsmen do not live as discrete atoms; they have formed an enormous number of new associations, through which they express not only those new interests occasioned by urban life and employment in the modern sector, but also those interests served in the rural area by the indigenous associations. The sheer variety of urban associations is somewhat bewildering: the ethnic or tribal associations; those representing new economic interests – craft guilds, trade unions, chambers of commerce; recreational clubs; youth organizations – Boy Scouts, the Life Brigade; the charities – Red Cross, R.S.P.C.A., Y.M.C.A.; the old boys' associations of the many secondary schools and universities; masonic orders; political parties and associations; the churches and sects with their Bible reading societies and social activities.

In some measure, each of these associations may be said to assist its members in adapting to town life. The values espoused are, broadly, appropriate to urban conditions. Through his membership, the recent immigrant learns the new values and patterns of behaviour expected of him. By their sanctions, of reward or censure, the older members check any deviance by the newcomer. The methods of organization of many urban associations differ radically from those of the rural area; formal rules of debate may be followed, minutes taken and recorded, new roles of secretary or treasurer created. Through practising these methods in, perhaps, a small dancing club, the member becomes accustomed to the similar roles expected in the larger bureaucratic structures of government and commerce and in parliament. Not all urban associations, however, serve to promote the values appropriate to the modern economy; some reaffirm in the urban area the values of the rural homes from which the migrants have come. Whilst such associations provide security for their members, they may do little to stimulate adoption of specifically urban patterns of behaviour. The urban associations offer a variety of new statuses from which the migrant may select those he wishes to assume, choosing perhaps between throwing himself whole-heartedly into urban life or restricting his relationships as far as possible to members of his own ethnic group. The choice open to the immigrant is, however, often circumscribed by criteria of wealth and education. The subscriptions of many clubs may be beyond the means of the unskilled labourer; when the majority of club members are literate and their conversation is in English or French, the illiterate will hesitate to join them. Yet multi-membership of urban associations is common. The Western-educated member of the elite belongs to his ethnic association as well as to the old boys' association of his former school. The semi-skilled worker may be active in his trade union and his Bible class, as well as in his ethnic association. This multi-membership inhibits too rigid a stratification of society into groups, each with its own sets of values and patterns of urban life; it fosters a degree of consensus about the new urban norms.

The variety and number of urban associations make their classification difficult. One criterion is that of origin. Many associations have been introduced by the expatriates, and some of these still form part of international bodies, uniformly organized in each country. Thus, the West African churches and schools have their Scout and Guide troops; the major charities, the Rotary Clubs and the Freemasons' lodges are affiliated to their parent bodies. Trade unions have been largely established and encouraged by union officials from the metropolitan countries, their services requested and financed by the colonial governments. Many associations, and especially the charities, were first established by the wives of expatriate officials who drew into membership the growing numbers of educated African women, eventually handing over to them the management.

Other associations are indigenous in their creation, with no expatriate influence or example at all evident. Among these are the ethnic associations and many of the dance companies and mutual aid societies. Qualifications for membership tend to be framed in terms of the traditional criteria of descent and age; and offices are distributed more according to ascribed status – age or length of residence in town – than to wealth, education or ability. The values inherent in the association are those of the rural area. Indeed, many of these urban associations seem to be but modifications of traditional associations – the differences between them being necessitated by urban conditions. One might compare the associations of modern towns like Lagos, Enugu or Kaduna with those of the contemporary Yoruba town which is being modernized *in situ*. In the latter, the traditional age groups have disappeared, their functions in war and public work having become obsolete; and in their place are the *egbe*, serving recreational purposes yet exhibiting a strong degree of social control over their members (much more, according to most young people, than does a Boy Scout troop). The craft guilds have adapted to the modern economy the traditional organization of market guilds and age groups. With the increasing value of land, many descent groups have developed modern methods of organization, with written records of meetings and land transactions, with membership and subscription lists and a bank account. It is in such organizations, without question developed from the indigenous associations, that one may see the closest parallels with some of the urban ones.

Alternatively, and perhaps more usefully, we may examine the functions which these urban associations perform for their members. Foremost is social security; the members of an association are expected to find employment for each other, to maintain the unemployed and sick, and to arrange and pay for the funerals of the deceased and the repatriation of their descendants. Recreation, too, is an important function. In varying degrees the associations provide offices for which those who aspire to leadership may compete; while some of these offices may confer prestige only within the association, others are more universally respected, and their holders may use them as a means to reaching even higher posts. Lastly these associations socialize their members, as we have already stated, to the norms of urban life, exercising a degree of social control and so enforcing these norms. Not all of the urban associations fulfil each of these functions. Most sports clubs confine themselves to the recreational sphere; they do not serve as mutual aid associations, nor do they question the behaviour of individual members outside the club. Ethnic associations, on the other hand, fulfil to a high degree each of the functions listed, though the functions served for members of different social categories may vary considerably. Thus, the unskilled worker sees in his membership of an ethnic association his only source of social security; the wealthy member from the elite gains little material benefit, and is more likely to use his ethnic association as a means of enhancing his prestige in his home area and so furthering perhaps his political aspirations.

It would be impossible to discuss all the associations to be found today in the modern West African towns. We may, however, examine a few examples from three broad categories: the traditionalist associations – usually of indigenous origin and generally looking back towards the rural areas; the associations serving the interests of the urban workers – for example, the trade unions; and the elitist associations – their membership largely confined to the well-educated and wealthy, and serving, apart from their overt charitable or recreational aims, to create new patterns of behaviour among the elite, to assist in the definition of new statuses, and to provide new avenues of advancement for the ambitious.

Traditionalist associations

Let us first examine the ethnic associations, of the type established by many of the peoples of the Guinea coast and exemplified by those of the Ibo- and Edo-speaking peoples of Eastern and Mid-Western Nigeria.[102, 103, 104]

The emigrant from the rural area rarely travels to the modern town without the hope of meeting some members of his own village. In selecting a town, indeed, the location of earlier emigrants and their success have probably constituted determining factors. The traveller descends upon his closest kin and expects them to maintain him until he finds work; an obligation then rests with his host to introduce the newcomer to prospective employers, to teach him the methods of securing a job, and perhaps to lend him the money necessary to bribe minor officials. The immigrant's first contacts in the town thus tend to be with members of his own descent group.

At the earliest opportunity the newcomer is introduced to the appropriate ethnic association and enrolled. These associations are formed on the basis of single villages or, where the numbers of immigrants in the town from such a unit are too small, of village groups; in the latter case, it is likely that the members of such a village group will trace descent from a common ancestor. In the French-speaking states, the basic unit may be the canton – a unit which is defined not in terms of descent but of locality. All members of the village or villages concerned who live in the town are expected to join the association; and most of the poorer members do, because the benefits of membership are so much greater than they could obtain from other sources. It is easier for members of the elite to reject their expected obligations, but they will do so only if they have little intention of returning to live in the village and can thus ignore the ostracism of their countrymen. Meetings tend to be held regularly, perhaps on a defined Sunday in each month. Sometimes the members of each village meet separately on one Sunday, while the members of the entire village group gather for a larger meeting on the Sunday following. Attendance figures are usually good, traditional methods of fining late or absent members being frequently employed. The meetings are held either in the houses of the presidents or in those of the other members in rotation. The host for the day may be expected to provide food and drink for the company.

The leading offices in the ethnic associations tend to be held by those members who are the oldest or who have lived for the longest period in the particular town. The meetings are almost always conducted in the vernacular, thus enabling all members to participate fully whatever their degree of education, but minutes and records are probably kept in English or French, because the school leavers generally find it easier to write in these languages than in their vernaculars. The offices of secretary and treasurer are held by the better-educated, and usually younger men, while other wealthy or educated men are accorded deference – perhaps a more comfortable chair than that to which their age would entitle them – but not necessarily office.

The meetings generally open with prayers similar to those used by traditional associations in the rural area, and procedure, too, tends to follow an indigenous pattern. Many of the topics which come up for discussion on the other hand pertain to urban life and its problems. With the more formal business of the meeting completed, the members relax in singing the songs of their village and in dancing. And this recreation is of greatest importance to the unskilled urban workers. Such men establish in their everyday life a large number of relationships – with employers and co-workers, with traders in the market, with neighbours. But these tend to be highly superficial and rarely develop beyond the initial specific contact. Their personal friends are almost exclusively drawn from members of their own small ethnic group, and may in fact be selected from among those most closely related to them. They may belong to no other association in the town, their lack of education barring them from sports clubs or Bible-study groups.

The members of the ethnic associations actively seek employment for the newcomers to the town, or those otherwise unemployed. Most expatriates in West Africa will not forget the numerous occasions on which an employee has introduced his 'brother' with fulsome praises of his ability – often, through loyalty to the employer, qualified as soon as the 'brother' is out of earshot. The unemployed man is supported by his kin. One who becomes, through age, physical weakness or incompetence, chronically unemployable, however, is urged to return to the village, and should he fail to go, being ashamed to return home without wealth, the association may forcibly repatriate him.

Upon the death of a townsman, it is the members of his ethnic association who arrange the funeral. Indeed, its officers will often act as executors of the deceased's estate, listing his property and sending a statement to the elders of his descent group in the village so that his assets may be distributed in the customary manner and not taken by unentitled persons living in the town. The widow is cared for and, where appropriate, repatriated to the village. The relative absence of ethnic associations in East, Central and Southern Africa may be due, in part, to the fact that industrial workers in these areas often live in settlements belonging to companies, and it is the companies' personnel departments which arrange funerals and the repatriation of descendants. Although kin and countrymen participate in these events, formal organization on their part is not called for.

The activities of the ethnic associations are financed both by regular contributions and by levies for specific purposes. Such funds may also be used to grant loans to members starting in business. An association may even form itself into a business company, perhaps purchasing a lorry, or function as a savings club, with each member paying a fixed monthly contribution and, in rotation, receiving the total contributed in any one month.

One of the most important functions of the ethnic association is to settle quarrels that arise between members. Not only are the members anxious to keep their disputes away from the urban police and courts (which may employ alien concepts of law in resolving them) but the police are usually themselves reluctant to intervene in matters that do not constitute a serious breach of the peace. In the settlement of disputes the ethnic associations apply the customary law of their home areas. They are themselves anxious to preserve the reputations of their own ethnic groups and will take strong measures to prevent any member from damaging them by theft or drunkenness. The small number of police stationed in a Nigerian town reflects, in part, the success of the ethnic associations as agents of social control.

Little formal use of the ethnic association seems, however, to have been made by governments. In some cases, where administrative officers ruled small townships, their advisory boards contained representatives of the major ethnic groups. A rather recent innovation has been the practice of the Social Welfare Department in Eastern Nigeria of handing over juvenile delinquents, caught in theft or sleeping in the market places, to the elders of the appropriate ethnic associations. These men investigate each boy's circumstances and either arrange to care for him in the town or send him back to his relatives. Only if neither course seems practicable, do they return a boy to the Welfare Officers, to be cared for by the state services.

We have been discussing, so far, the benefits received by the members of an ethnic association, the obligations of members to each other. A further and most important aspect of the activities of these associations lies in their relationship with their home areas. This is illustrated by the names adopted by many of them – the — Improvement Union, the — Progressive Association.

Much of the time of each meeting of the association is spent in discussing the news and affairs of the home town. In some Ibo villages surveyed in 1961, three-quarters of the absentee migrants had been at home within the past twelve months. Some villages organize a season of Christmas festivities, annually or biennially, which every member is expected to attend. Many villages, again, have important markets which are visited regularly by lorries from the modern town, facilitating the flow both of goods and gossip. The town dwellers, being better educated than those at home, feel obliged not only to gain improved social services for their villages but also to intervene in traditional matters, such as the settlement of a chieftaincy contest in which the dispute may be held to impede the progress of the village. Their own activities consist of giving advice to their elders, raising money for schools or scholarships, and influencing, through their own educated members, the relevant Ministers and civil servants.

The foundation of individual ethnic associations in the West African towns dates probably from an early period – indeed, from as soon as there were sufficient immigrants from a given area to constitute a formal association. Later, the number of literate men living in their home villages increased, and these formed home branches of the ethnic associations. Membership here was, however, restricted in practice to the educated and wealthy. The activities of the home branch were directed solely towards local political issues and the provision of social services; they did not provide social security for their members, since this was supplied in the traditional manner through descent and age group membership. The new home branches also tended to act as catalysts in the amalgamation of associations in all the modern towns of the state. Further amalgamations among the ethnic associations of larger territorial areas produced even stronger political pressure groups, culminating for the Ibo peoples in the Ibo State Union. In this case, a fairly well defined hierarchy exists, stretching up to the State Union from the village ethnic associations; among other peoples, the larger groups are not so linked. The Yoruba Egbe Omo Oduduwa, for instance, was started by a number of educated Yoruba from all parts of the country; its cultural and para-political aims were not directed towards the progress of any specific area within Yoruba country, nor were the members of the Egbe regarded as representatives of their home areas. Whilst leadership in the village ethnic association brings a man little prestige outside his own community, activity in the larger groups has become a well-worn ladder to a political career. Not surprisingly, therefore, these associations have attracted the West African elite.

Ethnic associations of the type outlined in the previous paragraphs are far more strongly developed in West Africa than elsewhere on the continent. One reason has already been suggested – the provision elsewhere of social security by employers. (In South Africa, the fostering of ethnic associations by the government is seen by the educated African elite as just another expression of *apartheid*, with its objective of segregating not only white from non-white, but non-whites from each other.) Another possible explanation lies in the greater wealth of many West African rural areas; town dwellers become involved in the improvement of their home areas because they feel that progress is possible – money is available, and local government councils provide a necessary institutional framework. But these associations are not formed by all West African peoples – not even all those from affluent rural areas. Their development is most marked among the coastal peoples, and in particular those with a tribal social structure. A man's links with his home area tend to be strongest when he can assume on his return a status determined by his descent and age, and thus unaffected by his absence. The links will be least strong where status in the local community is determined largely by ties of patronage;

the man living at home is continually attempting to improve his status in the community through his relationships with others, and the man who has been absent for several years is at a marked disadvantage. Thus among the Hausa one does not find a Kano Union, Zaria Union, or the like; the basis of their own organization in the modern towns is markedly different. A further factor in the establishment of ethnic associations may be the inferiority which people traditionally having dispersed settlements and a small-scale political organization feel when mixing with other migrants from indigenous towns and substantial kingdoms; the former peoples perhaps feel a stronger need for solidarity as a group, and to eradicate the 'backwardness' of their home area.

Ethnic associations as strongly developed as those described above seem to be found most often in southern Nigeria. Elsewhere the functions of individual associations may be slightly less extensive, perhaps stressing material aid at the expense of other functions. Less effort may be made to enrol all eligible members, and there may be a resultant trend for the members of the association to belong to socio-economic categories of a smaller range. Less often are the university lecturer, the prostitute and the cook members of one association.

For the migrants of some ethnic groups, formal organizations of this type are scarcely necessary. For instance, the Zabrama seasonal migrants to Ghana tend to come from a few localities; they share rented accommodation in the modern town, reject contact with men of other ethnic groups, and spend all their leisure time together talking of their homes.

The organization of the Hausa in southern Nigerian towns is typified, one suspects, by the Sabon Gari community in Ibadan. Unlike many other migrants in southern Nigeria, the Hausa are engaged in a very limited range of economic activity – the purchase and transport to the north of kola nuts, and the sale of cattle to the local Yoruba butchers. Again, unlike other migrants, they are residentially segregated; almost all the 6,000 Hausa of Ibadan live in or around Sabon Gari (the remainder living beyond the city at the larger rural markets, to purchase kola nuts). Among the older residents of Sabon Gari are about thirty 'landlords', men who own much of the housing rented by the more transient migrants, and who also act as entrepreneurs between the Fulani cattle owners and the local Yoruba butchers. Thus each 'landlord' heads a little business enterprise, each participant in which is related to him by ties of clientage. The community supports, too, a relatively large number of *mallam* (men learned in Koranic studies) – over five per cent of the occupied males. Indeed, each 'landlord' has a *mallam* as his private adviser in matters both spiritual and temporal. Most of the 'landlords' have, in addition, recently made the pilgrimage to Mecca (thus becoming *alhaji*). Although about three-quarters of the indigenous population of Ibadan is Muslim, the Hausa do not join them in prayers and are scornful of their laxity in rituals and observances. One of the 'landlords' is recognized as the chief for Sabon Gari, and it is through him that the City Council deals with the community. The chief, advised by the remaining 'landlord'-*alhaji*, is responsible for the administration of the community.

The Hausa of Ibadan's Sabon Gari retain their kin ties with relatives at home in the emirates, though many have such ties with several towns as a result of frequent intermarriages in the geographically mobile trading groups. Their cohesion, however, derives not from their membership of individual emirates, but from their ritual exclusiveness and economic specialization.[106, 107, 108]

Trade unions

One would not have been surprised if the West African trade unions had been in the forefront of the independence movements. Theirs was the opportunity to mobilize the rapidly increasing urban populations of literate men – men who had in some degree forsaken the rural areas and the traditional value systems. In fact, however, the overall impact of the unions was slight in almost every territory; Guinea provided the most marked exception. Again, one would expect the trade unions to play a dominant role in socializing the migrants to urban styles of life, in encouraging in them a commitment to town dwelling. But here, too, their impact has been slight.

Workers' protests have a long history in West Africa. A strike at Freetown in 1874 is recorded, and others followed in the rapidly expanding coastal towns. But these were regarded as illegal by the colonial governments and quelled, sometimes with considerable force. The aims and methods of collective bargaining were little understood in this period by the African worker. The withdrawal of his labour was his most effective means of protest. Trade unions themselves were legalized in the French colonial territories only in 1937 – a right later withdrawn by the Vichy regime and restored only in 1946. In the Gold Coast, a trade union ordinance was passed only in 1941, although occupational associations in the form of craft guilds or friendly societies had existed in earlier decades. A Nigerian Civil Servants Union dates from 1912; the railway workers were organized in 1921; and the Nigerian Union of Teachers was founded in 1931. It was, however, only in the 1940s and 1950s that trade union activity really began to develop.

In the early 1950s, between ten and twenty per cent of the employed workers in the West African territories were enrolled in trade unions. But most of the unions were small; two-thirds of those in Ghana and one-half of those in Nigeria had less than 350 members. Some of those listed in the annual returns today are clearly not trade unions at all but guilds of independent craftsmen; the Nigerian list contains, for instance, the Ijesha Goldsmiths Union and that of the Enugu Washermen. The unions tend to represent not specific categories of workers employed by a number of firms but the employees of each company, government department or public utility. Thus one finds the United Africa Company Workers Union and the Elder Dempster Lines African Workers Union, the Union of Posts and Telegraph Workers, and so on. The unions representing the public utilities and the professions tend to be the largest in scale and the best organized; all are national in scope. In Guinea, however, wage earners were affiliated directly to a central association, and organization was neglected at the level of the individual company. This situation may have resulted from the very rapid industrialization of the country with the exploitation of the bauxite mines. It certainly resulted in a much more coherent and politically effective unionism.

Guinea has produced a President in Sékou Touré who himself

rose to prominence through the trade union movement; in the early 1950s, the organization of his party (the Parti Démocratique de Guinée) was very closely interwoven with the trade union. Elsewhere, however, trade unionists have been conspicuously few among the nationalist leaders and within the membership of the elected parliamentary assemblies; four of 473 assemblymen in the French African states were, in 1958, former trade unionists, and only three of the eighty-four members in the Nigerian Federal House of Representatives from the Eastern and Western Regions had had trade union experience.

The political parties of the early elites, like the United Gold Coast Convention, tended to ignore the trade unions; their members and interests were of the professional 'middle class'. Parties seceding from these elite associations, however, did seek the support of the unions. In the late 1940s the Nigerian trade unions were affiliated to the National Council of Nigeria and the Cameroons, and this party, or more especially its radical Zikist wing, actively exploited the Enugu coal mine dispute of 1949 (in which many miners were shot) and a strike in 1950. In the Gold Coast, leaders of the Trades Union Congress called a general strike in support of the Convention People's Party's positive action campaign. In both countries the suppression of these strikes resulted in the disintegration of the central labour organization. Then, in the years following 1950, the nationalist leaders tended to ignore the trade unions – except, of course, in Guinea, and in Ghana where the C.P.P. progressively drew into its own structure first a section of and later the entire trade union movement.

In each territory the trade unions tended to be radically oriented. In as much as they were allied with political parties, it was with those of the left – with the P.D.G. in Guinea, the C.P.P. in Ghana, and the early N.C.N.C. in Nigeria. In Nigeria, Nduka Eze, who built up both the U.A.C. Workers Union and a strong central labour organization, finally broke with the N.C.N.C., criticizing its 'bourgeois' leadership. In the French territories, the unions urged their members to vote *non* in the 1958 referendum on joining the French Community; but apart from Guinea, only in Niger did the *non* votes form a substantial part, and still a minority, of the total. The radicalism of the trade union leaders has perhaps made them unacceptable partners of most of West Africa's present nationalist leaders.

The weakness of the trade unions may be illustrated by their political ineffectiveness, but cannot be ascribed to political leaders and their parties. The cause lies rather in the structure of industrial employment.

Much of West Africa's labour is unskilled, and workers are often barely literate. Only the semi-skilled and skilled are in permanent employment; the remainder are daily-paid. Most of such workers have, moreover, just recently left the rural areas for the towns, and their intention is to return to their home villages, perhaps in the very near future. Such men have little commitment to urban employment; they are not interested in the long-term improvement of working conditions. Their grievances tend to arise over day-to-day incidents – the unfair dismissal of a worker, or alleged insults. These men make up, of course, the large proportion who are not enrolled in trade unions; but they probably account, too, for many who are nominal members.

With the increasing flow of migrants to the town, the applicants for unskilled jobs tend to exceed the opportunities available. Employers can only too easily dismiss their discontented workers and hire others. Workers' protests thus tend to be ineffective. The lack of technological education, on the other hand, results in a severe shortage of skilled workers, especially in cities such as Lagos, where industry is currently expanding at rates between fifteen and twenty-five per cent a year. Here, newly arrived firms attempt to seduce staff from existing factories with promises of training in their European works, and the overseas experience raises the lucky recipients to the privileged status otherwise held only by those with high educational qualifications.

Despite the low wage levels of unskilled labour, employers regard such labour as relatively expensive. Most new factories are, therefore, highly mechanized. The plywood factory at Sapele in the Niger Delta, owned by a subsidiary of U.A.C., is one of the most advanced in the world. In such establishments, the wage rates are high compared with those in alternative local employment, and the prospects for promotion both in the workshops and in the offices are good. The factory had initially to employ men with little skill and education, and the management has actively embarked on a variety of training programmes. Contributory pension schemes have been instituted; two or three weeks' annual leave on full pay is granted to pensionable staff, with six days for others, and extra compassionate leave is often allowed. In factories with such relatively favourable working conditions, augmented in some cases by social services – a company hospital for instance – the rates of labour turnover and absenteeism tend to be very low. Not all employers, of course, measure up to these standards, but the majority of the larger firms do. The smaller and less generous firms are penalized by their failure to recruit skilled workers.

A high proportion of the labour force in each West African state is employed by the government, and conditions of work in the public sector have in general been relatively good. In the French colonial territories, a labour code fixed statutory minimum wages and determined the wage rates of all unskilled labour; but practice did not always follow precept, and the administration of these codes led to continual friction between unions and government. Minimum wages were not fixed in the British territories, but frequent reviews were made of the wages and conditions of work of government employees, and these had a strong influence in the private sector of the economy, where all but the largest companies were competing with the government for skilled workers and suffering the disadvantage of the greater prestige attached to government employment. Furthermore, the labour codes have enforced on all employers relatively high standards in their relationships with their workers.

Although individual trade unions have developed largely through the initiative of their West African leaders, much of the stimulus for their growth in the post-war years came from the colonial governments. In the French territories, many trade union headquarters were built with public funds, and many of the union officials were civil servants receiving regular salaries. The British Colonial Office posted in its own territories men whose task was to promote the development of trade unions; the Extra-Mural Departments of the new university colleges ran a large number of training courses. A direct effect of this activity was to urge the limitation of union activity to the economic sphere and to discourage intervention in nationalist politics. Many of the larger private companies, in fact, continued to oppose the organization of their own employees into unions; they cited, not altogether without justification, the success of their existing methods of joint consultative committees.

Official encouragement, however, such as it is, has not been enough to ensure a strong trade union movement. Poor attendance at union meetings and the consequent failure to pay regular dues have made most unions financially weak. Many rely on subventions from the international movements. The unions can thus have little to offer in the way of benefits to their members, who look instead to their ethnic associations for social security. The unions, too, are in general poorly led. Skilled workers who might provide leadership are too few, and often more interested in their promotion prospects within their own firm. The well-educated have usually been able to get government posts. The poorly paid union offices tend to attract the demagogues and the academic failures. Their inefficiency and, in many cases, corruption further strain the loyalty of the members. The more promising union official, sent to study overseas, has usually transferred to an occupation with higher pay and prestige on his return.

The inefficiency and corruption in many of the smaller unions have inhibited the development of trade union federations. The larger and better organized unions are less loath to become embroiled in political issues. Why, too, should the more strongly organized – and so probably better paid – workers strike in sympathy with those demanding wage levels or conditions of work far below what they themselves already enjoy, thus jeopardizing their own security? To rivalries among the local union leaders and in some cases ethnic groups has been added the competition between rival international associations – the World Federation of Trade Unions and the International Confederation of Free Trade Unions – for the allegiance of African unions. In their disorganization, the trade unions have not been able to form their own political parties. In fact, the nationalist parties have been competing with the unions for the support of the masses. Within the wider framework of their own political demands, they have proclaimed their dedication to raising the living standards of the workers. In most cases, the parties have appealed directly to the masses, rejecting the assistance of the unions. The success of the political leaders in achieving both political independence and an expansion in the modern sectors of the economy has muted the possible claims of trade unionists.

Elitist associations

The variety of the elitist associations, patronized by the wealthy and well-educated, contrasts markedly with the uniformity of the ethnic associations. The functions of the former tend, overtly, to be more specific than those of the latter. They are devoted to occupational interests – the civil service unions or Bar Association; to charity – the Red Cross; to recreation – the tennis clubs; to cultural pursuits – the dramatic societies. It is far more difficult to assess the contribution that they make towards elite self-consciousness.

A high proportion of the elitist associations were introduced into West Africa by the expatriate civil servants and trading communities; their organization still follows a Western pattern, and many associations continue to be affiliated to an international body. As Africans were admitted to membership, they regarded their participation as implying acceptance of their social equality by the Europeans. Such associations have come to be identified with the highest social ranks. In many cases membership is restricted – as in the occupational associations, or the old boys' societies of the leading secondary schools. And in general, though restrictive admission is openly abhorred, there are frequent splits in elitist associations when the higher ranking members complain of the predominance of less wealthy or cultured men, and secede in consequence to found a new association.

One feels that many men and women who have joined a charitable association have done so not from philanthropic motives, but because it is expected of those of their status. In such circumstances, it is usual that the membership of these associations should be restricted in practice to people enjoying very similar styles of life.

In Western societies one finds elitist associations of a type very similar to those in West Africa. But there also exist associations in which the membership extends from upper, through middle, to the lower classes. Leadership positions in these are usually held by the upper and middle classes, and such associations are usually based upon a local community – the neighbourhood church, or the village cricket team. One's impressions are that such associations are less common in West Africa. The suburbs of the modern town have yet to develop much local community spirit; people are willing to travel far to meet their friends rather than establish closer ties with their neighbours. The churches attract members from all social categories; but in many towns the elite form separate congregations, preferring to attend the little churches first built for the expatriate community or the university chapels rather than the larger parish churches. Sport tends, in West Africa as elsewhere, to be segregated by status – tennis and golf for the elite, football for the literate and semi-literate masses. It is, in fact, mainly in the ethnic associations that the elite mix socially with the more humble folk.

Whereas the illiterate, unskilled worker tends to belong to a single association – his ethnic association – and to satisfy within it all his needs for security and recreation, the member of the elite belongs to a large number of groups. In many of these, the demands of membership upon his time are slight; yet the relationship of common membership may be exploited upon numerous occasions. The old boys' societies may only meet once a year for a formal dinner, yet this is sufficient to maintain the cohesion of the group, and to keep alive in its members a sense of obligation to former schoolmates. The ethnic association assists the migrant to find acceptable compromises between the values of his home community and those demanded by urban life. Multi-membership of elitist associations encourages the elite, on the other hand, to form new sets of values, internally consistent and not related specifically to those of any single ethnic group. The associations are national in the limits of their membership, and it is a sense of national identity which they seek to inculcate in their participants.

Some associations, in fact, transcend national boundaries; graduates of the William Ponty School at Dakar are found throughout the French-speaking territories of West Africa; members of African Rotary Clubs are entertained on their travels abroad by foreign branches, thus developing an international outlook of a sort.

As has earlier been observed, most members of the present elite have come from humble homes; furthermore, once they have gained the educational qualifications appropriate to elite status, their promotion through the bureaucratic ranks has been rapid. These men seek from the elitist associations an assurance that they are really accepted into the highest levels of their society. Through the associations, as through informal friendship networks, they seek the collaboration of those similarly placed in establishing appropriate norms of behaviour. In the 'rat-race' for promotion, they believe that academic qualifications are not sufficient, but that one needs the patronage of those in the higher positions. None of these attitudes is peculiar to West Africa – one reads of them often enough in American society; the rapidity of social mobility in Africa does, however, tend to accentuate them. The West African civil servant probably spends more evenings away from home, either at formal meetings of associations or in informal drinking parties, than does his English or American counterpart. To some extent this may be ascribed to the lack of common interests shared with his wife. Yet inasmuch as he feels obliged to spend so much time with other men, establishing his reputation as a 'good type', the development of a more egalitarian marital relationship is impeded. (Though patronage exercised through elitist associations is not the only means of seeking promotion or security of tenure; loyalty to the political party and its leaders, or the exploitation of ethnic ties, may in many situations provide a more effective means of advancing one's status.)

Some of these functions of elitist associations are demonstrated even more markedly in those of the women. The wives of members of the elite are usually less well educated than their husbands. Their status in society is determined, however, not by their personal qualifications but by those of their husbands. In the charitable organizations, therefore, one usually finds the highest ranking offices occupied by the wives of the cabinet ministers, of the judges and senior civil servants. Such roles are accorded these women in the anticipation that they will develop that aptitude for leadership which their husband's status demands. Some associations have been deliberately founded to teach the new domestic arts to their members; in others, flower-arranging competitions or cookery demonstrations take place behind the cover of philanthropic work. The attendance at meetings in the homes of the leading office-holders is itself an educational experience for those merely aspiring to such status.

The urban role of voluntary associations

In a study of overall social change, it is not possible to discuss every type of modern urban voluntary association, and those selected here do illustrate extreme types. The ethnic associations tend to be exclusive; one may not join if one is not a member by birth of the village or town concerned. They are multi-functional, so that it is possible for a man to satisfy his social needs in the town within a single association. They are traditionalist, looking back to the rural area, providing for the migrant a home away from home. They encourage perhaps the minimal adaptation of rural patterns of behaviour to town life. On the other hand, the elitist associations are characterized both by more specifically described functions and by multi-membership. They, too, are exclusive, with lower limits of income and education observed, though not decreed. They aim to create new sets of values, perhaps to some extent African, but not identified with any particular ethnic group.

Members of the elite seem to participate infrequently in those associations dominated numerically by persons intermediate in wealth and education – the primary school teachers, clerks, skilled manual workers. They may, however, participate in the associations of their own ethnic groups, being expected to do so both by the humble members of these groups and also by co-members of the elite who hold that the denial of one's community of origin is demeaning. Many well-educated Yoruba, for instance, have taken chieftaincy titles in their home towns, thus earning not only the favour of the elders at home, who are gratified by this apparent acceptance of traditional values, but also a considerable prestige among the Yoruba elite.

It is significant that in many parts of West Africa the contact between the elite and the masses is provided more by ethnic relationships than by membership of associations ranked hierarchically through the socio-economic status of their members. Much of the strength of the ethnic associations derives, in West African towns, from the weakness of the trade union, since men feel far more confident of the security provided by the former. The unskilled urban workers tend to participate only marginally, if at all, in associations which directly foster a commitment to urban life and a rejection of the traditional values of their rural homes.

9 Political parties

Political power in the newly independent West African states has passed not to a federation of local traditional or traditionalist elites but to new national elites, largely Western-educated and identifying themselves with the new states rather than with ethnic groups or pre-colonial kingdoms. The creation of these elites has resulted in the development of new patterns of social stratification, in which wealth and power are distributed in a manner different both from that of the indigenous societies and from that of the colonial period. The growth, composition and structure of the political parties which have come to dominate each state reflect the new stratification.

The changes in West African society have so far been studies through examples – of family relationships or ethnic associations, for instance – drawn from specific areas; we can only guess how far these phenomena are common to the whole of West Africa, for so little research has as yet been carried out. In the political field, in contrast, there is an overwhelming amount of data collected by scholars. Lengthy monographs have described the political development of many states, which have, with the remainder, also been covered by numerous shorter essays. Together these explorations provide a guide through the pattern of changes as parties are born through secessions from existing groups and later amalgamate with erstwhile rivals. The fifteen West African states have had, in the past two decades, over sixty major parties and at least as many ephemeral ones. Our task here is neither to catalogue these parties nor to chronicle their rise or fall. Generalizing, to a degree which inevitably eliminates most of the flavour of political development in each particular state, we must try to correlate the growth of the successful parties with the existing social structure of their own states and examine the later effect of their dominance upon this structure. The elite which now wields power is everywhere Western-educated. But, as has already been shown, the present members of the elite do not always form a homogeneous group. Rivalry between political parties has often resulted from clashes between men of strong personality or from ethnic loyalties, but its roots have often lain in the competition for power between different groups within the elite. In this competition rival leaders have developed contrasting ideologies and sought by different methods the popular support of the masses.

Today the West African states have almost all reached the stage of single-party government – either *de facto* or *de jure*. In each case the educational levels and occupations of the present political leaders seem to follow a broadly similar pattern. But among the dominant parties themselves considerable differences exist in internal structure and membership, in ideology, and in the type of social structure which they seek to impose or confirm in their respective states. Nevertheless, each party claims to be the agent of modernization in its own society.

Early protest and nationalist movements

West Africans today tend to glorify the exploits of those of their forebears who forcibly resisted European penetration, often terming such men the first nationalists. But the term is hardly apt. Some of these men – Al Haj Omar, Samory, Behanzin the King of Dahomey, and the Fulani rulers of the Hausa emirates – were merely protecting the integrity of their own kingdoms and of their own power within them; their collapse was not always displeasing to the neighbouring peoples whom they had raided for slaves. Others who resisted were Jaja of Opobo and Nana of Warri, both of whom had established monopolistic control of the palm oil trade between the English merchants and the interior producers; their inability to increase the supply of oil led the merchants to try to bypass them, penetrating the interior themselves and thus destroying these commercial empires. During the colonial period, the imposition of taxes often resulted in rebellions, and these were then usually exacerbated by the failure of the colonial officers to understand the roles of indigenous chiefs, who were expected to exercise authority in spheres or among peoples where they had no traditional jurisdiction. Yet other forms of resistance took a religious form.

None of these protests can, however, properly be termed a nationalist movement; all were identified with local areas or issues, and most sought to preserve the *status quo ante* European penetration or rule. Nationalism connotes the consciousness of belonging to a particular nation, with pride in its cultural heritage (rather than in that of any particular ethnic group), together with an articulate demand for the self-government of that nation in place of alien colonial control. The first real 'nationalists' were thus drawn from among the members of the early Western-educated elites. As has already been observed, many of these elites were alien to the countries in which they resided – for instance, the creoles in Freetown, the Americo-Liberians in Monrovia, the Sierra Leoneans and Brazilians in Lagos. And hence, indeed, the development of national consciousness was fostered by the very fact that these men had no specific ties to local groups.

Within these early elites, attitudes towards the colonial power varied considerably. At one extreme were those who largely accepted the system of government but who sought for themselves a greater degree of participation, complaining of discrimination against Africans when Europeans with no higher educational qualifications were appointed to vacant posts. These were the 'Black Englishmen' or 'Black Frenchmen', who sought social acceptance from the European communities by faithfully copying their habits of dress and entertainment. Nevertheless, these men did not necessarily disown their cultural heritage; for some of them wrote valuable histories of their own people, compiled largely from oral evidence, or scholarly statements of indigenous legal systems. Stimulus at the other extreme came from certain West Indian and American intellectuals, who sought to arouse in West Africans a movement for Negro emancipation, implying the complete rejection of colonial rule and the institution of African self-government. In the early decades of this century, such sentiments were echoed more loudly in the British colonies than in the French – probably in consequence of the greater freedom given by the British colonial government to local political movements, and of the greater frustration felt by the much larger numbers of educated Africans. The official French doctrine of assimilation did much to mute the more extreme types of opposition to colonial rule. These rival viewpoints did not mean the existence of two or more distinct nationalist movements, however, as much as the weakening of the single movement whenever specific action against the colonial government was proposed.

The mid-colonial period saw the summoning of Pan African – and Pan West African – congresses, again partly stimulated by American Negro leaders. They indicate the degree to which the early nationalist elites sought to end colonialism more by combining among themselves than by organizing forces of resistance within their own territories. And so, in the process, the nationalists laid themselves wide open to criticism from the colonial governments that they could not possibly claim to represent the masses of their countries and accept power in their name.

The aims of these nationalist movements were usually expressed in very general terms, partly in an attempt to embrace all shades of opinion within the elite. Those of the Nigerian National Democratic Party of Lagos, led by Herbert Macaulay, the father of Nigerian nationalism, were as follows:—

1. in regard to Lagos: a) the nomination and election of the Lagos members of the Legislative Council;
b) the achievement of municipal status and complete self-government for Lagos.

2. in regard to Nigeria: a) the establishment of branches and auxiliaries of the party in all areas of Nigeria;
b) the development of higher education and the introduction of compulsory education throughout Nigeria;
c) economic development of the natural resources of Nigeria under controlled private enterprise;
d) free and fair trade in Nigeria and equal treatment for native traders and producers of Nigeria;
e) the Africanization of the civil service;
f) the recognition of the National Congress of British West Africa and the pledge to work hand in hand with that body in support of its entire programme.[124 p. 98]

In spite of the avowed intention to establish branches of the nationalist movements up country, very little seems to have been done in this direction; they remained tied to Lagos, Cape Coast and like towns, involved as often with local municipal issues as with those national in scope. In the British territories, the nationalists printed their own newspapers, often violent in their attacks on the colonial administrations; but these did not circulate widely outside the major coastal towns. The dissemination of nationalist ideas proceeded more effectively through traders who travelled between large towns and their hinterland than through any purposeful activity of the political leaders themselves.

In the Gold Coast, where the early elite did belong to the local ethnic groups, the nationalist movement drew the traditional rulers into its orbit to a greater degree than elsewhere. Allying themselves with the chiefs and speaking as their representatives, the nationalists fought the threatened transfer of control over land to the colonial government. But as the government drew the traditional rulers into closer association, by establishing advisory councils of chiefs and admitting educated rulers even to the Governor's executive council, the chiefs began to see themselves as heirs to the colonial power. Thus periods of alliance alternated with rivalry as the elite sought to restrain the growing influence of the chiefs in national politics. The chiefs sided with the political leaders in ensuring the success of the cocoa boycott in 1936; but the politicians had in 1927 opposed the introduction of a native authority system (as established in Nigeria) on the grounds that it would reinforce the power of the chiefs.

The organization of these early nationalist movements was crude in the extreme. They consisted of cliques surrounding a few active and prominent leaders, and their unity derived more from personal loyalty than any deep commitment to specific aims. Formal membership or the establishment of branches scarcely existed.

Militancy increased during the war years and those immediately following, though this was barely reflected in a higher degree of organization. Azikiwe and Nkrumah returned to their home countries from the United States, where they had become deeply influenced by the Negro emancipation movements, and both men eventually broke with the existing nationalist movements to found their own more radical parties. In the French territories the African political leaders were drawn into the political life of Paris, joining or affiliating with parties, usually of the left, and becoming versed in their ideologies and organizational methods. In both British and French territories the returning ex-servicemen formed a discontented group, often unable to find jobs commensurate with their education and experience, and frustrated by their restored subordination after fighting as equals alongside their colonial masters. They carried their discontent to their home areas, though they often became misfits in the still traditionally-oriented rural communities and were hence of limited influence. But as education expanded, so did the numbers of literates in interior towns; cash crops brought greater wealth to many of these areas; lawyers were no longer to be found only in the capitals – on his return from England, Awolowo settled and practised in Ibadan whilst remaining prominent in national movements. Azikiwe's N.C.N.C. by the late 1940s claimed the affiliation of trade unions and ethnic associations, and whilst these links seem to have had little direct political effect, they did encourage the urban workers to identify themselves with the nationalist movement.

Parliamentary government

The colonial systems of government did not postulate eventual self-rule by West Africans. The absence of organized national political parties reflected, indeed, the fact that only in a few towns were Africans able to elect their own representatives. The granting of parliamentary legislatures, with constituencies of approximately equal size covering the entire territory, and with the election of members, at first often indirectly, by almost universal suffrage and secret ballot, was a sudden break with the past. Constitutional advances demanded by the nationalist leaders were granted with increasing rapidity. But in most cases the development of political parties necessary to exploit the new situations lagged behind. In the initial stages the nationalist leaders, with their small cliques in the capital, were faced with the tasks of appealing to the masses for popular support and at the same time of welding those elected into a coherent party – for the parliamentarians from the rural areas were often men with almost no experience of nationalist politics, who had been chosen for their supposed ability to win social services for their home area, and who, their constituents believed, would place their local loyalties above national interests.

In West Africa, as in most of the underdeveloped world, certain characteristics distinguish the political process. The masses tend to be apathetic towards the new nationalist governments. Their lack of education and scant experience of the world beyond their own small communities make it very difficult to appreciate the new types of political structure and the ideologies which they represent. Their dominant attitude is – 'how will it affect us?' In many societies, the ending of colonial rule brought few benefits to the peasants. In the French colonies, the abolition of forced labour and the *indigénat* was appreciated, and the popularity of some present political leaders is still ascribed to their part in this reform. In British territories, the party leader campaigning in the rural areas was likely to be told that the permanent residence of an administrative officer in the locality was a source of prestige which the people were reluctant to lose. Few specific interest groups (save for ethnic ones) can be discerned among the mass of the population, and, the appeal being to an undifferentiated public, few clear statements of domestic policy are enunciated by the politicians. The title of Nkrumah's own movement – the Convention People's Party – was ambiguous; did it aim to attract all the people, or the common people as opposed to the chiefs and elite?

With the rapid intake of hitherto non-political men into the developing political parties, and the consequent conflicts between local and party loyalties, there lacks within the parties themselves, and even more so among the masses, a consensus on the legitimate means and ends of political activity. It is in such situations, where norms are poorly defined, that the emergence of the charismatic leader is facilitated. Such a status gives its holder considerable freedom in formulating the policies of his party, for these are not expected to be related to specific interest groups. Loyalty to the charismatic leader is an emotional one, with a high expressive content. He is expected to maintain the degree of pomp and ceremony that characterized the rulers of many traditional African societies.

At the threshold of the constitutional advance towards self-government and national independence, the nationalist movements of the various West African territories were usually divided into several factions, sometimes organized as political parties, sometimes as cliques around an individual leader. In some cases, the divisions coincided with personal rivalries for leadership in the national movements; in others, ethnic divisions formed the basis. (Save in the Regions of Nigeria, ethnic groups have not been large enough to provide the basis of a national political party.) The most significant divisions, however, were those which reflected differences in ideology. These differences were often latent in the earlier stages, but became apparent as the factions began to develop a party organization and direct their appeal to the masses. Three contrasting types would seem to characterize the range of West African parties at this stage.

The party of the traditional elite may well be led by men who have received Western education, but they nonetheless represent the ruling elite of the pre-colonial period. Such an elite, if it has not been destroyed by colonial rule, seeks to continue its dominance and to accept only such modernization of the economy and of the administrative system as will not threaten its power and status. The Northern People's Congress (N.P.C.) of Northern Nigeria was such a party; another, though rather different, example is the Liberian True Whig Party.

The second type of party is led by members of the Western-educated elite, predominant among whom are the lawyers, teachers, and some wealthy traders – a coalition nowadays often termed, though with some imprecision, a national bourgeoisie. Whilst they seek to control the administration of the modern sector, their plans to reform traditional society are almost non-existent. The political leaders rely heavily on the support of local elites – perhaps both traditional chiefs and wealthy traders. They seek not so much to control the various groups in the national society as to provide the arena wherein the differences among them may be reconciled.

The radical type of party tends to make its initial appeal to those who have become most divorced from their own traditional societies. It promises them a completely new, though African society, the creation of which is the main task of the party. And to achieve this task, the party seeks to control all spheres of activity – in the West African context, through the incorporation of trade unions and women's and youth associations into the party, and the establishment of village and ward councils which are both the local party branches and also the organs of local government and justice.

These three types of political party, which will be illustrated in the case studies presented below, differ not only in their ideologies but also in their methods of appealing for popular support. The party of the traditional elite will tend to use the existing administrative system through which to communicate with the masses. The party of the national bourgeoisie appeals indirectly to local elites. The radical party establishes a network of local branches, appealing directly to the masses and exploiting the charisma of its leader. A few case studies will illustrate the rivalry among political groups as the colonial territories began to move towards full independence.

Some case studies

Northern Nigeria. The emirates of Northern Nigeria were, for the British colonial administration, the showpieces for their policy of 'Indirect Rule'. The rulers of these somewhat feudal kingdoms had been maintained in office, and, within the native authority system here instituted, their traditional roles had been largely preserved. The independence which the emirs lost in the colonial situation was replaced by a far greater security in office. The vast complex of patronage which ensured the allegiance of chiefs and commoners was retained. So, too, was the pomp of office – the huge palaces busy with retainers of servile status, the elaborate and quasi-political durbars at the two Muslim *Id* festivals. The growing of cotton and groundnuts for export had relatively little effect on an already commercialized economy. Wealthy traders were commoners who sought no political office, but by gifts to the rulers protected their own privileges. Christian missions were not allowed to practise within the walled towns, and educational facilities were limited. However, teachers were needed for the few government and native authority schools, and many of these were trained in the Katsina College.

The social origins of the Northern Region's political leaders have reflected with uncanny exactitude the divisions within the emirates.[159]

Abubakar Tafawa Balewa was born to a minor slave office-holder (the keeper of the horses) of a Fulani chief in Bauchi, and as often happened he was sent to school because the Fulani aristocrats were reluctant to send their own sons. From Katsina College he became headmaster of the Bauchi primary school. He then studied at London in 1945–6 for his Diploma in Education, and on his return, was appointed first to the Emir's council and later to the Northern House of Assembly. Here he was vehemently critical of the inefficiency and corruption of the native authorities and of the British administration which protected such abuses. But he called for a reform of the system, not its abolition.

Aminu Kano was born into a patrician Fulani clan in Kano which is noted for its Islamic learning; its members do not hold political offices, but have provided many famous scholars and judges. It is from such men that criticism of the political behaviour of emirs, in terms of deviation from the Muslim law, has come; to them the victims of oppression look for a redress of their grievances. Aminu, born of a woman literate in Hausa and Arabic, received his first education in the traditions of Islam. His own home provided examples of conflict – his father, as Acting Chief Alkali, was often at variance on questions of justice with the reigning Emir of Kano. But Aminu went to Kaduna College and thence to London, to fall under the spell of Laski, the left wing of the Labour Party, and the writings of Marx.

In its early years, radical and reformist ideas had been prominent in the largely cultural Northern People's Congress. But on the threshold of independence, as the party came to control the new legislatures and regional government, the N.P.C. became the caucus of the holders of traditional offices in the emirates. Leadership passed to Ahmadu Bello, Sardauna of Sokoto, a product of

Katsina College but a member, too, of one of the ruling houses of Sokoto. He had unsuccessfully contested for the title of Sultan – a ruler who, tracing direct descent from Dan Fodio, leader of the *jihad*, not only governed his own emirate but, as *seriki mussalmani*, claimed the allegiance of all other emirs and their subjects. Abubakar Tafawa Balewa, a vice-president of the party, entered the Federal political arena to play, as Prime Minister from 1959 until his death in the military coup of 1966, a role of mediator between the Northern and Southern Regions. Aminu Kano was forced out of the N.P.C. and founded his own party, the Northern Elements Progressive Union.

As leaders of the N.P.C. government in the Northern Region, the emirs sought to modernize their roles and their societies, but only to such a degree as would not threaten their own dominant position. Local government was introduced in the non-Hausa areas, giving the people here a direct expression in their local affairs; but the native authority system, with its members still largely selected by the emirs, has been retained in the emirates. Many emirs today are, however, educated men; these and the less literate are more keen than hitherto to educate their sons. Local officials of the N.P.C. tended to be senior and educated officials of the native administrations, and their control over the parliamentary elections (indirectly until 1959) ensured the victories of the N.P.C. Elected office was added to the posts in the gift of an emir; and men have resigned even from ministerial office to take high ranking posts in the emirates.

Yet political opposition to the N.P.C. was growing. N.E.P.U.'s main support came from the urban workers, insecurely employed; but local grievances against the ruling aristocracies were exploited in the rural areas. The party claimed to be the organ of the commoners dedicated to the end of feudal rule. Its supporters refused to accord the traditional salutations to the traditional office-holders, while its legally trained members defended the victims of political oppression. The efforts of N.E.P.U. and the allied Action Group, together with the increasing penetration of new ideas into the emirates, resulted in a high percentage of votes – though rarely enough to constitute a constituency majority – being cast for N.E.P.U. in the first direct election of 1959.

To a large extent the N.P.C. Regional government was able to preserve the traditional social structure of the emirates. But conflicts were latent. The government contained ministers from non-Hausa areas, owing loyalty to the party but not to the emirs, and the civil servants tended to come from the non-Hausa areas, too, since in some of these, like the Yoruba Kabba Province, education was much more advanced. Regional government vied with the large and powerful native authorities of the emirates for the control of public services – the hospitals or water works; offices in these organizations usually fell within the patronage of the emirs. Between the two factions, the Sardauna was able to mediate, while keeping the issues out of public discussion. In 1963 the Emir of Kano was forced to abdicate – an example to others who, failing to modernize their roles, threatened the security of all; but the report into the administration of his emirate was never made public.

Southern Nigeria and Ghana. The political parties of southern Nigeria and Ghana developed from the nationalist movements under the control of the middle class professionals, and the N.C.N.C., led by Azikiwe, and the C.P.P. of Nkrumah were offshoots of these, having more radical ideologies.

To begin with, the N.C.N.C. appealed directly to the urban migrants and won the affiliation of trade unions and ethnic associations, especially of the Ibo. During the early 1950s, indeed, it described itself in Lagos elections as a party of the proletariat. But in the first parliaments, it developed into a predominantly Ibo party. Azikiwe himself, a native of Onitsha waterside (a settlement of immigrant Ibo) and reared in Northern Nigeria, became the charismatic leader of the Ibo, a saviour who would terminate Ibo inferiority – for at this period, higher education in the East lagged behind that of the West, and the national elite was predominantly Yoruba. No antecedent parties in Eastern Nigeria rivalled the N.C.N.C., which was able to win almost unanimous support. The local teachers and traders elected by the rural constituencies, however, overwhelmed both the radical 'Zikist' wing of the party and also the more independent intellectuals. The party lost its radical image. Its appeal to the rural Ibo lay in Azikiwe's charisma and in the support of local elites. Politicians held mass rallies throughout the villages but made little attempt to establish permanent local branches. In the Western Region, too, the radical image of the N.C.N.C. disappeared; it exploited rivalries between Yoruba towns and ethnic groups, albeit usually supporting the weaker or poorer faction. Claims by its opponents that an N.C.N.C. electoral victory would mean Ibo domination of the Yoruba, constituted a perpetual handicap. Opposition to the N.C.N.C. within the Eastern Region tended to follow ethnic divisions; the fears among non-Ibo of exploitation and domination by the larger ethnic group were voiced by locally based parties, often allied with the Action Group. Divisions occurred within the N.C.N.C.; Dr K. O. Mbadiwe, a very senior member of the party, broke away from it for a few years, his following identified with the Aro – an Ibo-speaking people who had, through trade and control of a powerful oracle, dominated the Ibo in the nineteenth century. In many elections, an N.C.N.C. candidate nominated by the party headquarters was defeated by a man more popular locally who stood as 'Independent N.C.N.C.' Chike Obi's Dynamic Party, advocating a Kemalist dictatorship (probably not understood by the electorate) and inveighing against corruption among politicians (a more popular theme) at one time won significant support in the Onitsha area.

The Lagos politicians, little known to the masses outside the city and unable to trace an ancestry in the rural areas, were eclipsed in Western Nigeria by the advent of parliamentary legislatures. Their place was taken by the Action Group – the political wing of the Egbe Omo Oduduwa, a Yoruba cultural association led by Obafemi Awolowo and supported by mainly Yoruba professional men, and wealthy and educated traders. Its organization in 1950 was most rudimentary, and in the early years its tactics were to seek the allegiance of men whom the local constituencies seemed likely to elect. In election campaigns the party leaders sought the support of the local elite, hoping that these men would urge their own followers to vote for the party. The party as a whole relied heavily on the allegiance of the many *oba*, and measures which would have considerably reduced their power were modified, even though the long-term impact of political modernization promised to spell the inevitable obsolescence of indigenous kingship. The party leaders, indeed, continually claimed to uphold the status of the traditional rulers; many of the intellectuals among them saw in kingship an important and distinctive element of the Yoruba heritage, worthy of preservation if any link with the past was to be maintained.

Opposition to the Action Group was usually exploited by the N.C.N.C. – most successfully in 1954, when the governing Action Group had considerably increased taxation but had not yet translated this into increased social services. At all times, however, the differences in ideology between the two parties and in their respective methods of organization were slight. Both parties placed their major emphasis on the provision of improved living standards, better social services, and more employment for educated youth; while individual members of parliament derived their electoral support from their success in bringing – or persuading voters of their powers to bring – benefits to their own constituencies.

An interesting contrast in political development may be made between Western Nigeria and southern Ghana. The indigenous social and political structure of each area was very similar; in both areas, the traditional rulers continued to wield considerable power in local affairs; and the export of cocoa brought considerable wealth to Akan and Yoruba farmers alike. Yet parties of a different type acceded to power.

The C.P.P. was born as a radical outgrowth of the nationalist movement controlled by the professional elite. Its appeal was mainly to the young men and women uprooted from traditional society, and in this it resembled the N.C.N.C. of the early days. But unlike the N.C.N.C., it was able to retain this appeal as it sought the support of the rural masses. A large proportion of the population in the cocoa-growing areas was immigrant and owed no allegiance to local chiefs. Furthermore, the prestige of these chiefs, in the eyes of their own people, was lower here than among the Yoruba. Since they had not been drawn into a native authority system, they were less often preserved in office by colonial administrators. Their high incomes from land and timber and mining royalties, moreover, gave rise to considerable local opposition over charges of corruption and selfish expenditure. This was exploited to the full by the C.P.P. The chiefs and the professional elite sought mutual support in the United Gold Coast Convention and were attacked by the C.P.P. as representing reformist elements, tepid in their support for emancipation from colonial rule. Against the charismatic appeal of Nkrumah and the advantages in electioneering usually held by the party in power, the U.G.C.C. steadily lost ground. Its final bid for power lay in supporting an ethnically based movement among the Ashanti for a greater decentralization of power and wealth from Accra through the grant of a federal constitution. The C.P.P. overtly claimed to support the traditional status of chiefs and welcomed those rulers who allied themselves with the party; but its legislation considerably reduced their powers. In adopting the title *Osagyefo*, and in exchanging Ghanaian (and predominantly Akan) for British symbols and ceremonies in Parliament, Nkrumah took upon himself, as it were, the quasi-traditional role of ruler of all Ghana.

Although Nkrumah himself long acknowledged Marxist beliefs, the concept of the C.P.P. as a radical type of party, mobilizing the support of the masses in the building of a new society, seems to have developed as the C.P.P. contested with the U.G.C.C. for the popular support of the electorate.

Some French-speaking territories. The French-speaking territories have many similarities in political development which distinguish them from British West Africa. Their elite came from the same few schools, notably the William Ponty School at Dakar. They formed cultural associations when political parties were illegal; initially they sought positions within a French political system rather than independence from it. As representatives in Paris, they were associated with the left wing parties and absorbed the language of Marxism. In Africa, their parties were both territorial and inter-territorial.

Poverty had resulted in the minimal development of a wealthy trading or farming category, save in the Ivory Coast, and educational backwardness resulted in the elites being very small. French administrative policy itself had either abolished traditional rulers or made them little more than figureheads; native administration was established by 'direct rule' through appointed chiefs. These chiefs, frequently literate, and often wealthy through the exploitation of their authority, constituted a local elite. In the early post-war years, the French colonial administration was allured by the prospect of eventually handing over power to these men, and supported the political parties of which they were members – to the extent, in some territories, of blatantly rigging the elections. In consequence, the nationalist leaders were obliged to seek the support of the rural masses with a directness unusual in British territories, and equipped with the greater understanding of party organization that they had gained in Paris, the French-speaking leaders often developed networks of party branches at an early period. Nevertheless, alongside these similarities, there arose within French-speaking Africa, as a result of local situations, some quite considerable differences in party structure and ideology.

In Senegal, Léopold Senghor won leadership from the veteran Lamine Guèye. Son of a prosperous, though 'subject', shopkeeper in the heart of the groundnut area, Senghor was a brilliant student. For several years he taught at secondary schools in Paris and elsewhere, becoming a naturalized French citizen, and returning to Africa after the war, having served in the French army and spent some time in a German prison. Whilst Guèye was identified with the 'citizens' and their desire to retain a monopoly of political power, Senghor won the allegiance of 'subjects' and exservicemen. He travelled through the rural areas in khaki shorts, eating with village elders, whilst Guèye retained his formal suit and tie. Senghor's Bloc Démocratique Sénégalais emphasized an African theory of socialism in opposition to the assimilationist values of its opponents. It sought to unite a variety of local Muslim and ethnic associations; it courted the marabouts and Tijaniya leaders. Within a very few years it had the support of the majority of voters. But the amalgamation of these many varied interest groups gave the party neither a coherent progressive ideology nor a well organized base in the villages. Younger men returning from France in the 1950s often with more pronounced Marxist beliefs first criticized Senghor's party, then were admitted to it. But in recent years the split between Senghor and the radicals has been widening.

Whereas so many of Senegal's political leaders are Christian (Senghor himself is a Roman Catholic) in a Muslim country, in Mali the political leadership has been strongly influenced by the puritanical reformist movements of nineteenth century Islam. The Union Soudanaise of Mamadou Konaté (d. 1956) and Modibo Keita found its early support in the urban areas (inviting comparison with the N.E.P.U. of Northern Nigeria) and among the Malinke, Songhai and other staunchly Islamic peoples. Its opponent, the Parti Progressiste Soudanais, drew its popular support from the rural areas, the largely pagan Bambara, and those peoples terrorized in the nineteenth century by Al Haj Omar; it was supported, too, by the canton chiefs and the French administration. The U.S. thus aggregated all the most anti-colonial elements – the educated, the wage-earners, and the Muslim intelligentsia – into a single party, on the one hand politically radical and, on the other, aspiring to an Islamic brotherhood. It was more active in establishing local party branches than was its rival the P.P.S., which was handicapped both by its French allegiance and its policies of supporting the canton chiefs; the chiefs, in fact, were often reluctant to see P.P.S. branches in their cantons, fearing that these might compete for power. Not surprisingly, therefore, in the 1957 elections to a Territorial Assembly, the U.S. won an overwhelming majority of seats.

In the decade following 1945, the political parties of backward Guinea were mostly based upon local ethnic interests; elected candidates had the support of the canton chiefs and less directly of the French administration. The rapid expansion of the mining industry, however, created both greater numbers of workers and more unemployed in the towns, and both categories were mobilized by the Confédération Générale du Travail trade union federation, led by Sékou Touré, its secretary general. A highly successful strike in 1953 brought popularity to Sékou Touré and his Parti Démocratique de Guinée, both in the towns and in the rural areas. The small ethnic parties fought back by combining, but here, too, their appeal to the masses was vitiated by the support of the chiefs and the French administration. In many areas the popularity of the P.D.G. was promoted by Sékou Touré's descent from Samory and by the support, as in Mali, of the Muslim teachers. The Marxist language of the urban-based party was modified with Muslim precepts, and in 1957, the P.D.G. won almost all the seats in the Territorial Assembly.

In 1946, Félix Houphouet-Boigny of the Ivory Coast, a Deputy from the Ivory Coast and Upper Volta in the French Parliament, founded the Parti Démocratique de la Côte d'Ivoire – an outgrowth of an African planters' association. During the following three years, the party mobilized all the anti-colonialist forces in this relatively rich colony, and the French administration, unable to build an effective single rival, supported five small parties with ethnic and religious bases. Between 1949 and 1951 extreme government repression against the P.D.C.I. ensued, with crudely rigged elections. Yet this served only to strengthen the party, and from 1952 the colonial government, recognizing their popular hold, increasingly pursued a policy favourable to the party leaders. Houphouet's own position as a Minister in Paris from 1956 gave him an advantage in checking the colonial government such as no politician in a British colony ever enjoyed. Yet victory seems to have cost the P.D.C.I. its unity. Rural membership of party branches declined, while ethnic and interest groups created a myriad of local factions. Instead of instituting collective leadership (as had the leaders in Mali and Guinea), Houphouet appealed directly to the masses, and thus every local leader became dependent on a personal relationship with him. The charisma of Houphouet was carefully developed as he became in effect the sole ruler and sole mediator. Opposition from intellectuals (recently returned students from France) and from the trade unions increased. Then, in 1959, the trade unions were drawn into the P.D.C.I., and the leaders of some civil service unions which refused amalgamation were arrested.

Liberia. Liberia has had no anti-colonial struggle. Its True Whig Party, founded in 1860, has been the governing party continuously since 1877. The parliament is elected by adult suffrage; but the coastal areas, where the Americo-Liberians live, are heavily over-represented, having thirty-three of the thirty-nine seats. The indigenous peoples of the interior share only marginally in schemes of economic and social development, though the new iron mines are in their area. Cooperative agriculture and the spread of plantation crops have not been encouraged. The *poro* society, the agent of government in the tribal areas, has been officially recognized, and the late President Tubman was head of all *poro*. The trade unions have a large Kru membership, but Tubman's own son is President of the Trade Union Congress. Strikes are ruthlessly repressed.

High political offices are almost entirely reserved for the Americo-Liberians and are open to others only if they can gain acceptance, preferably through intermarriage, by this group. Disputes within the True Whig Party are thus between competing Americo-Liberians, and are usually resolved by granting offices to the discontented. In recent decades the Americo-Liberians have come to fear the impact which economic development might have on their privileged position. Tubman, as 'managing director of the Americo-Liberian class', enabled them to reap the benefits of development, and whilst maintaining a more tolerant attitude towards the indigenous peoples and winning popularity among them, yet maintained their inferiority.

Towards one-party rule

The British and French governments, in setting up parliamentary systems in their West African colonies, presumed that multi-party states would exist. And they seemed justified in this belief by the rivalry which existed between parties in the early 1950s. Furthermore, it was held that two or more parties, forming government and opposition, were an essential characteristic of a democracy. In the years which followed the granting of independence, however, each new state has moved quickly towards a single party system. The parties not in office rapidly dwindled in strength. By 1960, for instance, Nkrumah gained over a million votes in the national referendum for President, against 125,000 for Dr Danquah, the candidate of a coalition representing the professional elite and certain ethnic groups. And the Ghanaian government subsequently outlawed all parties in opposition to the

C.P.P. In other states – in Senegal, Mali, and Guinea, for instance – some of the minority parties merged with those in office ostensibly to form a 'national front'. Other minority parties simply faded away, with their leaders taking no further part in national politics. The speed of this process was largely unexpected. But with the grant of complete independence, the peculiar restraints exercised by the colonial powers were removed, and the new rulers had a much freer hand in amending the constitution (by due law, for they usually commanded an overwhelming majority of parliamentary seats) to eliminate opposition.[118a]

A mundane reason for the trend towards one-party rule was the desire of the politicians to remain in office. There were few who had earned substantial incomes as doctors or lawyers, and whose salaries as ministers or members of parliament did not, therefore, represent a large increase in earnings. Most of the elected politicians had previously been schoolteachers, clerks, or traders, and their new salaries were three or more times their former incomes. Generous travel allowances and subsidized housing (official residences for ministers often cost £30,000) and the eternal round of cocktail parties (save in austere Mali) at which the government entertained visiting delegations created a style of life hitherto unexperienced in West Africa, even by the senior officials of the colonial administration. And added to this was the power of patronage held by the politicians. Politics became the most highly rewarded of all professions. The leaders of the new states lived in even more opulent style. The presidential palace of Houphouet-Boigny in Abidjan cost over £6 million – a contemporary Versailles. The late Sardauna of Sokoto built a wall costing over £30,000 around his Kaduna residence. Leading ministers rode in hugely expensive cars. One might accuse these men of megalomania. Yet it may be argued, too, that these great palaces symbolize the nationhood of the new states; in them, the new rulers may entertain without embarrassment the leaders of the world's most powerful nations. The magnificence of the presidency, often contrasted with the simple clothing of its incumbent, enhances the charisma which these heads of state feel essential to their roles.

The one-party state, criticized from abroad by those who see in it the negation of democracy, is justified by Africans. Their arguments provide, for the dominant party, the basis of the legitimacy of its power.

The colonial period left a legacy of authoritarian rule which the African governments felt bound to assume. It was felt, too, that the party which was largely instrumental in winning independence should continue to lead the country in its striving for economic and social development. The minority parties of the professionals and chiefs, castigated by their successful rivals for attempting to delay independence and for subservience to the colonial power, were in consequence, it was maintained, ill fitted for subsequent office.

The difficulties of development facing these new states need no emphasizing. African leaders argue that skills and talents are so scarce in their societies that all must be employed directly in the tasks of reconstruction. National unity, too, is essential. Africans repeat Western criticism of democracy as the least efficient form of government. And 'opposition' to most Africans denotes not an 'alternative government' but 'wrecking' or 'sabotage'; in many African vernaculars, it is translated by a word which, in other contexts, means 'hooligans'.

On an ideological plane it is argued that opposing interest groups – in the sense of an economic bourgeoisie and proletariat – do not exist. Traditional tribal African society, too, was classless, in that it did not often give rise to hereditary differences of wealth and power. In the Marxist thinking of many African leaders, classes can provide no basis for rival political parties, because they do not exist. Within each state, the competing parties were each dedicated to providing for their electorate the maximum improvements in living standards; such differencies in policies at have existed derived more from the means by which developmens might be achieved than from the proposed distribution of rewards among the various sections of the population. And in the last resort, development policies have been determined more by the willingness of expatriate firms to invest and the generosity of international aid agencies, than by the ideologies of the politicians.

It is claimed, too, that the conflicts and tensions latent in societies undergoing such rapid change are so great that if they were brought into the open for discussion in parliament and the press, the cohesion of the new state would be seriously threatened. The resolution of the conflicts within the framework of a single party is said to be more effective. The role of the charismatic leader is emphasized here; he alone can force agreement upon rival groups holding opposed opinions. And this process is justified by tradition, being likened to that in indigenous kingdoms where the ruler, often mistermed a 'despot' by European observers, mediated between rival descent groups. The council of chiefs in these kingdoms was not divided into permanently opposed groups or parties; alignments usually shifted with the issues. And the decisions of the leading chiefs or the king were accepted unanimously, not by majority vote. This process, the politicians now allege, is repeated in the single party.

Accession to government office has provided the successful parties with numerous methods of enhancing their own dominance and reducing the influence and effectiveness of their rivals. In distributing the new social services – tarred roads, schools, hospitals – the government may locate them in constituencies returning members of their party. Areas which return members of opposition parties thus see themselves, not entirely without justification, as doomed to backwardness; and either their sitting members will cross over to the governing party, or they may vote for others next time. Sanctions, too, may be wielded against members of local elites, in the expectation that they will sway the opinions of the masses in their own communities. Men loyal to the governing party will receive loans for trading or agricultural improvements, or contracts for minor public works; members of opposition groups are assessed for taxation on a high income, with the onus placed on them to prove any lower earnings, and are then harried in the customary courts for non-payment. This implies a control by the governing party of these courts and the machinery of local government; and this is achieved by statutory provisions, by the appointment to the courts of party loyalists (instead, in many cases, of the traditional chiefs), and by the success of the governing party in local council elections.

Political parties can collect little income from the periodic subscriptions of thousands of individual members; such methods rarely remain effective for long. Parliamentarians often provide a tithe from their salaries, and here the smaller parties are at a clear disadvantage. Moreover, parties in power receive gifts from commercial firms, both indigenous and expatriate, in return for favours expected and granted. And a subtle transfer of funds from government to party may often be effected through the acquisition by the government of land or a business at an inflated price, with most of the difference between this and the realistic market value being donated by the recipient to the party.

With greater financial resources, the governing party can mount a much more effective electoral campaign, employing more party agents, more bribes, and, in some cases, more thugs to intimidate opposition. The loudspeaker vans of the Information Ministries are partisan supporters of the party in power. In Northern Nigeria, the British administrative officers were usually overt supporters of the N.P.C. A stage is soon reached where it becomes impossible for an opposition party effectively to organize – its members being continually victimized – or contest an election on anything like equal terms with the governing party. Nigeria, until the army coup in 1966, was always cited as an example of a multi-party state; two parties (N.P.C. and N.C.N.C.) were in coalition to form the government, and the third (the Action Group and later the N.N.D.P.) was in opposition. But each of these parties had become overwhelmingly dominant in its own Region. From its home base, each could campaign in the neighbouring Regions; without this external aid, the minority parties within each Region would soon have succumbed.

A final method of ensuring the dominance of the single party lies in the cultural and ideological sphere; the party in power seeks to instil the values which it represents into the entire population. In the case of some parties – the C.P.P. of Ghana, the U.S. of Mali, the P.D.G. of Guinea – this was achieved by the control of modernist groups – youth associations, trade unions, farmers' societies, and the like. In Northern Nigeria the N.P.C. leaders endeavoured to convert to Islam the non-Muslim populations of the 'Middle Belt' – the areas of tribally structured societies outside the emirates. Muslim law was here enforced in all customary courts whereas during the colonial period indigenous law had prevailed; and Hausa insisted upon as a lingua franca. Pagan or Christian members of the House of Chiefs wore turban and riga when in Kaduna to avoid being shamed. In recent years the periodic tours of the Sardauna of Sokoto, the Regional Premier till his murder in the 1966 coup, through the non-Muslim areas were marked by a proselytizing zeal; tens of thousands of converts were announced at the formal completion. As an ethnic group the Hausa are defined in terms of culture – a common language, dress, religion – not of common descent or membership of a single political unit. New members are thus easily assimilated; and it seems, therefore, that the ultimate aim of the political leaders was to make all Northern Nigerians into Hausa. The most sustained opposition to this came, significantly, from the egalitarian Tiv people.

In the creation of one-party states, the Western-educated elites have played a surprisingly acquiescent role. Educated at universities in Western Europe or the United States, they learned to accept and value the concepts of democracy current there. And as the best-educated men in their own African states, they not only believed in the freedom to criticize their government, but thought that their views should carry weight with the less well-educated politicians. As civil servants they were, indeed, frequently offended when decisions were made on grounds not of economic logic but of party advantage. Yet their protests against the victimization of their own members have been weak and ineffectual. The reason lies in the control exercised by the government over elite employment. Many members of the elite are in the civil service and feel that overt political activity is wrong; those known to hold views hostile to the government are deemed 'unreliable' and denied promotion. Headmasters feel that if a member of their staff expresses views hostile to the party in power, their schools will not be approved for additional government subsidies. Only a few professions remain beyond official control, and these usually demand specialist training. They cannot provide a refuge for the vocally disaffected teacher or administrator.

Furthermore, the elite enjoys a privileged position in society. Its high salaries are defended by the government. The complete collapse of the government, resulting in general chaos, would terminate its offices and privileges, and its interest thus lies in maintaining a strong government. Any criticism, therefore, must not be so trenchant as seriously to threaten authority; in many states tensions exist which could easily produce a revolutionary situation, if sparked off by a rebellion within the elite.*

Throughout West Africa the dominant parties have, in general, used the same methods to attain their *de facto* or *de jure* superiority in a one-party state, and have justified their positions by similar methods. But just as these dominant parties differed in the early stages of struggle for self-government, so have they subsequently developed into organizations of diverse character.

The parties of the traditional elite have remained autocratic, though continuing to emphasize their role in the modernization of their countries. The dominance of the ideology of the traditional elite is maintained. Party organization is weakly structured; few congresses are held, and most decisions seem to result from informal contacts among party leaders or from the parliamentary members.

The major difference between parties is seen in the distinction between two types of political structure. On the one hand is the party which seeks to mobilize the entire population in the development of the country, producing in the process a distinctive ideology which stresses the leadership of the party, and seeking to achieve its end through the control of modernist associations which are used as agents of socialization. On the other hand, there is the party which accepts the independence of existing associations, conceiving its own role as the reconciliation of the incompatible interests of these associations; such a party does not develop any clearly formulated ideology. These two types of party – mobilization and reconciliation parties, to use Apter's terminology[115] – tend to develop respectively from the earlier radical and professional elite parties, though the correspondence is not exact. Nor are features of the mobilization party entirely absent from states with reconciliation parties, and *vice versa*.

The stress is placed by the mobilization parties – the C.P.P. of

---

* These are explored later in chapter 13.

Ghana, the P.D.G. of Guinea, the U.S. of Mali – upon the acceptance of modernizing values by the entire population. The party works through those – captive – associations which stress such values, and traditional loyalties to ethnic groups are disparaged (though the new state may claim descent from ancient kingdoms; the Gold Coast thus became Ghana, and the Soudan took the name of Mali). Some examples of the party-controlled associations may be cited.

In Ghana the 'New Structure' of the Trade Union Congress was created in 1958, making the T.U.C. an integral part of the C.P.P. organization, with the General Secretary of the T.U.C. a member of the party's central committee. A few unions only were recognized by the government, and their size, with the financial provisions created, made them more powerful than the earlier unions had ever been. The aim of the New Structure was that 'the energies and potentialities of all workers shall be collectively directed towards the economic reconstruction of Ghana'. Through its control of the unions, the government hoped to minimize industrial strife, which might otherwise weaken the economy. The tasks of the unions were thus to develop a highly disciplined labour force, committed to urban life, and to act as a vehicle for C.P.P. propaganda in all political matters.[111, 112]

The Ghana Workers' Brigade was founded in 1957 as a direct response to the growing unemployment among school leavers, which seemed to be exciting outbreaks of violence, frequently directed to ethnic ends. The Brigade, which had recruited over 10,000 members by 1960, was organized on para-military lines, with uniforms and regular drill; and in addition to athletic and recreational activities, it received lectures on the new ideology of Nkrumaism. The Brigade members were engaged in public works like road building and on state farms, and it was expected that they would learn trades which they could subsequently practise in civilian life. But the growth of the Brigade seems to have been hampered by ill-defined ideas of its ultimate purpose and by its high costs, which rose to £2 million in 1960–1.[134]

In Mali, the new youth movement formed in 1961 embraced all former associations – including, for instance, the Boy Scouts.

Compulsory membership was decreed for all eighteen-year-old youths, and, as in Ghana, a para-military life in camps was instituted. A sense of urgency, a need to protect the security of the nation, was conveniently provided by the coup which in 1960 ended Mali's federation with Senegal. In the camps themselves, the youths have learned the rudiments of literacy, craft techniques and new agricultural methods, with the aim of preventing an exodus from the rural areas to the towns, together with a respect for their own history and culture. The example of the Israeli youth movement, which has endeavoured to unite, behind a single system of values, immigrants of widely different cultures and economic backgrounds, has been consciously adopted by several West African states.

One of the greatest problems of any mobilization party is to establish itself in the rural areas. This may be achieved both through the development of government-sponsored cooperative societies and by the establishment of local party committees as the main instruments of local government and justice. In Mali, the rural cooperative is based upon the village and organizes collective farming, the development of new techniques, and the provision of credit. A local leader is appointed by the members, and at district and divisional levels, government agricultural workers provide instruction and organize the buying of supplies and selling of produce. The cooperatives are also active in promoting literacy and cultural activities.

In Guinea, the colonial chieftaincy system was abolished in 1958, and able office-holders loyal to the P.D.G. were absorbed into other administrative posts. In its place, village councils are annually elected by adult suffrage; they consist of ten persons – with three seats reserved for women and two for members of youth associations – and the candidate receiving the highest number of votes becomes the village chief. These councils are responsible for local law and order, public health, minor judicial matters, and the collection of taxes, while the village chief is both the agent of the party at the lowest level and also the most junior member of the administrative hierarchy. At this, and at the higher levels, confusion may arise over the respective authority of party officials on the one hand and administrative officers, responsible to the various ministers, on the other. The official reply is that the two streams complement each other rather than provide a system of checks and balances.

Economic planning in the West African states is impeded by the dependency on expatriate firms to initiate new projects, and by a failure of the government to exercise adequate controls, so that much foreign exchange is spent on importing luxuries used by the elite instead of on more useful machinery. The doctrinaire socialists call for state control of all industry and commerce. In Ghana, according to official policy statements in the years before the military coup, expatriate firms might operate only large-scale industrial enterprises (though the existing foreign trading companies were, in fact, allowed to continue). The country thus had fifty state corporations. But state control does not by itself render an enterprise economically viable; many projects, established for reasons of prestige, have made huge losses. Men trained as civil service administrators often have little aptitude for business. And increasing state control results in so much red-tape that bribery and corruption become rampant, damaging both the efficiency and the public image of the corporations. It is not an easy dilemma to resolve.

In the states with mobilization parties controlling the youth and women's associations, the trade unions, the farmers' cooperatives, the village councils and courts, the central committee of the party becomes the main focus of decision making. Parliament is a ratifying body. But here, it is argued, is true democracy, with the opinions of the masses, expressed through their associations, passing upwards to the higher party committees. It is difficult to discover how effective this process really is; it is much easier to envisage the decisions of the party central committees passing downwards to the local branches of the various associations. Certainly, this newly developed channel of communication engenders new loyalties, detracts from the traditional relationships, and fosters the acceptance of values appropriate to modernization. Much depends, however, on the successful operation of these associations; too often we have only the glowing description of them in government brochures. It is in these associations that the accommodation of traditional and modern values must take place;

and the tensions which develop within them or in their relationship with the higher party officials may negate their more positive achievements. The network of associations and party branches, articulated by fairly frequent congresses, at which (so it often appears) more pronouncements are made than decisions taken, provides in these new states one of the main avenues to high ranking office – an avenue distinct from that provided for the educated in the bureaucracies and stressing different criteria, such as loyalty to the party and leadership among the masses.

The reconciliation party – represented by those which won power in the southern Regions of Nigeria, in the Ivory Coast, and Senegal, for instance – differs from the mobilization type in that it does not seek to control, through incorporating them into its own structure, the major associations and interest groups of the society. At best, it attempts to win their allegiance or to attract formal declarations of support. The views of the people continue to be expressed primarily through the parliamentarians; M.P.s represent their constituencies, and commercial firms lobby ministers. Much that might properly fall within the sphere of administrative action is, in practice, influenced by the politicians. A member of parliament intervenes to get a university scholarship for a boy from his home town – and is recompensed by the parents for his trouble; the minister obtains a contract or licence for a firm – which in gratitude builds him a block of flats. As the party becomes more secure in its power, local branches, which had always been reactivated at election time, wither away. The party ceases to hold regular conventions; its organization becomes increasingly restricted to the parliamentarians. Electoral support tends to be gained more through the control of the police, the local courts and the local government machinery than through the canvassing for votes. Lip-service is paid to the ideals of democracy and socialism, but the policy of the party is essentially pragmatic – it seeks only those goals which can, without sacrifice, be realized.

Economic development is, of course, the main aim of the 'reconciliation party' states as well; but the initiative is expected to come largely from the independent associations, the indigenous or expatriate firms. Local communities may seek government aid to realize some project, and community development or welfare offices exist to stimulate such demands; but their efforts tend to be channelled through existing associations, exploiting perhaps traditional values or rivalries to spur the effort. Schemes of agricultural development take the form of state-owned farms or plantations divorced from existing villages, and little is done to reform the techniques of the mass of the farmers. This may be because state farms seem likely to yield more rapid returns than any reforms in traditional farming methods; but it might equally be attributed to the inability of politicians to mobilize the farmers for such activity as would yield visible benefits.

10 The strains of change

In previous chapters, we have seen how West Africans have adapted their institutions and their patterns of behaviour to the impact of the West on their societies. The relationships among members of the family have been altered as young couples set up their homes far from their kin. Traditional goals are sought by new means; the townsman no longer seeks social security through his descent group but through the ethnic association of men from his own village. New goals are formulated; the workers organize trade unions to bargain for better conditions, while the Western-educated elite found political movements and parties to wrest power from the colonial governments. Superficially these changes would seem to have been made with relative ease. But we are usually unable to assess the strain which each individual undergoes in making the adaptation from a tribal to modern society.

In situations of change, the individual is faced with difficult problems of choice. New goals are added to those already accepted by society. A man may have to choose between a high ranking status in a traditional and in a modern sphere; he may find it difficult to make up his own mind, being uncertain of the values in which he believes; he is given conflicting advice by his fellows, and will be mindful of the sanctions that these may employ should he fail to act according to their various expectations. Frustration arises when the individual fails to achieve his goal, though he may have followed the accepted means of attaining it; and added to this may be the guilt felt in failing to rise to the expectations of others. A few men and women are able to cope with these problems successfully. Others, however, express their anxiety in a number of physiological symptoms – headaches, stomach pains, and the like. Slightly less common are the psychoneurotic symptoms; and the small minority display symptoms of personality disorder – aggressive or compulsive behaviour, sociopathic conduct (drunkenness or drug addiction, for instance), or acute mental disorders. Most societies have methods by which the fears and anxieties of the individual are allayed – at least to the extent that they do not give rise to mental illness, which seriously impairs his daily work routine. In traditional African societies, beliefs in witchcraft and the practice of magic largely performed this function. Today these methods are falling into disuse, and new practices are developing to take their place. Some of these have clearly developed from traditional practices – the use, for instance, of the modern magic talismans and 'power pills'. Others have derived from Western institutions, such as the numerous religious sects which have seceded from Christian mission churches in an effort to meet demands that the churches themselves seem unable to satisfy.

Much of the strain experienced by individuals today derives from the open structure of their society – from the rapidity with which a man can rise from the humble home of his birth to a high office in a modern bureaucratic structure. Such a degree of social mobility was not altogether unknown in traditional societies; in fact, in many of the tribal societies of the West African forest belt, a meteoric rise to wealth or political power was not unusual. In these cases, however, the methods of achieving such rewards were well known to all in the society. Today, the educational system – the ladder for almost all success in the modern sphere – is poorly understood by all but the few who actually experience it. In the cash-crop-producing areas of Nigeria, Ghana and the Ivory Coast, hundreds of villages have now produced a university graduate. This man, resplendent in his Western suit and with his large car, is a frequent visitor to his home area; by young and old alike he is regarded as a model which the rising youth should aspire to emulate. This situation differs from that usually found in industrial societies, where the successful man moves away from the community of manual workers in which he grew up; he does not serve as a model for the youth of his home locality; the aspirations of the youth are here framed largely according to the type of jobs found by most of their peers. Such aspirations are substantially realistic. But the aspirations of most youth in West Africa today are unrealistic. The success of the few who have entered the Western-educated elite is real enough, and many of these, as we have already seen, have come from humble homes. The statistical chances that a youth from such a home will achieve such success are, however, extremely small. Nevertheless, the individual not only sets himself such high goals, but frequently persists in seeking them long after one would expect him to admit failure and lower his expectations; in societies where many men have won entrance to university at thirty years of age, it is the coward who gives up at twenty. The unrealistic goals of the young are not only enthusiastically supported by their kin but financially backed, too; the accumulated savings of a wide circle of relatives are often pooled to pay for the university education of the apparently bright youth. The pressures on him to achieve the expected success and to reward his kin, not only with prestige but with a financial return, are enormous.

Similarly, in the sphere of business, a few men, well known in their villages, have become wealthy. Yet much of their success has been due to sudden vagaries of the world market economy, or to the operations of the expatriate trading corporations; neither of these is understood in the village, and the wealth of the successful trader is attributed by the village folk – and, perhaps, by the trader himself – to personal luck. Thus, in a rapidly changing society it is not unusual that the goals set by individuals and valued by most members of the society are not attainable by the means which are generally regarded as legitimate.

How much tension is experienced by West Africans today? Usually it is presumed, without any measured proof, that there will be more tension in rapidly changing societies than in the more stable ones; and, following from this, that more tension will be experienced by those rapidly moving from a traditional to a modern way of life than by those whose life has remained relatively unchanged. Again, the complexities of modern life may be stressed in comparison with the 'simple life of the African villages'; the very complexity of modern life may, however, enable the individual to evade many difficult choices, whereas the village offers much less freedom of action. The traditional African villager feels himself much more at the mercy of uncontrollable natural forces than does the urban dweller today.

In 1961, a survey of psychiatric disorder was carried out in and around Abeokuta, south-western Nigeria, by a team of psychiatrists, medical doctors and social anthropologists from Cornell University, working in conjunction with the staff of the local mental hospital.[137] Their sample was drawn from Abeokuta itself – a Yoruba town largely retaining its traditional structure of compounds and descent groups, but today largely inhabited by people in urban occupations, such as crafts and trade; from the farm hamlets around Abeokuta, in which lived men and women whose home compounds were in Abeokuta itself; and from a small town politically dependent upon Abeokuta. The area selected is comparatively wealthy, even by the high standards of Yoruba country; most of its people are nominally Christian or Muslim. It does not, of course, represent the modern urban area with its high proportion of immigrants, working for salaries and wages in indnstrial or commercial employment. The results obtained in the Abeokuta survey were then compared with those from a similar project, carried out in previous years in Stirling County, Nova Scotia.

The conclusions reached by the Cornell study of Abeokuta are tentative but illuminating. The number of psychophysiological and psychoneurotic symptoms found among the Yoruba seemed greater than among the North American population. But the proportion of the sample population suffering from certain or probable psychic disorder was lower among the Yoruba (as sufferers often displayed more than one symptom). And the difference between the African and North American groups was even greater in the assessment of the proportion of persons who seemed to be significantly impaired by their disorders: the lowest figure of 15 per cent was given for the Yoruba hamlets; in Abeokuta town the proportion was 19 per cent; and in Stirling County, 33 per cent. Furthermore, whereas in the North American sample, significant impairment increased with the age of men and women, among the Yoruba men it was the youngest (below 39 years of age) and among the Yoruba women the 40–59 years age group which were most frequently impaired. In Abeokuta town the monogamous men had poorer health than the polygynous –

although the town-dwelling polygynous wives were in poorer health than the monogamous ones. Literate Yoruba men experienced more mental disorder than did the illiterate, but not to any very marked degree; the survey teams 'were impressed by the apparent ability of the culture to incorporate some aspects of education in non-disruptive ways'.[137, pp. 158–9].

The general picture that emerges from this study is that social and economic change – at least of the type experienced in Abeokuta – does not result in any great increase in individual tension, and that contemporary Yoruba society manages to assuage this tension with a high degree of success, so that the health of the majority is not significantly impaired. (And for those who do succumb to serious mental disorder, treatment by native doctors using healing methods handed down from the past, is often highly effective.)

Coping with tension

Magic. Today, we describe as magic any non-scientific means used to attain ends. The magic may be directed at increasing one's own personal power or ability to influence or affect other persons, or at controlling the impersonal world. And such use of magic was, of course, very widespread in traditional societies. Although the farmer often showed great skill in assessing soil fertility and deciding which crop variety to plant, he sought, too, to ensure favourable weather and a good harvest by burying, for example, a pot of 'medicine' in his field. He probably saw this latter action as no less rational than his assessment of fertility, even though he had far less empirical proof of the effect of the 'medicine' than of the correlation of crop varieties and soil conditions. We see his use of magic as a rite symbolizing the importance to him of the climate and assuaging his anxiety in situations of possible danger or misfortune.

Most of today's educated West Africans have grown up in homes where traditional attitudes were held towards magic; it is, therefore, hardly surprising that almost all these men and women still to some extent believe in magical forces. But to cope with the modern world, new methods are sought. The magazine *Drum*, though often featuring articles designed to reduce belief in magic and witchcraft and to stimulate the values more appropriate to modernizing societies, contains all the same scores of advertisements for talismans, Indian charms, power pills, memory cures, the later Books of Moses and other literature promising to reveal the secrets of the oriental religions. The scholar buys these, as well as the more humble potions sold perhaps in the local market, in order to ensure his success in examinations. He seeks the personal power to write impeccable answers; he aspires to influence the examiner; he hopes that the questions will be revealed to him in dreams. Similarly, magic is employed to ensure success in business.

Such use of magic does not seem to reduce the amount of more rational effort directed towards the desired goal. The student buys his charms, but still reads through the night. Indeed, the talisman may so allay his anxiety as to facilitate the increased effort. It is not likely, however, to make him re-evaluate his energies to see whether his effort is, in fact, well spent. And when the examination results produce disappointment, much of the blame may be attributed to the magic; either it was a useless charm, or one did not use it correctly.

Bribery. One can rarely read of contemporary West African states without finding references to bribery. Ministers receive from contractors whose bids have been successful a present in cash, or perhaps a block of flats to let. In local government all the councillors want to sit on the Establishment and Works Committee, where bribes are frequent; few are anxious to sit on the Education and Health Committees. The police constable delays the issue of a driving licence until considerably more than the statutory fee has been received. The scholarship applicant gets his influential friend to telephone education officials to ensure that they deal 'favourably' with his forms. And as political leaders fall, the call to end corruption rings forth.

In mitigation, it is argued that in African societies corruption is difficult to define. Office-holders in traditional societies received much of their remuneration in gifts for services rendered, and the ambitious regularly advanced their interests through the patronage of the more influential members of the community. In general, the lavishness of gift exchange greatly exceeded that in contemporary Western society (which is not without its system of bribes). And in contrast, the impersonality of bureaucratic relationships is alien to the African. Nevertheless, West Africans have accepted that officials should do their duty without extra remuneration, and the bribe is given unwillingly even when regarded as inevitable. Again, it is argued that the high degree of bureaucratic control inherited from and developed since the colonial period leads to administrative paralysis when so many civil servants are young and relatively inexperienced. Bribery and the use of personal influence cut through the red-tape so that some action is taken, even if the beneficiary is the person with the most pull rather than the one with the strongest claims.

Those who give bribes claim that, since everyone else does so, their own claims will be disregarded if they do not follow suit. Many illiterate persons, unable to understand printed forms, will bring gifts to the official to solicit his help, supposedly beyond his formal duty, in filling them in correctly. And those who receive bribes will in self-defence point to the practices of those in higher positions. Yet the degree of such corruption seems linked again with the speed of social mobility and the vast differences in income between those who are very successful and those who are only moderately so. The junior clerk or primary school teacher refers to the more successful man as a former colleague who was less diligent and ranked lower in class at school. How, therefore, has he managed to do so much better? Differences in the age at which a student reaches his peak academic form are not understood or used in explanation. The success of the other man is attributed to his use of patronage, his ability to bribe adequately; and inasmuch as he has got ahead by non-academic means, so is one entitled to redress the difference by the same means. Bribery is, perhaps, the correlate of the highly competitive society in which the means of success are not completely understood.

We have described both magic and bribery as methods used either to achieve success in the modern occupational sphere or to mitigate the anxiety produced by striving. In the first case, the methods used are non-scientific; in the second, non-bureaucratic.

By some of those employing these means, this analysis will not be accepted; they believe in the efficacy of magic, in the propriety of bribes. But most educated men will, if pressed, admit to an ambivalence in their attitude; they deny the magic, yet use it; they condemn bribery, yet practise it. This in itself can create tensions for which further remedies need to be found.

Aggression. The ruthlessness with which African political leaders are apt to repress opposition is usually exclaimed over with horror in the Western press, even though the methods are little different from those of the preceding colonial governments. In both periods the rulers have feared not only organized rebellion but, even more perhaps, outbreaks of mob violence, which are much more difficult to control. A few Nigerian examples will illustrate this phenomenon.

In 1960, when most Nigerians were celebrating Independence, the Tiv were fighting. A highly egalitarian people, they believed, traditionally, that any increase in the influence or power of one man could be attributed to his use of witchcraft against his near kin. In the pre-colonial period the Tiv lacked any institutionalized positions of authority; but colonial rule was impossible without such offices, and men were gazetted as village and district heads. The early rebellions against those in authority took the overt form of witch-hunts. Later, local government was introduced, and again the elected councillors became powerful, wealthy and entrenched; they allied themselves with the ruling N.P.C. although the masses, more than among any other Middle Belt people, voted against this party. Opposition to the councillors was undoubtedly stimulated by the leaders of rival political parties; but the resultant looting, murder and arson, directed in general against those in authority, was not led by these men and did not diminish following their arrest. Violence, indeed, continued sporadically for the next five years.

In 1957, Adegoke Adelabu, the charismatic political leader of Ibadan, was killed in a car accident. The Ibadan people had looked to him to restore their town to its former glory, ending its apparent exploitation by wealthier and better-educated neighbouring Yoruba groups. His loss was a bitter blow to Ibadan's prestige. As an immediate response, gangs of youths began to roam the streets, especially in the peripheral areas inhabited by strangers, overturning cars. And in the next few days some village tax collectors were killed, as individuals sought to use this period of apparent licence to settle old grievances.

University students have frequently marched through the streets of Lagos bearing placards that voice their disapproval of specific government policies. Many of these demonstrations have led to no disorder; but on some occasions, bystanders have joined the procession and begun throwing stones, thus creating a mêlée which the police have then sought to control with tear gas.

In the last weeks of 1965, and until the January 1966 army coup, the main road into Lagos was virtually closed by marauding gangs, who demanded large sums of money as the price of allowing a car to pass freely; travellers who refused to pay had their cars sprayed with petrol and fired. Similar violence occurred elsewhere in the Western Region. In the weeks before the Regional election of October 1965, the paid thugs of the political parties had been engaged in beating up leaders of rival parties, and in protecting their own leaders. The unemployment of these men after the election was cited as one cause of the continuing violence, but it seems likely that others had formed new groups. In the later period, the violence was directed not against political activists but against the persons and property of the prosperous elite.

Each of these outbreaks has been characterized by a lack of obvious leadership; it is difficult to discover who committed the first act of violence that set the example for others. After the events, no ringleaders are remembered as heroes. The marauders are not popular bandits robbing the rich to give to the poor; they destroy property rather than redistribute it. They have no clear social aims. Their violence seems to result from a mounting tension which has been able to find no other outlet. The likelihood of outbreaks would seem to increase as the politicians become more firmly entrenched in power and as elections give the masses less opportunity to express views hostile to those in power; they would seem to increase, too, with the growing number of unemployed primary school leavers who flock to the towns but are unable to find work. The much used social-psychological hypothesis that aggression is the result of frustration seems applicable. Much of the violence is directed against those in authority and against the existing government, but many of those who suffer are simply members of the elite. And it is from these people that the demands for strong repression come.

Conspicuous by their absence from West Africa are movements denying the benefits of Western technology. No major leaders have emerged arguing for a return to the simple life of the farm or the rejection of any untraditional tools. Perhaps West African technology was rather too simple to be so espoused. A small community living on the Nigerian coast according to basic communist principles possesses, indeed, as a result of its own effort, a highly mechanized sea fishing fleet and its own electricity plant; its members are, by the standards of neighbouring fishing communities, very prosperous. Nor has West Africa experienced movements such as the 'cargo cults' of Melanesia, where, frustrated by the inability to attain Western goods and unable to express the frustration through political channels, the people have retreated into a world of fantasy, believing that their 'white gods' will one day reappear with cargoes of goods for general distribution. For, in West Africa, European trade goods and luxuries have been, for many decades, widely available. The means of obtaining these (through migration for wages, or the growing of export crops) are both well known and available. Individuals have moved into the new elite to demonstrate that this route to success is open, albeit narrow. In recent years the nationalist political parties have promised to the masses a future of 'freedom' – implying in the minds of many illiterate men and women an immediate increase in wealth. For many, the adherence to the party and the adulation of its leader have characteristics of a millenary cult. Disillusion rapidly sets in after independence, however, as the improved living standards fail to materialize.

Fears of witchcraft

The great disparity between the aspirations of most West Africans and their real chances of success leads to a high rate of failure. And the response to these failures tends to be extra-punitive;

the individual does not blame his own shortcomings but shifts the responsibility to external agents. In the Cornell survey at Abeokuta, a half of those suffering certain or probable mental disorder believed that they were bewitched; nearly a quarter, that sorcery was being used against them. By many, talismans purchased to ensure success were described as 'not strong enough' to counter other forces. Rather fewer people ascribed their failures to their neglect of traditional deities, the omission of sacrifices or infringement of taboos. Witchcraft, however, is feared not only by those who fail but perhaps even more so by the successful. The young man who is financed at university by a large number of near kin fears the envy of his less fortunate half-brothers and cousins – or, more especially, that of their mothers. The wealthy man suspects that his relatives expect greater benefits from his affluence than he is willing to share with them.

Anxieties of this type certainly existed in traditional societies; the modern world has provided merely a new range of situations. It is impossible to tell whether witchcraft is more widely feared today than a few decades ago. In recent years, and especially at times of economic crisis, new anti-witchcraft agencies have been established; but many of these have been of a transitory nature, perhaps replacing earlier, equally ephemeral phenomena, and we cannot with certainty describe them as peculiarly twentieth century. There is, however, considerable evidence that many of the traditional methods of combating witchcraft are losing their effect.

To the spread of Christianity is attributed a general increase in moral laxity. Traditional deities were believed to punish swiftly and sternly. But the Protestant is taught that salvation can be gained through faith alone; the Roman Catholic confesses, and is forgiven his sins. Consequently one fears that one's enemies will be more likely to employ witchcraft or sorcery against one. Traditional methods of detecting witches are falling into abeyance. One such method, employed in southern Ghana and in the Niger delta, was to carry a corpse on a stretcher through the village; the deceased would 'direct' the carriers towards the house or person that had caused his death. Many oaths, once greatly feared, are no longer employed; some of these were used in customary courts in the early decades of this century, but were subsequently banned by the colonial governments. Parties to a case who made incompatible statements were required to swear the veracity of their own version before the local deity; the liar would, it was believed, die within a short period. Little fear attaches to oaths made on the Bible – unless, as many believe, it is opened at the story of Ananias and Sapphira, and the lips touch the verses describing their untruthfulness and subsequent sudden deaths. Trials by ordeal, in which all suspects were required to drink a poisonous potion such as sasswood, so that the guilty might die and the innocent be saved through vomiting, have been similarly banned by governments.

To allay these fears of increased insecurity against witchcraft and sorcery there has, in recent years, developed a profusion of new anti-witchcraft shrines and of religious sects. The former operate almost entirely within the context of traditional beliefs, while the latter, founded by men and women who have often been prominent church members, are syncretist in character. The growing popularity of both indicates the degree to which the mission-established churches have failed to respond to the needs of their congregations. Such shrines and sects would seem to be much less common in the Islamic areas, perhaps because these tend to be economically backward but more probably because the Muslim religion, as taught and understood in West Africa, is far more accommodating to traditional beliefs about witchcraft and magic.

Anti-witchcraft shrines and witch hunts. The development of new shrines in Ghana offering protection against witchcraft has been described very fully by Field.[141] Of twenty-nine shrines located within one small area of Ashanti, only three were ancient; three were established about the time of the 1918 influenza epidemic; and twenty-one were less than ten years old. All the recent shrines were privately owned and profit-making. The shrines fall into two categories. At one, the suppliant first seeks the support of the deity through sacrificing a chicken: if it eventually rests breast upwards, the deity's approval is assumed; if it falls otherwise, the suppliant must search his heart, confess more sins, and make a fresh sacrifice. The approval of the deity secured, the suppliant eats a consecrated kola nut or perhaps ritually bathes to symbolize the pact made with the deity. The priests at such shrines rank as private practitioners of native medicine and pay several guineas a year to their local government councils for licences to practise.

In the shrines of the second category, the priest becomes possessed by the deity and in his trance conveys to the suppliant the deity's advice or predictions. The seances are conducted with much ritual and pageantry. Elders and assistants control the flow of suppliants; the frenzied beating of drums facilitates the possession of the priest; chickens or eggs are offered to the deity to discover whether the requests have been propitiously received.

A popular shrine may be visited by a hundred suppliants in a day; others, by only half a dozen. Among those who come are both the illiterate and the educated, the rich and the poor. Most are not severely ill, but merely seek to allay anxieties; some of the most frequent complaints include general cases of 'not prospering', unspecified sicknesses, and infertility (all of which misfortunes may be attributed to witchcraft rather than to natural causes). And many of the suppliants come to the shrine to offer thanks for prayers answered, protection granted.

The protection offered by the deities of these shrines, and the requests made of them, are granted conditionally upon the suppliant's maintaining strict rules of conduct. He must not steal, commit adultery, or bear false witness against another person; he must not practise witchcraft or sorcery, and must not curse others. Should he break any of these rules, the deity will first make him sick or mentally disturbed, so giving him a chance to repent; if he fails to mend his ways, the deity will cause his death or permanent madness. Similar fates await anyone who wrongs, in these specified ways, the protected suppliant. And the forbidden acts are significant in reflecting the fears of men and women. The decline in traditional methods of divination is believed to result in more thefts passing undetected, while those who are brought before the courts seem lightly punished. In societies where a strong emotional relationship between husband and wife is unusual, men continually fear that their wives will leave them for men more wealthy or physically potent than themselves. Jealousies so aroused are believed to be a common cause of sorcery.

One of the better known of the new Ghanaian cults is *Tigari*. Adherents pay a fee for membership, and obedience to the rules of the deity, listed in a manner similar to the Ten Commandments, is obligatory for life. Paralleling this obvious Christian influence are Muslim elements, too, reflected in the dress of the priests and some of the rituals. The priest is possessed on ceremonial occasions, but the bond between suppliant and deity is usually made with the eating of a kola nut. The term *tigari* itself became used to describe any anti-witch shrines and also a witch-finding movement which in the late 1940s and early 1950s spread into Dahomey and Western Nigeria, in the latter area being known as *atinga*.

A band of people called *alatinga* arrived in the Egbado Division of Western Nigeria at the end of 1950. They claimed that they would only visit a town upon the request of its elders – a request often accompanied by a gift of hundreds of pounds (though this is said to have been returned to host chiefs in return for free board and lodging). They then erected a shrine and, after ritual sacrifices, prepared consecrated kola nuts which were sold for a shilling or two a piece. This kola protected one against one's enemies, as long as one observed the taboos on stealing, adultery and witchcraft. In addition, the *atinga* cult members danced themselves into states of possession in which they were allegedly able to recognize witches; in one town of ten thousand people, nearly five hundred women were so designated. When these women confessed, sometimes after further divinations, they were asked to bring all their evil materials to the cult shrine for destruction, to be cleansed by ritual washing and to eat the consecrated kola (so that any further witchcraft by them would be punished by *atinga* with death). Considerable force was used against some women to gain confessions.[142]

A corollary of the visitation by the *alatinga* was the destruction of many shrines to descent group deities, the wooden images and other paraphernalia being piled in heaps at the *atinga* shrines. Only those traditional cults largely concerned with witch-finding escaped relatively unscathed. And five years later, long after the end of the *atinga* movement, the traditional shrines had not been rebuilt. Thus this witch-finding movement not only developed in response to the weakness of the traditional deities (and may have found wide support among Christians and Muslims, because it was not directly associated with these deities) but in its turn reduced them to greater impotence, thus increasing the void left between the traditional and modern religions.

New sects

Whilst the priests of the anti-witchcraft shrines and movements claim to serve deities of traditional type, those of the modern sectarian movements acknowledge the Christian god. Many of them are men who have left the Mission churches because of rivalries for leadership, disagreement over doctrine, or failure to find emotional satisfaction. The number of such sects and of their congregations seems to have increased rapidly in recent years. In Ibadan, for instance, 8 congregations of *aladura* or 'prayer' sects existed in 1940; by 1950 the number had grown to 21, and by 1962 to 83. In Accra 17 different sects were counted in 1955. In their profusion, the new sects exhibit considerable variety. Whilst some substantially retain the liturgy of the Protestant churches, others are syncretist in character, with spirit possession among the priests (and perhaps the congregation) and dancing and drumming during services. Many of them base their doctrine almost completely upon the efficacy of prayer, and their function upon healing. In most cases, the priests are believed to be divinely inspired, their vocation having been described to them in dreams; sometimes the call takes a traditional form – a mild mental illness indicates to a man that he has been selected for leadership. Most congregations are small, and fission is common. Yet a few sects have succeeded in establishing a number of branches and in solving the problems inherent in providing successors to the original founders.

Most of the new sects have developed in areas which had already experienced a decade or more of mission influence; but there have been a few recorded instances of successful proselytizing in hitherto unevangelized areas. One of the most spectacular of these was the brief activity in the Ivory Coast and western Gold Coast of William Harris.

Harris was the nephew of a Methodist pastor in Liberia, and his life seems to have been uneventful until, about sixty years old, he began his mission. Clad in a long white gown and white turban, and carrying a roughly-hewn wooden cross and a Bible, he travelled between 1913 and 1915 through the villages of the southern Ivory Coast, living simply from the gifts offered to him on his journeys. He claimed no special authority for himself but described himself as the envoy of God, sent by the angel Gabriel. He preached the dignity of labour and obedience to authority; he condemned alcohol, theft and adultery, but permitted polygyny. He taught that Sunday should be a day of rest. He denounced all forms of traditional religion and called for the destruction of sacred groves. He baptized but did not practise healing, though stories exist of women who were convulsed and cured by touching his cross. In each village, Harris appointed twelve apostles to act as elders of the local church and continue his work until the coming of the missionaries. The French colonial government initially approved of his work, believing that much of the disorder in the country was due to 'witch doctors'. Later, however, they exiled him and made perfunctory attempts to destroy his churches. It seems that among his 100,000 converts were some dismissed government clerks who, claiming to be 'sons of God', alleged that the French would soon leave the country and that taxes would be reduced. Such sedition was not to be tolerated by the government in the early years of a world war. But the congregations started by Harris continued in good heart, their Bibles remaining the central objects of the little churches even though nobody could read them. Ten years after Harris's exile, Methodist missions began work in this area, building upon these earlier foundations. And to the present day, the traditional religious cults have not been revived.[141]

A somewhat similar movement occurred in south-western Nigeria in 1930. Joseph Babalola, literate only in Yoruba and employed driving a steam-roller, felt a call to preach; and an initial disinclination to obey was overcome when, as a sign from God, his roller was disabled. Baptized into the Faith Tabernacle sect, he attended a meeting of the leaders at Ilesha and suddenly began dramatic healings. News spread rapidly, and for six weeks he healed, praying over water brought by the suppliants. Some alleged that witches who did not confess but who drank the consecrated water would die. Like Harris, he commanded people to turn from their traditional beliefs and burn their idols and charms.

One of the Ghanaian sects, the Church of the Twelve Apostles, was founded by two converts of Harris himself, and after their death leadership passed to John Hackman, an illiterate who remained Bishop until his death in 1957. In these decades the sect established a large number of sub-stations, but its central organization and discipline became, after Hackman's death, very lax. Today, educational levels among members of the sect tend to be very low. The sect claims to subscribe to the same articles of faith as does the Methodist church, but in fact emphasis is laid almost exclusively upon the activity of the Holy Spirit in enabling men and women to predict the future, detect evil and cure illness. The Bible plays a prominent part in the meetings but is not read; it is held over the head of those seeking baptism or cure. Priests and congregation possess gourd rattles which are used in rituals and which would seem to possess the power to chase away evil spirits. Certain foods are tabooed; smoking is prohibited; wine and beer are allowed in moderate quantities only; and fasting is enjoined. Polygyny is permitted, but no divorced person may marry another member of the same local congregation.

Each priest maintains a 'garden', a compound wherein live ten or twenty people seeking healing through the church. A huge white cross stands in the centre of the compound, and at its foot is a basin of consecrated water. A large shed serves as the main place of worship for the regular services of prayer, and for the healing sessions which are usually held on Fridays. The Church of the Twelve Apostles does not prohibit the use of Western medicine or traditional herbal remedies, but will have nothing to do with people who have sought help from the traditional shrines. Suppliants strip to the waist and carry a basin of consecrated water on their heads; the priests begin with prayers, and then the drummers whip up a frenzied rhythm, while the priests move among the suppliants sprinkling them with water. The suppliants go into trances until physically exhausted, and their states of ecstasy, aided by the consecrated water, are held to effect the desired cures.

This Ghanaian example could be both contrasted and paralleled with many others in that country and in its neighbours. But, whatever their differences in liturgy and ritual, the new sects share many common functions.[145]

Unlike the anti-witchcraft shrines which are tolerant of other religions, their priests regarding their own protecting deity as one among many, the sects tend to be exclusive. In some cases membership is compatible with adherence to a mission-established church; but, generally, the sects forbid their members to make any use of traditional religious practices. Observers feel that these injunctions are upheld, and that sectarians patronize the native doctors and priests much less than do church members. The emphasis is placed upon faith and prayer as the means of healing. Supported by the references to miracle healing in the New Testament, the priests of the sects cure both by teaching the afflicted and by inducing states of possession in which the evil spirit is thought to leave the body. And by similar means they are supposedly able to ward off witchcraft or sorcery threatened against their suppliants.

Members of the sects are expected to uphold a strict moral code. Their frequent meetings together as congregations enable effective informal sanctions to be applied among members, and less emphasis seems to lie on supernatural sanctions than in the edicts of the shrines. The ban on the remarriage of the divorced to local members is an obvious attempt to forestall the coveting of other men's wives. The priests, divinely inspired, are always available to advise on courses of action when the prevailing norms are vaguely expressed and conflicting. Again, strictly literal interpretations of Biblical passages may be used to justify unorthodox behaviour. Many of the sects, whilst rejecting the Western values of the Mission Churches, do serve to facilitate the modification of traditional behaviour patterns. The Church of the Twelve Apostles, for example, stresses the obligation of the father to provide for his children until their marriage, and of children to care for their fathers in their old age; these are radical innovations in matrilineal Akan society. Generally the sects permit polygyny but some try to limit the number of wives a man may take. One Ghanaian sect prohibits divorce among its members but ameliorates the traditional customs which widows are expected to observe, reducing the mourning period from a year to two or three months and omitting several repugnant rites.

In most of the sects women constitute a majority of the congregation. In part, this is because their demands for conception, for safe delivery and for the health of their children are most persistent. In addition, however, the sects offer to their women members roles, of priestess and acolyte, which are usually closed to them both in traditional religious cults and in the Christian churches.

In societies where stratification by wealth is becoming increasingly dominant, the sects promote egalitarian sentiment. In some there are few officers, and members wear rough clothes or simple white gowns. Others have a complex hierarchy of priestly offices, with robes appropriately distinguished; but the offices are rarely held by men who have attained high ranking status in secular spheres. Many priests are humble men whilst their congregations attract rich and poor alike. This contrasts with the mission-established churches, where offices tend to be held by the wealthy and educated, and where these same men use the church as a place in which to display their power or affluence, with the apparent connivance of the churches themselves. Inasmuch as the membership of the sects is stratified, it is a stratification which differs in its basis of recruitment from that of the secular world. Those who have failed to realize their aspirations in this sphere, may be rewarded with new opportunities or with a more egalitarian atmosphere in the sects. Membership of these sects would seem, therefore, to be more attractive to the barely literate clerical and manual workers; nevertheless, those who have been more successful may be drawn by the reputations of one or other of the sects for healing and granting prayers for further prosperity.

The use of magic and the shrines provide for the individual the means of supposedly manipulating the real world and of allaying anxieties. To a large extent the sects fulfil the same functions. But whereas most suppliants at the shrines attend only when they have specific requests to make or thanks to offer, the sects have continuing congregations of members. For many, if not perhaps all of these members, the sect provides a community in which they can withdraw to some extent from the real world. The moral code of this community, validated by superhuman authority, is at variance with that of the outside world, being better adapted to the needs of its members, more rigidly defined, and ethically superior. The sect dominates the whole life of its members. To its faithful adherents, it promises rewards in the life to come, in the form of a status more privileged than that available to other men. (The shrines, in contrast, provide benefits only in this world.) Furthermore, it offers to its urban members much of the emotional support that might otherwise be gained from kinsmen.

Shrines and sects, magic, bribery and aggression all serve as means whereby the anxieties and frustrations of the changing society may be alleviated. To the extent that they relieve individual tension and reduce the amount of severe mental illness, these agencies are obviously beneficial to the society. But on other counts they may be maladjustive, inhibiting rather than promoting rapid social and economic development. To what extent, for instance, may the reliance on external factors in accounting for failure to realize one's goals inhibit both the rational reassessment of one's chances, with the modification of those goals, and the examination of one's own inadequacies? How far may the successful man's fears of witchcraft impede rational action? On the other hand, may not the channelling of discontent into religious movements diminish the force of direct political action, thus contributing to the stability of the state? How far do beliefs in supernatural forces prevent the growth of a scientific mode of thought? Or will beliefs in witchcraft disappear rapidly with the spread of education?

Part 4

Stagnation or Revolution

11 Ideologies

We have seen how some of the indigenous institutions of West Africa are being transformed as they adapt to the changing economic and political structures of societies. Relationships within the family are adjusted to accord with new patterns of residence; as some of the traditional methods of coping with frustration and anxiety become obsolescent, new ones develop. In the modern urban areas men and women have, in seeking for economic security, formed new associations, some of these – the trade unions – being of Western introduction, and others – the ethnic associations – being traditionalist. The growing Western-educated elite have created the political parties which won independence for their countries and political power for their own members. We have examined each of these institutional spheres, isolating them to a considerable degree from the total society to which they belong. We must now try to see these West African societies in their totality, and to encompass within a single framework all the processes of change taking place within them.

The question that all must ask is 'What is the future of the independent West African states?' Will the hopes of their people, that their standards of living will rise to meet those of the industrial nations, ever be realized? Will their leaders successfully accomplish the revolution from tribal to modern society? Or will these states stagnate economically, their political life punctuated by repeated rebellions which bring new men into power but no new solution to the problems of poverty? Economically, the future of West African states does not seem very bright. Though their leaders hope for rapid industrialization, the markets offered by their small and poor populations are inadequate to support the manufacture of most consumer goods; only in Nigeria is such a market commercially attractive. Again, it seems improbable that rich mineral resources remain to be discovered; and if they were to be found, they would increase natural wealth but also perpetuate the 'colonial' type of economy. These forecasts are, however, made in terms of the technology we have today; we cannot imagine what new inventions and processes may radically alter the location of industry in the coming century.

In the immediate future, the rate of development will depend to a large degree upon the role played by the Western-educated elites – upon their size and their levels of education and training, and upon the ability of their members to analyse the problems facing their countries. They face a task that seems peculiar to the developing nations of the twentieth century; in nineteenth-century Western Europe, it was the craftsman and small entrepreneur who promoted industrial development, not the university graduate with his liberal education. The small size of these new elites necessitates cohesion and enthusiasm among their members, but these will be vitiated by continual struggles for power between different groups or by the retreat of the frustrated into bureaucratic ritualism. In few countries have such high proportions of the well-educated entered the public services with such a sense of their mission to improve the living standards of their people; yet these hopes can so easily turn within a few years to cynicism as efforts seem thwarted or ineffectual. Much will depend, too, upon the relationship that exists between the elites and the masses; upon the extent to which the former can obtain, at least the acquiescence of the people in their leadership, at best their active support in the tasks of modernization.

In earlier sections we have noted the conflicts that already exist or that may develop, both within the elites and between the elites and the masses. Competition exists between groups of the elite for control of political power; and this may be analysed in terms of the criteria by which the highest offices are distributed. Conflict thus exists between different generations of elite – the older claiming authority by virtue of their seniority; the younger, by their higher educational levels. Conflict exists, too, between civil servants, whose right to office is seen to be based upon educational criteria, and the senior party members and officials who have been rewarded for their loyalty to their leader and cause. The majority of the contemporary elite were born into humble families, and although they now live in affluence, they still retain close ties with their homes areas. Yet the gap between their salaries and privileges and those of the peasant farmer or urban labourer shows few signs of decreasing. The educational system operates, indeed, to ensure that the children of the elite have marked advantages in gaining admission to secondary schools and universities and thus retaining the status of their parents. Thus the elite becomes far less open to the recruitment of new members and may become, within a few decades, an all but closed aristocracy. The sense of frustration among the masses increases, for not only does their own standard of living fail to rise (as they believed it would after Independence) but also the opportunities seem to grow less for themselves and their children to enter the privileged elite. With each decade the members of the elite draw further away from the masses, and the pride once shown in the success of the local boy turns to anger as the expected benefits fail to materialize.

Competition within the elites and conflict between the elite and the masses could, in each West African state, lead to such overt hostility as would halt the modernizing process or, in the last resort, cause the collapse of the entire modern sector of the economy. One method of avoiding such overt hostility lies in the development of procedures through which conflicts are mediated, so that each faction supports, at least for the time being, an agreed solution. Secondly the consciousness of the conflicting interests may be reduced through the acceptance of ideologies stressing unity or through the cross-cutting of other divisions with society – in the West African case, especially, of ethnic divisions which, in stressing primordial loyalties, counter national unity but also obscure national distinctions of wealth and privilege.

Ideological themes

An ideology enshrines the popularly accepted ideas about the structure and processes of society, interpreting the society's history and providing a basis for the evaluation of new experience. It incorporates a statement of the goals and values approved by the society. The Western-educated elites of West Africa have fashioned ideologies which define their own role in their societies. Unlike the ideologies of societies undergoing only slow change, which tend to be implicit – few Englishmen could describe their own national ideology – the ideologies of West Africa are the subject of constant discussion and explanation, however vaguely they may sometimes appear to be formulated. They would seem to fulfil two functions.

First, the members of the new elites seek an ideology which will provide them with an identity. As individuals they have experienced both the life of traditional African society and that of the industrial Western world. All have rejected at least some of the values of the former and consequently experienced reproof from their elders or feelings of guilt. In accepting the technology of the West and acknowledging its superiority, they feel drawn towards declaiming the superiority of Western values, too. In their uncertainty they seek for guiding principles, defining the relationship between African and Western society. This uncertainty is experienced most markedly by those who have become most assimilated to Western ways – those members of the elite of the French-speaking territories, for instance, who have lived for several years in Paris – and least, by the educated Fulani of the northern Nigerian emirates, whose local schooling has scarcely divorced them from their Muslim heritage, or by the Americo-Liberian of Monrovia and creole of Freetown, whose forebears have already institutionalized a syncretist culture.

Secondly, the elites seek to legitimize their rule. They have attained political power, as politicians and civil servants, by virtue of their education and by the ballot box, neither of which existed in traditional society. No traditional sanctions, therefore, exist by which the new leaders may justify their rule, although some have, after their accession to power, sought to assume the traditional symbols of chieftaincy. The elite must thus espouse a doctrine that purports to explain and justify its leadership, converting political power into authority. And the ideology must find acceptance not only among the elite but also among the masses. For the alternative to a general acceptance of the legitimacy of government is rule by coercion.

In those states where the government seeks to mobilize the entire population in the task of modernization, and controls those associations directed to this end, the ideology of the elite is fashioned as a mass religion. The political philosophy of the leaders, espoused by a militant party organization, becomes a cause with which the entire population may identify itself. The whole of social life is politicized. The leader becomes a messiah – a man of the people, yet remote from them. With the acceptance of such an ideology, primordial ethnic loyalties are discouraged and weaken.

It is thus in Guinea, Mali and Nkrumah's Ghana that the new ideologies have been most precisely defined and enunciated, becoming the official doctrines of the ruling parties rather than the individually expressed opinions of members of an elite. The younger intellectuals in other countries have been continually attracted by the formulations of the leaders of the mobilizing states, and critical of the lack of any clear lead from their own more pragmatic leaders.

Two fundamental themes dominate current West African ideologies – *Négritude* or the African Personality, and African Socialism.[151]

The term *Négritude* was coined by the West Indian poet Aimé Césaire in 1939, was almost immediately adopted by Léopold Senghor, and has since held sway among the French-speaking elite of West Africa. The concept of the African Personality has developed among English-speaking West Africans since it was first popularized by Nkrumah in 1958. The current usages of these two related concepts range widely. At one extreme are those who use the term African Personality simply to denote the equality of Africans with all other peoples of the world, thus justifying their right to self-determination and their claim that their voices should be heard in world councils with the same attention accorded those of other nations. Those who use the term in this way would not necessarily imply that the paramount values in African society are any different from those of Western society. Others, however, and here one would include the proponents of *Négritude*, would hold that African values are different from, and morally equal to, those of the West. Indeed, some would assert that many of these values are superior to those of the West and ought to be construed as Africa's contribution to human society. A recurrent theme in the exposition of *Négritude* is thus the preservation of these values in a modern economy. Less positively, the African Personality may be used to justify ends and means which are diametrically opposed to those of the Western ideologies; those who basically accept Western values, but fear that Africans will fall short in their efforts to uphold them, use the term to cover their embarrassment at seeking what they themselves consider to be less worthy goals.

Most of the African governments, with the notable exceptions of the Liberian and Northern Nigerian, have claimed to be socialist. Yet the 'Colloquium on Policies of Development and African Approaches to Socialism', attended at Dakar in December 1962 by intellectuals and political leaders from a wide variety of African states, failed to provide any clear or concise definitions of African Socialism. The term is popular inasmuch as it implies a scientific approach to human problems; and it is also identified with planning and specific codes of action. It seems an appropriate term when so much of the ideology of the West African elite is phrased in Marxist language. Yet it is realized by the proponents of African Socialism that Marx's analysis of Western-European capitalism in the mid-nineteenth century is scarcely relevant to twentieth-century West African societies, where land is still corporately held by descent groups, and industry – owned by the state or by expatriate companies – is a small portion of the economy. Educated Africans hope, indeed, that they may be able to modernize their societies without causing the human suffering that characterized the growth of towns in Western Europe or the compulsion associated with the development of the U.S.S.R. Again, the stress on the African-ness of their socialism safeguards the West African intellectuals against criticism that it falls short of connotations the term usually has in the West. Socialist forms are sought in traditional African societies and are reaffirmed as the basis of the new society.

The content of these ideologies must be seen in relation to the experiences of the Western-educated elites during the past century; it cannot be divorced from the intellectual background and the emotional needs of these men. But backgrounds and needs are uniform neither in place nor in time. We may, in fact, postulate four stages. In the first, appropriate to English-speaking territories in the nineteen thcentury and to French-speaking territories until the end of the Second World War, the African ideologies are a reaction against assimilation. The African is permitted social equality with Europeans and may attain high ranking offices, but only insofar as he accepts European styles of living and denies his African culture. Some men have been quite ready to make this sacrifice; others with a sudden shock realize their alienation from their past only after years of Western education. A second stage, appropriate to the colonial period, especially in British territories, is one of discrimination against the African in public offices, with the consequent frustration of those who feel that they are denied the legitimate rewards of their academic achievements. Ideologies of political protest are typical. In the third stage, with the end of colonialism, the positive aspects of building the new society are stressed. But as these aims, like independence and Africanization of the elite posts, are realized, the emphasis shifts, in a fourth stage, towards the preservation of the new structures.

Many ideological themes are common to each of these stages. For not only do the present leaders claim intellectual descent from the early nationalist writers, but many of those whose voices were loudest in the protest movements are now the heads of governments in the new states. Dennis Osadebay, first Premier of Nigeria's Mid-Western Region, was one of Nigeria's foremost poets of earlier decades. Senghor expressed the themes of *Négritude* in a collection of poems that he published in the late 1940s, and made African Socialism the dominant theme of his writings in the following decade. Whilst in the United States Azikiwe wrote articles for the *Journal of Negro History* on Nigerian history and political institutions, and on the ethics of imperialism. Then, in the early 1940s, he produced books and pamphlets on political reform; his *Political Blueprint of Nigeria* appeared in 1943. Four years later, Awolowo published his own manifesto, *Path to Nigerian Freedom*. But such men, once in power, produced not further political programmes but autobiographical works. The task of elaborating the ideologies of the independence period fell primarily to the leaders trying to mobilize the masses of their states – to Nkrumah and Sékou Touré.

The African ideologies are expressed in the intellectual language of twentieth-century Europe and America; but their themes may differ widely from those usually expressed in such language, and a Westerner may easily be misled. Hodgkin has argued that many of the basic ideas in the African ideologies closely parallel the central theses of Rousseau; though there is little evidence that even the French-speaking Africans were directly influenced by this philosopher. 'A certain kind of historical situation, certain fundamental human problems to be resolved, tend to stimulate a particular way of thinking about the situation and its problems.'[150] Contemporary African ideologies are most often expressed in Marxist terms. French-speaking Africans gained a close acquaintance with Marxist ideas during their student days in Paris; the intellectual traditions of that city led them to seek an integrated and consistent philosophy. African elected politicians sat with Communist deputies in the French Parliament; African scholars communed with Sartre and existentialism. Their counterparts in London were often attracted by the left wing political parties, but succeeded in gaining no more than a basic set of terms which later seemed inapplicable to Africa. Nkrumah claimed, on his return to England from his studies at American Negro universities, to be a 'Marxist socialist'. His view of Communism, however, was to be shaped in part by his association with George Padmore. A middle class West Indian intellectual, Padmore had spent several years in Moscow during the 1930s, but had become disillusioned by the manner in which the U.S.S.R. seemed to use the colonial peoples as tools for its own ends. He turned instead to Pan-Africanism, and, living in Accra from the early 1950s until his death, was active in establishing the various Pan-African agencies associated with the Ghanaian government and in developing Pan-Africanist ideologies. The terminology of Marxism has, however, proved useful to Africans in portraying the evils of capitalist society – its exploitation of the underdeveloped world and its alienation of man – while from Lenin have been sought the precepts of party organization.

An equally powerful influence has come from the Negro movements of the Americas. A few West Indian Negroes, notably Edmund Blyden, became prominent in nineteenth- and early twentieth-century West Africa. Africans in Paris met other scholars from the French American colonies; it was here that Senghor met Aimé Césaire from Martinique, the originator of *Négritude*. From the British colonies a few Africans began to attend American Negro universities in the 1930s and early 1940s. Not only did they here contact the movements of Marcus Garvey and W. E. B. DuBois, but on their return to their home territories found that their American degrees were regarded less highly than British ones. After teaching in American colleges, Azikiwe was refused a post in King's College, Lagos. Such a situation which continued into the 1950s (though not always without justification, for many Africans gained their degrees from American universities with poor academic reputations) served to enhance the militancy of the graduate from the United States, strengthening him in a commitment to the Pan-Negro struggle. Nkrumah's own respect for DuBois was manifest in his appointment of this aged leader as Director of the *Encyclopaedia Africana* – an enterprise established in Accra under the auspices of the Ghanaian Academy of Sciences.

In spite of their oft-avowed Marxism, none of the West African leaders is anti-religious. Senghor remains a sincere Roman Catholic, drawing much inspiration from Teilhard de Chardin. Awolowo has continued to be a staunch Methodist. Others, owing less ardent allegiance to the Mission churches, acknowledge traditional religious practices, pouring libations on public occasions. But in societies where so many of the educated elite are the product of mission-established schools (with churches themselves as agents of change and progress), and where the technological ignorance of the masses inhibits agnostic thinking, an attack on religious beliefs is likely to be highly unpopular.

The experience of the elite

The themes of *Négritude* were developed in Paris among the Negro scholars and students who felt assimilated to Left Bank intellectual society, and yet were painfully conscious of having denied their own traditional culture. It was essentially an expression of expatriates, to lose its meaning once they returned home and revived their relationships with their kin and communities. In Nigeria during the 1950s, interest in *Négritude* was confined largely to those men and women who had adopted an essentially European style of life – in the composition of their households, the furnishings of their homes, their modes of entertainment. The contemporary artistic florescence in this country has, however, come not from these men but largely from others who received their university and professional training in Nigeria. Thus 'Wole Soyinka, a graduate of the University of Ibadan, could cynically remark, 'I don't think a tiger has to go around proclaiming his tigritude'. Yet whether they are reacting against their own assimilation of Western ways, or, whilst feeling more secure in their membership of their traditional society, are consciously borrowing from the West those elements of culture which they deem appropriate, the educated West Africans discover a dilemma in the experience of their contact with the Western world.

In Africa, the young man soon registers the technological superiority of the white man, and imputes a corresponding moral superiority which legitimizes colonial rule. Disillusion follows when, on his visits to the metropolitan country, he sees white men performing the most menial tasks and even, perhaps, meets his senior colonial administrator strap-hanging in the Métro or Underground. Attitudes of racial superiority, tolerated in Africa where they were often blurred by political and economic domination, become more blatant in Europe. It is here the African learns that 'whites' hold negroid colouring and features more repugnant than those of the 'yellow' peoples of Asia. In those countries in which the Protestant ethic has been institutionalized, the African discovers that the poverty and technical backwardness of the colonial peoples are correlated with their moral failings.

A natural reaction to isolation and rejection is nostalgia. The life of one's African childhood is idealized. The warmth and succour provided by the wide circle of relatives in the village, the happiness of the playing children, are potent images in the cold foreign town. Senghor, in his poem *Femme Noire*, glorifies the Negro woman –

Naked woman, dark woman
Ripe fruit with firm flesh, sombre ecstasy of dark red wine, mouth
which makes mine lyrical.

And in much of his poetry, Senghor sees the ancestors as the bridge between himself and the society from which his education has drawn him away.[161]

As these themes are developed, characteristic traits of Western society are denigrated. African visitors to Europe are appalled by the emptiness of residential suburbia, its inhabitants each locked behind his own front door; they are shocked by the individualism stressed in family life – as when brothers educate their own, but not each other's children. For Senghor, the ills of Western society can be ascribed to the alienation of man, which derives from material progress and reaches its apogee in capitalist society. Not only has Africa so far escaped these ills, but the values inherent in traditional society are ones which could restore man to his true dignity in the modern industrial world. The values of Africa and Europe are thus judged not by the degree to which they are appropriate to their respective societies but by transcendent standards.

African definitions of socialism stem from the economic realities of the African states. The basic task of the new leaders is to increase the wealth of their people, but the redistribution of wealth is not a practical issue when the elite is so small. The economy is already largely state-controlled – a legacy of the colonial period. African entrepreneurs are few, and their number seems unlikely to increase very far very fast. Nationalist governments have often made loans to indigenous businessmen, but few of their enterprises have been successful; their failures have been due as much to their technical ignorance and entrepreneurial inefficiencies as to the inability to compete with the established expatriate companies. Political leaders have come to rely on state initiative not only from ideological conviction but also from expediency. Economic development thus rests with the Western-educated elite and its political organ, the party.

The years of colonial rule have convinced African leaders that *laissez-faire* policies will not lead to a reasonable rate of development. Planning of the economy is essential. Stimulus must be provided for industry either by creating favourable conditions for foreign investors or by direct state intervention in manufacturing. But few states can provide locally the capital necessary for such developments. The small but wealthy elite spends heavily on prestige symbols, and on the education of children; it saves little, though the recently introduced stock market in Nigeria is beginning to attract investment. The masses are too poor to save much, and politicians are reluctant to deny them some few tokens of increasing affluence. West African states, therefore, continue to rely heavily on foreign capital. In Ghana, the national plan ascribed to the foreign capitalists the role of providing the major industrial development – a field in which they were not likely to compete with indigenous enterprises and in which the managers of state corporations lacked the technological skills. In Guinea, the bauxite mines, accounting for one-half of the country's exports, are foreign-owned. Yet the ambivalence of political leaders who proclaim the need for state ownership and control of industry, whilst encouraging foreign enterprises, probably deters many private investors.

In spite of their hopes for industrialization, West African politicians realize that their countries will remain basically agricultural, and that improved farming must be a major contributor to economic development. Yet the methods of raising agricultural productivity are far from being clearly established. One country, Ghana, has emphasized the development of state farms; another, Nigeria (in the Western Region), has established settlements of peasant farmers who might be expected to gain an income similar to that of a skilled artisan. Yet developments of this type frequently require as much capital investment for each participant as do manufacturing industries. The poorer states are obliged to seek agricultural improvement through the establishment of village cooperatives and collective activities.

The assertion of an African form of socialism also enables the political leaders to pursue foreign policies of non-alignment. With their newly won independence, they are anxious that they should not appear subordinate to foreign powers – least of all to the former metropolitan countries. Yet it is these countries which still have the greatest financial stake in the erstwhile colonies, and which are most able and usually willing to provide technical assistance. Although the African leaders inveigh against the capitalist countries and their apparent reluctance to see the developing nations emerge from the bondage of a colonial economy, it is these same countries which, too, seem most likely to provide the capital for development. Though to balance their dependence on the West, they might turn for aid to the great socialist powers – the U.S.S.R. and China – the West African leaders remain suspicious of them. They are fearful of being used by them in the game of world politics. Neither the U.S.S.R. nor China is experienced in the problems of tropical development; and stories of the delivery of snow ploughs to Conakry spread rapidly. The social changes taking place in West Africa today do not fit easily into any of the classic Marxist patterns.

Myths of traditional society

The exponents of *Négritude*, the African Personality and African Socialism turn equally to traditional African societies, to seek an indigenous origin of those values which they seek now to extol and propagate. Such values thus provide a bridge between the Western living-styles adopted by the elite and the cultures in which they seek an identity. The image of traditional societies which is presented is, however, not one that accords with the studies of sociologists and anthropologists. In the early colonial period, men such as Sarbah and Ajisafe described with considerable accuracy the political and legal systems of Fanti and Yoruba kingdoms respectively. Today, the novels of Chinua Achebe show a deep insight into the social organization of the Ibo village in the precolonial and early colonial period. But such contributions have not come from any of those men who now lead the West African states and who usually belong to the generation most divorced from, and most ambivalent in their attitude to, their indigenous societies.

Stress is placed on the lack of conflict in indigenous African society. Social classes are seen by many African intellectuals as peculiar to Europe and to industrial society, and their possible introduction into Africa is viewed with repugnance. It is argued that traditional African societies were but minimally stratified, having little economic heterogeneity. Those scholars who admit that considerable differences in wealth and power could exist in traditional societies, add that the classes so created were not antagonistic and therefore not productive of a class conflict. Marxists who feel obliged to retain and use terminology of class and exploitation use it to describe the relationship between African states and the colonial or neo-colonial powers. The Africans are thus members of a single class, the consciousness and cohesion of which are fostered. In traditional society, the chiefs were not exploiting the masses; the leisure which they enjoyed was the just reward for the efforts of their youth; they are seen not as tyrants but as the defenders of their people, feeding them in times of poverty, safeguarding them from the attacks of their enemies.

Furthermore, African society differs from that of Europe in the treatment of the individual. For Senghor, European society

> is an assembly of individuals. ... Negro-African society puts more stress on the group than on the individual, more on solidarity than on the activity and needs of the individual, more on the communion of persons than on their autonomy. Ours is a community [*communitaire*] society. ... The member of the community society ... claims his autonomy to affirm himself as a being. But he feels, he thinks he can develop his potential, his originality, only in and by society, in union with all other men.[153, pp. 93–4]

Alienation did not exist in traditional African societies; and inasmuch as it exists in Africa today, it is the result of colonialism, of the domination of one country by another.

Seen in such simplistic terms, African society appears homogeneous; ethnic differences are only minor; ethnic hostilities are the result of the divide-and-rule policies pursued by the colonial powers. The values of African societies are Negro values (or Negro-Berber, in Senghor's terms, for he has had to accommodate the non-Negro populations of Senegal, and for a brief period, of Mali). They would seem to be dependent upon the biological characteristics of Negro peoples, and not upon their widely divergent social and political structures.

It is not difficult to see what such interpretations of traditional society imply in the contemporary social setting. African society, it is reasoned, remains classless, for the elite are not seen as exploiting the masses. The people are united against external powers; ethnic divisions within should soon, therefore, disappear. The political party is synonymous with the nation, and the efforts of the individual can only be achieved within the party. The uniformity of African societies, in their struggle against colonialism and in their own values, provides a basis for Pan-Africanist ideologies and organizations, transcending the political rivalries of neighbouring states and the difficulties of economic cooperation.

Contrasts in ideologies

The limited variety in the educational experiences of West African intellectuals, along with their common situation in the elites of developing nations with similar economic and social problems, has restricted the range of ideological expression. If we contrast the views of Senghor with those of Nkrumah, we are struck by the convergence of their philosophies in the past decade.

Senghor is, *par excellence*, the philosopher of *Négritude* and of African Socialism. In his long years in France, first as a student and later as a teacher, he developed, following his associations with Aimé Césaire and Sartre, as the poet of *Négritude*. Significantly the titles of his early volumes signified darkness – *Chants d'Ombres Hosties Noires, Éthiopiques*. The power of his poems does, in fact, derive from the degree to which he had been assimilated to French culture, and later sought to rediscover his Africa. *Négritude* does not, however, imply a return to all traditional ways; too much has already been borrowed from the West. Of imported religions, Senghor writes:

> Islam and Christianity gave us spiritual values as substitutes [for Negro animism]: more elaborate religions, more rational or, to repeat, more attuned to the present age. Once we have chosen them, it's our own task to adapt these religions to our historical and sociological conditions: it is our task to Negrophy them.[153, pp. 72–3]

But the African can give as well as receive.

> The problem which now faces us, Negroes of 1959, is to know how we can integrate Negro-African values into the world of 1959. There is no question of reviving the past, of living in a Negro-African museum; the question is to inspire this world, here and now, with the values of our past.[162, p. 291]

Senghor's analysis of the causes of Africa's backwardness and subjection developed but slowly. His scholarly appreciation of Marx was deepened with his political activity. But it is the humanistic themes of the pre-1848 Marx that attract him – the themes of ethical as well as economic redemption. Later economic analyses of capitalist society are not relevant to Africa.

> The error . . . is to start from European socialism without having analysed it . . . . The error is to want to transplant as they stand the institutions which it advocates. The part of European socialism which should be retained is, above all, its method. And that requires us to begin by analysing the Negro-African realities.[162, p. 292]

Only then may one understand how to adapt foreign institutions to African needs.

As has been noted already, Senghor stresses the classlessness of traditional African society; though he does warn of a possible clash between the elite and workers on one hand and the peasant masses on the other, should the former exploit the latter. He stresses, too, the communal nature of African society. Alienation, the scourge of both capitalist and colonial societies, is absent from the true community.

> The suppression of the second alienation of [colonial status], the solution of these new contradictions, can be found only in creative activity, the practical and social activity of the producers, of individuals organized as a community.[153, p. 118]

In 1962, Senghor advocated the development of the dominant party within a multi-party system. Socialism does not necessarily imply either a one-party state or a party of cadres, for the single party becomes dominated by a clique, and the party of cadres ceases to be a party of the masses. The dominant party rejects violence; it appeals to nationalist sentiment, it *is* the party of the masses, 'a political organization of the nation working towards the nation's construction by socialization . . . with the nation and each individual citizen progressing from underdevelopment to development'.[153, p. 145] The party must be the consciousness of the masses. The trade unions should not be agencies for grievances:

> as the best educated and therefore most conscious group, the wage earners must transcend their own group interest . . . Placing themselves at a higher level, they will embrace all the interests of all social groups, and, first, those of the under privileged: the peasants, shepherds, fishermen and artisans.[153, p. 97]

African Socialism integrates the contribution of European socialism with African nationalism and with *Négritude*, 'defined as the common denominators of all Negro Africans whatever their race, religion or country'.[153, p. 133] *Négritude* becomes the call with which to awaken the national conscience, permitting that development which is a 'combination of peoples' mental and social changes'. A major means of realizing the development plan thus lies through *animation rurale* – involving the creation of community development centres throughout the country. In Senegal the policies of *l'investissement humain* stress the role of the individual. Economic development means more than the pursuit of concrete objectives. Senegal needs a doctrine which gives her people enthusiasm, dynamism and a consciousness of their liberation.

In his autobiography, Nkrumah describes the influences on his 'revolutionary ideas and activities' of Hegel, Engels, Marx and Lenin, of Mazzini and of the American Negro leaders, Marcus Garvey and, to a lesser extent, the socialist DuBois. He described himself as a 'non-denominational Christian and a Marxist socialist', finding no contradiction between the two. Nkrumah's early ideology came much closer to orthodox Marxism than did that of Senghor. He argued that Ghana was not at present a socialist state; it would become one only with complete industrialization and an agricultural revolution and with the means of production under popular control. A socialist state can be built only by socialists – by cadres working within the society. But socialism cannot be successfully built within a single African country. Pan-African themes are expressed in Nkrumah's belief that only a continent-wide, single mass political party can achieve socialism and economic independence for the whole continent.

The development of socialism rests with the elite of the country and especially with the single political party. But Nkrumah's own C.P.P. did not originate as a party founded upon Marxist principles. Nor were all the elite convinced of the merits of socialism; most of the older generation have fully accepted Western ideas of individualism and of private enterprise – values not lacking, of course, among the thousands of traders in Ghana who strongly resent any suggestion that the state should control their activities. The spearhead in the ideological doctrination of the country was thus constituted by groups of intellectuals closely associated with Nkrumah himself. Whilst still in London, Nkrumah had formed 'The Circle' of dedicated followers, the vanguard of the independence movement. Later in Ghana this role passed to the leaders of the National Association of Socialist Students Organization, succeeded by the Party Vanguard Activists, founded in 1959 when N.A.S.S.O. seemed in danger of being controlled by careerists. N.A.S.S.O. and P.V.A. members did not generally hold ministerial posts or seats in parliament. They were stationed strategically in party organizations, in the press and radio, in Pan-Africanist organizations – the Bureau of African Affairs, for instance – and in the party training centres such as the Ideological Institute at Winneba.

The nationalization of most sectors of the economy, envisaged in the Seven Year Plan, intensified the need for ideological acceptance of socialist principles. But the members of the C.P.P. were divided between the N.A.S.S.O. and P.V.A. leaders, enjoying the special patronage of Nkrumah, on the one hand, and many ministers and civil servants, paying only lip-service to socialism, on the other. The purges, which the famous Dawn Broadcast of April 1961 seemed to herald, never completely materialized. From December 1962 *The Spark*, published by the Bureau of African Affairs, became the theoretical voice of the party press. It took an orthodox Marxist line, rejecting all notions of a specifically African Socialism and arguing that traditional African society was not classless nor collective but feudal. The contributors to *The Spark*, a minority group within the C.P.P. and even N.A.S.S.O., seem to have enjoyed the personal protection of Nkrumah, although he never publically endorsed their views. In fact, his own opinions were undergoing considerable modification, bringing him much closer to Senghor.

In the early 1960s, Nkrumah seemed to be seeking for a doctrine of socialism which would be of general application to Africa, reconciling this with Pan-Africanism through a philosophy which would establish him as a messianic leader of the whole continent. Nkrumah's own initial definition of 'Nkrumaism' was pragmatic.

> In Ghana we have embarked on the socialist path to progress; but it is socialism with a difference. Some have called it 'Nkrumaism'. It is not socialism for the sake of socialism but a practical solution of the country's problems. We want to see full employment, good housing and equal opportunity for education and cultural advancement for all the people up to the highest levels possible.[151, p. 141]

A later official definition placed the emphasis more on Pan-Africanism.

> Nkrumaism is the ideology for the New Africa, independent and absolutely free from imperialism, organized on a continental scale, founded upon the conception of One and United Africa, drawing its strength from modern science and technology and from the traditional African belief that the free development of each is conditioned by the free development of all.[151, p. 141]

Nkrumah described traditional African society as communistic and rejected the notion of a class struggle in African society. Socialism is the defence of communalist principles in modern society, safeguarding the society against the class cleavages which would otherwise result from economic and political inequalities. Violent revolution is inevitable only when a society passes from a structure in which the principles of socialism are negated, as in a capitalist or colonial society. For those societies traditionally based upon socialist principles, peaceful evolution to modernity is possible. These expressions of a specifically African socialism were set forth in the new philosophy 'consciencism', together with the method of achieving such socialism throughout Africa by the single mass party for the continent.[151]

The impact of the ideologies

It is not easy to measure the success of these ideologies, either in producing a sense of cohesion among the educated elite or in mobilizing the masses. The themes of *Négritude* have little meaning for the young West African educated in secondary schools no longer dominated by missionary teachers and, perhaps, graduate of a local university. For him, the need to rediscover African values does not arise. Nor is he so naive about the homogeneity of African societies. Nevertheless, he accepts the notion that African society of the future will not be a replica of Western industrial society, and the challenge remains to develop specifically African institutions to meet Africa's special needs. Marxism and American Negro movements probably have less impact upon students at present studying abroad than they had two or three decades ago. Today's student is not involved in the struggle for independence, he belongs to the rising bureaucracy and technocracy. He is more inclined to be impatient with the expositions of his political leaders, which, reflecting their own intellectual and emotional problems, seem to have little practical relevance to the tasks before him. Yet whilst the young Ghanaian was cynical about 'Nkrumaism' and 'consciencism', his Nigerian counterpart is apt to be equally disturbed at the lack of any theoretical orientation among the leaders of his own country; and he was apt to admire Ghana and its leaders for their sense of purpose (without displaying any sympathy towards Nkrumah's bid for African leadership).

For the masses, *Négritude* has no meaning at all; nor can they appreciate the effort of reinterpreting European theories of socialism in the African context. The ideological pronouncements of the political leaders tend to be so protracted and abstruse that few, even among the elite, can fully comprehend them. Inasmuch as they are reducible to slogans, such as African Personality, these tend to be so vague or diffuse in meaning as to be incapable of mobilizing support for specific action. The substantial rejoicing at the military coup in Ghana suggests the weak hold of Nkrumaism on the minds of the people, even in this comparatively well-educated country with one of the most highly organized political parties.

African Socialism, as usually expounded, is sufficiently diffuse and pragmatic to permit most forms of economic development which seem likely to increase the wealth of the West African nations. Expatriate private enterprise is unwelcome only to the extent that it may compete unduly with nascent African enterprises. Where, as in Ghana and Guinea, socialist objectives were sought through the nationalization of commerce, services, and manufacturing industries, the lack of entrepreneurial skills among the elite, together with the unwieldy size of the bureaucracy, has resulted in serious financial losses, damaging the entire economy. African Socialism inspires variously the state farms of Ghana and the cooperatives of Senegal and Mali.

The values of traditional African societies stressed in the philosophies of *Négritude* and African Socialism are those of, albeit idealized, tribal societies. Are these compatible with modernization? They have been selected by the intellectuals because they fill their emotional needs or because they support certain convenient propositions about contemporary society. They have not been selected by economists designing institutions capable of ensuring rapid development, nor have sociologists judged them consistent with an industrial society. Is the modern society based upon traditional African values but a fantasy, incapable of realization? Time alone will finally tell, yet there is ample evidence that, in West Africa's towns, modes of life and thought are taking root which have more in common with those of the West than with Africa. It is perhaps those traditional values which are most threatened that are being most vociferously defended today. Yet it is, perhaps, only through the assertion of traditional values and their subsequent modification that Africans can enter tomorrow without serious trauma.

12 Tribalism

The ideologies of the Western-educated elite stress the unity of the newly independent states; conflicts within their boundaries between different classes or ethnic groups are denied, ignored or belittled. Yet, in their search for identity, members of the elite explore the past of their own societies, often creating myths of past greatness or idealized traditional values. In this process, stress is inevitably placed upon primordial attachments – those that arise from a sense of natural affinity, deriving from one's birth into a given family, religious community or language group, rather than from personal affections or common interests. In the modern state, national unity is usually maintained by routine allegiance to the civil power supplemented by ideological exhortation; a lifting of the primordial ties to the level of political supremacy is regarded as pathological. Yet in the modernizing states of Africa and Asia, these primordial attachments are repeatedly proposed as bases for political units, with arguments that legitimate authority, acceptable to the masses, flows only from the inherent coerciveness of such attachments. In West Africa, such political units are almost invariably smaller than the present independent states, and proposals for their creation constitute separatist and fragmenting tendencies.

In the years following the first definite moves towards independence, 'tribalism' appears to have increased in West Africa. Furthermore, it has come to be regarded as one of the major social ills of the new states, one against which politicians continually inveigh. It is used as a term of abuse – as might 'bourgeois', 'capitalist', or 'communist' be used in other parts of the world. Yet the term is vague, and its current usage embodies a number of separate concepts. One may describe a man as a 'tribalist' if he adheres to the norms of his traditional society where – as in the modern town – these tend to be inappropriate. Thus a man who uses his influence to secure a job for a close kinsman is accused of nepotism by those who assert the supremacy of bureaucratic values. Or, again, one may use the term tribalist to describe the man who does adapt his behaviour to modern situations yet retains an allegiance to chiefs and elders in his rural home. Tribalism is perhaps most commonly used, however, to connote loyalty to an ethnic group (or tribe) which parallels or transcends loyalty to the new state. The term 'ethnicity' is frequently used here by sociologists, though it has yet to find its way into colloquial usage in the English-speaking states.

As has been shown, cultural differences between neighbouring West African peoples are often very considerable. Thus between the Yoruba and Edo languages, the similarities are as slight as between English and Russian. From Dakar to Lake Chad the range in types of social system, dress, diet, and language, far exceeds that to be found between Ireland and the Urals. Nor have events in the twentieth century diminished these differences. The indigenous languages are still spoken by almost the entire West African population; many of them are taught in primary school. Styles of life have not, for the majority of people, altered to such a degree as to produce appreciably greater uniformity. Even in those areas where the export of cocoa, coffee or groundnuts has brought rapidly increasing cash incomes, a large proportion of the farmers still live in their traditional compounds in the villages of their ancestors. In few areas are there large groups of strangers owing no loyalties to local elders or chiefs. Men usually choose their wives from settlements within a very few miles radius from their own, and almost invariably from their own ethnic group. The stranger who settles permanently in a rural area still tends to adopt the culture of the host group; the temporary migrant maintains his ties with his own people. In West Africa's rural areas, primordial attachments remain as strong as ever.

It is in the towns that one might expect a weakening of these ties. Yet, as has already been indicated, this is not always so. Most residents of the modern urban areas are recent immigrants, men and women who were born and grew up to adolescence in the rural villages; only a minority of the present adult population is urban-born. The immigrant usually claims that he intends to return to his home village in his old age, if not earlier; and he maintains close contacts with those at home, so ensuring that his rights to land and to political status do not lapse through his presumed renunciation of his group. Such links are reinforced by the ethnic associations.

Nevertheless, it is in the modern towns that the people of diverse ethnic groups come together. In few cases are the members of any single group residentially segregated; the Hausa are, here, an exception. In fact, one frequently finds considerable ethnic mixing in tenement buildings, with members of different groups sharing washing or cooking facilities. Yet despite the numerous inter-ethnic contacts, the social life of the urban immigrant, and especially of the unskilled worker, tends to be shared with members of his own ethnic group. English and French may each be a lingua franca, but neither provides the basis for intimate relationships. Again, marriage tends to be within the ethnic group, and even townsmen choose their spouses from their own or neighbouring home villages. Only among the best-educated does the number of mixed marriages become appreciable. And so even in the towns it is unusual to find a man who is not closely identified with an ethnic group, and very rare to find one who identifies only with the modern state.

Stereotypes of neighbouring peoples have always existed; but in the past a villager rarely saw men and women from places more than a few miles distant. Ethnic mixing is a contemporary phenomenon. In the towns the new immigrant is unfamiliar with the urban roles expected both of himself and of others. Only slowly does he learn to categorize people by their wealth or occupation. In the transitional period, ethnic categorization is the one which most readily comes to him. Hence it is not surprising that competition for jobs and the frustrations of failure tend to be seen in ethnic terms, with the resulting tensions merely increasing the tendency to categorize individuals primarily by ethnic criteria. Tribalism is thus to a large extent an urban phenomenon, and one which develops with increasing modernization of the economy.

Ethnic nationalism

The early intellectuals of West Africa usually traced the origin of their peoples and cultures from civilizations of prestige in the Middle East. In so doing, they asserted, perhaps only implicitly, the equality of their own cultures with those of the Western world, and Biblical legends of the dispersion of the sons of Noah lent credence to their hypotheses. Thus, for instance, the religion of the Yoruba people has been shown by one author to have extraordinarily close affinities with that of Egypt in the second millennium B.C. Alternatively, the Yoruba are said to have originated in the Nile kingdom of Meroe. Others again would derive West African peoples from the Hebrews. The arguments for such origins are drawn variously from rather literal interpretations of myths current in West African kingdoms (and influenced, in many cases, by a general Islamic mythology); from the specious equation of modern African names for places, peoples and deities, with those of the supposed ancestral cultures; and from parallels drawn between the social structures and traits of present and past cultures – similarities which, in most cases, are expressed in terms so general as to be applicable to tribal peoples in any part of the world. Later intellectuals tended to look for the origins of contemporary culture not in the non-Negro civilizations but in the medieval kingdoms of the western Sudan, ruled by Negroes and thus inferring a purely Negro origin of African culture. Chiek Anta Diop has, indeed, gone so far as to postulate that Egyptian civilization was largely of Negro origin, so that the Western world is thus indirectly the cultural heir of Negro Africa.

These hypotheses, formulated on the most meagre evidence, have found little support from recent research. Whilst it is, indeed, likely that cultural influences both from the Nile valley and from the medieval kingdoms of the western Sudan (and through them from North Africa and the Mediterranean shores) did reach the forest areas of the Guinea coast, linguistic and archaeological evidence suggests long settlement of these areas. But whilst current African scholarship is recognizing the importance of recent findings, the tendency remains among historians to see each ethnic group as possessing its own peculiar origin, as developing over the centuries its own culture, and retaining to a substantial degree its biological purity. Thus some scholars portray the ancestors of their own ethnic group as a small band of migrants who travelled from the east; others see the ethnic groups of West Africa linked genealogically one with another. It is rarely suggested by these men that West African societies, as we know them today, have developed over the centuries as the result of successive population contacts. The arguments of anthropologists favouring a gradual evolutionary development and postulating a most complex pattern of interaction among peoples and cultures, do not find wide popular support.

The intellectuals among the elite have been responsible not only for stressing the exclusiveness of each ethnic group but for creating, in many cases, cohesive groups much larger than those that existed in the pre-colonial era. Thus the term Yoruba was formerly used only of the kingdom of Ọyọ; no single term seems to have existed to describe the diversely structured kingdoms whose peoples spoke closely related dialects and whose rulers claimed common descent from the mythical Oduduwa. Individual loyalties were directed to one's own kingdom, and members of other kingdoms were seen as foreigners. But the early C.M.S. missionaries used the term Yoruba to embrace all these related peoples, and the usage has won almost universal acceptance. Schools have taught a standardized dialect which is quickly superseding local variations. The Yoruba dress adopted by the elite has a range of styles, but differences between the kingdoms are no longer apparent. The search for 'the origin of the Yoruba people' tends to take priority over the histories of the individual kingdoms. In the past, it is probable that kingdoms on the margins of Yoruba country felt a closer affinity with their non-Yoruba neighbours than with other Yoruba-speaking groups two hundred miles away. But the development of a Yoruba consciousness creates not only greater internal cohesion but much more starkly defined cultural boundaries with neighbouring ethnic groups.

A similar process has occurred within other ethnic groups. Thus throughout much of West Africa individuals have been drawn into modern society and into membership of new states, whilst continuing to proclaim the uniqueness of their own ethnic groups. The distinctions between pride in one's own group and claims of its superiority become difficult to draw.

None experience the competition of loyalties to state and ethnic group so much as do the educated elite. They are a national elite, identified with the state and its government. Yet they are also largely responsible for the development of ethnic nationalism in their respective groups. Many, indeed, still prefer to identify primarily with their ethnic group rather than with the state. In Nigerian hotel registers, one often finds 'Ibo', 'Yoruba', or 'Hausa', in the column headed 'Nationality'. As we have already seen, the educated man is expected to be active in the affairs of his home town, using his ability and influence in its attempts to achieve social and economic development. But if he is a highly placed civil servant, for instance, others will accuse him of using his office to gain favoured treatment for his town.

Fears of domination

Colonial governments stood apart from African society, ruling arbitrarily and relatively impartially. Each community and ethnic group was equal in its subordination to the alien power. Now independence has granted to West Africans not only a direct participation in government, but also participation in governments which wield greater powers and control larger resources than did the colonial instruments which they replaced. Popular interest in the government of the new states thus runs at a high level; and for many, 'self-government' implies defining the relationship between one's own community or ethnic group and the new locus of power. One of the facets of ethnic nationalism is the claim for equality with other groups. Yet modern political constitutions may be used as the most potent agents of domination.

Competition for power between ethnic groups is usually recorded at the national level; yet identical processes are at work within the smallest communities. A local government ward may consist of two villages, one of which is larger than the other, and each will probably put forward one of its own members as a candidate. Every voter will feel a primary loyalty to the candidate of his own village (though other factors may complicate the situation), and so the larger village will see its representative elected. Everyone will subsequently expect that the new councillor will not only seek to secure the maximum benefits for his own ward, but that his own village will be especially favoured; the new school and well will be close to his own village, and his kin will be preferred in the granting of licences. If he fails to fulfil the expectations of his electorate, another candidate will replace him at the next election. In the ethnically heterogeneous modern town, it is feared that licences for market stalls will be granted only to members of that ethnic group which dominates the town council.

Fears at a national level merely replicate those at local levels. Each member of a legislative assembly is expected to win favoured treatment for his own constituency – if not always for his own section within it (although one does hear of newly tarred roads which stop at the house of the minister responsible for such works). A cabinet in which one ethnic group is dominant is thought to expedite the social and economic development of that group at the expense of others. Members of minority groups feel that they can never be better than second-class citizens; they cannot alter their ethnic status, but they may seek a greater share of power by joining the political party associated with the dominant ethnic group and so facilitate a general tendency towards one-party government.

In the past, the villager probably felt that men living more than ten miles from his own home were strangers, while those living more than thirty miles away were foreigners. His loyalties lay to relatively small political groupings. The ethnic groups recognized today are not only varied in size but in some cases very large indeed – the ten million Yoruba, for instance, or the ten million Ibo. The degree of inter-ethnic hostility arising from fears of political domination is dependent upon the relative sizes of the groups. In one state, the ethnic groups may be so small that none can assert a dominant role; nor perhaps are permanent coalitions between culturally related ethnic groups likely to develop. Here ethnic hostilities are likely to be minimal. In other states, however, one ethnic group may be dominant. Nigeria provides a triple example, for in each of the three regions originally created, one ethnic group constituted a majority of the population – the Yoruba in the West, the Ibo in the East, the Hausa and the population of the emirates in the North. The ethnic minority areas claimed that they were discriminated against. Often with reason, they felt that legislation on matters relating to personal status or land tenure was drafted to accord with the social structure of the dominant group. They feared a loss of their cultural identities. Yet the minority ethnic groups rarely achieved unity in demands for a separate region, since among themselves they were similarly divided. Within Nigeria's Western Region, the non-Yoruba comprised Edo-speaking groups, Ibo and Ijoh. The traditional rulers of Benin saw in the proposed Mid-West State a revival of the Benin empire, and this was resented by Edo-speaking peoples who no longer paid allegiance to the *oba* of Benin. Others feared the dominance of the achievement-oriented Ibo. The Ijoh wanted to join other members of their ethnic group in Eastern Nigeria, or hoped to form with them a separate Delta State. The eventual creation of the Mid-West State was due to a number of factors, of which local demands were but one.

Fears of ethnic domination are most widely reported in the political sphere. But they may be found, of course, in any power structure – in trade unions, in student associations, or in religious synods – where those holding high office are felt to be in a position to discriminate in favour of members of their own ethnic group. That they would so discriminate is probably presumed until other loyalties, not based upon primordial attachments, take obvious precedence.

Competition for employment

The modern West African towns are ethnically heterogeneous. And with the expansion of primary and secondary schools, an ever increasing flow of literate immigrants moves townwards. These youths not only seek work but often have, as least at the outset, an unrealistic knowledge of the employment market and of the type of work currently correlated with specific levels of education. Many primary school leavers still expect to enter a clerical career, as did their elder brothers and cousins a decade or two earlier; in fact, in areas such as southern Nigeria or Ghana, they may find difficulty in being hired as unskilled labour.[82] The ensuing frustrations are liable to be attributed to tribalism.

There is no sound evidence that members of one West African ethnic group are inherently more apt in either academic or mechanical skills than any other. Some people with the most rudimentary indigenous technology have with training made surprisingly good artisans. University examination results do not show that one ethnic group produces better scientists, whilst another provides the more brilliant arts graduates. Any irregularities in the distribution of talent can usually be attributed to the different quality of secondary schools and to the vagaries of the selection processes. On the other hand, some parts of West Africa – in general, the coastal areas – have enjoyed Western education for a much longer period than others; and the tendency has been for these parts to maintain their earlier advantages, so that at the present time they produce more secondary school- and university-educated persons in proportion to their total population. They may even appear to dominate certain fields of employment.

If differences in innate skill are difficult to specify differences in attitudes towards achievement certainly seem to be more apparent. Members of certain ethnic groups appear more aggressive in their desire to make good. Some people seem less reluctant to start right at the bottom; some shun manual labour, maintaining in this a traditional attitude of superiority over neighbouring peoples; others do not mind dirty work when the rewards seem promising. Such qualities usually dominate the stereotypes held of neighbouring peoples. It is believed, furthermore, that in the town every man has an obligation to find work for others from his own village, and these obligations are expressed through the ethnic associations which provide a focus for primordial loyalties. The image is thus created of the chief clerk or foreman who endeavours to establish an ethnic 'closed shop' among his own subordinates – an endeavour which fails to succeed only to the extent that the higher officials insist rigidly on ability and education as criteria for appointment and promotion.

Ethnic rivalries are not confined to the less skilled among the urban people, those one might expect to find more attached to primordial sentiments. They may be equally strong among the most highly educated. As has already been observed, the rapid rates of promotion in the expanding civil services have created extremely intense competition. Many men have been appointed to posts for which, by generally accepted Western standards, they were inadequately qualified. Some have owed their good fortune to the lack of more suitable candidates; others, to policies of Africanization which have eliminated better qualified but expatriate rivals. One's failure is easiest to bear when the successful man is obviously fit for the office; it leads to bitter resentment when the mediocre are rewarded.

Failure can, however, be rationalized as the effect of nepotism and tribalism. It is rarely difficult to find one or two members of the board making the appointment who belong to the same ethnic group as the successful applicant and who may even have some tenuous ties of kinship with him. Their willingness to place ethnic loyalties above other criteria is held responsible for the outcome of the contest. Such arguments are used by the disappointed, indeed, even when the successful candidate seems to have been chosen on his merits. They find even greater scope in processes, such as the award of scholarships, which are inevitably somewhat haphazard, owing to the difficulties in finding valid measures of ability. The appointment committees are probably less partial towards their kin and ethnic groups than is commonly presumed. But it is the common presumptions which encourage men to improve their chances of appointment or promotion by seeking the aid of influential members of their own ethnic groups. A decade or more ago it seems probable that, at least in southern Nigeria, men personally manipulated their relationships within elite associations to seek advancement. Today, they are more likely to urge the senior members of their own ethnic group to press their claims, so that the group does not fall behind others in the general competition for elite status and a better livelihood.

Competition of this type seems most bitter when two ethnic groups are equally large and have similar levels of education. Such is the case with the Ibo and Yoruba of Nigeria. And rivalry is exacerbated by the different personality type of the two peoples, together with the fact that the Ibo were later in developing their educational system and feel a need to catch up with the Yoruba. In recent years the public corporations and some of the universities have been riven with inter-ethnic hostilities to the extent that these have become major political issues.

In the modern towns, the ethnic protagonists are usually on neutral ground; all are equally strangers. Nevertheless, situations do occur where the more favoured types of employment are held by recent immigrants, whilst the locally resident population is left with the menial tasks; differences in educational level are, in most cases, responsible. The outcome of the tensions generated, however, may be serious ethnic rioting.

Thus, the prohibition of Christian missionary work in the Muslim emirates of Northern Nigeria has resulted in their scholastic backwardness. Clerical workers and artisans from the southern Regions fill posts not only in the government service and expatriate commercial firms, but even in the native authorities. In 1945, nearly one-half of the employees in Zaria's Public Works Department were southerners. The Hausa feared, with some justification, the control exercised by the southern immigrants over all the strategic sectors of the North's modern economy, and the more insistent demands for self-government by the politicians of the southern Regions raised the possibility that southerners would effectively control the new Federal government structure, in spite of the Northern Region's allocation of half the seats in the House of Representatives. Thus, when the southern political parties campaigned at Kano in 1953 for immediate independence, riots were triggered off which resulted in thirty-six deaths and 240 wounded.

Riots at Abidjan in 1958 seem to have been inspired by minor clerical workers who were frustrated following the end of a boom in employment opportunities. Their own targets were the Dahomeyan and Togolese clerks. For literates from these countries, with more advanced primary schooling than was available in most parts of the French West African empire, had migrated from their own economically more backward areas to the capitals of the other territories. On subsequently returning home, they constituted a dissatisfied group, a further source there of political instability.

Political exploitation

The political leaders of the newly independent states must arouse sentiments of national unity and loyalty, in their attempts to establish for the masses the legitimacy of their rule. To the extent that party leaders seek to mobilize the masses, using the single party to socialize new values and stressing the absence both of class and ethnic conflicts in the allegedly homogeneous society, ethnic loyalties are repressed and their manifestations discouraged. But most politicians have, at some time or another, attempted to manipulate ethnic loyalties in order to increase their popular support.

It is, in fact, difficult for leaders to claim an aura of traditional legitimacy without arousing ethnic loyalties and fears. When Modibo Keita asserts his descent from the early rulers of the empire of Mali, or Sékou Touré exploits the resistance of his ancestor Samory to French colonization, the peoples subject to these past rulers are not likely to be impressed. In employing traditional symbols of dress or political ceremony, it is difficult to avoid an identification with a specific ethnic group. The adoption of the name Ghana, for the former Gold Coast, was in some respects a stroke of genius, for it identified the new nation not with any ethnic group inside its boundaries but with an empire far distant in the past. Similarly, in replacing the English symbols and ceremonials of parliament with those of Ghana, an attempt was successfully made to incorporate motifs from all parts of the country; the dominance of Akan themes reflected the numerical superiority of this group in the state. It would be a far harder task to design Nigerian symbols which incorporated motifs from the cultures of the Hausa, Ibo and Yoruba.

When parliamentary constituencies elect influential local men to the legislatures, it is tempting for the government to reward such supporters not only with social services but with ministerial office. The result is that a very high proportion of the members of the dominant party tend to hold such office, and parliament tends to be an expensive institution. Rivalry between ethnic groups is manifested in the demands that one of their own members should be among the occupants of the most powerful offices. And the impression is thus further enhanced that members of parliament represent the interests of ethnic groups and localities before all others. In Treichville, the major African suburb of Abidjan, branches of the Parti Démocratique de la Côte d'Ivoire are reported to be ethnically based, emphasizing primordial ties in those areas where one would most expect occupational interests to be dominant. The deliberate fostering of ethnic loyalties probably contributes to the absence of organizations based upon other criteria of recruitment.

Ethnic resentments provide, of course, a ready weapon for the politican unsure of his majority. In some cases he may advance the claims of the dominant group in his constituency, hoping to win its entire vote. In others he may whip up feelings of antagonism against outsiders, in order to resolve or obscure divisions within his own constituency.

In the Gold Coast, the rapidly declining party of the older Western-educated elite, led by men like Dr Danquah, seized upon the disaffection in Ashanti for a last bid for power. The Ashanti complained that too much of the country's revenue, gained from their cocoa crops, was being spent in Accra; and that the status of traditional chiefs was being undermined. The National Liberation Movement accordingly sought a more federal type of constitution, which would not only grant greater local autonomy, but also weaken the nationally organized C.P.P. In Northern Nigeria when, in 1959, the Action Group campaigned in the Hausa areas on the issue of class, attempting to rouse the commoners against the Fulani aristocracy, N.P.C. propaganda stressed in reply that a vote for a southern party would lead to southern dominance and the quick elimination of Hausa and Islamic culture.

The rift in the Action Group in Western Nigeria between Akintola and Awolowo culminated in the reinstatement of the first as Regional Premier by the Federal Government and in the gaoling of the second with several supporters, on charges of treason. The Yoruba remained divided in their loyalties to these two leaders, and it seems certain that Akintola never enjoyed the support of the majority. Soon after Awolowo's trial, the opposing factions tried to rally Yoruba unity behind a new culture hero, substituting Olofin for Oduduwa, who was associated with the Egbe Omo Oduduwa, the Pan-Yoruba cultural movement that Awolowo had founded. But this ploy met with little success. Then, at the first regional election held after Akintola's triumph, the propaganda of his party emphasized the need for Yoruba unity. Some cartoons showed an Ibo and a Hausa dipping into a full bowl of soup, with a Yoruba man on the floor picking up the falling scraps. (The implication being that until Akintola's party, supreme in the Western Region, entered the Federal coalition, the Yoruba would be discriminated against in the allocation of services and in the location of new industry. Awolowo's desire to convert the Action Group into a national party, whilst Akintola favoured the development of Regional parties, each supreme in its own area, was one of the causes of their disagreement.) Other cartoons were bitterly anti-Ibo, implying that most Yoruba ills might be attributed to exploitation by Ibo traders and lorry owners – a situation which equally called for greater Yoruba unity behind their incumbent rulers.

The consequences of tribalism

Those who on some occasions use tribalism as an epithet of abuse, at others stress the positive value of ethnic loyalty. The term embraces a variety of meanings, according with different aspects or theories of modernization process.

Ethnic loyalties provide for West African peoples a sense of identity, of the values of their own cultures, which balance the feelings of inferiority that derive from the continual borrowing of Western technology and the acceptance of Western styles of living. Allegiances have been developed to ethnic units far larger than existed in the pre-colonial era. Many associations based upon these and smaller units, the para-political elite cultural associations or the urban ethnic associations, are modern in purpose and structure and are conducive in less direct ways to the acceptance of new norms and values within an apparently traditional framework. Much of the enthusiasm in the building of new schools, indeed, has derived not so much from appreciating those values of modern society that stress education, as from a rivalry between neighbouring villages or ethnic groups in which neither wishes to appear the more backward. When the incumbent of a modern office is criticized in terms of his ethnic origin, the new role of the office is tacitly accepted; were attacks upon the failings of the modern sector to be directed against its structure rather than the individual traits of its personnel, the survival of the new state would be seriously jeopardized.

Yet these positive contributions may be balanced by others, apparently inimical to modernization. The large ethnic units are united by cultural features which are also what distinguish them sharply from neighbouring groups. The factors which have united the various Yoruba-speaking peoples cannot, at a higher level, unite them with the Ibo. The particular segmentary structure of Ibo society, which has engendered such strong sentiments of cohesion, cannot be replicated at a level which would unite all Nigerian peoples. Ethnic exclusiveness provides a ready basis for political separatist movements. The supremacy of ethnic loyalties may be convenient to ruling groups who fear opposition from the underprivileged, for they may exploit these divisive factors. Progressive movements may accordingly be weakened. Furthermore, it becomes difficult to stress ethnic loyalties without implying acceptance of tribal values like nepotism. The efficiency of any modern organization is likely to be impaired if appointments are made on the basis of ethnic allegiance rather than ability. In many cases the reduction in efficiency may be slight; but the apparent disregard of bureaucratic values by those in power leads many educated men and women to view their supporters with cynical contempt. Ethnic rivalries may produce schools and the like, but enthusiasm can overreach itself, and the development of such social services may injure the total economic effort. A new manufacturing plant of marginal economic viability is severely handicapped when its location is determined by ethnic considerations rather than industrial ones. It is to obviate these destructive features of tribalism whilst retaining some of the beneficial aspects that political leaders have sought to emphasize a general African culture, not identified with particular ethnic groups; ethnic rivalries are then contained within the smallest units, where they are least disruptive to the nation and its economy.

13 Conflicts

With economic development, the conflicts inherent in traditional society are often intensified, while new conflicts arise in the modern sector. In the traditional sectors, new methods are found for the pursuit of indigenous interests and values; wealth may now be gained from the growing or marketing of export crops, and an office in the local church may be as prestige-laden as a traditional chieftaincy title. With the growing of cash crops and the increasing population, land shortage may intensify the conflicts between the descent groups constituting the community. Rulers whose actions were severely constrained by their councils of chiefs have been able to exploit their relationships with the colonial administrators and, sometimes, the politicians of the independent states, to enhance their local power.

It is, however, with the conflicts of modern West Africa that this book is primarily concerned – with the developing stratification of society into haves and have-nots, rich and poor, privileged and underprivileged. Among the wealthy and privileged Western-educated elite, we see the competition for power between rival groups, each basing its claims upon different criteria of ascription or achievement. The goals of one individual or group are incompatible with those of another when the two goals cannot be attained simultaneously, and the success of one party necessitates the failure of the other. The term conflict is, in some ways, unfortunate, since it implies to the non-sociologist a relationship of violence. The resolution of conflict, the mediation of the incompatible interests and demands, however, may take a variety of forms, ranging from the most amicable discussion within a committee to the use of physical force. It is through the resolution of conflicts that societies change in their structure. And as we described earlier, such changes may vary in their scope and in their magnitude. The more powerful group may concede some demands of the weaker group whilst not relinquishing its basic position; or it may meet the demands by introducing individuals of the weaker group into its membership. But such changes in the policies or the personnel of more powerful groups may not be effective in reducing the degree of tension in the society; new organizations may emerge producing far more radical changes in the structure of the society. The magnitude of the change is not necessarily correlated with the degree of peaceful arbitration or violence through which it may be effected. Military coups may preserve the *status quo*, whilst committees may produce revolutionary changes.

In considering the extent of tension and of change in West African societies, we must consider three variables. Firstly we must evaluate the degree to which interests are opposed: the differences of poverty and wealth in the society, and the degree to which such differences are becoming hereditary; the degree, too, to which various groups within the Western-educated elite are differentiated. Secondly, we must ascertain the manner in which the interests of these different groups are articulated; are individuals conscious of their interests and have they the appropriate channels through which to express them? Or is the perception of interests inhibited by countervailing factors, as when economic interests are obscured by religious or ethnic divisions? Thirdly, we must assess the degree to which the tensions engendered by the conflicts in society may be resolved through institutionalized procedures. Traditional societies had their methods by which disputes and incompatible demands were mediated. But in rapidly changing societies, the evolving of new procedures often fails to keep pace with the development of conflicts. The agents of mediation, and in particular political parties and trade unions, may fail to perform the tasks expected of them.

These variables are difficult to evaluate with any real precision. Were we able to obtain the necessary data, indeed, and to construct a method of measurement, we could probably predict the future patterns of stability and violence, stagnation and change in the West African states. Instead, we tend to rely on hindsight in assessing the forces of change at work in these societies. The sociologist who analyses the changes taking place in developing countries is, furthermore, in an ambivalent position. For his reports become one of the factors in the process. If he stresses the conflicts inherent in the society, he may give an impression of instability to the outside world, thus conditioning its attitude to the developing country; equally, he may facilitate the expression of interests within the developing country, so raising the level of tension without supplying any new methods of alleviating it. On the other hand, these countries, and the West African states are here no exception, have probably been ill-served by writers who attributed stability to situations which later events have shown to be on the verge of military coups.

Incipient class conflict

The development of new forms of social stratification in the West African states is producing an incipient class conflict – a conflict between the new elites and the mass of the population, particularly in the urban areas. In using the term 'class conflict', we do not, of course, imply that the classes of West Africa are to be defined in exactly the same manner as those of Western Europe, or that they necessarily possess the same characteristics of living styles, behaviour patterns, and values.

We have already seen that manual workers in the towns of West Africa live at a level of severe poverty. The Morgan Commission in Nigeria estimated that the wages of unskilled labourers comprised only half of the sum needed to provide a married man with a minimum level of subsistence. Yet these labourers are men who left the rural areas to seek a better livelihood. In the towns they enjoy modern services – piped water and electricity – and better educational and health facilities than are usually obtained in the rural areas. But in the past decade their real wages have barely risen at all, and their diets are probably now inferior to those in the villages. The increased provision of primary education has now led to an ever-increasing migration of school leavers to the towns, while land shortage in many areas has produced an additional factor in attracting men away from farming. Yet the towns are unable to provide employment. In the years before and immediately after Independence, the level of government services expanded rapidly, as accumulated savings were used to build new offices, schools, health centres. But these savings are now exhausted, and much of each country's revenue and foreign aid is spent on servicing its external debts. Urban unemployment is growing rapidly. Poverty and unemployment are, of course mitigated by the continuing links which the town dweller retains with his rural area. For most men the possibility still remains, however reluctantly accepted, of returning to their village to farm in the traditional manner. And whilst they remain in the town, their compatriots from their home areas will, through the ethnic associations, succour them in times of need.

The poverty of the urban migrants must be seen, though, not only in absolute terms but also as relative to their aspirations. Many of these men, and in particular those of tribally organized ethnic groups, belong to traditional societies in which the attainment of great wealth or high political office is open to all members. Thus, in the towns too, they see no limit to the heights of prestige to which their 'fates' might lead them; they actively aspire to and compete for advancement. Education is seen as the prime condition of success and is avidly sought by parents for their children, and by adolescent workers for themselves. Yet, as in each decade the increase in numbers of school leavers surpasses the increase in newly created jobs, the qualifying standards for these jobs also rise. The primary school leaving certificate, which once ensured a clerical post, now becomes the qualification for semi-skilled manual work. And when the migrant returns to visit his village, he is more likely to tell of the excitement and pleasures of the city than of his own struggle to earn a livelihood, of his failure to achieve the expectations both of himself and of his kin.

Politicians, drawn from the new elites and endeavouring to attract the support of the masses, have portrayed the benefits of independence in such terms as to give many of the less literate people a quite unrealistic image of their prospects in the coming years. The rewards have been stressed; the efforts necessary have been mentioned less often. The level of political interest among West Africans has been very high during the past two decades, as the gaining of independence and the consequent constitutional changes have reverberated to the most remote villages. The high attendance at the polls affirms in a way the support of the masses for their leaders and their desire to participate in the promised rewards of the new nations.

Levels of aspiration have been maintained, too, through the close contact which the developing countries of Africa and Asia have retained with the industrial nations. They are too poor to isolate themselves and raise their living standards solely by their own efforts. And whilst expatriate advisers and businessmen live in developing countries at standards even higher than they would expect at home, and whilst students and politicians frequently travel abroad, the living standards of the industrial countries become the target for the people of Africa.

In practice, those who have attained high educational qualifications have achieved a style of life very similar to that of men and women similarly employed in the industrial nations. As their numbers have grown and their residential suburbs developed, a pattern of living has evolved which is in extravagant contrast to that of either the urban poor or the villagers – a far greater contrast, indeed, than usually existed in traditional societies between the wealthy and powerful and the ordinary farmer. The urban poor live literally on the fringes of elite society, contemplating its wealth and never quite losing hope that they, too, might achieve such a status – for have not so many members of the elite come from rural homes as humble as those which raised the poor urban migrant?

But meanwhile, access to the elite is becoming progressively more difficult. To the extent that the elite increases at a decreasing rate, the number of recruits from humble homes will correspondingly fall. For education is the principal condition of success, and those who have attained elite status are best able to ensure that their children will be similarly favoured. The chances that a young person will gain a secondary school or university education are directly related to the education of his parents. Well-educated families still seem to be fairly large; in the coming decades their members could easily fill any vacancies in the slowly growing elite. In contrast, the son of the unskilled urban worker, among all occupational categories, has the poorest chances of receiving a good education. And so the poor urban father not only sees his own chances of success rapidly receding, but begins to feel, too, that his children are handicapped by his own poverty – a situation which did not apply in tribal society.

An unrealistically high level of aspiration is perhaps the inevitable concomitant of rapid economic development. Many are certain to be frustrated in their attempts to achieve goals by methods which are new and but poorly understood. Lack of success may be attributed either to one's personal insufficiency or, as we have seen to be common in West Africa, to the machination of others, through witchcraft, sorcery or corruption. Slowly, personal aspirations will become more realistic. But as the ostentatious life of the elite ceases to appear a possibility for oneself or one's children, so opposition to it is likely to grow. Hopes of entertaining the elite change to demands that it be shorn of many of its privileges.

The resolution of tensions

The demands of the urban workers are, first, for increased wages, and then, when these demands are not met, for a reduction in the privileges of the elite. The first demand is likely to be unrealistic. The members of the Morgan Commission recognized that the Nigerian government could not be expected to decree a minimum wage double that already in existence; they recommended wages midway between the existing levels and the desirable ones, while the government itself felt able to grant only one-third of the recommended increase. Wage increases on a scale which would substantially alleviate poverty are possible only with considerably increased productivity; taxing the small elite or reducing their privileges will not alone yield sufficient revenues. But as governments are unable to meet the demands of their peoples, so they are drawn into repressing the demands, often by force.

West African trade unions tend, as we have already seen, to be poorly organized. Furthermore, a high proportion, often over one-half, of the wage-earning population is in government employment. Bargaining for higher wages takes place in general therefore, not with a private employer, under the arbitrating control of the government, but with the government itself. It becomes easy for the politicians in power to interpret wage demands as acts threatening the well-being of the state. One response is to draw the trade union movement into the dominant political party, conceiving it primarily as an agent in socializing the values of the party; another is to weaken the unions with endless repression. Neither response seems completely effective in preventing the expression of demands for improved conditions, but each is a substantial deterrent.

In mid-1961, the Ghanaian government introduced a harsh budget, partly as a result of falling cocoa prices. Duties were levied on a wide range of consumer goods, and all who earned more than £120 a year were to have five per cent of their wages deducted as contributions to a compulsory savings scheme. Both measures reduced real incomes, bearing heavily on skilled and semi-skilled workers, and in September, a major strike broke out among the railway and dock workers of Sekondi-Takoradi, causing widespread paralysis of the country's transport system. Under the trade union legislation of 1958 the strike was illegal; a state of emergency was declared, and violence broke out between the strikers and police. In two or three weeks funds ran out, and the strikers returned to work, admonished by several of the T.U.C. leaders and by Nkrumah himself. Shortly afterwards many of the strike leaders, together with market women who had supported them, were arrested, and over fifty members of the opposition United Party were placed in detention.

The delay of the Nigerian government, first in publishing the report of the Morgan Commission and then in announcing its own decisions, led to a nationwide strike in June 1964. Personal appeals by the Prime Minister, Sir Abubakar Tafawa Balewa, went completely unheeded. In fact, the somewhat cavalier attitude of the government only attracted widespread support for the strikers, and the original limited demands of the union leaders developed into general disgust with the corruption and inefficiency of the politicians. The strikers returned to work only when the government promised negotiations on the basis of the Morgan report. But a few days later, Dr Allen, an English university lecturer studying the Nigerian trade union movement, and three minor union leaders were arrested and charged with attempting to overthrow the government. All were convicted; though a year later Allen won his appeal and was released. The charges were felt by most to have been magnified out of all proportion, but they served to frighten other union leaders.

In February 1966, the Firestone rubber tappers of Liberia struck for a wage of 15 cents an hour, instead of the existing 65 cents a day – a demand which would have doubled their earnings. They were ultimately awarded an increase of 4 cents a day. Here, too, the President declared the strike illegal, and riot troops were used, one worker being shot. Following the return to work, President Tubman called for a week of prayer and fasting, 'considering the existence of a state of tension, unrest, turmoil and disturbance in many parts of the world'; Liberians were urged to worship 'with lowly and contrite hearts, garbed in sackcloth and ashes or ordinary apparel'.

Thus the attempts of the urban workers to express their grievances through their trade unions and by utilizing the conventional method of the strike are met with threats, force, and accusations of national sabotage.

In the years following Independence, the political parties of West Africa have tended to become less, rather than more, representative of public opinion. Founded by nuclei of educated elite, the parties were obliged to seek popular support as they competed with each other for the heritage of colonial power. And success usually rewarded the party with the best organization throughout the villages and urban suburbs, the party whose members most effectively reflected the aspirations of the masses. But with the dominance of single parties within each government, politicians have often grown remote from their electorate, and party organization has fallen into decay.

In the one-party states, it is anticipated that conflicts which develop within society will be mediated within the party committees; they will be withdrawn from such public discussion as may arouse increasing tension. It is implied here that the party is not only an agent of socialization, but equally the vehicle for the expression of popular grievances. It may, indeed, perform the latter role, if the officially presented descriptions of village meetings are a reality – electing their own chairmen and representatives to party committees, and discussing national policies both in abstract and as they affect their own lives. But it seems likely that in many areas villages have lost interest in such meetings. If this is the case, the party becomes merely an avenue for the advancement of the few, and local leaders do little more than publicly announce the directives of the central committee.

Where parliamentary institutions are still important, the elected members become firmly entrenched; nominated by the dominant party and rich enough to buy sufficient local support, they are ensured of victory at each election. A high proportion of them are rewarded with ministerial office, and this demands their residence in the capital for most of the year; but the remaining members, too, tend to live in the capital, arguing that only here can they properly urge the claims of their constituents.

With their high salaries, often free or subsidized housing, and generous allowances for travelling, politicians tend, in many of the West African capitals, to live in ostentatious luxury. In his 1961 Dawn Broadcast, which seemed to herald a more puritanical era, Nkrumah ruled that party members should not own more than two houses with a combined value of £20,000 or more than two cars. Such limits seem significantly generous for men whose previous careers, often as teachers or clerks, would have earned them salaries below £500 a year. Initially, people accepted the affluence of their elected representative, feeling that it symbolized not only his own success but also the dignity of his constituency; it was merited by the benefits which he attracted for his people. But as the benefits cease to flow, and the representative grows wealthier and more remote from his constituents, these people do not forget that he owes his position to their votes. They may flatter him when they seek favours, but their general attitude becomes one of disillusion.

It is easy for the masses to castigate their political leaders as corrupt men seeking to promote only their own interests. One does not hear the frank confessions of the politicians. Most of them entered the spheres of government with little or no previous experience. Probably most of them seriously misjudged the difficulties of carrying out their promises to their electorate, imagining that the lack of progress during the colonial period was due solely to the restraints imposed by the expatriate administrators. Their subsequent sense of failure and inadequacy may perhaps be manifest in a craving for popularity, expressed in flamboyant living, and a reluctance to advocate policies which might prove unpopular. Exposed corruption is cynically defended by them as no different from the undiscovered practices of others.

The creation of new political parties, perhaps better fitted to express popular grievances, is, as we have already seen, almost impossible. In some states dominance of the single party is preserved by law; rivals are illegal. In others, the financial resources of the dominant party, its control over the means of propaganda, and its unchecked use of violence against opponents, render ineffective the efforts of a small rival party. Leadership of such rival parties tends, indeed, to come from discontented intellectuals. Where, as in Nigeria, the major parties have tended to be ideologically weak, the new parties have stated their claim on a more revolutionary doctrine. Thus the Dynamic Party of Dr Chike Obi, a university mathematics lecturer, sought to impose a 'Kemalist' regime, based upon the doctrines of the Turkish modernizer, Ataturk. The manifestoes of Dr Tunji Otegbeye's Socialist Workers and Farmers Party are paraphrases of the Communist Manifesto. Neither ideology arouses much popular enthusiasm, and in seeking votes the leaders of these parties have tended to stress the corruption of the existing politicans. But the cynical voter is apt to reply that a new set of politicians is likely to be no less corrupt than the former one.

The non-consciousness of class

As the conflicts develop between the mass of the people and the wealthy educated elite, the mediating instruments – the trade unions and the political parties – are seen increasingly to fail in providing satisfactory channels for the grievances of the poor. These grievances are ill-expressed, often in a manner not conducive to logical action. The values of traditional society and the ideologies formulated by the elites are jointly responsible.

Throughout West Africa, primordial loyalties to the ethnic group remain powerful. Most men have not moved away from the villages of their ancestors in which the traditional social structure is strongly maintained. Those in the towns find security and recreation in the ethnic associations; occupational associations among manual workers are but weakly developed. Failure to achieve desired goals in the towns can be ascribed to the ethnic loyalties of those who make appointments or to the competition of other ethnic groups. The organization of trade unions within firms rather than on an occupational basis promotes a relationship of patronage between employer and employee. In the rural areas one can hardly expect to find national associations of farmers, instituted to protect their common interests. The illiteracy of the villagers and the vast range of vernacular languages makes combination difficult.

The concepts of class conflict are largely absent from vernacular languages. In the stratified societies of the savana, the terminology of caste may perhaps be adapted; the Hausa terms – *talakawa* (commoner) and *sarakuna* (office-holders and their kin) – form concise categories into which the population may be divided. Tribally structured societies, on the other hand, tend to have a variety of terms with which to designate men of prestige, emphasizing variously their wealth, their moral standing, or their generosity. And these are applied to individuals and not to groups. The term elite is gaining currency among the educated themselves; in southern Nigeria, literates usually use the term 'senior service' to denote the man who earns more than £500 a year and whose office entitles him to a loan for buying a car.

An ideology of classlessness is, as we have seen, being developed by the intellectual elite of several West African states. And those who endeavour to keep within the limits of orthodox Marxism usually see the class struggle as being between the developed industrial nations and their underdeveloped former colonies. But the use of class terminology to describe conflicts within West African societies is not entirely absent. In Northern Nigeria, the N.E.P.U. based its policies upon the conflict between the Fulani aristocracy and the commoners. During its campaigns in the Northern Region before the Federal election of 1959, the Action Group exploited the same themes within the emirates, whilst elsewhere trying to arouse anti-Hausa ethnic loyalties. In its 1961 manifesto outlining 'Democratic Socialism', it defined three incipient classes – the 'self-employed' (the bulk of the population); the 'workers'; and the 'employers' (including private and public corporations, industrialists and contractors). These are economic categories and replace Awolowo's much earlier threefold division, based upon education – the 'educated'; the 'enlightened' (traders and artisans); and the 'ignorant' masses. Otegbeye's Socialist Workers and Farmers Party is more orthodox in its Marxism, describing the adherents of the N.C.N.C. and Action Group as a '*compradore* national bourgeoisie'. Analyses of the 'new class' by Djilas or the strictures of the Martinique psychiatrist Fanon do not seem, as yet, to have made much impact upon African intellectuals. In the West African context, classes cannot be defined in terms of ownership of the means of production – for most of the elite are salary earners, and it is the peasantry in tribal societies who are the corporate owners of land. Classes can only be defined in terms of power. Furthermore, whilst the elite has the cohesion, the consciousness of privilege and distinct style of life to merit the term class, it is not balanced by another recognizable class – unless one restricts one's use of such terminology to the modern sector, and terms the urban manual workers an incipient class.

Classes, representing incompatible interests, are conceptually closed groups. Class consciousness is minimal when movement from the underprivileged into the privileged class is believed to be easy and frequent. Men are rarely apt to oppose privileges which, they believe, may one day be shared by themselves. West African society is still seen as an open society. The chances which a farmer's son has of obtaining a good education and a well-paid office are, as we have seen, far less than he imagines them to be. But most of the successful elite are still identified with their home areas, serving for the youth as models of possible achievement. So many men have graduated when nearer forty years of age than thirty, that others in their twenties still assiduously prepare for university entrance examinations, ever postponing the age when they will have to admit that they have lost the chance. It is significant that those who aspire to elite status are the skilled manual workers, the junior clerks and teachers – the very people one would expect to find active in radical political and protest movements; revolutionary leadership has rarely been drawn, anywhere in the world, from the most depressed and poverty-stricken groups.

The continued evocation of nationalist sentiments is a further factor inhibiting the development of class consciousness. The attainment of independence is seen as a national struggle, not as the effort of specific ethnic groups nor even of the elite alone, for it was the success of the last in arousing popular support which legitimized, in the sight of the colonial powers, their right to govern. Their achievement of independence has constituted one of the major claims of political leaders to continue in office, and their electorates have usually conceded this point. Party workers have subsequently developed the charismatic appeal of their leaders, who are seen as 'men of the people', humbly dressed in their public appearances, yet living apart in exotic palaces. They symbolize the fusion of the traditional glories of their people and the expectations of the modern world; but neither their public images nor their pronouncements give the ordinary man a clear guide to action or belief. Often the charismatic leader is seen as a miracle worker; C.P.P. propagandists at one time attributed a virgin birth to Nkrumah. The emphasis lies on the rewards which the leader will bring, and so the leaders are personally identified with the most grandiose projects, with the Volta Dam or Pan-African unity. They delegate to others the explanations of high taxes or reduced prices for export crops. And they become highly vulnerable when the affluence promised to the masses fails to materialize.

There is a tendency for the symbols of national unity to consist more of persons than of physical objects or ideas. In Nigeria the newspapers display photographs of cocktail parties at which the local elite, glasses in hand, mix on equal terms with visiting dignitaries. Their success in reaching the highest circles is thus demonstrated to their kin and supporters at home. Most West Africans could, one suspects, name those men native of their own home area who are prominent in the capital; fewer would recognize a photograph of the national parliament or other public buildings; and very few indeed would be able to recite the words of their national anthems (which are not even in the vernacular languages).

The outlets for tension. As conflicts develop with economic changes and the evolution of new forms of social stratification, so do tensions increase. Yet numerous factors inhibit the articulation of grievances in specifically economic terms and the development of sentiments of class consciousness. Furthermore, the institutionalized channels for the expression of such grievances are becoming less effective, so that protests are not directed against the structure of society by organized political movements. Instead, individual frustrations are expressed through charges of tribalism and corruption, of witchcraft and sorcery. Action lies in developing one's own relationships with influential patrons and in seeking from supernatural agencies protection against evil forces and support in one's aspirations. Outbreaks of aggressive behaviour tend to lack coherent leadership or organization, to be without any class ideology or goals – save a general attitude of destruction directed against those with wealth, power or property. Violence of this type is most difficult to control and constitutes a major threat to the stability of the new states. But before examining further the consequences of such aggression, it is necessary to look briefly at the tensions developing within the elites of the new states.

Competition within the elite

The elites of the West African states each possess a considerable internal homogeneity. Their occupations have a limited range, with a marked preponderance of bureaucratic posts and certain professions. There is little variety in their educational background. Members enjoy very similar styles of living. Their families tend to intermarry. An intricate network of relationships links members through friendship and formal associations.

The elites are highly privileged groups, their members enjoying an affluence which would have been beyond the comprehension of their fathers and grandfathers. Yet these privileges stem directly from the governments, which employ the majority of the well-educated men and set the pattern for conditions in other spheres. The elite are thus beholden to the politicians in power, and dependent on them not only to preserve these privileges but also to ensure the expansion of the economy, so that new offices may be created, and promotion prospects enhanced. A few independent voices have argued that the educated receive excessive salaries, disproportionate to the earnings of the masses. But no general move to renounce their privileges has been made by the elite. For most of the elite, the assumption of the privileges enjoyed by the colonial administrators is the surest sign of their equality with their former masters.

The elite are certainly conscious of their position in their society, and of the power and responsibility that has befallen them. Many members tend to be disparaging in their references to the illiterate farmers and craftsmen of their country. Yet most of them are only first-generation recruits to the ranks of the privileged, and so whilst they deny any fundamental cultural differences between themselves and the remaining members of their ethnic groups, they are training their children to occupy an elite status, giving them the best schooling and often restricting their interaction with children of humble parentage. It is very difficult to measure the degree to which individual members of the elite are committed to the evolving values of the group or to which they see the elite as merely a means to the advancement of their personal careers.

In the 1950s the rapid expansion of the bureaucracies resulted in the creation of more posts than there were qualified men to fill. It was easy to find employment, but the rapidity of promotion at this period created a highly competitive atmosphere in all the offices. Now, a declining rate of expansion, together with the increased output of secondary schools and universities, has created in the more advanced West African states a relative shortage of vacancies and strong competition to fill them. In such situations, the criteria upon which appointments and promotion are based become matters of deep concern. Traditional criteria vie with those which are believed more appropriate to modern institutions. Within the elite, accordingly, there exists a competition for power, for control over the apparatus of the new states, between groups basing their claims upon incompatible criteria of achievement.

These rival criteria have already been outlined in previous chapters. Elite status is, by definition, almost impossible in modern West African society without education. But this criterion may in certain situations be subordinated to that of birth. It is difficult in Monrovia for a man who is not an Americo-Liberian to obtain high office. In Lagos the Northern Nigerian politicians who dominated the Federal government distrusted the loyalty of a civil service almost entirely staffed by southerners. They introduced northerners to redress the balance, and southerners replaced by men of considerably less education and experience felt accordingly aggrieved. With the recent expansion of higher education, many of the recent entrants to the bureaucracies are more highly qualified than their superiors. Yet the latter move ahead to the highest offices by virtue of their age and length of service. In societies where education is keenly felt to be the touchstone of modernization, the respect paid to other criteria of achievement is not well received by the educated. The early political leaders came from the ranks of the educated elite; they were teachers, lawyers or doctors. Modernization has led to a growth in the numbers not only of African bureaucrats but also, in some states, of party functionaries, men owing their rise in the hierarchy to their loyalty, organizing abilities, or local popularity. When the decisions of these men, made in terms of political expediency, govern the policies to be followed by the bureaucrats, the latter feel that their commitment to rational action is threatened.

The tensions which derive from these conflicting criteria of achievement are experienced by men who feel, in many cases, doubts of their own adequacy in tackling the problems that face their country, fears that their ability may not match that of Europeans in similar situations. Their early enthusiasm for the tasks of government may well turn to apathy, as they withdraw into ritualistic attitudes towards their work. In seeking to redress their grievances, these men are unable, by virtue of their employment, to take direct action against their governments; even those who are self-employed often rely heavily on official patronage. They seek to attain their ends by informal means through the networks of friendship. Yet in these states where such values as liberty of expression have been most seriously assailed by the political leaders, the educated elite, who have earlier vocally supported such values, have often remained curiously silent and inactive. They are probably unwilling that any dispute with the political leaders should become so overt as to arouse mass feelings and threaten the stability of the government, with inevitable consequences for their own status in society.

Military coups

In January 1966, the President of Upper Volta handed over power to his military leaders. Commenting upon both this coup and that in the Central African Republic of a few days earlier, the British press tended to stress both the economic poverty of these small states, and their sudden and unprepared attainment of independence from French rule. But within the same month, whilst Lagos was still enjoying the publicity of the Commonwealth Conference, the army seized power in Nigeria, and the Federal Prime Minister, his Minister of Finance, and the Premiers of the Northern and Western Regions were killed in the process. A month later, during Nkrumah's absence from his country, the Ghanaian army and police deposed him, detaining his Ministers and closest supporters and formally abolishing the C.P.P. The political systems of Nigeria and Ghana were markedly different from each other; and these two states were among the richest in West Africa. The lesson of the three coups seems to be that no one type of government is significantly less susceptible to takeover than any other.

The role of the military must be described in relation to the tensions which we have seen to exist in West African states. Army officers, resident in their barracks often far from the capital, are not associated with the 'high life' of the politicians and educated elite. Their duties impinge little upon the everyday lives of the people, and they are free from the taint of corruption and nepotism associated with the administration of social services. In Nigeria the army won popular acclaim for its peace-keeping role in the Congo. In most of the newly independent states, the army was one of the last institutions to be fully Africanized. Its indigenous officers were men highly trained in the staff colleges of the metropolitan country. Their appointments and promotions were believed to rest entirely on ability; the introduction of political factors, as when Nkrumah replaced both the British G.O.C., General Alexander, and later his Ghanaian Chief-of-Staff, General Ankrah, caused resentment within the army. The senior army officers tend to be men conservative in outlook; their training has imbued them with a strong *esprit de corps*. It was reported that the Sardauna of Sokoto tried to remove the southern heads of the Nigerian army and police force, sending them on extended leave and promoting northern officers; but the northerners concerned themselves foiled this attempt. The discipline of the army stands in contrast to the schismatic tendencies in most elite protest movements, where each young intellectual believes that his opinions are as valid as anyone else's. But the army is not only a disciplined body of men; it also controls the use of physical force. And the ease and speed of the coups demonstrate how little force is needed to topple governments in these states.

Cohesive as the military elite may appear in contrast with other elite groups, it is not without its own divisions. Many of the most senior officers have risen from the ranks, having joined the army as clerks on leaving primary school in the early 1940s. Many of the junior officers are thus more highly educated, with several of them university graduates. Their military training and promotion has been far more rapid as armies have grown in size and been Africanized, and they tend to be more radical than their superior officers.

Nigeria. The Nigerian military coup of January 1966 was the consequence of a complex situation in which most of the conflicts cited previously were represented. There has, however, been a tendency to ascribe it overwhelmingly to ethnic divisions in the country, at the expense of incipient class conflicts.

The feudal structure of the emirates in the Northern Region, substantially preserved under colonial rule, contrasts with the tribal organizations of the more southerly societies. The latter, and especially those nearer the coast, accepted Western education early and thus dominate the modern sector of the economy. The N.P.C. leaders, representing the Fulani aristocracy, were initially reluctant to accede to Nigeria's independence, but agreed when it appeared that the Northern Region would have at least half the seats in the Federal Legislature (on the basis of its population in the 1952 census) and that each Region would have considerable powers of self-government. The dominant position in the Federation of the N.P.C. then became more apparent as the party won the allegiance of almost all areas in the Northern Region; after the 1959 election, it emerged as the senior partner in the Federal government, allied with the N.C.N.C., while the Action Group led by Awolowo constituted the opposition.

The status of the Fulani aristocracy, protected by the British, was seriously threatened by the modernization of the 1950s – by increasing industrialization and by the growing power of Federal and Regional governments. But during this period the N.P.C. leaders realized that the preservation of their status lay not in isolation but in control of the Federal government and of the modern sector of the economy, so that the emirates would experience only those changes which their rulers could accommodate. This realization was expressed in demands for a greater share of the administrative posts and in the census issue. The results of the 1962 census were never released but were believed to have given the southern Regions a majority in population over the North – thus legitimizing a demand by the southern politicians for a majority of seats in the federal legislature and the relegation of the N.P.C. to the status of a minority party. A later census gave the Northern Region the same share of the total population as had that of 1952, and southerners immediately claimed that these figures had been rigged. Nor were fears of total Northern domination eased by the Sardauna's references to the continuance of the *jihad* and the megalomania of his aspirations to the role of Dan Fodio. The Muslims of the North, however, though united by the dire predictions of their own politicians on the fate of

Islam should the southerners ever achieve control of the North, were divided by their sectarian movements, with the vast membership of the Tijaniya only lukewarm in their support for the orthodox Sardauna.

The Nigerian crisis of 1965- early 1966 did not stem immediately from the situation in the North, however, but from events in the Western Region and, in particular, from the rift between its two leading politicians, Awolowo and Akintola. Personal, and to some extent ethnic rivalries divided these men. A complex constitutional relationship existed between them since Awolowo, after 1959, was Leader of the Opposition in the Federal Parliament and Leader of the Action Group, while Akintola was Premier of the Western Region and subordinate to Awolowo in the party. The more vital difference was an ideological one. Having solidly established the Action Group in the Western Region, Awolowo sought to make it a national party, campaigning in the 1959 Federal election on tribal issues in the non-Ibo East and in the Middle Belt, but on class issues, in alliance with N.E.P.U., in the emirates. The size of the Action Group vote in some of the wealthier constituencies displayed cracks in the solidarity of Hausa society. Akintola, however, sought to retain the Action Group as a regional party, with the ultimate aim of forming a national coalition of the dominant parties in each Region.

A fracas in the Ibadan parliament in June 1962 led the Federal Government to declare a state of emergency and to impose six months of administrative rule. All politicians were temporarily exiled; but whilst Akintola was then restored to power, apparently loyal to N.P.C. leadership, Awolowo was gaoled for conspiring to overthrow the state and acquired thereby an aura of martyrdom. These events left the Yoruba divided in their allegiance between the two rival leaders. In power, Akintola then sought to win support by appealing to Yoruba ethnic loyalties. But over two years of rule seem to have done little to increase his popular support. The first Regional election following his reinstatement as Premier was held in October 1965; it was marked by considerable violence before polling day, and the subsequent victory of his party was widely believed to have been rigged. Violence continued, and was clearly not limited to party thugs. The bands of lawless youths who waylaid traffic on the main roads demonstrated a complete breakdown in the authority of the government.

An underlying cause of tension in Nigeria has thus been the Fulani aristocrats' fear for the integrity of their traditional social structure, together with the corresponding fear among the southerners of Fulani domination, vocalized most frequently in ethnic terms and representing the supremacy of values in a premodern society. But the southerners have been unable to combine effectively to resist the Northern threat, for although their political parties contain the same range of ideologies, competition, in particular among the Yoruba and Ibo elite, has been most intense. Elite protests against the census debacle quickly fizzled out, though leaving some deep resentment. The masses grew disgusted with the corruption and inefficiency of their politicians, but no issues mobilized them into action. The tense political atmosphere undoubtedly aggravated the violence of the reactions to poverty and unemployment. But this violence was directed randomly against the affluent elite (though Hausa communities in Lagos and Ijebu towns were also attacked).

The coup was apparently organized by junior army officers. It seems possible that they had planned to confront Akintola and the Federal Prime Minister with the gaoled Awolowo, in an attempt to force the formation of a national government. The killing of the Sardauna removed the main threat of counter-action. But the logistics of the operation were very complicated. Within a few hours General Ironsi had gained control of the situation. The rump of the Federal cabinet abdicated power to him, and military rule was instituted.

It is still not clear whether the rebel army officers saw themselves acting primarily as Ibo – as most of them were – or as radicals. However, in the ensuing months, military rule seemed to the other ethnic groups to look like an Ibo bid for power. The rebel officers were arrested but not charged; to the army officers from the North the rebels were the murderers of their colleagues; to many in the south they were national heroes. The death of the Sardauna provoked surprisingly little open resentment in the North, indicating perhaps both the growing opposition to his megalomania and the religious divisions in Hausa society; but the Hausa did resent the rejoicing by some Ibo in the streets.

Ironsi, though an Ibo, had never been identified as a protagonist for his ethnic group. But, in the months of military government, he seemed to lean most heavily on his Ibo advisers. Other Ibo tried to exploit ethnic relationships in their own interests. The promotion of army officers to fill the gaps left by the coup seems to have favoured the Ibo. Plans were hurriedly advanced to promote the administrative unity of Nigeria; regional government was to be abolished and much of the Native Authority system of the North seemed threatened. To the Northerners it seemed that the Ibo would be able to increase their domination of the North through their control of high civil service offices. With each month there was growing disenchantment with military rule as it not only failed to take measures which markedly improved living standards but also, through the investigations into the workings of the public corporations, showed that corruption was not confined to the politicians but was equally rife among the senior civil servants. But it was the specific fears of the Northerners which sparked off the May massacres of Ibo in the Northern towns.

At the end of July, a group of young army officers of Northern origin abducted General Ironsi at Ibadan, together with his host, the Military Governor of the Western Region, killing them both. Several Ibo officers and men were also killed in their stations. The Northern officers claimed that they had discovered a plot among young radical Ibo officers to displace General Ironsi; their own action was to forestall this. Colonel Gowan, son of a Christian evangelist from one of the small ethnic groups of the Jos plateau, succeeded as the new military ruler. This coup made overt the deep ethnic divisions within the Nigerian army. Ibo troops were repatriated to the East and it was held that, as far as possible, each of the Regions should have garrisons of local men. (However, with so few Yoruba in the army, battalions of Northerners at Ibadan and Lagos were inevitable.) The further loss of senior officers and the displacement of the survivors led to some men being promoted over the heads of their seniors; in particular, Colonel Ojukwu, Military Governor of the Eastern Region, was senior in rank to Colonel Gowan and reluctant on this, as well as other grounds, to accept his superiority.

The Ibo seem to have been unaware of the ethnic hostility which was building up against them, and the May massacres and the July coup came as a profound shock. They closed ranks and began moving back to their own Region; threats of secession were made with the corollary that the Easterners could only continue membership of a united Nigeria if reparations were made. Secession would have given the East full control over the oil revenues, making it richer than either West or North. (Though within the Eastern Region the Ijoh and Ibibio argued that the oil came from their land and they renewed their claim for a separate state.) In this period of tremendous political tension, Colonel Gowan managed to assemble a conference of politicians and notable men not closely identified with the parties most recently in power. (Awolowo was a leading member of the Western delegation.) But near the close of its meetings – at which progress towards reconciliation seemed apparent – rumours of Hausa deaths in Onitsha and Port Harcourt led to a renewed and far more vicious massacre of Ibo in the North. At least ten thousand were murdered and the remainder, numbering several hundred thousand, fled, usually without any possessions, back to their homes in the East. Very many Ibo senior civil servants in Lagos, university staff and students in Ibadan, also returned to the East, where commensurate posts were found for them.

Nigeria entered 1967 still formally intact, but with the Regions barely on speaking terms. A meeting of the Military Governors with their advisers, at ex-president Nkrumah's residence at Aburi, near Accra, indicated a slight thaw in the relationship between the East and the rest of the country. However the Ibo felt that their demands for reparations were not being met by the Federal military government and after successive threats, the Eastern Region seceded, proclaiming itself Biafra. The Federal Government launched a 'police action' to restore the integrity of the Nigerian state but this developed slowly into a bitter war as each side mobilized armies of unprecedented size and sought arms and aid from foreign powers. As Federal armies pushed slowly into Ibo country, Biafran claims that the northerners in the army were pursuing a policy of genocide further intensified the ethnic hostility in the country. These claims have been shown, by foreign observers, to be without foundation.

A political solution which both gives the Ibo the independence and security which they seek and yet preserves the integrity of Nigeria seems increasingly difficult to conceive. The Federal military government abolished the Regional structure of the country, instituting in its place twelve States with a high degree of local autonomy. The Western Region, almost completely Yoruba, constitutes one such State; but the Hausa-Fulani emirates of Northern Nigeria are divided between three whilst Bornu and two Middle Belt amalgamations cover the rest of the erstwhile Northern Region. The Eastern Region was divided into three States, two of these being largely of non-Ibo people. By this move the domination of Northern Nigeria has, it is presumed, been removed. The Middle Belt peoples enjoy a higher political status. In the Hausa-Fulani States the ruling Fulani aristocracy may perhaps hope to retain their privileged position; but increasing Federal control of local police and customary courts withdraws from the emirs their former coercive powers.

Ghana. Ghana's first coup ended a period during which Nkrumah's rule rested increasingly on coercion. But no specific event, save perhaps Nkrumah's absence, seems to have precipitated military action. To be sure, the state of the economy was such that outbreaks of violence were only to be expected. During the late 1950s and early 1960s, Ghana's sterling balances – her savings from the earlier high cocoa prices – were rapidly spent, to a significant degree on the infrastructure essential to a modern economy, but also on prestige buildings and unprofitable industries. Much of the development was paid for with external loans, and debt servicing became an increasing item of state expenditure; but falling cocoa prices reduced government revenues. In this condition of near-bankruptcy, a harsh budget was predicted. Higher taxes or enforced savings would have been added to the already rapidly rising cost of living in the major towns. The extravagant living of the political elite was, however, continuing unchecked, despite the occasional demands for genuine austerity.

The coup here seems to have been organized by the most senior officers of the army and police with no opposition from within the services, save from Nkrumah's own presidential guard at his official residence.[173a, 173b]

Upper Volta. An economic crisis more obviously led to the coup in Ouagadougou. An austerity budget in 1963 had been accepted without much protest; but that of 1965, cutting all salaries of public employees by twenty per cent and reducing family allowances, met with a hostile reception, in spite of the reductions made, on this occasion, in the salaries of the President and his Ministers. In this one-party state, the opposition to the government had developed largely within the trade unions, whose membership consisted almost entirely of civil servants. The union leader Ouedraogo, a political opponent of President Yameogo since Independence, had once been mayor of Ouagadougou. The threat of a strike was met by the President with a declaration of a state of emergency, making any strike illegal. But the workers filled the streets, clashing with the police; marched to the palace calling for the army to take power; and then marched to army headquarters, where their spokesman won the agreement of the army commander to assume the powers of the head of state – a decision which the President is said to have welcomed.

Sierra Leone. In March 1967 elections resulted in a very close result between the Sierra Leone People's Party of Albert Margai and the All People's Congress of Siaka Stevens. When the Governor-General invited the latter to form the Government, power was seized by Brigadier Lansana; but he too was soon replaced by Brigadier Juxon-Smith when the military coup seemed but an attempt to confirm Margai in power. A judicial commission held later that Stevens' party had in fact won the election but the military rulers seemed reluctant to restore power to a civilian government. In April 1968 a group of junior soldiers imprisoned most of the officers in the army and police, declared themselves an Anti-corruption Revolutionary Movement and ultimately placed Siaka Stevens in office. The unpopularity of the military government seems to have arisen from its apparent inability to cope with the country's social and financial problems and from the feeling that senior army officers were enjoying the luxuries of power in a manner associated hitherto with the corrupt politicians. In placing Stevens in office as Prime Minister the soldiers were not merely recognizing his declared success in the elections of a year previously but were giving power to a party which, drawing its support from the urban workers, reflected their own interests. In contrast, the Sierra Leone People's Party was traditionalist, supported by the chiefs and creoles.

The results of the coups. The military coups won popular acclaim. In Ghana many people celebrated in the streets with the same fervour as they had displayed in the C.P.P. demonstrations of a few years earlier. In Western Nigeria, violence almost immediately ceased – only in part because of army threats to shoot the disorderly on sight. Political corruption was made the scapegoat for all national shortcomings, and leading politicians were either detained or rusticated to their villages. Political appointees were removed from public corporations, local government councils and courts. Decisions were made by military councils depending very heavily upon the advice of senior civil servants – re-creating, in fact, a colonial type of administration. The new regimes were thus popular with the elites; property was now safeguarded from attack, and political decisions were more likely to be based upon administrative or economic logic than on political expediency.

The coups certainly lowered the levels of tension in the countries concerned. But it remains to be seen whether the military governments will effect any major changes in the structure of their societies. In Upper Volta, the new regime cancelled the twenty-per-cent salary cuts. In neither Nigeria nor Ghana were any measures announced either to curb the privileges of the elite or impose a heavier burden on the masses, in a coherent and persuasive programme of sacrifice for national development. The military leaders seem to envisage their rule as a holding operation, until the permissible return of elected government; though this is rendered difficult with the banning of all political activity – both of the erstwhile governing parties and of their rivals. In Ghana a civilian Political Advisory Committee has been set up to advise the military government; its first Chairman is Dr Busia, hitherto the exiled leader of the banned United Party. In Nigeria leading politicians of the Action Group and its allies have been appointed as Commissioners in the Federal Ministries.

In general, however, the military coups reinforced the status of the Western-educated elites in West African societies, by staving off the complete collapse of governments threatened by the ineptitude of the politicians. Yet the conflicts inherent in these societies demanded that decisions must be made which would be unpopular either with the elite or with the masses. Rival groups examined the military pronouncements for signs of bias. In Nigeria it was soon alleged that the new regime was favouring the Ibo, since most of the prominent officers seemed to be from this ethnic group. In Ghana, it was rumoured that the coup was plotted at the race course – thus identifying the military rulers with the older professional elite and suggesting their aversion from radical change.

Dahomey was the first West African state to undergo military rule. With the exceptions described above, and of Togo and Mali, the other states are still (in February 1972) ruled by elected leaders. But the conflicts outlined here would seem to be present in each one of them. That they have not so far resulted in marked political instability may be due to a number of factors. Wealthier countries, such as the Ivory Coast, are better able to satisfy the aspirations of their people. The poorest countries, which have been unable or unwilling to increase educational facilities, are spared the problem of unemployed school leavers with unrealistic aspirations drifting to the towns. In some states, the political activity at village level gives the masses a sense of participation in government which is lacking in other states. The politicians of some states live in the wildest extravagance, whilst in others a more spartan style of life is enjoined. It is perhaps in the wealthier states, in those which have progressed furthest in the modernizing process that the conflicts become most acute. Crises occur when the means of mediating the conflicts and resolving the tensions are not equal to the tasks set.

14 Postscript: 1972

With the passage of years slow quantitative changes in the structure of society develop, often imperceptibly, into qualitative changes. But our perception of society and of the social processes ongoing within it alters, not only because that society changes but also because we bring to our study new concepts and new propositions. With each new decade we pose different questions, highlight different themes. In the six years since the foregoing pages were written little has happened which encourages me to alter radically the general framework of my argument. But there are a number of themes which I mentioned but briefly or by implication – themes which seem likely to dominate discussion in the 1970s. In this brief postscript I hope to present some of these.

In 1946, Margery Perham, doyen of writers on colonial affairs and, for her day, an outspoken liberal, could still write in her Foreword to Awolowo's blueprint for constitutional development 'I do not mean . . . that the British Government will or should in the immediate future hand over final responsibility for this vast region with its still unintegrated groups of peoples to the first small group of African officials and professional men who emerge at the centre.'[156] Yet this is exactly what did happen – in fourteen years Nigeria was independent. The speed of political development in the 1950s, in most of the West African colonies, filled both the African elite and expatriate observers with a sense of euphoria. Furthermore, there seemed to be wealth abounding – from savings husbanded by the Colonial powers, from increased foreign aid and from favourable terms of trade. The politicians' promises of 'Life More Abundant' filled one with hope. In this situation the attention of scholars was focused on the process of modernization, presumed to be progressing smoothly, and on the tactics and strategies of the elite in wresting power from the colonial rulers.

These hopes, in retrospect rather wild ones, have not been fulfilled. Military regimes have replaced elected parliaments in half of the independent states, the economies are stagnating and the flamboyant schemes of the fifties seem to be petering out. To the visitor coming to West Africa for the first time it is still one of the most colourful and vivacious quarters of the world. But for the expatriate with long contacts, as for the educated African, active participation in the events of the past quarter century ends at best with a sober realization of unpleasant facts, at worst with cynicism and disillusion.

One aspect of this change can be seen in the relative decline in scholarly interest in West Africa. Africanists for a time turned their attentions to Tanzania, the one state which seemed intent on developing socialism. Today Latin America attracts the Western scholar for, with its various guerrilla movements, its one communist government in Chile and an apparently radical military regime in Peru, that is where the action lies. West Africa is left to the journalists, recording civil wars but failing to explain them. One vein in current literature is cynical. Africa's predicament is ascribed to the venality of her educated elites – a venality which is ascribed more to the moral weakness of individuals than to the structure of society. This literature is unhelpful. More pertinent is the literature which examines the relationship between the African states and the industrial nations of the world, including here the erstwhile metropolitan powers. In the fifties and sixties we focused upon the background and the achievements of Africa's leaders; today we stress the importance of the rigid constraints within which these men operate, constraints which contribute to their failure to achieve the promised goals. This change in approach is world-wide and not limited to Africa. It is manifest, furthermore, at many levels – in the increased popularity of radical organizations devoted to the problems of the Third World, in the writings of economists and sociologists, such as Andre Gundar Frank, who ascribe the continuing poverty of the underdeveloped nations to their relationships with the industrial nations and, at a level of academic abstraction, in the swing away from explanations of social process exclusively in terms of structure and function to those which focus upon individual action and the factors which guide and constrain it. This changed intellectual climate influences our perception of African society. But whilst the liberals of the fifties erred in postulating an almost inevitable process of evolutionary modernization, the radicals in the seventies may err equally in imposing their concepts, of class and conflict for instance, on African data. I do not wish to deny the usefulness of such concepts, but merely to warn against the presumption that concepts and propositions developed to explain the development of industrial society will *neatly* fit the contemporary African scene. There is no alternative to the study of Africa itself. It is perhaps a sad reflection upon the state of our knowledge that the comments in the following pages rest more upon my own impressions gained from recent visits to Nigeria than upon rigorous analysis by sociologists.

The economy

Statistics of the Gross National Product of African states, though but a crude guide, demonstrate nevertheless the declining rate of development. In many states a rate of growth of between 4 per cent and 8 per cent had declined noticeably in the mid-sixties. For instance, Nigeria was experiencing a slower rate even before the onset of the civil war; and for Dahomey it has been argued that the G.N.P. in real terms has declined absolutely in recent years. If we break down these figures into the component sectors of the economy the general picture is as follows: traditional agriculture is virtually stagnant, as few means of improving yield have been successful and as young men migrate to the towns; in contrast, the manufacturing sector has increased, often by between 10 per cent and 20 per cent a year, but its beginnings were so small that its contribution to the national wealth is still minimal; some countries have been lucky in developing new exports, such as oil, whilst the unfortunate ones have witnessed falling prices for their existing commodities. This last factor largely accounts for the disparity in the fortunes of individual states. Concurrent with it is a cycle within the manufacturing sector. From negligible beginnings import substitution industries are established but the home market is eventually satiated and inter-state trade is still almost non-existent. Thus the apparent comparative affluence of the Ivory Coast in the past two decades reflects this period of rapid industrialization – a period which may now be ended.

Set against this rate of economic growth is the rapidly increasing population. Family planning programmes are fostered in many states, but these rarely reach the mass of the people and the educated elite who do adopt these measures still *prefer* a family of four children and often have more. When economic growth of 3 per cent is matched by population growth of 2·5 per cent the effect on the average man is imperceptible.

The economies of the African states are still firmly dominated by the industrial nations. The success of the manufacturing sector, cited above, rests largely upon expatriate firms which provide most of the capital and initiative even though local bodies are accepted as willing partners. New exports, too, are due to foreign initiative. In spite of setbacks caused by the civil war, oil now accounts for half of Nigeria's exports; though the Nigerian government has now set up its own company to exploit this resource, its development so far has rested with the major international companies. In this case the political repercussions have been obvious. Though obviously not the prime cause of the civil war, the promised wealth of the oilfields first encouraged the Ibo leaders to secede in as much as their new state would be one of the wealthiest in Africa, and then enabled them to bargain for the support of foreign powers, notably France, in return for the concessions to be seized from the existing holders. The cocoa-producing countries of the world have, in spite of repeated conferences, been unable to combine to control output and curb falling prices. In Nigeria, the government has not been able to reduce the price paid to the farmers; the revenue of the Western state has fallen dramatically, with a consequent constraint upon development in the public sector. Though yields of cocoa have increased, the costs of disease control reduce the farmer's net return. African governments still find it extremely difficult to generate private savings and this obliges them to remain dependent on foreign assistance.

One aspect of disillusion with Africa is the slight fall in the total annual amount of foreign aid received in the late 1960s. Traditional donors – Britain, France and the U.S.A. – reduced their aid quite substantially, whilst some other countries – notably West Germany, Italy and Canada – increased theirs, though not on a scale to match that of the traditional donors. Much of this aid is spent in the donor country. Past aid has produced the chronic indebtedness in which many states now find themselves. As the forerunner in the race to Independence, Ghana industrialized at a relatively early period and her debts have accumulated; many of the foreign-financed state enterprises have been unprofitable. Busia's collapse resulted from this indebtedness. His personal leanings are very pro-Western and in seeking the support of the West he could not renounce his country's debts. The military regime has announced the cancellation of a substantial part of the debts. National accounts are notoriously difficult to compile but it seems likely that, in some West African states, the income from aid is more than balanced by debt-repayment, and the repatriation of profits and savings. It is sometimes the African state which is the donor country!

Most of the West African states did not sever, dramatically, their ties with their metropolitan countries, though several have diversified their overseas relationships. At one extreme the Ivory Coast remains very closely associated with France; the dominance of French administrators is still a political issue here, long after it has died elsewhere. Of the states which said '*non*' to France, Mali has re-entered the franc zone and Guinea is increasingly dependent on the U.S.A. Within each state, too, there are differences of opinion. The independent businessman is apt to favour closer ties with private overseas firms, seeing these to be to his own advantage. The civil servant, whether from ideological beliefs in state planning and socialism, from a personal desire to control the economy or from an interest in the lucrative gains which this control can yield, often puts obstacles in the path of this private development, though rarely achieving any tangible alternative. Businessmen and civil servants are, however, agreed on policies of restricting small-scale business to indigenes, as have recently been enacted in Nigeria and Ghana.

Continued dependence upon the industrial West has constrained the development of close ties between the African states. In fact, considerable antagonism has been produced when, for instance, one country in an overt but probably misdirected effort to solve unemployment, expels (as Ghana and the Ivory Coast have done) migrants from neighbouring territories. Again, France's closest associates, the Ivory Coast and Gabon, supported Biafra in the Nigerian civil war. The Organization of African Unity, founded in 1963, is united on few issues; one is the liberation of Africans in Rhodesia and the Republic of South Africa, but even here unity is broached by the arguments of the Ivory Coast that a dialogue with South Africa is possible.

Political developments

Seven of West Africa's fourteen independent states have experienced military regimes; six are still (in March 1972) so ruled. In the others, the political leaders who led the independence movements from the beginning of the 1950s are (save for exceptions due to deaths) still in power. Opposition groups are weak and seem unlikely to produce alternative governments in the near future. Even in those states with military regimes, the political leaders brought in to assist the soldiers, and in some cases to succeed them, are men long prominent in the nationalist movement but who had fallen foul of the ousted political regimes. Thus we see Awolowo reinstated in Nigeria – as senior civilian in the military government; Busia elected as Prime Minister of Ghana. In those states which have experienced governmental continuity, the changes in the political scene are not easy to detect. It would appear that in some states there is a growing conflict between the members of the party organization and the civil servants and professionals – a conflict similar to that seen in East European countries. To introduce young technocrats into the government, as elderly presidents such as Senghor and Houphouet-Boigny are reported to be doing, assuages the demands of the bureaucracy, but at the expense of loyal party workers. This is, however, a process which merits much more study.

The military coup should not be seen as an attempt by an external body to mediate between two antagonistic elite groups or between politicians and masses. The officer corps is a part of the educated elite and its intervention occurs to maintain the existing privileged position of that elite in the society. Intervention occurs in a variety of situations (which can be compounded since they are not mutually exclusive): firstly, when political groups begin, or seem likely to begin, to fight among themselves so that there is a breakdown of law and order – this occurred in Nigeria in late 1965 and was threatened in Sierra Leone in 1967; secondly, when skilled workers and clerks, the only groups in society effectively able to mount an organized protest, strike against austerity cuts and so threaten to bring the nation (or at least the modern sector) to a standstill; thirdly, when the status of the army itself is threatened by pay cuts, or by being supplanted by a politically recruited force.

In a brilliant study of the Nigerian army, Luckham has shown that the officers have come from the same range of social backgrounds as other members of the educated elite – the fathers of some were illiterate farmers, of others, prosperous businessmen. Their formal schooling usually ended at the secondary level, very few being university graduates. For them the army was an alternative route to high status, for officers' salaries are on a par with those of senior civil servants. Their military training was brief and limited in scope and they tend to envy the education of the civil servant or professional; they emphasize that 'officers are gentlemen'.[181]

In acceding to power, the military bans all political activity and (in an an effort to cleanse the Augean stables) often institutes commissions of inquiry into corruption. With the dissolution of parliaments and local government councils an autocratic colonial-type regime is restored. Councils of officers replace cabinets as superior decision-making bodies, but administration below this level is left to the civil service – one does not find the officers acting as provincial and district administrators for there are too few of them. The military leaders thus rely heavily on the permanent secretaries, whose reaction is to bring forward their plans which the politicians had shelved. Lacking the education of the civil servant or the intuition of the politician, the military leadership tends to be neither far-sighted nor astute.

The initial wave of popular enthusiasm at the time of the coup soon wanes, and the military leaders begin to feel the need of popular support. Officers, living in barracks, are not as accessible to individual representations as were the politicians; nor is the sanction of withdrawal of popularity particularly effective – in fact, the sanction of force rests with the soldiery. In Nigeria, 'leaders of thought' were first selected to advise the military government and these developed into Commissioners who were, in most cases, well-known politicians who functioned as Ministers, even occupying the same office in the Secretariat buildings.

As an elite group the officer corps is liable to the same internal divisions as other such groups. A few years in seniority represents a wide gap in rank, and so junior officers resent their seniors; this is exacerbated when political postings interfere with normal promotion practice. Ethnic or regional differences are, in fact, as real for officers as for others in spite of their overt solidarity. Finally, the officers find themselves divided in their attachment to the political leaders to whom, at some future date, they promise the reins of government. And as military leadership becomes less effective, so does popular discontent increase. This is especially so when, as happens, many senior army officers become as ostentatious and apparently corrupt as the politicians whom they displaced, building grand houses and establishing their wives as wealthy traders. In Ghana, charges against General Ankrah forced him to retire.

Military regimes have often, on their accession, implemented those austerity measures which the displaced politicians have been unable or unwilling to accept. But thereafter there seems to be little overall difference between the policies of military and civilian governments. Economic plans are drawn up but often remain little more than window-dressing; the fate of specific projects so often depends on foreign aid or private investment. The one target frequently overfulfilled is the growth of the administration. The social services continue to expand rapidly, the proportion of children in school rises, but at less than the projected rates. Nigeria has met its target of 10,000 university students by 1970, but, of these, under 50 per cent, rather than the planned 75 per cent, are scientists and technologists. Schemes for state industries and state farms have generally been dropped. Less is heard of mobilizing the entire population into creative activity, though Guinea did experience a 'cultural revolution' in 1967. Among the elite, *négritude* and African socialism have become dead issues. Finally, little or nothing has been done to alter *radically* the prevailing patterns of income distribution. Again, Nigeria furnishes a clear example. Senior civil service and university salaries had remained static since 1960, although wage earners had won increases during the decade. Rapid inflation after the civil war led to widespread though muted protest and undeniable hardship. The Adebo Commission, in its interim report, stated that whilst there was intolerable suffering at the bottom of the income scale, this was aggravated by the manifestations of affluence by the elite which could not be explained on the basis of visible and legitimate income; but it finally awarded increases ranging from 30 per cent for those earning £200 per year, to between 10 per cent and 20 per cent for those earning above £1,000.[184]

Social polarity

In my earlier discussion of the educated elite I stressed their varied social origins, the rapidity of their rise to their present status and the bureaucratic nature of most employment. Today I would emphasize a growing differentiation within these elite groups and a consolidation of their privileged position.

Mention has already been made of the greater significance of the military elite. The commercial elite too has been growing as Africans establish their own businesses, either as satellites of expatriate firms or as independent enterprises at a level between these firms and the local craftsmen. Recent studies of such entrepreneurs have tended to show that education is not apparently a qualification for their success. Significant, too, is the commercial activity of the salaried elite. On the security of their salaries these men can easily obtain loans to build houses – for themselves but also for renting to expatriates and urban wage earners. With rents exceeding mortgage repayments they become affluent landlords with ease. Though usually barred from secondary employment, these same men can establish their wives or close relatives as traders, contractors and the like. The prerequisites are capital or security and the influence to win government or industrial contracts.

The wealth so gained enables such men not only to educate a larger number of kin but also to ensure the perpetuation of their status in their children. Private primary schools flourish and it is the products of these which now dominate the annual entry to the more prestigious secondary schools.

Within the educated elite one can thus see a growing differentiation between the affluent property-owning members and those who rely solely on salaries eroded by inflation. The former can enjoy an international 'middle-class' style of life; the poor promotion prospects of the latter, usually the later entrants to the bureaucratic cadres, make such styles for them an almost unrealistic goal.

The continuing links of the educated elite with their home towns and villages was stressed earlier. The ribbon development along the roads from provincial Yoruba towns is now of modern houses of the city-based elite; these are their country houses to which at weekends they return to participate actively in local affairs. Conversely, the local elite of traditional chiefs, traders and lorry-owners is much less in evidence. Probably they are poorer relative to the 1950s; they invest more in education or in city property than in flamboyant houses at home; their business is dependent more on government contracts and licences, less on local patronage. This eclipse of the local elite and the penetration of the countryside by the national elite is probably a widespread phenomenon, though not as yet widely reported.

The discussion above of economic changes has already indicated that real incomes of farmers and urban workers have not markedly increased during the past decade; for many they have fallen. Groundnut farmers, for instance, are slightly better off, cocoa and palm producers are poorer. In a debate on the movement of urban wage rates in Nigeria and the effectiveness of trade unions, it is argued that rates of real income for unskilled labour in Lagos rose, in the 1950s and 1960s, by less than the growth of the G.N.P.; thus, although the unions had frequently bargained for, and won, higher wage rates, they had not improved the relative status of their members.[177]

West African governments, both military and civilian, continue to assert strong control over trade unions, strikes of urban workers being one of the most effective modes of protest against the government. For this reason workers are apt to have little confidence in their leaders. Furthermore, trade unionists who leave the shop floor for high-ranking union offices are seen as aspiring to elite status and rejecting the workers. However, distrust of the union leadership is not incompatible with quite highly organized activity within individual factories (in fact unions tend to be encouraged by those firms with the best working conditions and high rates of pay, discouraged by those, often Asian, firms with lower standards). But when protests are directed more against the government than against the individual firm, there is apt to be poor coordination between unions and their branches.

The spectre of growing urban unemployment has haunted both expatriate scholars and city-based politicians. In the absence of proper registration of the jobless, the ever widening gap between the number of school leavers and of employees in recognized establishments has been taken as the unemployment index. But this postulated army of unemployed is not so apparent in African city streets and one is obliged to assume that many urban migrants find work of some kind, as employees of petty traders and craftsmen, and in performing services. Undoubtedly, many are irregularly employed; many too are engaged in activities which Western economists would not deem productive but which may well be socially beneficial in the African context. Almost all are very poor. But this is yet another of those fields in which there have been far too many pronouncements by experts – both expatriate and of the African elite – and far too little study of what is actually happening on the ground.

The growth of manufacturing industries increases the number

of skilled and semi-skilled workers in permanent employment; the substitution of highly mechanized modes of road building and the like for labour intensive modes has reduced the numbers of temporary and migratory unskilled workers. For many commentators, the labour force is developing the characteristics of an urban proletariat in the Western sense of that term. Indeed, the modes of work and the terms of employment are similar to those of Western industry. But this wage-labour force is still but a small minority of the urban population, most of whom are self-employed traders, craftsmen or professionals or employees of such small operators. The factory worker sees little or no opportunity to progress beyond the shop floor; the clerk sees himself on a bureaucratic ladder up which, by passing exams, he might rise; the self-employed man sees living in his own quarter wealthy traders, lorry-owners, who have risen to affluence from a social level similar to his own. The factory worker thus aspires to use his savings and skills and move into this 'open' sector of self-employment; he has no permanent commitment to the 'closed' sector of industrial employment.

How in a few concluding sentences can one sum up the contemporary West African scene? Once more I must stress that in generalizing about states with widely differing characteristics I am indicating the variables which I believe to be important. The disparity between rich and poor remains as wide as ever. Most of the rich have humble origins but the poor grow increasingly disillusioned as their own living standards fail to rise, and their admiration of the success of the elite turns to envy as they realize that they and their children cannot hope to reach similar heights. Military regimes and one-party civilian regimes have closed or curtailed the avenues of popular protest which existed when one could lobby, publicly abuse and vote against one's local politician. In several states there have been peasant rebellions, but these have been local and weakly coordinated, lacking positive and clearly formulated goals of changed social structure.[185] It has been relatively easy for their leaders to be bought off or removed by death or imprisonment. Similarly, national industrial strikes are rarely possible with the trade union leadership cowed into submission or allied with the government; furthermore, the workers' demands are limited to immediate monetary gains – the structure of society is accepted rather than criticized. Finally, organized political groups in opposition to the present regimes, which might canalize grass-roots discontent and protest to its own ends, are non-existent.

There continue to be tensions within the elite along several lines of cleavage – between ethnic groups, between elected politicians and bureaucrats, between private businessmen and civil servants controlling the economy, between the army and any ruling body which threatens its status. Each military regime in West Africa has promised to hand government back to elected politicians and some have already done so. With its monopoly of armed force it could continue to rule indefinitely but it seems concerned with its public image and prefers to retire to its barracks before public hostility becomes too embarrassing. One possible outcome, suggested by events in Ghana for instance, is an alternation of military and civilian rulers as each fail to cope effectively with their country's economic problems. The Nigerian example shows how politicians may, through their corruption and blatant attempts to maintain power, lose almost all support. In those countries still with civilian regimes, the politicians have evidently been more successful in maintaining the allegiance of bureaucrats and the masses.

Radical change in the immediate future seems unlikely. It is possible that a particular configuration of forces in any one country, generated internally but perhaps stimulated externally (for instance, by a sudden affluence through the exploitation of a new resource, by poverty through the decline of an existing one), could set in train a process of revolutionary development; but such changes cannot be predicted.

Appendix

The following notes contain brief comparative data on the states discussed in this book. Most of the statistics are taken from the *U.N. Statistical Year Book, 1964*. Population figures for some of the towns are from the *Statesman's Year Book 1965–66*; the figures for wage labour are from V. I. Junod and I. N. Resnick (eds.), *Handbook of Africa* (1963). The figures for Gross National Product (G.N.P.) have been converted from *Estimates of Gross National Product* prepared by the Agency for International Development for April 1963 and published in *Africa Report*, August 1963. Among the best up-to-date reference books now available are the annual *Africa Contemporary Record* (ed. Colin Legum) and *Africa South of the Sahara* (1971).

Dahomey

Area	44,000 sq. miles
Population	2·2 million
Chief towns	Porto Novo (cap.) (58,000); Cotonou (86,000); Abomey (19,000)
Principal ethnic groups	Fon (41%); Adja (13%); Yoruba (9%); Bariba
Economy	G.N.P. £28 million (£14 *per capita*) Value of exports £4·6 million (£2·1 *per capita*) Electricity production 9·6 million kwh. (4·3 kwh. *per capita*) Wage labour 22,000 (10 per 1,000 population)
Social services	Post-primary school enrolment 6,300 (2,900 per 1,000,000 population) Doctors 85 (39 per 1,000,000 population) Newspaper circulation 3,000 (1,400 per 1,000,000 population)

Government The French territory of Dahomey opted to join the French Community in 1958 and subsequently became independent in 1960. Dahomeyan politics have been dominated by the parties of Hubert Maga – drawing support from the northern parts of the state; of S. M. Apithy – supported in particular by southern Catholics; and of Justin Ahomadegbe – supported by the urban workers. These parties have changed titles, coalesced and broken apart in a confusing manner. Apithy and Maga jointly formed the Parti Dahoméen de l'Unité in 1960, and this party won all seats at the ensuing election; Maga became President and Apithy Vice-President of the Republic. Ahomadegbe's party, after a brief period of belonging to Maga's coalition government, was dissolved by government decree in 1961. In 1963, after military intervention, Ahomadegbe joined Maga and Apithy to form a national party, but senior army officers took control of the government in 1965; these were in turn replaced by younger officers in 1967. After a succession of abortive elections and military takeovers, a Presidential Commission, comprising the three politicians cited above, was set up in 1970.

Gambia

Area	4,000 sq. miles
Population	0·32 million
Chief towns	Bathurst (cap.) (40,000)
Principal ethnic groups	Mandingo (33%); Fulani (16%); Wolof (10%)
Economy	G.N.P. figure not available
	Value of exports £3·2 million (£10 *per capita*)
	Electricity production 7·4 million kwh. (23 kwh. *per capita*)
	Wage labour 6,000 (18 per 1,000 population)
Social services	Post-primary school enrolment 2,900 (8,700 per 1,000,000 population)
	Doctors 17 (51 per 1,000,000 population)
	Newspaper circulation 1,500 (4,500 per 1,000,000 population)

Government The Gambia, Britain's oldest West African territory, gained independence in 1965. The United Party, led by Pierre N'Jie, had its main strength among the Catholics of Bathurst and the Colony, while the Progressive Party, now led by Sir Dauda Jawara, was dominant in the Protectorate. In the 1960 elections each won overwhelmingly in its respective area and the two leaders first joined in coalition. Jawara became successively Prime Minister and President, whilst N'Jie later led the opposition party.

Ghana

Area	92,000 sq. miles
Population	7·3 million
Chief towns	Accra (cap.) (337,000); Kumasi (190,000); Sekondi-Takoradi (76,000); Tamale (40,000)
Principal ethnic groups	Akan; Ewe; Ga
Economy	G.N.P. £490 million (£71 *per capita*)
	Value of exports £97 million (£13 *per capita*)
	Electricity production 470 million kwh. (64 kwh. *per capita*)
	Wage labour 253,000 (35 per 1,000 population)
Social services	Post-primary school enrolment 180,000 (25,000 per 1,000,000 population)
	Doctors 315 (43 per 1,000,000 population)
	Newspaper circulation 201,000 (27,000 per 1,000,000 population)

Government The British Colony and Protectorate of the Gold Coast became independent in 1957, taking the name of Ghana, and was declared a Republic in 1960. The Convention People's Party, founded in 1949 by Kwame Nkrumah, was successful in all elections after 1951, Nkrumah becoming successively Prime Minister and President. Opposition came initially from the United Gold Coast Convention (of which Nkrumah had been General Secretary), and later from the United Party, a coalition of regional and ethnic parties led by Dr Kofi Busia. The C.P.P. government was overthrown by a military coup in 1966. Civilian rule was restored in 1969 and Busia became Prime Minister. His government was overthrown in a military coup in 1972.

Guinea

Area	96,000 sq. miles
Population	3·4 million
Chief towns	Conakry (cap.) (112,000); Kankan (25,000); Kindia (25,000)

Principal ethnic groups	Mande (including Malinke, Susu) (48%); Fulani (29%)
Economy	G.N.P. £66 million (£21 *per capita*)
	Value of exports £19·5 million (£5·7 *per capita*)
	Electricity production 147 million kwh. (42 kwh. *per capita*)
	Wage labour 109,000 (32 per 1,000 population)
Social services	Post-primary school enrolment 13,000 (3,800 per 1,000,000 population)
	Doctors 154 (45 per 1,000,000 population)
	Newspaper circulation 2,500 (740 per 1,000,000 population)

Government The French territory of Guinea became independent in 1958, having opted out of the French Community by voting '*non*' in the referendum. Sékou Touré became Prime Minister in 1958 and President in 1961. He had, in 1952, assumed the leadership of the Parti Démocratique de Guinée, founded in 1946 by Madeira Keita (now Minister of the Interior in Mali). Sékou Touré was elected Deputy in the French Assembly in 1956. In 1957 the P.D.G. overwhelmingly won the elections to the Guinean Territorial Assembly instituted under the *loi-cadre*.

Ivory Coast

Area	128,000 sq. miles
Population	3·7 million
Chief towns	Abidjan (cap.) (180,000); Bouaké (70,000)
Principal ethnic groups	Agni; Kru; Mande; Baole; Dan
Economy	G.N.P. £220 million (£66 *per capita*)
	Value of exports £82 million (£22 *per capita*)
	Electricity production 159 million kwh. (43 kwh. *per capita*)
	Wage labour 171,000 (46 per 1,000 population)
Social services	Post-primary school enrolment 14,000 (3,800 per 1,000,000 population)
	Doctors 123 (33 per 1,000,000 population)
	Newspaper circulation 4,000 (1,100 per 1,000,000 population)

Government The French territory of the Ivory Coast became independent in 1960, having voted in 1958 to remain within the French Community. The Parti Démocratique de la Côte d'Ivoire was founded in 1946 by Félix Houphouet-Boigny. It was successful in the 1946 elections to the French Assembly, Houphouet-Boigny being elected as a Deputy; he served in French cabinets between 1956 and 1959. The P.D.C.I. won all the seats in the elections to the Territorial Assembly in 1957, Auguste Denise becoming Vice-President and later Prime Minister. In 1959 Houphouet-Boigny returned from France to assume the leadership of party and government; he became President in 1960.

Liberia

Area	43,000 sq. miles
Population	1·0 million (estimates vary between 0·75 and 2·5 million)
Chief town	Monrovia (cap.) (80,000)
Principal ethnic groups	Mandingo; Gissi; Gola; Kpelle; Kru; Greboes
Economy	G.N.P. £57 million (£57 *per capita*) Value of exports £29 million (£29 *per capita*) Electricity production 84 million kwh. (84 kwh. *per capita*) Wage labour figure not available
Social services	Post-primary school enrolment 3,700 (3,700 per 1,000,000 population) Doctors 80 (80 per 1,000,000 population) Newspaper circulation 3,000 (3,000 per 1,000,000 population)

Government Liberia has been independent since 1847 and the True Whig Party has governed continuously from 1860, save for a period of Republican Party dominance from 1871–7. William V. S. Tubman was President from 1943 until his death in 1971, when he was succeeded by the Vice-President, William Tolbert.

Mali

Area	465,000 sq. miles
Population	4·4 million
Chief towns	Bamako (cap.) (120,000); Kayes (28,000); Segou (19,000)

Principal ethnic groups	Bambara (23%); Fulani (12%); Songhai (5%); Tuareg
Economy	G.N.P. £88 million (£21 *per capita*) Value of exports £4 million (£0·9 *per capita*) Electricity production 21 million kwh. (5 kwh. *per capita*) Wage labour 42,000 (9·5 per 1,000 population)
Social services	Post-primary school enrolment 4,100 (900 per 1,000,000 population) Doctors 110 (25 per 1,000,000 population) Newspaper circulation 2,000 (450 per 1,000,000 population)

Government The French territory of Soudan opted in the 1958 referendum to remain within the French Community. In January 1959 it federated with Senegal to form Mali, and the federation gained independence in June 1960. But in August of the same year, the federation split, and the Soudan assumed the name of Mali. The Union Soudanaise was founded in 1946 by Mamadou Konaté, who died in 1956 having become a Deputy in the French Assembly. Leadership of the party passed to Modibo Keita who was also elected to the French Assembly. The U.S. won a majority of the seats in the 1957 election to the Territorial Assembly, and Keita became Prime Minister; the party won all seats in the 1959 elections and minor opposition parties merged with it to make it the sole party. An army coup deposed Keita in November 1968.

Mauretania

Area	419,000 sq. miles
Population	0·77 million
Chief towns	Nouakchott (cap.). (population figure not available); Kaedi (8,000)
Principal ethnic group	Moor (82%)
Economy	G.N.P. figure not available Value of exports £4 million (£5 *per capita*) Electricity production figure not available Wage labour 4,800 (6·2 per 1,000 population)
Social services	Post primary school enrolment 900 (1,200 per 1,000,000 population) Doctors 26 (34 per 1,000,000 population) Newspaper circulation figure not available

Government The Islamic Republic of Mauretania became independent in 1960, having been a constituent territory of French West Africa until 1958 and then a member of the French Community. The Parti du Regroupement Mauritanien was founded in 1947 (as the Union Progressiste Mauritanienne), and had the support of the French administration and of the Moorish traditional elite. The party was victorious in the elections to the Territorial Assembly in 1957, and Mokhtar Ould Daddah became the Prime Minister.

Niger

Area	490,000 sq. miles
Population	3·1 million
Chief town	Niamey (cap.) (30,000)
Principal ethnic groups	Hausa (47%); Songhai (23%), Fulani (18%); Tuareg (10%)
Economy	G.N.P. £43 million (£14 *per capita*) Value of exports £7 million (£2·3 *per capita*) Electricity production 14 million kwh. (4·5 kwh. *per capita*) Wage labour 13,600 (4·4 per 1,000 population)
Social services	Post-primary school enrolment 2,500 (800 per 1,000,000 population) Doctors 45 (15 per 1,000,000 population) Newspaper circulation 1,000 (320 per 1,000,000 population)

Government The French territory of Niger became independent in 1960. The Parti Progressiste Nigérien was founded in 1946. Its radical General Secretary, Bakary Djibo, left the P.P.N. to found the Union Démocratique Nigérienne in 1951. The P.P.N. narrowly won the 1956 elections to the French Assembly, but in the 1957 elections to the Territorial Assembly the U.D.N. won two thirds of the seats and formed the government. This party campaigned for a vote of *non* in the 1958 referendum and lost heavily, the chiefs having transferred their allegiance to the P.P.N.; the government resigned and won only 5 of 60 seats in the ensuing elections. It became known as the Sawaba party and was declared illegal in 1965 by the P.P.N. government of Hamani Diori.

Nigeria

Area	357,000 sq. miles
Population	55·6 million (Northern Region, 29·8; Western Region, 10·3; Eastern Region, 12·4; Mid-Western Region, 2·5; Lagos 0·67)
Chief towns	Lagos (cap.) (675,000); Ibadan (600,000); Kano (130,000); Onitsha (77,000); Port Harcourt (72,000); Enugu (63,000); Aba (58,000); Maiduguri (57,000)
Principal ethnic groups	Hausa-Fulani (27%); Ibo (17%); Yoruba (16%)
Economy	G.N.P. £1,180 million (£29 *per capita* [based on a pop. of 40 million])
	Value of exports £190 million (£3·4 *per capita*)
	Electricity production 929 million kwh. (17 kwh. *per capita*)
	Wage labour 466,000 (8·3 per 1,000 population)
Social services	Post-primary school enrolment 237,000 (4,300 per 1,000,000 population)
	Doctors 1,354 (24 per 1,000,000 population)
	Newspaper circulation 370,000 (6,700 per 1,000,000 population)

Government Elections to Regional and Federal parliaments were first held in 1951. Then, in 1957, the Regions became self-governing, and in 1960 Nigeria gained her independence. A Republic was declared in 1963. In the Northern Region the Northern People's Congress has been consistently victorious in regional elections, with its leader, Ahmadu Bello, Sardauna of Sokoto, in office as Prime Minister. Similarly in the Eastern Region the National Council of Nigeria and the Cameroons (later, with the secession of the Cameroons, the National Convention of Nigerian Citizens) has been continuously in power, with Nnamdi Azikiwe as the first Prime Minister. The Action Group of Obafemi Awolowo was victorious in the West. A split in the party occurred in 1962 between Awolowo, then leader of the Opposition in the Federal Parliament, and the Regional Premier, Samuel Akintola; the latter formed the Nigeria National Democratic Party and remained in power, being successful in the 1965 elections.

The Mid-West Region was excised from the Western Region in 1962, and Dennis Osadebay became Premier in an N.C.N.C. government. Sir Abubakar Tafawa Balewa, Vice-President of the N.P.C., became a Federal Minister in 1952. In 1957 he was appointed Chief Minister in a National Government of the three major parties, and following the 1959 Federal elections, became Prime Minister in a coalition government formed by the N.P.C. and N.C.N.C. After Independence Azikiwe became successively Governor-General and President.

Federal and Regional governments were overthrown by the military coup of January 1966.

Portuguese Guinea

Area	14,000 sq. miles
Population	0·55 million
Chief towns	Bissau (cap.) (population figure not available)
Principal ethnic groups	Balante; Pepel
Economy	G.N.P. figure not available
	Value of exports £2·8 million (£5 *per capita*)
	Electricity production figure not available
	Wage labour figure not available
Social services	Post-primary school enrolment 1,500 (2,700 per 1,000,000 population)
	Doctors 27 (49 per 1,000,000 population)
	Newspaper circulation 2,000 (3,600 per 1,000,000 population)

Government Portuguese Guinea is formally an overseas province of Portugal. Its Governor, responsible to the Minister of Overseas Territories in Lisbon, is advised by a council representing the military and civil administration. Political parties, in exile in neighbouring states, are engaged in subversive and revolutionary activity within the colony.

Senegal

Area	76,000 sq. miles
Population	3·4 million
Chief towns	Dakar (cap.) (380,000); Rufisque (48,000); St Louis (48,000); Kaolack (47,000); Thies (39,000)

Principal ethnic groups	Wolof (32%); Fulani (15%); Serer (14%); Toucouleur (11%); Dioula (5%)
Economy	G.N.P. £118 million (£63 *per capita*)
	Value of exports £40 million (£12 *per capita*)
	Electricity production 175 million kwh. (51 kwh. *per capita*)
	Wage labour 100,000 (29 per 1,000 population)
Social services	Post-primary school enrolment 19,500 (5,700 per 1,000,000 population)
	Doctors 145 (43 per 1,000,000 population)
	Newspaper circulation 20,000 (5,800 per 1,000,000 population)

Government The French territory of Senegal opted in 1958 to remain within the French Community. In 1959 it federated with Soudan to form Mali, and this gained independence in 1960. The federation, however, broke apart in the same year. The Bloc Démocratique Sénégalais was founded in 1948 by Léopold Senghor and Mamadou Dia, and was successful in the 1951 and 1956 elections to the French Assembly. It was then joined by Lamine Gueye's Section Française de l'Internationale Ouvrière (from which Senghor had originally seceded) in 1958 to form the Union Progressiste Sénégalaise. The U.P.S. won all seats to the Senegalese legislature in 1959, Senghor ultimately becoming President, and Dia, Prime Minister of the independent state. Dia was later ousted by Senghor.

Sierra Leone

Area	28,000 sq. miles
Population	2·2 million
Chief towns	Freetown (cap.) (128,000)
Principal ethnic groups	Mende (30%); Temne
Economy	G.N.P. £63 million (£25 *per capita*)
	Value of exports £29 million (£13 *per capita*)
	Electricity production 72 million kwh. (33 kwh. *per capita*)
	Wage labour 44,000 (20 per 1,000 population)
Social services	Post-primary school enrolment 10,400 (4,700 per 1,000,000 population)
	Doctors 112 (51 per 1,000,000 population)
	Newspaper circulation 18,000 (8,200 per 1,000,000 population)

Government Sierra Leone became an independent state in 1961. In 1951 Milton Margai formed the Sierra Leone People's Party, a party which successfully allied the interests of the creoles in the Colony and of the people in the Protectorate. Margai became Chief Minister when Sierra Leone gained internal self-government in 1954; then, as a result of a split in 1958 within the S.L.P.P., Albert Margai (brother of Milton) and Siaka Stevens formed the more militant People's National Party. Albert Margai's faction was, however, reunited with the S.L.P.P. in 1960, to form the United National Front. Stevens, supported by young radicals and trade unionists, formed the All People's Congress, which was in opposition to the U.N.F. After Milton Margai's death in 1964, his brother Albert became Prime Minister. A military coup took place in March 1967. A military counter-coup a year later placed in office Siaka Stevens and his P.N.P.

Togo

Area	22,000 sq. miles
Population	1·6 million
Chief town	Lomé (cap.) (80,000)
Principal ethnic groups	Cabrai (20%); Ewe (19%)
Economy	G.N.P. £37 million (£25 *per capita*)
	Value of exports £6·4 million (£4 *per capita*)
	Electricity production 11 million kwh. (7 kwh. *per capita*)
	Wage labour 12,000 (7·5 per 1,000 population)
Social services	Post-primary school enrolment 7,000 (4,400 per 1,000,000 population)
	Doctors 45 (28 per 1,000,000 population)
	Newspaper circulation 14,000 (8,750 per 1,000,000 population)

Government The major part of the German Colony of Togo was administered by France as a Trust Territory. (The remainder was subsequently integrated into Ghana.) The Comité de l'Unité Togolaise was formed by Sylvanus Olympio in 1946 and formed the governing party of the Territorial Assembly for that year. The party was then beaten in the 1951 elections to the French Assembly by the Parti Togolais de Progrès of Nicolas Grunitsky, which enjoyed the support of the French administration. Grunitsky was Prime Minister from 1956–8, but in the 1958 elections Olympio was successful and formed a government, becoming Prime Minister in 1958 and President, upon Togo's independence, in 1961. Olympio was assassinated in 1963. Grunitsky became President but was deposed in an army coup in 1967.

Upper Volta

Area	106,000 sq. miles
Population	4·5 million
Chief towns	Ouagadougou (cap.) (51,000); Bovo Dioulasso (51,000)
Principal ethnic groups	Mossi (50%); Bobo; Gurunsi
Economy	G.N.P. £63 million (£14 *per capita*) Value of exports £3·2 million (£0·7 *per capita*) Electricity production 16 million kwh. (3·5 kwh. *per capita*) Wage labour 25,000 (5·5 per 1,000 population)
Social services	Post-primary school enrolment 3,400 (750 per 1,000,000 population) Doctors 58 (13 per 1,000,000 population) Newspaper circulation 1,500 (330 per 1,000,000 population)

Government The French territory of Upper Volta became a member of the French Community in 1958 and independent in 1960. The Union Démocratique Voltaique was formed in 1956 through a merger of pre-existing parties and was led first by Ouezzin Coulibaly and, after his death in 1958, by Maurice Yameogo. The party was successful in elections to the Territorial Assembly in 1957 and in all subsequent elections. Yameogo became President in 1959, and abdicated in favour of a military government in December 1965. After elections in 1970 a government was formed in which government offices were shared between army officers and politicians (mostly opponents of Yameogo), pending a return to full civilian rule.

References and Further Reading

The literature on contemporary West African society grows apace yet the quality is uneven. Relatively little is based upon solid research, compared for instance with the anthropological studies of traditionally structured societies. More emphasis has been placed upon superficial political developments than upon the underlying tensions and changes in societies. The works cited below are those which have proved most useful in writing this book; the list is thus an idiosyncratic one. Many of the more stimulating articles from journals have been reprinted in readers and for ease of reference it is their latter location that I quote.

(*Italic numbers are cross-references to descriptions in the main numerical order.*)

General

[1] Guy Hunter, *The New Societies of Tropical Africa* (1962, Oxford University Press, London, for the Institute of Race Relations) and [2] G. H. T. Kimble, *Tropical Africa* (1960, The Twentieth Century Fund, New York, and in abridged form, 1962, Anchor Books, New York) both provide admirable introductions to contemporary African society. [3] Virginia Thompson and Richard Adloff, *French West Africa* (1958, Allen and Unwin, London) is a useful compendium on the French territories, though becoming rather dated. A more vivid analysis of the processes of change is to be found in [4] Thomas Hodgkin, *Nationalism in Colonial Africa* (1956, Frederick Muller, London) and [5] Peter Worsley, *The Third World* (1964, Weidenfeld and Nicholson, London). Broader perspectives however may be obtained from some of the rapidly growing number of symposia and readers. [6] Simon and Phoebe Ottenberg (eds.), *Cultures and Societies of Africa* (1960, Random House, New York) contains articles, mostly by social anthropologists, describing aspects of traditional and contemporary

African society, together with a long introduction by the editors outlining the structure of African traditional society. The readings in [7] Pierre L. van den Berghe (ed.), *Africa: Social Problems of Change and Conflict* (1965, Chandler Publishing Company, San Francisco) and the contributions to [8] William R. Bascom and Melville J. Herskovits (eds.), *Continuity and Change in African Cultures* (1959, University of Chicago Press, Chicago) stress, as their titles indicate, social change; the former is more sociologically oriented with sections on family structure, social stratification, urbanization and political movements, while the latter, largely the work of social anthropologists, focuses on the adaptation of traditional African institutions. Another reader in a sociological vein (covering Asia as well as Africa) is [9] Immanuel Wallerstein (ed.), *Social Change: The Colonial Situation* (1966, Wiley, New York). [10] Hidla Kuper (ed.), *Urbanization and Migration in West Africa* (1965, University of California Press, Berkeley and Los Angeles) deals largely with the mechanics of labour migration and the absorption of the migrants into urban life. [10a] Horace Miner (ed.) *The City in Modern Africa* (1967, Pall Mall Press, London) is an interesting symposium reporting recent research in a variety of spheres. The articles in [11] K. L. Little (ed.), 'Urbanization in West Africa', *Sociological Review* vol. 7, 1959, are more oriented towards changing family patterns and new religious movements. [12] William John Hanna (ed.), *Independent Black Africa: The Politics of Freedom* (1964, Rand, McNally, Chicago) is politically oriented but contains a number of sociologically important articles of relevance to West Africa. [13] Clifford Geertz (ed.), *Old Societies and New States: The Quest for Modernity in Asia and Africa* (1963, The Free Press, Glencoe) contains several articles of considerable theoretical importance. Finally [14] Ruth P. Simms, *Urbanization in West Africa: A Review of Current Literature* (1965, Northwestern University Press, Evanston) provides a descriptive, if idiosyncratic, bibliography of over 200 books and articles.

Chapter 1. Traditional society

The Ottenbergs in their Introduction to [6] provide a good summary of traditional African social structures. [15] Daryll Forde, 'The Cultural Map of West Africa', in the same volume is excellent. Six of the contributions to [16] James L. Gibbs (ed.), *Peoples of Africa* (1965, Holt, Rinehart and Winston, New York) give brief, 15,000-word sketches of individual West African peoples – Gibbs: 'The Kpelle of Liberia', and Simon Ottenberg: 'The Afikpo Ibo', M. G. Smith: 'The Hausa', D. Stenning: 'The Pastoral Fulani', P. J. Bohannan: 'The Tiv', P. C. Lloyd: 'The Yoruba' – all of Nigeria. The anthropological mongraphs on West African ethnic groups have tended to be by English-speaking writers on peoples in British territories; French writers have, in comparison, provided more ethnographic descriptions. A selection of the better-known works would include the following: – [17] Paul Bohannan, *Justice and Judgement among the Tiv* (1957, Oxford University Press, London, for the International African Institute); [18] Daryll Forde, *Yako Studies* (1964, Oxford University Press, London, for the International African Institute); [19] M. J. Field, *Akim Kotoku: an oman of the Gold Coast* (1948, Government Printer, Accra); [20] Meyer Fortes, *The Dynamics of Clanship among the Tallensi* (1945, Oxford University Press, London, for the International African Institute) and [21] *The Web of Kinship among the Tallensi* (1949, Oxford University Press, London, for the International African Institute); [22] M. M. Green, *Ibo Village Affairs* (1947, Sidgwick and Jackson, London); [23] Kenneth Little, *The Mende of Sierra Leone* (1951, Routledge and Kegan Paul, London); [24] S. F. Nadel, *A Black Byzantium: The Kingdom of Nupe in Nigeria* (1942, Oxford University Press, London, for the International African Institute); [25] Elliot P. Skinner, *The Mossi of the Upper Volta* (1964, Stanford University Press, Stanford); [26] M. G. Smith, *Government in Zazzau 1800–1950* (1960, Oxford University Press, London, for the International African Institute) a study of Zaria in Northern Nigeria; [27] Derrick J. Stenning, *Savannah Nomads* (1959, Oxford University Press, London, for the International African Institute), on the Fulani of Western Bornu, Nigeria; [28] Jacques Lombard, *Structures de Type 'Féodal' en Afrique Noir* (1965, Mouton, The Hague), on the Bariba of Dahomey; [29] V. C. Uchendu, *The Igbo of Southeast Nigeria* (1965, Holt, Rinehart and Winston, New York).

Specific aspects of traditional social structure are discussed in: – [30] Meyer Fortes, 'The Structure of Unilineal Descent Groups' in Ottenberg [*6*]; [31] M. G. Smith, 'On Segmentary Lineage Systems', *Journal of the Royal Anthropological Institute* vol. 86, 1956; [32] P. C. Lloyd, 'The Political Structure of African Kingdoms: an Exploratory Model' in M. Banton (ed.), *Political Systems and the Distribution of Power* (1965, ASA Monographs 2, Tavistock Publications, London); and for social stratification see [33] Lloyd Fallers, 'Equality, Modernity and Democracy in the New States' in Geertz [*13*]; and [34] M. G. Smith 'The Hausa System of Social Status', *Africa* vol. 29, 1959. For the concept of achievement see [35] David C. McClelland, *The Achieving Society* (1961, Van Nostrand, New York) [35a] R. A. LeVine applies this concept in *Dreams and Deeds: Achievement Motivation in Nigeria* (1966, University of Chicago Press, Chicago).

Chapter 2. Trade and colonization

[36] Roland Oliver and J. D. Fage, *A Short History of Africa* (1962, Penguin Books) provides the best outline of West African history, though with the increased teaching of the subject in the higher classes in African secondary schools, the number of textbooks is rapidly increasing. Detailed histories have been written of individual countries, the most outstanding being [37] David Kimble, *A Political History of Ghana: The Rise of Gold Coast Nationalism 1850–1928* (1963, Clarendon Press, Oxford). [38] K. Onwuka Dike, *Trade and Politics in the Niger Delta 1830–1885* (1956, Clarendon Press, Oxford) describes British mercantile and consular activity for a limited area and period while [39] G. I. Jones, *The Trading States of the Oil Rivers* (1963, Oxford University Press, London, for the International African Institute) describes the development of the Ijoh society of the Niger delta in response to European contact.

A comparison between British and French methods of native administration is made by [40] M. Crowder in 'Indirect Rule – French and British Style', *Africa* vol. 34, 1964. An early analysis of colonial policies is contained in [41] Raymond L. Buell, *The Native Problem in Africa* (1928, Macmillan, New York); whilst for the later workings of the British system [42] M. Perham, *Native Administration in Nigeria* (1937, Oxford University Press, London), and for the French [43] Robert Delavignette, *Freedom and Authority in French West Africa* (1950, Oxford University Press, London, for the International African Institute – a translation of *Service Africain*, 1946) are both valuable. [44] L. Gray Cowan, *Local Government in West Africa* (1958, Columbia University Press, New York) compares post-war developments in British and French territories. The impact of colonial administration on indigenous patterns of government is discussed in several of the anthropological monographs cited above [*24*, *25*, *26*, *28*] and especially in [45] K. A. Busia, *The Position of the Chief in the Modern Political System of the Ashanti* (1951, Oxford University Press, London, for the International African Institute) and by [46] P. C. Lloyd in 'Traditional Rulers' in Coleman and Rosberg [*120*]. A historical account of the interaction between the British colonial administration and the chiefs of Ashanti is given in [47] William Tordoff, *Ashanti under the Prempehs 1888–1935* (1965, Oxford University Press, London). See too, for Sierra Leone, [48] V. R. Dorjahn, 'The Changing Political System of Temne' in Wallerstein [*9*].

A good overall view of the geography and economy of West Africa is contained in [49] William H. Hance, *The Geography of Modern Africa* (1964, Columbia University Press, New York). Two volumes of papers discussing the problems of economic development are [50] Melville J. Herskovits and Mitchel Harwitz (eds.), *Economic Transition in Africa* (1964, Routledge and Kegan Paul, London) and [51] E. A. G. Robinson (ed.) *Economic Development for Africa South of the Sahara* (1963, Macmillan, London). In Hanna [*12*], [52] Joseph A. Kahl discusses 'Some Social Concomitants of Industrialization and Urbanization' and [53] Pius Okigbo outlines 'The Social Consequences of Economic Development in West Africa', while [54] Elliot J. Berg in 'The Economic Basis of Choice in French West Africa' describes the ties which bind France and her former colonies. [55] P. T. Bauer, *West African Trade* (1954, Routledge and Kegan Paul, London) is now a classic. [56] René Dumont, *False Start in Africa* (1966, André Deutsch, London) is a provocative essay on the problems of African development.

Chapter 3. The changing rural scene

Descriptions of the changing rural economy are implicit in most of the anthropological monographs. [57] Polly Hill, *The Migrant Cocoa Farmers of Southern Ghana: A Study in Rural Capitalism* (1963, Cambridge University Press, Cambridge) describes the migration of men into the forest areas to grow cocoa and the adaptation of traditional land tenure. [58] R. Galletti, K. D. S. Baldwin and I. O. Dina, *Nigerian Cocoa Farmers* (1956, Oxford University Press, London) is a compendium of information about both the cocoa growing and food production of Yoruba farmers. Two contrasting interpretations of the impact of change upon Yoruba towns are provided by [59] W. B. Schwab, 'Continuity and Change in the Yoruba Lineage System', *Annals of the New York Academy of Science* vol. 94, 1962 (and also in 'Oshogbo – an Urban Community' in Kuper [*10*]) and by [60] P. C. Lloyd, 'The Yoruba Town Today' in Little [*11*]. Good articles which analyse the factors which promote or inhibit acceptance of change are [61] Simon Ottenberg, 'Ibo Receptivity to Change' in Bascom and Herskovits [*8*] and [62] Philip J. Foster, 'Status, Power and Education in a Traditional Community' in *School Review* vol. 72, 1964. [63] Phoebe Ottenberg, 'The Changing Economic Position of Women among the Afikpo Ibo' in Bascom and Herskovits [*8*] shows how the introduction of new crops may alter marital roles. [64] P. C. Lloyd, 'Craft Organization in Yoruba towns' in Wallerstein [*9*] illustrates the indigenous development of guilds in modern crafts.

Works on the Christian churches and sects are cited in later sections. Two works by J. Spencer Trimmingham – [65] *Islam in West Africa* (1959, Clarendon Press, Oxford) and [66] *A History of Islam in West Africa* (1962, Oxford University Press, London, for the University of Glasgow) – survey the impact of Islam in the savana regions.

The impact of colonial and independent governments upon the rural areas is described in works cited for chapters 2 and 7. A good illustration of the translation of traditional cleavages into modern political rivalries is provided in [67] Dennis Austin, 'Elections in an African Rural Area' in Hanna [*12*] and in [68] Dennis Austin and William Tordoff, 'Voting in an African Town', *Political Studies* vol. 8, 1960.

Some effects of labour migration on a rural society are illustrated in [69] Elliot P. Skinner, 'Labour Migration and its Relationship to Socio-Cultural Change in Mossi Society' in Wallerstein [*9*].

Chapter 4. Urban life

A number of monographs have been written in recent years about the modern towns of West Africa. [70] M. Banton, *West African City* (1957, Oxford University Press, London, for the International African Institute) deals with Freetown and its immigrant population. [71] Merran Fraenkel, *Tribe and Class in Monrovia* (1964, Oxford University Press, London, for the International African Institute) deals largely with the tribal peoples of that city. More in the nature of urban surveys are [72] Ione Acquah, *Accra Survey* (1958, University of London Press, London) and [73] I. Neustadt and E. N. Omaboe, *Social and Economic Survey of Tema* (1959, Government Statistician's Office, Accra). Two Dahomeyan towns are treated in [74] Claude Tardits, *Porto Novo* (1958, Mouton, The Hague) and [75] J. Lombard, 'Cotonou Ville Africaine', *Études Dahoméennes* vol. 10, 1953. [76] Peter Marris, *Family and Social Change in an African City* (1961, Routledge and Kegan Paul, London) deals with slum clearance in central Lagos and the resettlement of people in the city's suburban estates. [77] P. C. Lloyd, A. L. Mabogunje and B. Awe (eds.), *The City of Ibadan* (1967, Cambridge University Press, Cambridge) contains articles describing the life in both the traditional and modern quarters of Africa's largest Negro town.

Patterns of migration into towns are described in Kuper [*10*] and also in [78] R. B. Davidson, *Migrant Labour in the Gold Coast* (1954, Department of Education, University College of the Gold Coast, Achimota) and [79] R. Mansell Prothero, *Migrant Labour from Sokoto*

Province, Northern Nigeria (1958, Government Printer, Northern Region of Nigeria, Kaduna). The migration of the Toucouleur of the Senegal valley to Dakar is described by [80] Abdoulaye Diop in 'Enquête sur la Migration Toucouleur à Dakar', *Bulletin de l'IFAN*, vol 22 ser. B, 1960. Data on urban wages and consumption patterns may be culled from a variety of government publications. Wage rates are the theme of the Morgan Commission's Report. In [80a] Leonard Plotnicov, *Strangers to the City: Urban man in Jos, Nigeria* (1967, University of Pittsburgh Press, Pittsburgh) biographies of eight migrants demonstrate their adaptation to town life. [81] *Report of the Commission on the Review of Wages, Salary and Conditions of Service of the Junior Employees of the Governments of the Federation and in Private Establishments, 1963–1964* (1964, Federal Ministry of Information, Lagos). The rising incidence of unemployment is discussed in [82] A. C. Callaway, 'Unemployment among African School Leavers', *Journal of Modern African Studies* vol. 1, 1963.

Other aspects of urban life are contained in works cited in chapters 7, 8 and 10. For a comparative study of a very different area see [83] P. Mayer, *Townsmen or Tribesmen* (1961, Oxford University Press, London) on South Africa.

Chapter 5. The Western-educated elite

[84] P. C. Lloyd (ed.), *The New Elites of Tropical Africa* (1966, Oxford University Press, London, for the International African Institute) contains a lengthy introduction and individual papers discussing the rise of the elites, patterns of social mobility and styles of living, and the status of the elite in their communities; West Africa is strongly represented in these contributions. Historical works and those tracing the development of political activity often discuss the growth of the elites – as does Kimble [*37*] for Ghana and Coleman [*124*] for Nigeria. [85] Arthur T. Porter, *Creoledom* (1963, Oxford University Press, London) graphically analyses the development of the creole society in Freetown from the original settlements of freed slaves. The role of this same group as evangelists in Nigeria is described in [86] J. F. Ade Ajayi, *Christian Missions in Nigeria, 1841–1891: The Making of a New Elite* (1965, Longmans Green, London). [87] Philip Foster, *Education and Social Change in Ghana* (1965, Routledge and Kegan Paul, London) discusses the development of the educational system and gives the most comprehensive data on social mobility, measured in the recruitment to secondary schools, available for West Africa. Comparison with the Ivory Coast is provided by [88]

Remi Clignet and Philip Foster, 'Potential Elites in Ghana and the Ivory Coast: a Preliminary Comparison', *American Journal of Sociology* vol. 70, 1964. This study is fully reported in [88a] Remi Clignet and Philip Foster, *The Fortunate Few: a study of secondary schools and students in the Ivory Coast* (1966, Northwestern University Press, Evanston). The background of entrants to the University of Ghana is described by [89] G. Jahoda, 'The Social Background of a West African Student Population', *British Journal of Sociology* vols. 5 and 6, 1954–5, and for a later period by [90] M. Peil, 'Ghanaian University Students: the Broadening Base', *British Journal of Sociology* vol. 16, 1965.

[91] G. Jahoda, *White Man* (1961, Oxford University Press, London) discusses the reactions of West Africans to the European; but few writers have discussed the European communities in West Africa. Exceptions are [92] Paul Mercier, 'The European Community of Dakar', in van den Berghe [7] and an interesting description of the tensions arising from the introduction of Africans to a European club in Freetown by [93] L. Proudfoot and H. S. Wilson, 'Clubs in Crisis: Race Relations in the New West Africa', *American Journal of Sociology* vol. 66, 1961.

Chapter 7. The family

Traditional family relationships form a major part of most anthropological monographs and several of the urban monographs discuss changing roles, especially Fraenkel [*71*]. Articles on the family are included in the symposia already cited:—in Little [*11*], containing [94] Kenneth Little, 'Some Urban Patterns of Marriage and Domesticity in West Africa' and [95] Tanya Baker and Mary Bird, 'Urbanization and the Position of Women'; in Lloyd [*84*] containing, [96] Kenneth L. Little, 'Attitudes towards Marriage and the Family among Educated Young Sierra Leoneans', [97] Barbara B. Lloyd, 'Education and Family Life in the Development of Class Identification among the Yoruba', and [98] Claude Tardits, 'Parenté et Classe Sociale à Porto-Novo'; and in van den Berghe [7]. A useful addition to this selection is [99] G. Jahoda, 'Images of Marriage Partners and Girls' Self-Images in Ghana', *Sociologus* vol. 8, 1958. A brief description of elite family relationships is in [100] P. C. Lloyd, 'The Elite' in Lloyd *et al.* [77].

Chapter 8. Urban associations

The literature describing urban voluntary associations has been admirably synthesized in [101] K. Little, *West African Urbanization* (1965, Cambridge University Press, Cambridge). Added detail is exemplified in [102] S. Ottenberg, 'Improvement Associations among the Afikpo Ibo', *Africa* vol. 25, 1955, [103] C. Okonjo, 'The Western Ibo', in Lloyd *et al.* [77] and [104] W. T. Morrill, 'Immigrants and Associations: the Ibo in Twentieth-Century Calabar', *Comparative Studies in Society and History* vol. 5, 1963. A further summary of the role of voluntary associations in the urbanizing process is given by [105] I. Wallerstein, 'Voluntary Associations', in Coleman and Rosberg [*120*]. The organization of the Hausa in Ibadan has been described by Abner Cohen in [106] 'The Hausa' in Lloyd *et al.* [77] and in [107] 'The Social Organization of Credit in a West African Cattle Market', *Africa* vol. 35, 1965 and [108] 'Politics of the Kola Trade', *Africa* vol. 36, 1966.

[109] Ioan Davies, *African Trade Unions* (1966, Penguin Books) is the first book in English to deal with the whole continent. A further summary is given by [110] Elliot J. Berg and Jeffrey Butler in 'Trade Unions' in Coleman and Rosberg [*120*]. Articles dealing with the trade union reorganization in Ghana are [111] D. Rimmer, 'The New Industrial Relations in Ghana', *Industrial and Labour Relations Review* vol. 14, 1961, and [112] L. N. Trachtman, 'The Labour Movement in Ghana: A Study in Political Unionism', *Economic Development and Cultural Change* vol. 10, 1962. The Sekondi strike of 1961 is described in [113] St Clair Drake and Leslie A. Lacey, 'Government Versus the Unions' in Carter [*123*]. A comparison of labour conditions in contrasting Nigerian industries is to be found in [114] F. A. Wells and W. A. Warmington, *Studies in Industrialization: Nigeria and the Cameroons* (1962, Oxford University Press, London, for the Nigerian Institute of Social and Economic Research).

Chapter 9. Political parties

The literature on West African political development is increasing rapidly. Many general works on the politics of the underdeveloped countries are based heavily upon African data – for example [115] David E. Apter, *The Politics of Modernization* (1965, University of Chicago Press, Chicago). In a similar vein are a number of articles by Shils and Eisenstadt: for instance [116] E. Shils, 'Political Development in the New States', *Comparative Studies in Society and History* vol. 2, 1960 (and his contributions to Hanna [*12*]); and [117] S. N. Eisenstadt, 'Sociological Aspects of Political Development in Underdeveloped Countries' in Wallerstein [*9*]. [118] Lucien W. Pye, 'The Non-Western Political Process' in Hanna [*12*] is equally valuable. [118a] Aristide R. Zolberg, *Creating Political Order* (1966, Rand McNally, Chicago) is the most up-to-date account of the development of single-party rule in West Africa.

In [119] Gabriel A. Almond and James S. Coleman (eds.), *The Politics of the Developing Areas* (1960, Princeton University Press, Princeton) the first editor sets out a framework of analysis whilst the second editor contributes 'The Politics of Sub-Saharan Africa' and summarizes the findings of all the contributors.

A number of symposia contain chapters on individual African states. [120] James S. Coleman and Carl G. Rosberg (eds.), *Political Parties and National Integration in Tropical Africa* (1964, University of California Press, Berkeley and Los Angeles) contains, in addition to articles on associations already cited [*46*, *105*, *110*], chapters on Senegal (William J. Foltz), Ivory Coast (Aristide R. Zolberg), Sierra Leone (Martin Kilson), Guinea (Victor du Bois,) Mali (Thomas Hodgkin and Ruth Schachter Morganthau), Ghana (David E. Apter), Liberia (J. Gus Leibenow), Nigeria (Richard L. Sklar and C. S. Whitaker). The editors conclude with a comparative analysis of the states described. Three volumes have been edited by Gwendolen C. Carter: [121] *African One-Party States* (1962, Cornell University Press, Ithaca) with essays on Senegal (Ernest Milcent), Guinea (L. Gray Cowan), Ivory Coast (Virginia Thompson) and Liberia (J. Gus Liebenow); [122] *Five African States* (1963, Cornell University Press, Ithaca) with an essay on Dahomey (Virginia Thompson); [123] *Politics in Africa* (1966, Harcourt, Brace and World, New York) containing seven case studies on African crises or key problems.

Of the mongraphs on individual African states, the following are the most valuable:

on NIGERIA – [124] James S. Coleman, *Nigeria: Background to Nationalism* (1958, University of California Press, Berkeley and Los Angeles); [125] Henry L. Bretton, *Power and Stability in Nigeria* (1962, Praeger, New York); [126] K. W. J. (Ken) Post, *The Nigerian Federal Election of 1959* (1963, Oxford University Press, London, for the Nigerian Institute of Social and Economic Research); [127] Richard L. Sklar, *Nigerian Political Parties* (1963, Princeton University Press, Princeton); [128] John P. Mackintosh, *Nigerian Government and Politics* (1966, George Allen and Unwin, London)

on GHANA – [129] David E. Apter, *The Gold Coast in Transition* (1955, Princeton University Press, Princeton); [130] Dennis Austin, *Politics in Ghana 1946–1960* (1964, Oxford University Press, London, for the Royal Institute of International Affairs)
on SIERRA LEONE – [130a] Martin Kilson, *Political Change in a West African State* (1966, Harvard University Press, Cambridge)
on the FRENCH-SPEAKING TERRITORIES – [131] Ruth Schachter Morganthau, *Political Parties in French-Speaking West Africa* (1964, Clarendon Press, Oxford); [132] Aristide R. Zolberg, *One-Party Government in the Ivory Coast* (1964, Princeton University Press, Princeton)

An account of the early growth of the Action Group is given in [133] P. C. Lloyd, 'The Development of Political Parties in Western Nigeria', *American Political Science Review* vol. 49, 1955. An interesting description of later youth organizations is [134] Peter Hodge, 'The Ghana Workers' Brigade: A Project for Unemployed Youth', *British Journal of Sociology* vol. 15, 1964.

West African political development has been summarized in [135] Ken (K. W. J.) Post, *The New States of West Africa* (1964, revised 1968, Penguin Books). A most useful reference work is [136] Ronald Segal, *Political Africa* (1961, Stevens, London) containing notes on the leading political figures and on the principal parties in each state.

Chapter 10. The strains of change

This field is poorly documented with few works of high quality. Outstanding, at least as an exercise in method, is [137] Alexander H. Leighton *et al.*, *Psychiatric Disorders among the Yoruba* (1963, Cornell University Press, Ithaca). Corruption has been discussed by [138] C. Leys, 'What is the Problem about Corruption?' *Journal of Modern African Studies* vol. 3, 1965, and by [139] M. McMullan, 'A Theory of Corruption' in Hanna [12]. A view of corruption in a traditional society is given in [140] M. G. Smith, 'Historical and Cultural Conditions of Political Corruption among the Hausa', *Comparative Studies of Society and History* vol. 6, 1964.

A fascinating study of new shrines in Ghana has been given by [141] M. J. Field, *Search for Security* (1960, Faber and Faber, London), whilst in [142] P. Morton-Williams, 'The Atinga Cult among the South-Western Yoruba', *Bulletin de l'IFAN* vol. 18, ser. B, 1956, a witch-hunting cult is analysed. For the role of modern magic see [143] G. Jahada, 'Social Aspirations, Magic and Witchcraft in Ghana: A Social Psychological Interpretation' in Lloyd [*84*].

In [144] Geoffrey Parrinder, *Religion in an African City* (1953, Oxford University Press, London) we have a summary of the various religions, traditional, mission and separatist, practised in Ibadan; [144a] J. D. Y. Peel, *Aladura: a religious movement among the Yoruba* (1968, Oxford University Press, London) describes one such faith. A description of some separatist sects is given in [145] C. G. Baeta, *Prophetism in Ghana: a study of some spiritual churches* (1962, S.C.M. Press, London) and in [145a] H. W. Turner, *African Independent Church* (1967, Oxford University Press, London), a study of the Aladura church, with particular reference to Sierra Leone. Two contributions to Bascom and Herskovits [*8*] discuss the syncretism of traditional and modern religions: [146] James Boyd Christensen, 'The Adaptive Functions of Fanti Priesthood' and [147] John C. Messenger, 'Religious Acculturation among the Anang Ibibio'. [148] B. Holas, 'Bref Aperçu sur les Principaux Cultes Syncrétiques de la Basse Côte d'Ivoire', *Africa* vol. 24, 1954, provides comparative material.

Chapter 11. Ideologies

A general discussion of the ideologies of the elite of developing nations may be found in Worsley [*5*]; [149] Basil Davidson, *Which Way Africa?: The Search for a New Society* (1964, Penguin Books) elaborates the African themes. [150] Thomas Hodgkin, 'A Note on the Language of African Nationalism' is contained in Hanna [*12*].

[151] William H. Friedland and Carl G. Rosberg (eds.), *African Socialism* (1964, Oxford University Press, London) provides definitions of African socialism and its interpretation in Ghana (Colin Legum), in Guinea and Senegal (Charles F. Andrain) and in Mali (Kenneth W. Grundy). Grundy has also summarized Marxist analyses in [152] 'The Class Struggle in Africa: an Examination of Conflicting Themes', *Journal of Modern African Studies* vol. 2, 1964. The writings of the African leaders themselves may be illustrated by [153] Léopold S. Senghor, *On African Socialism* (1964, Praeger, New York, translated by Mercer Cook); [154] Kwame Nkrumah, *Africa Must Unite* (1963, Heinemann, London) and [155] *Consciencism* (1964, Heinemann, London); [156] Obafemi Awolowo, *Path to Nigerian Freedom* (1946, Faber and Faber, London); and by the autobiographies – [157] Obafemi Awolowo, *Awo* (1960, Cambridge University Press, Cambridge), and [158] Sir Ahmadu Bello, Sardauna of Sokoto, *My Life* (1962, Cambridge University Press, Cambridge). A comparison of the outlook of three Northern Nigerian leaders is given in [159]

S. Whitaker, 'Three Perspectives on Hierarchy', *Journal of Commonwealth Political Studies* vol. 3, 1965.

For the role of history in modern ideologies see [160] J. F. Ade Ajayi, 'The Place of African History and Literature in the Process of Nation Building in Africa South of the Sahara' in Wallerstein [*9*]. The quarterly *Présence Africaine* is a rich source both of the poetry of *Négritude* and of expositions of these philosophical themes; see for instance [161] Lilyan Lagneau, 'The *Négritude* of L. S. Senghor', *Présence Africaine* vol. 11, no. 39, and [162] L. Sedar Senghor, 'Constructive Elements of a Civilization of Negro-African Inspiration', *Présence Africaine* vol. 24–5, 1959.

Chapter 12. Tribalism

[163] Clifford Geertz, 'Primordial Sentiments and Civil Politics in the New States' in Geertz [*13*] provides a general background to ethnic loyalties. Several articles in van den Berghe [7] discuss African tribalism, notably [164] Max Gluckman, 'Tribalism in Modern British Central Africa' (also in Wallerstein [*9*]), [165] Paul Mercier, 'On the Meaning of "Tribalism" in Black Africa', and [166] Immanuel Wallerstein, 'Ethnicity and National Integration in West Africa'. See too [167] Richard L. Sklar, 'The Contribution of Tribalism to Nationalism in Western Nigeria' in Wallerstein [*9*].

Chapter 13. Conflicts

The development of social classes in modern African society is discussed in the Introduction to Lloyd [*84*] and in two papers in this symposium – [168] P. C. Lloyd, 'Class Consciousness among the Yoruba' and [169] Paul Mercier, 'Elites et Forces Politiques'. By the latter author too is [170] 'Problems of Social Stratification in West Africa' in Wallerstein [*9*]. Also in [*9*] is [171] M. L. Kilson, 'Nationalism and Social Classes in British West Africa'.

The development of specific crises in the West African states is best traced in the weekly *West Africa.* Two articles by Richard L. Sklar are a useful background for Nigerian events – [172] 'Contradictions in the Nigerian Political System', *Journal of Modern African Studies* vol. 3, 1965, and [173] 'Nigerian Politics: The Ordeal of Chief Awolowo 1960–65' in Carter [*123*].

An analysis of the Ghana coup is given in [173a] B. Fitch and M. Oppenheimer, *Ghana: End of an Illusion* (1966, Monthly Review Press, New York); [173b] Col. A. A. Arifa in *The Ghana Coup* (1966, Frank

Cass, London) gives the viewpoint of one of the leading participants.

The role of the military in African states is discussed by [174] W. Gutteridge, *Armed Forces in New States* (1962, Oxford University Press, London, for the Royal Institute of International Affairs), and [175] Morris Janowitz, *The Military in the Political Development of New Nations* (1964, University of Chicago Press, Chicago).

Additional bibliography

Books on Nigeria continue to predominate, both in quantity and in quality. Valuable background material to recent events is contained in [176] G. K. Helleiner, *Peasant Agriculture, Government and Economic Growth in Nigeria* (1966, Richard D. Irwin, Inc., Homewood, Illinois), and in a series of articles [177] on industrial relations and wage determination by P. Kilby, J. F. Weeks and R. Cohen in the *Journal of Developing Areas*, 1 July 1967, 3 October 1968 and 5 January 1971; and by E. J. Berg and W. M. Warren in *Economic Development and Cultural Change*, 17 July 1969. Political development in Northern Nigeria is described in [178] B. J. Dudley, *Parties and Politics in Northern Nigeria* (1968, Cass, London) and [179] C. S. Whitaker, *The Politics of Tradition* (1970, Princeton University Press, Princeton). The civil war is discussed in [180] S. K. Panter-Brick (ed.), *Nigerian Politics and Military Rule: Prelude to the Civil War* (1970, Athlone Press, London); [181] R. Luckham, *The Nigerian Military* (1971, Cambridge University Press, Cambridge); and [182] J. de St Jorre, *The Nigerian Civil War* (1972, Hodder & Stoughton, London); [183] Ruth First, *The Barrel of a Gun* (1970, Allen Lane the Penguin Press, London) analyses African coups with specific reference to Nigeria and Ghana. Industrial and agrarian unrest is the subject of two government commissions: [184] *Second and Final Report of the Wages and Salaries Review Commission 1970–71* (Adebo Report) (1971, Lagos) and [185] *Report of a Commission of Enquiry into Civil Disturbances which Occurred in Certain Parts of the Western State of Nigeria in the Month of December 1968* (Ayoola Report) (1969, Ibadan).

Other valuable works recently published include:

[186] D. Cruise O'Brien, *The Mourides of Senegal: The political and economic organization of an Islamic brotherhood* (1971, Clarendon Press, Oxford); [187] C. Meillassoux (ed.), *The Development of Indigenous Trade and Markets in West Africa* (1971, Oxford University Press, London); [188] J. C. Caldwell, *African Rural-Urban Migration: the movement to Ghana's towns* (1969, Hurst, London); [189] R. Cruise O'Brien, *White Society in Black Africa: the French in Senegal* (1972, Faber and Faber, London).

Index

Penguin African Library

The Discarded People

An Account of African Resettlement in South Africa

Cosmas Desmond

One aspect of South African *apartheid* is the resettlement of Africans in Bantu 'homelands'. What this pretty concept entails and has entailed for about 1,000,000 black people in human suffering, poverty and starvation is here described by a Franciscan priest.

Early in 1968 the black population – tenants and parishioners – were arbitrarily removed from the author's mission in Natal and 'resettled' on an unprepared stretch of veld twenty miles away. This first-hand experience of a brutality which recalls Hitler or Stalin set Father Desmond off on a journey of inquiry through the Republic.

The Discarded People factually records what he found – thousands of families uprooted (with fire and force, where necessary) and dumped on bleak, barren sites which offer little hope of food, shelter, work or even water.

Like the television programmes based upon it, this is a book to shock and disgust. As Nadine Gordimer writes in her foreword: 'The physical conditions of life described in this book are such an appalling desolation that one is almost unable to think beyond bread and latrines.'

Penguin African Library

The Barrel of a Gun

Political Power in Africa and the Coup d'État

Ruth First

'The 1960s represented a decade not only of African independence but of widespread military intervention in the politics of newly independent states. More than a score of coups d'état caused speculation as to whether Africa would repeat the pattern of Latin America. Ruth First . . . has spent much of her enforced exile in examining the events and assessing the significance of these military incursions into African politics.

'In this long book Miss First describes in detail three major coups, those of the Sudan, Nigeria and Ghana; she also refers more briefly to the others . . . The stories themselves rivet the reader like the best fiction . . . Those who would understand the factors underlying African crisis, and especially African leaders themselves, should read this close analysis of a continent's sickness – John Hatch in the *New Statesman*

Ruth First effectively enlivens her text with interviews and from her examination of actual coups is able to offer a general theory of power for newly independent states which exposes their vulnerability.

Penguin African Library

Angola's People

In the Eye of the Storm

Basil Davidson

'This book is the product of Basil Davidson's twenty years of continuing concern with the Angolan problem . . . has all the virtues that one is accustomed to associate with Basil Davidson's work and one or two extra ones' – *Guardian*

'Basil Davidson writes with a warm commitment to the guerrilla cause, but without illusion . . . [He] has done a magnificent job in making their experiences available to us in such a vivid form' – *New Statesman*

'A brilliant account of the struggle in Angola' – *Observer*

'There is probably no Englishman who knows as much about the three Portuguese territories as he does' – *Economist*

Not for sale in the U.S.A. or Canada

Penguin African Library

A Short History of Africa

Roland Oliver and J. D. Fage

Third Edition – Revised

This concise history of Africa has been in constant demand since it first appeared in 1962. Much had already been written on different regions of the continent and different periods of its long development, including colonial histories of the European powers, ephemeral articles on the emergent countries, studies of Africa's pre-history, etc.: but there had previously been nothing that offered the general reader an overall view of African history from the earliest times to the establishment of the Organization of African Unity and the events of the late 1960s.

The authors, who are both professors of African history, have drawn on the whole range of literature about Africa and on the evidence provided by archaeology, oral traditions, language relationships, social institutions, and material cultures to write this volume. *A Short History of Africa* not only marshals the most authoritative views of African specialists into an absorbing narrative: it also puts forward original conclusions that take the study of Africa a stage further.

'Admirable in its quality, its balance, and its scholarship' – *Sunday Times*

Penguin African Library

Africa in Prose

Edited by O.R. Dathorne and Willfried Feuser

This original Penguin collection covers writing in European and native languages from the whole African continent in the last hundred years. It adds depth and perspective to our understanding of Africa's current literary revolution. This, as the editors make clear, is not a spontaneous creation but was produced over a period of time by minds grappling with the changing realities of emergent Africa, and adapting to their own use the received linguistic tools to express them. This anthology reveals the beginnings of the African novel written in French and English, the recent attempt to write prose in vernacular languages, and the experimental writing which is now taking place. Many of the translations have never appeared in English.

Penguin African Library

Rhodesia

White Racism and Imperial Response

Martin Loney

The late 1950s and early 1960s saw the rapid and, in most cases, peaceful decolonization of Africa. But today Rhodesia remains colonized, no longer controlled by the imperial power, but still governed by white settlers. Martin Loney describes the history of the colony and of the continuous African opposition to the invaders.

Central to his theme is the development of the power of the intransigent white rulers: in his words, this book is about the historical development of that power, the systematic use which has been made of it to build a prosperous white society in Africa, and the consequent impoverishment of the African population. It is also about the complicity of the British governments, Labour and Conservative, in this process.

In its assessment of the British sell-out and of the growing sense of national identity on the part of the African population, this is a book which will upset many of the comfortable ideas held about Rhodesia in this country.

Penguin African Library

Which Way Africa?

The Search for a New Society

Basil Davidson

Revised Edition

A man would have to be very brave or very foolhardy to try to forecast precisely the pattern of Africa's future. Where events outrun the printing-presses, discretion is the better part of omniscience.

In *Which Way Africa?* Basil Davidson, the well-known writer on African affairs, has steered clear of political ju-ju. Instead – and definitely more to the purpose – he has made what is the only up-to-date and comprehensive analysis in English – and probably in any language – of the social, economic, and political motives, myths, ideas, and beliefs which underlie modern African nationalism.

Events in almost every corner of the continent have shown the world an Africa poised on the threshold of new ventures, an Africa in flux. Only such an analysis as the author has sucessfully achieved in this volume can help to delineate the kind of societies which will now tend to emerge there.